A Textbook of
Translation

For my daughter Clare

A Textbook of
Translation

Peter Newmark
Centre for Translation and Language Studies
University of Surrey

Pearson Education Limited
Edinburgh Gate
Harlow
Essex CM20 2JE
England
and Associated Companies
throughout the World

www.longman.com

First published 1988 by Prentice Hall Europe
This edition published by Pearson Education Limited
Eighth impression 2003

Twelfth impression 2008

Printed in Malaysia, PP

Library of Congress Cataloging-in-Publication Data

Newmark, Peter
   A textbook of translation.

   Bibliography: p.
   Includes index.
   1. Translating and interpreting.   I. Title.
P306.N474   1987   418'.02   86-30593

ISBN 978-0-13-912593-5

British Library Cataloguing in Publication Data

Newmark, Peter
   A textbook of translation.
   1. Translating and interpreting
   I. Title
   418'.02   P306

Contents

Preface   xi
Acknowledgements   xii

Part I Principles

1 Introduction   3

2 The Analysis of a Text   11

Reading the text   11
The intention of the text   12
The intention of the translator   12
Text styles   13
The readership   13
Stylistic scales   14
Attitude   15
Setting   15
The quality of the writing   16
Connotations and denotations   16
The last reading   17
Conclusion   17

3 The Process of Translation   19

Introduction   19
The relation of translating to translation theory   19
The approach   20
The textual level   22
The referential level   23

The cohesive level 23
The level of naturalness 24
Combining the four levels 29
The unit of translating 30
The translation of texts 32
The translation of proper names 35
Revision 36
Conclusion 37

4 *Language Functions, Text-categories and Text-types* 39

The expressive function 39
The informative function 40
The vocative function 41
The aesthetic function 42
The phatic function 43
The metalingual function 43

5 *Translation Methods* 45

Introduction 45
The methods 45
Comments on the methods 47
Equivalent effect 48
Methods and text-categories 50
Translating 51
Other methods 52

6 *The Unit of Translation and Discourse Analysis* 54

Introduction 54
Coherence 55
Titles 56
Dialogue cohesion 57
Punctuation 58
Sound-effects 58
Cohesion 59
Referential synonyms 59
Enumerators 60
Other connectives 60
Functional sentence perspective 60
Contrasts 63
The lower units of translation 65
Conclusion 66

7 *Literal Translation* 68

Introduction 68
Varieties of close translation 69
The translation of poetry 70
Faithful and false friends 72
Words in their context 73
Elegant variations 73
Back-translation of text (BTT) 74
Accepted translation 74
Constraints on literal translation 75
Natural translation 75
Re-creative translation 76
Literary translation 77
The sub-text 77
The notion of the 'no-equivalent' word 78
The role of context 80

8 *The Other Translation Procedures* 81

Transference 81
Naturalisation 82
Cultural equivalent 82
Functional equivalent 83
Descriptive equivalent 83
Synonymy 84
Through-translation 84
Shifts or transpositions 85
Modulation 88
Recognised translation 89
Translation label 90
Compensation 90
Componential analysis 90
Reduction and expansion 90
Paraphrase 90
Other procedures 90
Couplets 91
Notes, additions, glosses 91

9 *Translation and Culture* 94

Definitions 95
Cultural categories 96
General considerations 96
Ecology 97
Material culture 97

Social culture   98
Social organisation – political and administrative   99
Gestures and habits   102
Summary of procedures   103

10 *The Translation of Metaphors*   104

Definitions   106
Translating metaphors   106
Types of metaphor   106

11 *The Use of Componential Analysis in Translation*   114

Introduction   114
Lexical words   117
Cultural words   119
Synonyms   120
Sets and series   121
Conceptual terms   121
Neologisms   122
Words as myths   123
Conclusion   123

12 *The Application of Case Grammar to Translation*   125

Introduction   125
The translation of missing verbs, i.e. verbal force   126
The translation of case-gaps   129
Various types of case-partner   132
Contrast and choice in translation   134
Some related issues   135
Case partners of adjectives and nouns   136
A remark on Tesnière   138
Conclusion   138

13 *The Translation of Neologisms*   140

Introduction   140
Old words with new senses   141
New coinages   142
Derived words   143
Abbreviations   145
Collocations   145
Eponyms   146
Phrasal words   147

Transferred words 147
Acronyms 148
Pseudo-neologisms 148
The creation of neologisms 149
A frame of reference for the translation of neologisms 150

14 *Technical Translation* 151

Introduction 151
Technical style 151
Terms 152
Varieties of technical style 152
Technical and descriptive terms 153
Beginning technical translation 154
Translation method 155
The title 156
Going through the text 158
Conclusion 160
Appendix: sample test 161

15 *The Translation of Serious Literature and Authoritative Statements* 162

Introduction 162
Poetry 162
The short story/novel 170
Drama 172
Conclusion 173

16 *Reference Books and their Uses; Tracing the 'Unfindable' Word* 174

Introduction 174
Resources 175
'Unfindable' words 176

17 *Translation Criticism* 184

Introduction 184
Plan of criticism 186
Text analysis 186
The translator's purpose 186
Comparing the translation with the original 187
The evaluation of the translation 188
The translation's future 189
Marking a translation 189
Quality in translation 192

18 *Shorter Items*   193

Words and context   193
The translation of dialect   194
You and the computer   195
Function and description   198
The translation of eponyms and acronyms   198
Familiar alternative terms   201
When and how to improve a text   204
Collocations   212
The translation of proper names   214
The translation of puns   217
The translation of weights, measures, quantities and currencies   217
Ambiguity   218

19 *Revision Hints for Exams and Deadlines*   221

20 *By Way of a Conclusion*   225

Part II   Methods

Introductory note   229
Text 1   'Power needs clear eyes', *The Economist*   231
Text 2   'Upper gastrointestinal endoscopy', *British Medical Journal*   234
Text 3   *Brideshead Revisited* (Waugh)   238
Text 4   'Une certaine idée de la France' (De Gaulle)   242
Text 5   'Le Parti Socialiste' (Source unknown)   245
Text 6   *A la Recherche du Temps Perdu* (Proust)   248
Text 7   'Présentation d'un cas de toxoplasmose', *Bordeaux Médical*   250
Text 8   'Dialysebehandlung bei akutem Nierenversagen', *Deutsche
          Medizinische Wochenschrift*   254
Text 9   *Alexander von Humboldt* (Hein)   259
Text 10   *L'Adoration* (Borel)   264
Text 11   *Die Blasse Anna* (Böll)   267
Text 12   *La Société Française* (Dupeux)   272
Text 13   'Zum Wohle aller', *SCALA*   277

Glossary   282
Abbreviations   286
Author's Published Papers   287
Medical terminology   288
Bibliography   289
Name index   291
Subject index   292

Preface

This book has been five years in the writing. Sections of it have twice been stolen during travel (once at knife point) and have been rewritten, hopefully better than the first time – the fond hope of all writers who have had their MSS lost, stolen or betrayed. Its 'progress' has been further interrupted by requests for papers for conferences; four of these papers have been incorporated; others, listed in the bibliography are too specialised for inclusion here. It is not a conventional textbook. Instead of offering, as originally planned, texts in various languages for you to translate, I have supplied in the appendices examples of translational text analyses, translations with commentaries and translation criticism. They are intended to be helpful illustrations of many points made in the book, and models for you to react against when you do these three stimulating types of exercise.

If the book has a unifying element, it is the desire to be useful to the translator. Its various theories are only generalisations of translation practices. The points I make are for you to endorse or to reject, or simply think about.

The special terms I use are explained in the text and in the glossary.

I hope you will read this book in conjunction with its predecessor, *Approaches to Translation*, of which it is in many respects an expansion as well as a revision; in particular, the treatment of institutional terms and of metalanguage is more extensive in the earlier than in this book.

I dislike repeating myself writing or speaking, and for this reason I have reproduced say the paper on case grammar, about which at present I haven't much more to say, and which isn't easily come by.

This book is not written by a scholar. I once published a controversial piece on Corneille's *Horace* in *French Studies*, and was encouraged to work for a doctorate, but there was too much in the making that didn't interest me, so I gave up. And a German professor refused to review *Approaches* because it had so many mistakes in the bibliography; which is regrettable (he was asked to point them out, but refused; later, he changed his mind and reviewed the book), but academic detail is not the essential of that or this book either.

I am somewhat of a 'literalist', because I am for truth and accuracy. I think that words as well as sentences and texts have meaning, and that you only deviate from literal translation when there are good semantic and pragmatic reasons for doing so, which is more often than not, except in grey texts. But that doesn't mean,

xi

as Alex Brotherton (Amsterdam) has disparagingly written without evidence, that I believe in the 'absolute primacy of the word'. There are no absolutes in translation, everything is conditional, any principle (e.g. accuracy) may be in opposition to another (e.g. economy) or at least there may be tension between them.

Much as at times I should like to get rid of the two bugbears of translation, the dear old context and the dear old readership, alas, we never can. I can only go as far as saying that some words in a text are far less context-bound than others; and that some readerships (say of a set of instructions, of which the readership is the reason for its existence) are more important than others (say a lyric) where the poet and his translator may only be writing for himself.

Again when Halliday writes that language is entirely a social phenomenon and consequently collapses or conflates Bühler's expressive and appellative functions of language into the interpersonal function, stating that there is no distinction between the first two functions in language, I can only say that this is a matter of belief or philosophy as the expression of belief, and that I disagree. But all this is to some extent a matter of emphasis (and reaction) rather than (diametrical) opposition. The single word is getting swamped in the discourse and the individual in the mass of society – I am trying to reinstate them both, to redress the balance. If people express themselves individually in a certain type of text, translators must also express themselves individually, even if they are told they are only reacting to, and therefore conforming with, social discourse conventions of the time.

Writing a book about translation, I am aware that this is a new profession, though an old practice, and that the body of knowledge and of assumptions that exists about translation is tentative, often controversial and fluctuating.

This book is intended to be reasonably comprehensive, that is, to discuss most of the issues and problems that come up in translating. (In this aim, at least, the book is original.) In spite of the controversial nature of several of its chapters, it is therefore designed as a kind of reference book for translators. However, some of the shorter pieces in Chapter 18 are inadequate and can only offer you a few pointers. I hope to expand the book (my last one on translation) for a second edition, and I would welcome suggestions for its improvement.

Acknowledgements

I warmly thank Pauline Newmark, Elizabeth Newmark and Matthew Newmark, whom I have consulted so frequently; Vaughan James, who has helped so much at every stage; Vera North, who coped so superbly with the ins and outs of my handwriting; Mary FitzGerald; Sheila Silcock; Margaret Rogers, Louise Hurren; Mary Harrison; Simon Chau, Hans Lindquist, René Dirven, Robin Trew, Harold Leyrer, David Harvey, Jean Maillot, Christopher Mair, Geoffrey Kingscott.

The author and publisher would like to thank the copyright holders who gave their permission to reproduce extracts in Part II.

PART I

Principles

Figures appear in Part I as follows:

1	The dynamics of translation	4
2	A functional theory of language	20
3	Language functions, text-categories and text-types	40
4	The translation of metaphor	105
5	Scalar diagrams	116
6	Equation diagram	116
7	Matrix diagram	117
8	Parallel tree diagram	117
9	Meals diagram	122

CHAPTER 1

Introduction

My purpose in this book is to offer a course in translation principles and method-ology for final-year-degree and post-graduate classes as well as for autodidacts and home learners. Further, I have in mind that I am addressing non-English as well as English students, and I will provide some appropriate English texts and examples to work on.

I shall assume that you, the reader, are learning to translate into your language of habitual use, since that is the only way you can translate naturally, accurately and with maximum effectiveness. In fact, however, most translators do translate out of their own language ('service' translation) and contribute greatly to many people's hilarity in the process.

Further, I shall assume that you have a degree-level 'reading and compre-hension' ability in one foreign language and a particular interest in one of the three main areas of translation: (a) science and technology, (b) social, economic and/or political topics and institutions, and (c) literary and philosophical works. Normally, only (a) and (b) provide a salary; (c) is free-lance work.

Bear in mind, however, that knowing a foreign language and your subject is not as important as being sensitive to language and being competent to write your own language dexterously, clearly, economically and resourcefully. Experience with translationese, for example,

> Strauss' Opus 29 stands under the star of Bierbaum who in his lyric poems attempted to tie in the echoes of the German love poetry with the folk song and with the impressionistic changes.
>
> *Opus 29 steht im Zeichen Bierbaums, der als Lyriker versuchte, Nachklänge des Minnesangs mit dem Volkslied und mit impressionistischen Wendungen zu verknüpfen.*
> (Record sleeve note)

shows that a good writer can often avoid not only errors of usage but mistakes of fact and language simply by applying his common sense and showing sensitivity to language.

Being good at writing has little to do with being good at 'essays', or at 'English' as you may have learned it at school. It means being able to use the appropriate words in the appropriate order for the object or process you are attempting to describe; continuously trying to improve your writing (a translation is never finished); and increasing your own English vocabulary co-extensively with your knowledge of new facts and new foreign-language words. And it means making flexible use of the abundant grammatical resources of your language, which are enriched by contemporary speech. It is something which, like translation, you can learn: you are not born a good writer; you do not have to be one now; you have to be determined to become one, to relate new experience to fresh language.

Finally, it means having a sense of order and pertinence – learning to construct a specific (*gezielt*, purposeful) beginning, body and conclusion for your subject: a beginning that defines and sets the subject out; a 'body' that gives and illustrates the pros and cons of the argument; a conclusion that states your own verdict – and all without irrelevance.

A translator has to have a flair and a feel for his own language. There is nothing mystical about this 'sixth sense', but it is compounded of intelligence, sensitivity and intuition, as well as of knowledge. This sixth sense, which often comes into play (*joue*) during a final revision, tells you when to translate literally, and also, instinctively, perhaps once in a hundred or three hundred words, when to break all the 'rules' of translation, when to translate *malheur* by 'catastrophe' in a seventeenth-century text.

I cannot make you into a good translator; I cannot cause you to write well. The best I can do is to suggest to you some general guidelines for translating. I shall propose a way of analysing the source language text; I shall discuss the two basic translation methods; and I shall set out the various procedures for handling texts, sentences and other units. I shall at times discuss the relation between meaning, language, culture and translation. By offering plenty of examples I hope to provide enough practice for you to improve your performance as a translator.

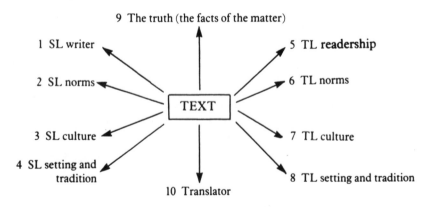

Figure 1. The dynamics of translation

What is translation? Often, though not by any means always, it is rendering the meaning of a text into another language in the way that the author intended the text. Common sense tells us that this ought to be simple, as one ought to be able to say something as well in one language as in another. On the other hand, you may see it as complicated, artificial and fraudulent, since by using another language you are pretending to be someone you are not. Hence in many types of text (legal, administrative, dialect, local, cultural) the temptation is to transfer as many SL (Source Language) words to the TL (Target Language) as possible. The pity is, as Mounin wrote, that the translation cannot simply reproduce, or be, the original. And since this is so, the first business of the translator is to translate.

A text may therefore be pulled in ten different directions, as follows:

(1) The individual style or idiolect of the SL author. When should it be (a) preserved, (b) normalised?

(2) The conventional grammatical and lexical usage for this type of text, depending on the topic and the situation.

(3) Content items referring specifically to the SL, or third language (i.e. not SL or TL) cultures.

(4) The typical format of a text in a book, periodical, newspaper, etc., as influenced by tradition at the time.

(5) The expectations of the putative readership, bearing in mind their estimated knowledge of the topic and the style of language they use, expressed in terms of the largest common factor, since one should not translate down (or up) to the readership.

(6), (7), (8) As for 2, 3 and 4 respectively, but related to the TL.

(9) What is being described or reported, ascertained or verified (the referential truth), where possible independently of the SL text and the expectations of the readership.

(10) The views and prejudices of the translator, which may be personal and subjective, or may be social and cultural, involving the translator's 'group loyalty factor', which may reflect the national, political, ethnic, religious, social class, sex, etc. assumptions of the translator.

Needless to say, there are many other tensions in translations, for example between sound and sense, emphasis (word order) and naturalness (grammar), the figurative and the literal, neatness and comprehensiveness, concision and accuracy.

Figure 1 shows how many opposing forces pull the translation activity (*l'activité traduisante*) in opposite directions. The diagram is not complete. There is often a tension between intrinsic and communicative, or, if you like, between semantic and pragmatic meaning. When do you translate *Il fait froid* as 'It's cold' and when as 'I'm cold', 'I'm freezing', 'I'm so cold', etc., when that is what it means in the context? All of which suggests that translation is impossible. Which is not so.

Why a book of this sort? Because I think there is a body of knowledge about translation which, if applied to solving translation problems, can contribute to a translator's training. Translation as a profession practised in international organisations, government departments, public companies and translation agencies (now often called translation companies) began only about thirty years ago; even now, the idea that all languages (there are 4000) are of equal value and importance, and that everyone has a right to speak and write his own language, whether it is a national or a minority language (most countries are at least 'bilingual') is not generally recognised. Translation as a profession has to be seen as a collaborative process between translators, revisers, terminologists, often writers and clients (literary works have to be checked by a second native TL reviser and desirably a native SL speaker), where one works towards a general agreement. Nevertheless, finally, only one person can be responsible for one piece or section of translation; it must have the stamp of one style. The principle with which this book starts is that everything without exception is translatable; the translator cannot afford the luxury of saying that something cannot be translated.

Danila Seleskovitch, a brilliant interpreter and writer, has said: 'Everything said in one language can be expressed in another – on condition that the two languages belong to cultures that have reached a comparable degree of development.' The condition she makes is false and misleading. Translation is an instrument of education as well as of truth precisely because it has to reach readers whose cultural and educational level is different from, and often 'lower' or earlier, than, that of the readers of the original – one has in mind computer technology for Xhosas. 'Foreign' communities have their own language structures and their own cultures, 'foreign' individuals have their own way of thinking and therefore of expressing themselves, but all these can be explained, and as a last resort the explanation is the translation. No language, no culture is so 'primitive' that it cannot embrace the terms and the concepts of, say, computer technology or plainsong. But such a translation is a longer process if it is in a language whose culture does not include computer technology. If it is to cover all the points in the source language text, it requires greater space in the target language text. Therefore, whilst translation is always possible, it may for various reasons not have the same impact as the original.

Translation has its own excitement, its own interest. A satisfactory translation is always possible, but a good translator is never satisfied with it. It can usually be improved. There is no such thing as a perfect, ideal or 'correct' translation. A translator is always trying to extend his knowledge and improve his means of expression; he is always pursuing facts and words. He works on four levels: translation is first a science, which entails the knowledge and verification of the facts and the language that describes them – here, what is wrong, mistakes of truth, can be identified; secondly, it is a skill, which calls for appropriate language and acceptable usage; thirdly, an art, which distinguishes good from undistinguished writing and is the creative, the intuitive, sometimes the inspired, level of the translation; lastly, a matter of taste, where argument ceases, preferences are expressed, and the variety of meritorious translations is the reflection of individual differences.

Whilst accepting that a few good translators (like a few good actors) are 'naturals', I suggest that the practical demands on translators are so wide, and the subject still so wrapped up in pointless arguments about its feasibility, that it would benefit students of translation and would-be translators to follow a course based on a wide variety of texts and examples. This book claims to be useful, not essential. It attempts to set up a framework of reference for an activity that serves as a means of communication, a transmitter of culture, a technique (one of many, to be used with discretion) of language learning, and a source of personal pleasure.

As a means of communication, translation is used for multilingual notices, which have at last appeared increasingly conspicuously in public places; for instructions issued by exporting companies; for tourist publicity, where it is too often produced from the native into the 'foreign' language by natives as a matter of national pride; for official documents, such as treaties and contracts; for reports, papers, articles, correspondence, textbooks to convey information, advice and recommendations for every branch of knowledge. Its volume has increased with the rise of the mass media, the increase in the number of independent countries, and the growing recognition of the importance of linguistic minorities in all the countries of the world. Its importance is highlighted by the mistranslation of the Japanese telegram sent to Washington just before the bomb was dropped on Hiroshima, when *mokasutu* was allegedly translated as 'ignored' instead of 'considered', and by the ambiguity in UN Resolution 242, where 'the withdrawal from occupied territories' was translated as *le retrait des territoires occupés*, and therefore as a reference to all of the occupied territory to be evacuated by the Israelis.

Translation has been instrumental in transmitting culture, sometimes under unequal conditions responsible for distorted and biased translations, ever since countries and languages have been in contact with each other. Thus the Romans 'pillaged' Greek culture; the Toledo School transferred Arabic and Greek learning to Europe; and up to the nineteenth century European culture was drawing heavily on Latin and Greek translations. In the nineteenth century German culture was absorbing Shakespeare. In this century a centrifugal world literature has appeared, consisting of the work of a small number of 'international' writers (Greene, Bellow, Solzhenitsyn, Böll, Grass, Moravia, Murdoch, Lessing, amongst those still living, succeeding Mann, Brecht, Kafka, Mauriac, Valéry, etc.), which is translated into most national and many regional languages. Unfortunately there is no corresponding centripetal cultural movement from 'regional' or peripheral authors.

That translation is not merely a transmitter of culture, but also of the truth, a force for progress, could be instanced by following the course of resistance to Bible translation and the preservation of Latin as a superior language of the elect, with a consequent disincentive to translating between other languages.

As a technique for learning foreign languages, translation is a two-edged instrument: it has the special purpose of demonstrating the learner's knowledge of the foreign language, either as a form of control or to exercise his intelligence in order to develop his competence. This is its strong point in foreign-language classes, which has to be sharply distinguished from its normal use in transferring meanings and conveying messages. The translation done in schools, which as a discipline is unfortunately usually taken for granted and rarely discussed, often encourages absurd, stilted renderings, particularly of colloquial passages including proper names and institutional terms (absurdly encouraged by dictionary mistranslations such as *Giacopo* for 'James' and *Staatsrat* for 'Privy Councillor'). Even a sentence such as:

> *Qu'une maille saûtat parfois à ce tissu de perfection auquel Brigitte Pian travaillait avec une vigilance de toutes les secondes, c'était dans l'ordre et elle s'en consolait pourvû que ce fût sans témoin.*
>
>   (Mauriac, *La Pharisienne*)

might produce something like this from a sixth-former:

> That a stitch should sometimes break in that tissue of perfection at which Brigitte Pian was working with a vigilance to which she devoted every second, this was in order and she consoled herself for it provided it was without witness.

which proves that each word construction is understood, where a more likely reading would be:

> If Brigitte Pian sometimes dropped a stitch in the admirable material she was working on with such unremitting vigilance, it was in the natural order of things and she found consolation for it, provided she had no witnesses.

A translator, perhaps more than any other practitioner of a profession, is continually faced with choices, for instance when he has to translate words denoting quality, the words of the mental world (adjectives, adverbs, adjectival nouns, e.g. 'good', 'well', 'goodness'), rather than objects or events. In making his choice, he is intuitively or consciously following a theory of translation, just as any teacher of grammar teaches a theory of linguistics. *La traduction appelle une théorie en acte*, Jean-René Ladmiral has written. Translation calls on a theory in action; the translator reviews the criteria for the various options before he makes his selection as a procedure in his translating activity.

The personal pleasure derived from translation is the excitement of trying to solve a thousand small problems in the context of a large one. Mystery, jigsaw, game, kaleidoscope, maze, puzzle, see-saw, juggling – these metaphors capture the 'play' element of translation without its seriousness. (But pleasure lies in play rather than in seriousness.) The chase after words and facts is unremitting and requires imagination. There is an exceptional attraction in the search for the right word, just out of reach, the semantic gap between two languages that one scours *Roget* to fill. The relief of finding it, the 'smirk' after hitting on the right word when others are still floundering, is an acute reward, out of proportion and out of perspective to the satisfaction of filling in the whole picture, but more concrete. The quality of pleasure reflects the constant tension between sentence and word.

You may have heard of a relatively new polytechnic/university subject called Translation Theory ('Translatology' in Canada, *Traductología* in Spain, *Über-*

setzungswissenschaft in German-speaking countries, 'Translation Studies' in the Netherlands and Belgium); this book is intended to introduce it to you.

In a narrow sense, translation theory is concerned with the translation method appropriately used for a certain type of text, and it is therefore dependent on a functional theory of language. However, in a wider sense, translation theory is the body of knowledge that we have about translating, extending from general principles to guidelines, suggestions and hints. (The only rule I know is the equal frequency rule, viz. that corresponding words, where they exist – metaphors, collocations, groups, clauses, sentences, word order, proverbs, etc. – should have approximately equal frequency, for the topic and register in question, in both the source and target languages.) Translation theory is concerned with minutiae (the meanings of semi-colons, italics, misprints) as well as generalities (presentation, the thread of thought underlying a piece), and both may be equally important in the context.

Translation theory in action, translation theory used operationally for the purpose of reviewing all the options (in particular, sensitising the translator to those he had not been aware of) and then making the decisions – in fact the teeth of the theory – is a frame of reference for translation and translation criticism, relating first to complete texts, where it has most to say, then, in descending level, to paragraphs, sentences, clauses, word groups (in particular, collocations), words – familiar alternative words, cultural and institutional terms, proper names, 'non-equivalent words', neologisms and key conceptual terms – morphemes and punctuation marks. Note that metaphor, perhaps the most significant translation problem, may occur at all levels – from word to text, at which level it becomes an allegory or a fantasy.

What translation theory does is, first, to identify and define a translation problem (no problem – no translation theory!); second, to indicate all the factors that have to be taken into account in solving the problem; third, to list all the possible translation procedures; finally, to recommend the most suitable translation procedure, plus the appropriate translation.

Translation theory is pointless and sterile if it does not arise from the problems of translation practice, from the need to stand back and reflect, to consider all the factors, within the text and outside it, before coming to a decision.

I close this chapter by enumerating the new elements in translation *now*, as opposed to, say, at the beginning of the century:

(1) The emphasis on the readership and the setting, and therefore on naturalness, ease of understanding and an appropriate register, when these factors are appropriate.
(2) Expansion of topics beyond the religious, the literary and the scientific to technology, trade, current events, publicity, propaganda, in fact to virtually every topic of writing.
(3) Increase in variety of text formats, from books (including plays and poems) to articles, papers, contracts, treaties, laws, notices, instructions, advertisements,

publicity, recipes, letters, reports, business forms, documents, etc. These now vastly outnumber books, so it is difficult to calculate the number or the languages of translations on any large scale.

(4) Standardisation of terminology.

(5) The formation of translator teams and the recognition of the reviser's role.

(6) The impact of linguistics, sociolinguistics and translation theory, which will become apparent only as more translators pass through polytechnics and universities.

(7) Translation is now used as much to transmit knowledge and to create understanding between groups and nations, as to transmit culture.

In sum, it all adds up to a new discipline, a new profession; an old pursuit engaged in now for mainly different purposes.

CHAPTER 2

The Analysis of a Text

READING THE TEXT

You begin the job by reading the original for two purposes: first, to understand what it is about; second, to analyse it from a 'translator's' point of view, which is not the same as a linguist's or a literary critic's. You have to determine its intention and the way it is written for the purpose of selecting a suitable translation method and identifying particular and recurrent problems.

Understanding the text requires both general and close reading. General reading to get the gist; here you may have to read encyclopaedias, textbooks, or specialist papers to understand the subject and the concepts, always bearing in mind that for the translator the function precedes the description – the important thing about the neutrino in context is not that it is a stable elementary particle, preserving the law of conservation of mass and energy, but that now the neutrino has been found to have mass, the Universe is calculated to be twice as large as previously thought. 'Chair', *chaise, Stuhl, Sessel, sedia, silla, stul* – they all present somewhat different images, lax bundles of shapes that differ in each culture, united primarily by a similar function, an object for a person to sit on plus a few essential formal features, such as a board with a back and four legs. A knife is for cutting with, but the blade and the handle are important too – they distinguish the knife from the scissors.

Close reading is required, in any challenging text, of the words both out of and in context. In principle, everything has to be looked up that does not make good sense in its context; common words like *serpent* (F), to ensure they are not being used musically or figuratively (sly, deceitful, unscupulous) or technically (EEC currency) or colloquially; neologisms – you will likely find many if you are translating a recent publication (for 'non-equivalent' words, see p. 117); acronyms, to find their TL equivalents, which may be non-existent (you should not invent them, even if you note that the SL author has invented them); figures and measures, converting to TL or *Système International* (SI) units where appropriate; names of people and places, almost all words beginning with capital letters – 'encyclopaedia' words are as important as 'dictionary' words, the distinction being fuzzy. (Words like 'always', 'never', 'all', 'must' have no place in talk about translation – there are 'always' exceptions.) You can compare the translating activity to an iceberg: the tip is the translation – what is visible, what is written on the page – the iceberg, the activity, is all the work you do, often ten times as much again, much of which you do not even use.

THE INTENTION OF THE TEXT

In reading, you search for the intention of the text, you cannot isolate this from understanding it, they go together and the title may be remote from the content as well as the intention. Two texts may describe a battle or a riot or a debate, stating the same facts and figures, but the type of language used and even the grammatical structures (passive voice, impersonal verbs often used to disclaim responsibility) in each case may be evidence of different points of view. The intention of the text represents the SL writer's attitude to the subject matter.

A piece about floors may be 'pushing' floor polishes; about newspapers, a condemnation of the press; about nuclear weapons, an advertisement for them – always there is a point of view, somewhere, a modal component to the proposition, perhaps in a word – 'unfortunately', 'nevertheless', 'hopefully'.

What is meant by 'That was clever of him'? Is it ironical, openly or implicitly? (In a text showing that BBC Radio 2 is a pale imitation of commercial radio, the irony may only be implicit and obscure to a non-British reader, and the translator may want to make the point more explicitly.) '*Clémente, notre justice répressive?*', writes a journalist meaning 'Our repressive judicial system is far from lenient', or is it a bluff, mainly nonsense, for amusement? It may be 'iceberg' work to find out, since the tone may come through in a literal translation, but the translator has to be aware of it.

Again, in a detailed, confused piece about check-ups on elderly patients who may have to undergo chemotherapy the author's intention is to show that patients must have a thorough physical check-up before they start a course of drugs: if physical problems are cleared up first, there may be no need for psychiatry.

A summary of this nature, which uses only a few key words from the original, appears to be isolated from the language, simply to show what happens in real life, and it is indispensable to the translator. But he still has to 'return' to the text. He still has to translate the text, even if he has to simplify, rearrange, clarify, slim it of its redundancies, pare it down.

THE INTENTION OF THE TRANSLATOR

Usually, the translator's intention is identical with that of the author of the SL text. But he may be translating an advertisement, a notice, or a set of instructions to show his client how such matters are formulated and written in the source language, rather than how to adapt them in order to persuade or instruct a new TL readership. And again, he may be translating a manual of instructions for a less educated readership, so that the explanation in his translation may be much larger than the 'reproduction'.

TEXT STYLES

Following Nida, we distinguish four types of (literary or non-literary) text:

(1) *Narrative*: a dynamic sequence of events, where the emphasis is on the verbs or, for English, 'dummy' or 'empty' verbs plus verb-nouns or phrasal verbs ('He made a sudden appearance', 'He burst in').
(2) *Description*, which is static, with emphasis on linking verbs, adjectives, adjectival nouns.
(3) *Discussion*, a treatment of ideas, with emphasis on abstract nouns (concepts), verbs of thought, mental activity ('consider', 'argue', etc.), logical argument and connectives.
(4) *Dialogue*, with emphasis on colloquialisms and phaticisms.

THE READERSHIP

On the basis of the variety of language used in the original, you attempt to characterise the readership of the original and then of the translation, and to decide how much attention you have to pay to the TL readers. (In the case of a poem or any work written primarily as self-expression the amount is, I suggest, very little.) You may try to assess the level of education, the class, age and sex of the readership if these are 'marked'.

The average text for translation tends to be for an educated, middle-class readership in an informal, not colloquial style. The most common variety of 'marked' error in register among student translators tends to be 'colloquial' and 'intimate', e.g. use of phrases such as 'more and more' for 'increasingly' (*de plus en plus*), 'above all' for 'particularly' (*surtout*); 'job' for 'work'; 'got well' for 'recovered' and excessively familiar phrasal verbs ('get out of', 'get rid of'). The other common error, use of formal or official register (e.g. 'decease' for 'death'), also shows signs of translationese. These tokens of language typify the student-translators instead of the readership they are translating for; they may epitomise their degree of knowledge and interest in the subject and the appropriate culture, i.e. how motivated they are. All this will help you to decide on the degree of formality, generality (or specificity) and emotional tone you must express when you work on the text.

STYLISTIC SCALES

The scale of *formality* has been variously expressed, notably by Martin Joos and Strevens. I suggest:

Officialese	'The consumption of any nutriments whatsoever is categorically prohibited in this establishment.'
Official	'The consumption of nutriments is prohibited.'
Formal	'You are requested not to consume food in this establishment.'
Neutral	'Eating is not allowed here.'
Informal	'Please don't eat here.'
Colloquial	'You can't feed your face here.'
Slang	'Lay off the nosh.'
Taboo	'Lay off the fucking nosh.'

As always, the distinctions are fuzzy. In not so informal language, translate *de moins en moins* by 'decreasingly', *tout à fait* by 'entirely', *d'un seul coup* by 'at one attempt' or 'simultaneously.'

Similarly, I suggest the following scale of *generality* or *difficulty*:

Simple
'The floor of the sea is covered with rows of big mountains and deep pits.'
Popular
'The floor of the oceans is covered with great mountain chains and deep trenches.'
Neutral (using basic vocabulary only)
'A graveyard of animal and plant remains lies buried in the earth's crust.'
Educated
'The latest step in vertebrate evolution was the tool-making man.'
Technical
'Critical path analysis is an operational research technique used in management.'
Opaquely technical (comprehensible only to an expert)
'Neuraminic acid in the form of its alkali-stable methoxy derivative was first isolated by Klenk from gangliosides.' (Letter to *Nature*, November 1955, quoted in Quirk, 1984.)

I suggest the following scale of *emotional tone*:

Intense (profuse use of intensifers) ('hot')
'Absolutely wonderful . . . ideally dark bass . . . enormously successful . . . superbly controlled'
Warm
'Gentle, soft, heart-warming melodies'
Factual ('cool')
'Significant, exceptionally well judged, personable, presentable, considerable'

Understatement ('cold')
'Not . . . undignified'

Note that there is some correlation between formality and emotional tone, in that an official style is likely to be factual, whilst colloquialisms and slang tend to be emotive. In translating, the effusiveness of Italian, the formality and stiffness of German and Russian, the impersonality of French, the informality and understatement of English have to be taken into account in certain types of corresponding passage.

ATTITUDE

In passages making evaluations and recommendations, you have to assess the standards of the writer. If he writes 'good', 'fair', 'average', 'competent', 'adequate', 'satisfactory', 'middling', 'poor', 'excellent', are his standards – relative to the context – absolute, generally accepted in his culture, or arbitrary? Often there is only a thin line in the critical difference between a positive and a negative opinion, which is not clarified by the 'middle' words I have listed.

Similarly, approximately the same referent may often be expressed positively, neutrally or negatively in many languages; thus 'plump/fat'; *rondelet/gras*; *mollig/dick*; 'slim/slender/thin'; *svelte/mince/maigre*; *schlank/dünn/mager*. (The process develops as writers become more aware of their language.) *Régime* ('government') is neutral in French but negative in English.

SETTING

You have to decide on the likely setting: Where would the text be published in the TL? What is the TL equivalent of the SL periodical, newspaper, textbook, journal, etc?, or Who is the client you are translating for and what are his requirements? You may have to take account of briefer titles, absence of sub-titles and sub-headings, shorter paragraphs and other features of the TL house-style.

You have to make several assumptions about the SL readership. From the setting of the SL text, as well as the text itself, you should assess whether the readership is likely to be motivated (keen to read the text), familiar with the topic and the culture, and 'at home' in the variety of language used. The three typical reader types are perhaps the expert, the educated layman, and the uninformed. You then have to consider whether you are translating for the same or a different type of TL readership, perhaps with less knowledge of the topic or the culture, or a lower standard of linguistic education. Finally, if you are translating a poem or an important authoritative statement, should you consider the TL reader at all, apart from concessions or cultural 'scraps' to help him out (e.g. translating 'a half-holiday' as *un après-midi libre*)?

THE QUALITY OF THE WRITING

You have to consider the quality of the writing and the authority of the text, two critical factors in the choice of translation method. The quality of the writing has to be judged in relation to the author's intention and/or the requirements of the subject-matter. If the text is well written, i.e., the manner is as important as the matter, the right words are in the right places, with a minimum of redundancy, you have to regard every nuance of the author's meaning (particularly if it is subtle and difficult) as having precedence over the reader's response – assuming they are not required to act or react promptly; on the contrary, assuming hopefully that they will read your translation at least twice. Deciding what is good writing is sometimes criticised as 'subjective' but it is a decision, like many others, not subjective but with a subjective element (the area of taste) which you have to make, using any experience of literary criticism you may have had but bearing in mind that the criterion here is meaning: to what extent does the web of words of the SL text correspond to a clear representation of facts or images? If a text is well written, the syntax will reflect the writer's personality – complex syntax will reflect subtlety (Proust, Mann) – plain syntax, simplicity. Words will be freshly used with unusual connotations. A badly written text will be cluttered with stereotyped phrases, recently fashionable general words and probably poorly structured. Note that language rules and prescriptions have nothing much to do with good writing. What matters is a fresh reflection of the reality outside language or of the writer's mind.

The authority of the text is derived from good writing; but also independently, unconnectedly, from the status of the SL writer. If the SL writer is recognised as important in his field, and he is making an ex-cathedra or official statement, the text is also authoritative. The point is that 'expressive' texts, i.e. serious imaginative literature and authoritative and personal statements, have to be translated closely, matching the writing, good or bad, of the original. Informative texts, statements that relate primarily to the truth, to the real facts of the matter, have to be translated in the best style that the translator can reconcile with the style of the original.

CONNOTATIONS AND DENOTATIONS

Bear in mind that whilst all texts have connotations, an aura of ideas and feelings suggested by lexical words (crudely, 'run' may suggest 'haste', 'sofa' may suggest 'comfort'), and all texts have an 'underlife' (viz. as much of the personal qualities and private life of the writer as can be derived from an intuitive/analytical reading of a text), in a non-literary text the denotations of a word normally come before its connotations. But in a literary text, you have to give precedence to its connotations, since, if it is any good, it is an allegory, a comment on society, at the time and now, as well as on its strict setting.

From a translator's point of view this is the only theoretical distinction between a non-literary and a literary text. In fact, the greater the quantity of a language's resources (e.g. polysemy, word-play, sound-effect, metre, rhyme) expended on a text, the more difficult it is likely to be to translate, and the more worthwhile. A satisfactory restricted translation of any poem is always possible, though it may work as an introduction to and an interpretation of rather than as a recreation of the original.

THE LAST READING

Finally, you should note the cultural aspect of the SL text; you should underline all neologisms, metaphors, cultural words and institutional terms peculiar to the SL or third language, proper names, technical terms and 'untranslatable' words. Untranslatable words are the ones that have no ready one-to-one equivalent in the TL; they are likely to be qualities or actions – descriptive verbs, or mental words – words relating to the mind, that have no cognates in the TL, e.g. words like 'fuzzy', 'murky', 'dizzy', 'snug', 'snub'; many such English words arise from Dutch or from dialect. You underline words that you have to consider out of as well as within context, in order to establish their semantic range, their frontiers: unlike Humpty, you cannot normally decide to make any word mean what you want, and there are normally limits to the meaning of any word. The purpose of dictionaries is to indicate the semantic ranges of words as well as, through collocations, the main senses.

I should say here whilst the meaning of a completely context-determined word may appear to be remote from its non-contextual (core) meaning there must be some link between the two meanings. Thus it might appear to be beyond reason that the French word *communication* could possibly mean 'fistula', but it can be translated as such if the fistula is a way of communication between the aorta and the pulmonary artery. Sometimes the link is a secret code.

I am not claiming that you should carry out this analysis on every part of the text; much of it may be intuitive or unnecessary in the case of a particular text. Underline only the items where you see a translation problem, and bear in mind that it is often helpful to study such an item first in context, then in isolation, as though it were a dictionary or an encyclopaedia entry only, and finally in context again.

CONCLUSION

In principle, a translational analysis of the SL text based on its comprehension is the first stage of translation and the basis of the useful discipline of translation criticism. In fact, such an analysis is, I think, an appropriate training for translators, since by underlining the appropriate words they will show they are aware of difficulties they might otherwise have missed. Thus you relate translation theory to its practice. A professional translator would not usually make such an analysis explicitly, since he would need to take only a sample in order to establish the properties of a text. A translation critic, however, after determining the general properties – first of the text and secondly of the translation (both these tasks would centre in the respective intentions of translator and critic) – would use the underlined words as a basis for a detailed comparison of the two texts.

To summarise, you have to study the text not for itself but as something that may have to be reconstituted for a different readership in a different culture.

CHAPTER **3**

The Process of Translating

INTRODUCTION

My description of translating procedure is operational. It begins with choosing a method of approach. Secondly, when we are translating, we translate with four levels more or less consciously in mind: (1) the SL text level, the level of language, where we begin and which we continually (but not continuously) go back to; (2) the referential level, the level of objects and events, real or imaginary, which we progressively have to visualise and build up, and which is an essential part, first of the comprehension, then of the reproduction process; (3) the cohesive level, which is more general, and grammatical, which traces the train of thought, the feeling tone (positive or negative) and the various presuppositions of the SL text. This level encompasses both comprehension and reproduction: it presents an overall picture, to which we may have to adjust the language level; (4) the level of naturalness, of common language appropriate to the writer or the speaker in a certain situation. Again, this is a generalised level, which constitutes a band within which the translator works, unless he is translating an authoritative text, in which case he sees the level of naturalness as a point of reference to determine the deviation – if any – between the author's level he is pursuing and the natural level. This level of naturalness is concerned only with reproduction. Finally, there is the revision procedure, which may be concentrated or staggered according to the situation. This procedure constitutes at least half of the complete process.

THE RELATION OF TRANSLATING TO TRANSLATION THEORY

The purpose of this theory of translating is to be of service to the translator. It is designed to be a continuous link between translation theory and practice; it derives from a translation theory framework which proposes that when the main purpose of the text is to convey information and convince the reader, a method of translation must be 'natural'; if, on the other hand, the text is an expression of the peculiar innovative (or clichéd) and authoritative style of an author (whether it be a lyric, a prime minister's speech or a legal document), the translator's own version has to reflect any deviation from a 'natural' style. The nature of naturalness is discussed in detail in my exposition of the theory of translating below; 'naturalness' is both grammatical and lexical, and is a touchstone at every level of a text, from paragraph to word, from title to punctuation.

The level of naturalness binds translation theory to translating theory, and translating theory to practice. The remainder of my translating theory is in essence psychological – the relationship between language and 'reality' (though all we know of 'reality' is mental images and mental verbalising or thinking) – but it has practical applications.

If one accepts this theory of translating, there is no gap between translation theory and practice. The theory of translating is based, via the level of naturalness, on a theory of translation. Therefore one arrives at the scheme shown in Figure 2.

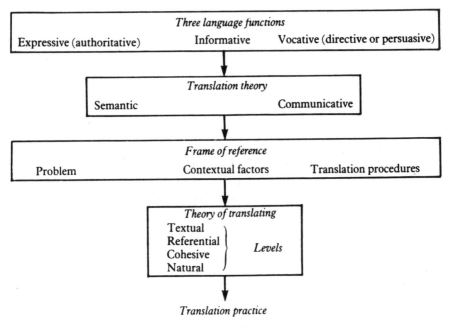

Figure 2. A functional theory of language

THE APPROACH

A translation is something that has to be *discussed*. In too many schools and universities, it is still being imposed as an exercise in felicitous English style, where the warts of the original are ignored. The teacher more or less imposes a fair copy which is a 'model' of his own English rather than proposing a version for discussion and criticism by students, some of whom will be brighter than he is.

Translation is for discussion. Both in its referential and its pragmatic aspect, it has an invariant factor, but this factor cannot be precisely defined since it depends on the requirements and constraints exercised by one original on one translation. All one can do is to produce an argument with translation examples to support it. Nothing is purely objective or subjective. There are no cast-iron rules. Everything is more or less. There is an assumption of 'normally' or 'usually' or 'commonly' behind each well-established principle; as I have stated earlier, qualifications such as 'always', 'never', 'must' do not exist – there are no absolutes.

Given these caveats, I am nevertheless going to take you through my tentative translating process.

There are two approaches to translating (and many compromises between them): (1) you start translating sentence by sentence, for say the first paragraph or chapter, to get the feel and the feeling tone of the text, and then you deliberately sit back, review the position, and read the rest of the SL text; (2) you read the whole text two or three times, and find the intention, register, tone, mark the difficult words and passages and start translating only when you have taken your bearings.

Which of the two methods you choose may depend on your temperament, or on whether you trust your intuition (for the first method) or your powers of analysis (for the second). Alternatively, you may think the first method more suitable for a literary and the second for a technical or an institutional text. The danger of the first method is that it may leave you with too much revision to do on the early part, and is therefore time-wasting. The second method (usually preferable) can be mechanical; a translational text analysis is useful as a point of reference, but it should not inhibit the free play of your intuition. Alternatively, you may prefer the first approach for a relatively easy text, the second for a harder one.

From the point of view of the translator, any scientific investigation, both statistical and diagrammatic (some linguists and translation theorists make a fetish of diagrams, schemas and models), of what goes on in the brain (mind? nerves? cells?) during the process of translating is remote and at present speculative. The contribution of psycholinguistics to translation is limited: the positive, neutral or negative pragmatic effect of a word (e.g. *affecter*, 'affect', 'brutal', *befremden*, *drame*, *comédie*, *favoriser*, *dénouement*, *extraordinaire*, 'grandiose', *grandioznyi*, 'potentate', *pontif*, 'pretentious', 'arbitrary/arbitration', *proposer*, *exploit*, *hauteur*, 'vaunt') e.g. Osgood's work on semantic differentials is helpful, since the difference between 'positive' and 'negative' (i.e. between the writer's approval and his disapproval) is always critical to the interpretation of a text. The heart of translation theory is translation problems (admitting that what is a problem to one translator may not be to another); translation theory broadly consists of, and can be defined as, a large number of generalisations of translation problems. A theoretical discussion of the philosophy and the psychology of translation is remote from the translator's problems. Whether you produce a statistical survey through questionnaires of what a hundred translators think they think when they translate, or whether you follow what one translator goes through, mental stage by mental stage, I do not see what use it is going to be to anyone else, except perhaps as a corrective of freak methods – or ideas such as relying entirely on bilingual dictionaries, substituting encyclopaedia descriptions for dictionary definitions, using the best-sounding synonyms for literary translation, transferring all Graeco-Latin words, continuous paraphrasing, etc. But there is never any point in scientifically proving the obvious.

THE TEXTUAL LEVEL

Working on the text level, you intuitively and automatically make certain 'conversions'; you transpose the SL grammar (clauses and groups) into their 'ready' TL equivalents and you translate the lexical units into the sense that appears immediately appropriate in the context of the sentence.

Your base level when you translate is the text. This is the level of the literal translation of the source language into the target language, the level of the translationese you have to eliminate, but it also acts as a corrective of paraphrase and the parer-down of synonyms. So a part of your mind may be on the text level whilst another is elsewhere. Translation is pre-eminently the occupation in which you have to be thinking of several things at the same time.

THE REFERENTIAL LEVEL

You should not read a sentence without seeing it on the referential level. Whether a text is technical or literary or institutional, you have to make up your mind, summarily and continuously, what it is about, what it is in aid of, what the writer's peculiar slant on it is: say, *L'albumine et ses interactions médicamenteuses* (It.: *L'albumina e le sue interazioni medicamentose*) – it may be the action of drugs on blood, the need to detect toxic effects, the benefits of blood transfusion. Say, *La pression quantitative* – the large number of pupils in schools, the demand for better-quality education, the need for suitable education for all. Say, *Recherches sur un facteur diurétique d'origine lymphatique* – the attempt to find a substance in the body fluid that promotes urine production, the disorders that inhibit the formation of the substance, the attempts to isolate the substance. Always, you have to be able to summarise in crude lay terms, to simplify at the risk of over-simplification, to pierce the jargon, to penetrate the fog of words. You get an abstraction like *Ce phénomène s'avère; ce phénomène, exact pour cellules et fibres* – referring to a tumour becoming so large that it compresses the parenchyma next to it. Usually, a more specific reference is desirable in the translation: the tumour's swelling, deterioration, etc. Thus your translation is some hint of a compromise between the text and the facts.

For each sentence, when it is not clear, when there is an ambiguity, when the writing is abstract or figurative, you have to ask yourself: What is actually happening here? and why? For what reason, on what grounds, for what purpose? Can you see it in your mind? Can you *visualise it*? If you cannot, you have to 'supplement' the linguistic level, the text level with the referential level, the factual level with the necessary additional information (no more) from this level of reality, the facts of the matter. In real life, what is the setting or scene, who are the actors or agents, what is the purpose? This may or may not take you away temporarily from the words in the text. And certainly it is all too easy to immerse yourself in language and to detach yourself from the reality, real or imaginary, that is being described. Far more acutely than writers wrestling with only one language, you become aware of the awful gap between words and objects, sentences and actions (or processes), grammar and moods (or attitudes). You have to gain perspective (*distacco, recul*), to stand back from the language and have an image of the reality behind the text, a reality for which you, and not the author (unless it is an expressive or an authoritative text), are responsible and *liable*.

The referential goes hand in hand with the textual level. All languages have polysemous words and structures which can be finally solved only on the referential level, beginning with a few multi-purpose, overloaded prepositions and conjunctions, through dangling participles ('reading the paper, the dog barked loudly') to general words. The referential level, where you mentally sort out the text, is built up out of, based on, the clarification of all linguistic difficulties and, where appropriate, supplementary information from the 'encyclopaedia' – my symbol for any work of reference or textbook. (Thus in *pour le passage de Flore*, you find that Flore/Flora was an Italic goddess of flowers and gardens. As it is in Claudel you translate: 'for the goddess Flora to pass' and leave the rest to the reader.) You build up the referential picture in your mind when you transform the SL into the TL text; and, being a professional, you are responsible for the truth of this picture.

Does this mean, as Seleskovitch claims, that 'the (SL) words disappear' or that you 'deverbalize the concepts' (Delisle)? Not at all, you are working continuously on two levels, the real and the linguistic, life and language, reference and sense, but you write, you 'compose', on the linguistic level, where your job is to achieve the greatest possible correspondence, referentially and pragmatically, with the words and sentences of the SL text. However tempting it is to remain on that simpler, usually simplified layman's level of reality (the message and its function) you have to force yourself back, in as far as the readership can stand it, into the particularities of the source language meaning.

THE COHESIVE LEVEL

Beyond the second factual level of translating, there is a third, generalised, level linking the first and the second level, which you have to bear in mind. This is the 'cohesive' level; it follows both the structure and the moods of the text: the structure through the connective words (conjunctions, enumerations, reiterations, definite article, general words, referential synonyms, punctuation marks) linking the sentences, usually proceeding from known information (theme) to new information (rheme); proposition, opposition, continuation, reiteration, opposition, conclusion – for instance – or thesis, antithesis, synthesis. Thus the structure follows the train of thought; determines, say, the 'direction' of *d'ailleurs* ('besides', 'further', 'anyway') in a text; ensures that a colon has a sequel, that *ultérieur* has a later reference; that there is a sequence of time, space and logic in the text.

The second factor in the cohesive level is mood. Again, this can be shown as a dialectical factor moving between positive and negative, emotive and neutral. It means tracing the thread of a text through its value-laden and value-free passages which may be expressed by objects or nouns (Margaret Masterman (1982) has shown how a text alternates between 'help' and 'disaster'), as well as adjectives or qualities. You have to spot the difference between positive and neutral in, say, 'appreciate' and 'evaluate'; 'awesome' and 'amazing'; 'tidy' and 'ordered'; *sauber* and *rein*; 'passed away' (indicating the value of the person) and 'died'. Similarly you have to spot differences between negative and neutral in say 'potentate' and 'ruler'. These differences are often delicate, particularly near the centre, where most languages have words like 'fair', 'moderate', *mäßig, passable, assez bon* whose value cannot always be determined in the context.

My third level, this attempt to follow the thought through the connectives and the feeling tone, and the emotion through value-laden or value-free expressions, is, admittedly, only tentative, but it may determine the difference between a humdrum or misleading translation and a good one. This cohesive level is a regulator, it secures coherence, it adjusts emphasis. At this level, you reconsider the lengths of paragraphs and sentences, the formulation of the title; the tone of the conclusion (e.g. the appropriateness of *à tout prendre, en définitive* (often tricky), *en fin de compte, enfin*(!), *à la fin, en somme, en tout état de cause* to summarise an argument at the beginning of a final sentence). This is where the findings of discourse analysis are pertinent.

THE LEVEL OF NATURALNESS

With all that, for all texts (except the ones you know are 'odd' or badly written but authoritative, innovatory or 'special', e.g., where a writer has a peculiar way of writing which has to be reproduced – so for philosophy, Heidegger, Sartre, Husserl; so for fiction any surrealist, baroque, and certain Romantic writers) – for the vast majority of texts, you have to ensure: (a) that your translation makes sense; (b) that it reads naturally, that it is written in ordinary language, the common grammar, idioms and words that meet that kind of situation. Normally, you can only do this by temporarily disengaging yourself from the SL text, by reading your own translation as though no original existed. You get a piece like: *Une doctrine née dans une fraction du clergé de l'Amérique latine qui foisonne sous diverses plumes et dans diverses chapelles et qui connaît déjà un début d'application autoritaire sous la tutelle de l'Etat.* (*L'Express*, July 1985.) The passage has various misleading cognates, and you can reduce it to sense by gradually eliminating all the primary senses (*fraction, née*, *plumes*, *chapelles*, *connaît*) to: 'A doctrine originating amongst a fraction of the clergy of Latin America which proliferates among various writers and in various coteries and which already experiences the beginnings of an authoritarian application under the tutelage of the State'.

Now you still have to make that passage sound natural, which will usually depend on the degree of formality (see p. 14) you have decided on for the whole text. But you might consider: 'A doctrine originating in a group of Latin American clergy and proliferating among various writers and coteries, which is now just beginning to be put into practice in an authoritarian fashion under the auspices of the State' (note that *déjà* often translates as 'now').

A word on 'naturalness'. A translation of serious innovative writing (maybe Rabelais, Shakespeare, Thomas Mann, maybe Hegel, Kant, maybe any authority) may not sound natural, may not be natural to you, though if it is good it is likely to become more so with repeated readings:

The funnel unravels an enormous mass of black smoke like a plait of horsehair being unwound.

La cheminée dévide une énorme fumée noire, pareille à une tresse de crin qu'on détord.
(G. F. Ramuz, 'Le retour du mort', from *Nouvelles*.)

A still new patient, a thin and quiet person, who had found a place with his equally thin and quiet fiancée at the good Russian Table, proved, just when the meal was in full swing, to be epileptic, as he suffered an extreme attack of that type, with a cry whose demonic and inhuman character has often been described, fell heavily on to the floor and struck around with his arms and legs next to his chair with the most ghastly contortions.

Ein noch neuer Patient, ein magerer und stiller Mensch, der mit seiner ebenfalls mageren und stillen Braut am Guten Russentisch Platz gefunden hatte, erwies sich, da eben das Essen in vollem Gang war, als epileptisch indem er einen krassen Anfall dieser Art erlitt, mit jenem Schrei dessen dämonischer und aussermenschlicher Charakter oft geschildert worden ist, zu Boden stürzte und neben seinem Stuhl unter den scheusslichsten Verrenkungen mit Armen und Beinen um sich schlug.
(Thomas Mann, *Der Zauberberg*.)

You may find both these sentences unnatural. Yet, in spite of numerous lexical inadequacies (we have no word for *mager* nor any as vivid as *schildern*, and few parallel sound effects) this is what Ramuz and Thomas Mann wrote, and we cannot change that.

When you are faced with an innovatory expressive text, you have to try to gauge the degree of its deviation from naturalness, from ordinary language and reflect this degree in your translation. Thus in translating *any* type of text you have to sense 'naturalness', usually for the purpose of reproducing, sometimes for the purpose of deviating from naturalness. In a serious expressive text, in the sentence: *il promenait son regard bleu sur la petite pelouse*, '*son regard bleu*' has to be translated as 'his blue gaze', which is a deviation from the normal or natural *les yeux bleus*, 'his blue eyes'. Again *Si le regard du pasteur se promenait sur la pelouse, était-ce pour jouir de la parfaite plénitude verte ou pour y trouver des idées* (Drieu la Rochelle) is translated as something like: 'If the pastor's gaze ran over the lawn, was it to enjoy its perfect green fullness, or to find ideas', rather than 'Whenever the pastor cast a glance over the lawn it was either to enjoy its perfect green richness, or to find ideas in it'.

Again, *son visage était mauve*, 'his face was mauve', *sein Gesicht war mauve* (*malvenfarben*) are virtually precise translation equivalents. 'Mauve' is one of the few secondary colours without connotations (though in France it is the second colour of mourning, 'his face was deathly mauve' would be merely comic), and normally, like 'beige', associated with dress – compare a mauve woman, a violet woman ('shrinking violet'?), but a scarlet woman is different. In the 'mauve' example, a retreat from the unnatural 'mauve' to the natural 'blue' would only be justified if the SL text was both 'anonymous' and poorly written.

You have to bear in mind that the level of naturalness of natural usage is grammatical as well as lexical (i.e., the most frequent syntactic structures, idioms and words that are likely to be appropriately found in that kind of stylistic context), and, through appropriate sentence connectives, may extend to the entire text.

In all 'communicative translation', whether you are translating an informative text, a notice or an advert, 'naturalness' is essential. That is why you cannot translate properly if the TL is not your language of habitual usage. That is why you so often have to detach yourself mentally from the SL text; why, if there is time, you should come back to your version after an interval. You have to ask yourself (or others): Would you see this, would you ever see this, in *The Times*, *The Economist* (watch that *Time–Life–Spiegel* style), the *British Medical Journal*, as a notice, on the back of a board game, on an appliance, in a textbook, in a children's book? Is it usage, is it common usage in that kind of writing? How frequent is it? Do *not* ask yourself: is it English? There is more English than the patriots and the purists and the chauvinists are aware of.

Naturalness is easily defined, not so easy to be concrete about. Natural usage comprises a variety of idioms or styles or registers determined primarily by the 'setting' of the text, i.e. where it is typically published or found, secondarily by the author, topic and readership, all of whom are usually dependent on the setting. It may even appear to be quite 'unnatural', e.g. take any article in *Foreign Trade* (Moscow): 'To put it figuratively, foreign trade has become an important artery in the blood circulation of the Soviet Union's economic organism', or any other example of Soviet bureaucratic jargon; on the whole this might occasionally be tactfully clarified but it should be translated 'straight' as the natural language of participants in that setting.

Natural usage, then, must be distinguished from 'ordinary language', the plain non-technical idiom used by Oxford philosophers for (philosophical) explanation, and 'basic' language, which is somewhere between formal and informal, is easily understood, and is constructed from a language's most frequently used syntactic structures and words – basic language is the nucleus of a language produced naturally. All three varieties – natural, ordinary and basic – are formed exclusively from modern language. However, unnatural translation is marked by interference, primarily from the SL text, possibly from a third language known to the translator including his own, if it is not the target language. 'Natural' translation can be contrasted with 'casual' language (Voegelin), where word order, syntactic structures, collocations and words are predictable. You have to pay special attention to:

(1) Word order. In all languages, adverbs and adverbials are the most mobile components of a sentence, and their placing often indicates the degree of emphasis on what is the new information (rheme) as well as naturalness. They are the most delicate indicator of naturalness:

> He regularly sees me on Tuesdays. (Stress on 'regularly'.)
> He sees me regularly on Tuesdays. (No stress.)
> On Tuesdays he sees me regularly. (Stress on 'Tuesdays'.)

(2) Common structures can be made unnatural by silly one-to-one translation from any language, e.g.:
   (a) Athanogore put his arm *under that of* (*sous celui de*) the young man: ('under the young man's').
   (b) After *having given his meter a satisfied glance* (*après avoir lancé*): ('after giving').
   Both these translations are by English students.
   (c) The packaging *having* (*étant muni de*) a sufficiently clear label, the cider vinegar consumer could not confuse it with . . . : ('as the packaging had . . .').

(3) Cognate words. Both in West and East, thousands of words are drawing nearer to each other in meaning. Many sound natural when you transfer them, and may still have the wrong meaning: 'The book is actually in print' (*Le livre est actuellement sous presse*). Many more sound odd when you transfer them, and are wrong – *avec, sans supplément, le tome VII*, 'with, without a supplement, Vol.7' ('without extra charge'). Thousands sound natural, have the same meaning, are right.

(4) The appropriateness of gerunds, infinitives, verb-nouns (cf. 'the establishment of', 'establishing', 'the establishing of', 'to establish').

(5) Lexically, perhaps the most common symptom of unnaturalness is slightly old-fashioned, now rather 'refined', or 'elevated' usage of words and idioms possibly originating in bilingual dictionaries, e.g.

> *Il fit ses nécessités*: 'He relieved nature.'
> *Je m'en sépare avec beaucoup de peine*: 'I'm sorry to part with it.'
> *Er sträubte sich mit Händen und Füssen*: 'He defended himself tooth and nail.'

Note (a) the fact that the SL expression is now old-fashioned or refined is irrelevant, since you translate into the *modern* target language; (b) however, if such expressions appear in dialogue, and are spoken (typically or say) by middle-aged or elderly characters, then a correspondingly 'refined' translation is appropriate; (c) naturalness has a solid core of agreement, but the periphery is a taste area, and the subject of violent, futile dispute among informants, who will claim that it is a subjective matter, pure intuition; but it is not so. If you are a translator, check with three informants if you can. If you are a translation teacher, welcome an SL informant to help you decide on the naturalness or currency (there is no difference), therefore *degree* of frequency of an SL expression.

(6) Other 'obvious' areas of interference, and therefore unnaturalness, are in the use of the articles; progressive tenses; noun-compounding; collocations; the currency of idioms and metaphors; aspectual features of verbs; infinitives.

How do you get a feel for naturalness, both as a foreigner and as a native speaker? The too obvious answer is to read representative texts and talk with representative TL speakers (failing which, representative TV and radio) – and to get yourself fearlessly corrected. Beware of books of idioms – they rarely distinguish between what is current (e.g. 'keep my head above water') and what is dead (e.g. 'dead as a door nail').

There is a natural tendency to merge three of the senses of the word 'idiom': (a) a group of words whose meaning cannot be predicted from the meanings of their constituent words (e.g. dog in the manger; *Spielverderber*; *l'empêcheur de tourner en rond*; (b) the linguistic usage that is natural to native speakers of a language; (c) the characteristic vocabulary or usage of a people. (*Elle avait frappé à la bonne porte.* (*Ça, c'est du français!*) when the original was merely *Elle avait trouvé la solution* ('She had found the solution'), which is also perfectly good French.) The danger of this procedure is that it tends to devalue literal language at the expense of 'idiomatic' language, as though it were unnatural. If anything, the reverse is the case. Certainly, idiomatic language can, being metaphor, be more pithy and vivid than literal language, but it can also be more conventional, fluctuate with fashion, and become archaic and refined ('he was like a cat on a hot tin roof') (*sur des charbons ardents*; *wie auf glühenden Kohlen sitzen*), and, above all, it can be a way of avoiding the (literal) truth. In translating idiomatic into idiomatic language, it is particularly difficult to match equivalence of meaning with equivalence of frequency.

Check and cross-check words and expressions in an up-to-date dictionary (Longmans, Collins, *COD*). Note any word you are suspicious of. Remember, your mind is furnished with thousands of words and proper names that you half take for granted, that you seem to have known all your life, and that you do not properly know the meaning of. You have to start checking them. Look up proper names as frequently as words: say you get *Dax, cité de petites H.L.M.* – 'Dax, a small council flat estate' may sound natural, but looking up Dax will show you it is incorrect, it must be 'Dax, a town of small council flats' – always assuming that 'council flat' is good enough for the reader.

Naturalness is not something you wait to acquire by instinct. You work towards it by small progressive stages, working from the most common to the less common features, like anything else rationally, even if you never quite attain it.

There is no universal naturalness. Naturalness depends on the relationship between the writer and the readership and the topic or situation. What is natural in one situation may be unnatural in another, but everyone has a natural, 'neutral' language where spoken and informal written language more or less coincide. It is rather easy to confuse naturalness with: (a) a colloquial style; (b) a succession of clichéd idioms, which some, particularly expatriate teachers, think is the heart of the language; (c) jargon; (d) formal language. I can only give indications:

(avant tout) (F)
(a) first of all
(b) before you can say Jack Robinson
(c) in the first instance
(d) primarily
plus ou moins (F)
(a) more or less
(b) give or take
(c) within the parameter of an approximation
(d) approximately

COMBINING THE FOUR LEVELS

Kunststück, *tour de force*, 'feat of skill', *dimostrazione di virtuosismo*: summarising the process of translating, I am suggesting that you keep in parallel the four levels – the textual, the referential, the cohesive, the natural: they are distinct from but frequently impinge on and may be in conflict with each other. Your first and last level is the text; then you have to continually bear in mind the level of reality (which may be simulated, i.e. imagined, as well as real), but you let it filter into the text only when this is necessary to complete or secure the readership's understanding of the text, and then normally only within informative and vocative texts. As regards the level of naturalness, you translate informative and vocative texts on this level irrespective of the naturalness of the original, bearing in mind that naturalness in, say, formal texts is quite different from naturalness in colloquial texts. For expressive and authoritative texts, however, you keep to a natural level only if the original is written in ordinary language; if the original is linguistically or stylistically innovative, you should aim at a corresponding degree of innovation, representing the degree of deviation from naturalness, in your translation – ironically, even when translating these innovative texts, their natural level remains as a point of reference. For *sincérité explosive*, 'impassioned, enthusiastic, intense or violent, sincerity' may be natural, but *sincérité explosive* is what the text, a serious novel, says, so 'explosive sincerity' is what you have to write, whether you like it or not (you will get accustomed to it, *on s'y fait à tout*) – unless, of course, you maintain (I disagree) that the figurative sense of *explosif* (*tempérament explosif*) has a wider currency than the figurative sense of 'explosive' ('an explosive temperament'), when you are justified in translating *explosif* by another word you claim comes within its semantic range ('fiery sincerity'?).

Paradoxically, it is at the 'naturalness' rather than the 'reality' stage of translating that accuracy becomes most important – therefore at the final stage. When you (reluctantly!) realise that a literal translation will not do, that it is either unnatural or out of place, there is a great temptation to produce an elegant variation simply because it sounds right or nice; say, for *Si mince, si dépourvu de chair, qu'on est bien obligé de comprendre les petits copains féroces de la communale, qui l'ont surnommé Bâton.* (Bazin, *L'Eglise verte.*) You translate: 'So thin, so deprived of flesh that you really can't blame his spiteful little friends at the local primary school who have nicknamed him "Stick".' Here the main trouble is 'spiteful' for *féroces*: 'spiteful' simply isn't in the word *féroce*, it will not stretch that far and it is unnecessary. The pragmatic (not the referential) component of *copain* is missed (but 'pals' or 'mates' won't fit). *On est obligé* is stretched a little too far, whilst *dépourvu de* is deceptive, it is such a common construction that even 'lacking in' is a little 'refined' or elevated. I would suggest: 'So thin, so fleshless that you have to show understanding for his fierce (alt. 'ferocious') little friends at the local primary school, who have nicknamed him "Stick".'

This is a stab at accuracy as well as naturalness, and in the case of the *on est obligé de comprendre*, it is not at the colloquial level of the first translation, but one could maintain that the French is not racy or colloquial either. Admittedly, except for technical terms and for well-used words for culturally overlapping familiar objects and actions, accuracy in translation lies normally within certain narrow ranges of words and structures, certain linguistic limits. It is not so precise as precise, it is not 'this word and no other'. It is not an absolute (there are no absolutes in translation). It represents the maximum degree of correspondence, referentially and pragmatically, between, on the one hand, the text as a whole and its various units of translation (ranging usually from word to sentence) and, on the other, the extralinguistic 'reality', which may be the world of reality or of the mind. Admittedly it is harder to say what is accurate than what is inaccurate – translation is like love; I do not know what it is but I think I know what it is not – but there is always the *rappel à l'ordre*, usually to bring you back to a close translation, and at least to show you there is a point beyond which you can't go.

THE UNIT OF TRANSLATING

Normally you translate sentence by sentence (not breath-group by breath-group), running the risk of not paying enough attention to the sentence-joins. If the translation of a sentence has no problems, it is based firmly on literal translation (the literal translation of *compréhensif* is 'understanding' and of *versatile*, 'fickle'), plus virtually automatic and spontaneous transpositions and shifts, changes in word order etc. Thus:

MB, arrêté à Périgueux le 13 février, observe actuellement une grève de la faim.

MB, who was arrested in Perigueux on 13th February, is at present observing a hunger strike.

The first sign of a translation problem is where these automatic procedures from language to language, apparently without intercession of thought (scornfully referred to as *transcodage* by the ESIT School of Paris), are not adequate. Then comes the struggle between the words in the SL – it may be one word like 'sleazy', it may be a collocation like 'a dark horse', it may be a structure like 'the country's government' (who governs what?), it may be a referential, cultural or idiolectal problem – in any event, the mental struggle between the SL words and the TL thought then begins. How do you conduct this struggle? Maybe if you are an interpreter, a natural communicator (I write half-heartedly), you try to forget the SL words, you deverbalise, you produce independent thought, you take the message first, and then perhaps bring the SL words in. If you are like me, you never forget the SL words, they are always the point of departure; you create, you interpret on the basis of these words.

You abandon the SL text – literal translation if you like (which, for the purpose of this argument, I couple with mandatory or virtually mandatory shifts and word-order changes) only when its use makes the translation referentially and pragmatically inaccurate, when it is unnatural, when it will not work. By rule of thumb you know literal translation is likely to work best and most with written, prosy, semi-formal, non-literary language, and also with innovative language; worst and least with ordinary spoken idiomatic language. Further, it is more often effectively used than most writers on translation, from Cicero to Nida and Neubert, (but not Wilss) lead you to believe.

Since the sentence is the basic unit of thought, presenting an object and what it does, is, or is affected by, so the sentence is, in the first instance, your unit of translation, even though you may later find many SL and TL correspondences within that sentence. Primarily, you translate by the sentence, and in each sentence, it is the object and what happens to it that you sort out first. Further, if the object has been previously mentioned, or it is the main theme, you put it in the early part of the sentence, whilst you put the new information at the end, where it normally gets most stress:

Die Vignette hatte Thorwaldsen 1805 in Rom entworfen.

The vignette was designed by Thorwaldsen in 1805 in Rome.

Your problem is normally how to make sense of a difficult sentence. Usually you only have trouble with grammar in a long complicated sentence, often weighed down by a series of word-groups depending on verb-nouns. Grammar being more versatile than lexis, you can render a sentence like the following in many versions:

L'abolition de ce qui subsistait des tutelles et la réorganisation du contrôle de légalité, notamment par la création des chambres régionales des comptes, le transfert aux présidents d'assemblées délibérantes de la fonction exécutive, la création de régions de plein exercice, l'extension de la capacité d'intervention économique des collectivités territoriales, le transfert par blocs aux différentes catégories de collectivités de co:npétences antérieurement exercées par l'Etat, le transfert aux mêmes collectivités des ressources d'Etat correspondantes, l'introduc-

tion de particularismes dans la législation, la création d'une fonction publique territoriale, l'adaptation des règles antérieures de déconcentration aux nouveaux rapports entre Etat et collectivités locales ont créé une effervescence institutionnelle comme notre administration locale n'en avait pas connue depuis un siècle.

(M. Duverger, *Les Institutions françaises*.)

You can either plough through this sentence, keeping roughly to the French grammar and keeping the reader guessing, or you can make compromises, or, at the other end of the spectrum, in order to clarify the sentence as far as possible, you can try:

The following measures have profoundly shaken French institutions in a way that has not been known in local government for a century: what has remained of government supervision has been abolished; control of procedural legality has been reorganised and regional audit offices established; executive power has been transferred to the chairmen of deliberative assemblies; regions with full powers have been created; powers of economic intervention have been extended to regional and local authorities; powers previously exercised by the State have been transferred in complete stages to the various types of authorities; corresponding State resources have been transferred to these authorities; specific local characteristics have been introduced into legislation; a territorial civil service has been created and previous devolution regulations have been adapted to the new relations between the State and the local authorities.

The above translation has converted a dozen verb-nouns into verbs, which goes against the noun-forming tendency of most languages but perhaps clarifies the sentence.

Below the sentence, you go to clauses, both finite and non-finite, which, if you are experienced, you tend to recast intuitively (see Chapter 8 on shifts or transpositions) as in the previous long sentence, unless you are faced with an obscure or ambiguous sentence. Within the clause, you may take next the two obviously cohesive types of collocations, adjective-plus-noun or verb-plus-object, or the various groups that are less context-bound. (I think Masterman's breath-group units may be more applicable to interpreters than to translators.)

Other difficulties with grammar are usually due to the use of archaic, little used, ambiguously placed or faulty structures. You should bear in mind, however, that if long sentences and complicated structures are an essential part of the text, and are characteristic of the author rather than of the norms of the source language, you should reproduce a corresponding deviation from the target language norms in your own version (as in Proust).

THE TRANSLATION OF LEXIS

However, the chief difficulties in translating are lexical, not grammatical – i.e. words, collocations and fixed phrases or idioms; these include neologisms and 'unfindable' words, which I deal with separately.

Difficulties with words are of two kinds: (a) you do not understand them; (b) you find them hard to translate.

If you cannot understand a word, it may be because all its possible meanings are not known to you, or because its meaning is determined by its unusual collocation or a reference elsewhere in the text.

We have to bear in mind that many common nouns have four types of meaning: (a) physical or material, (b) figurative, (c) technical, (d) colloquial; thus:

	Physical	*Figurative*	*Technical*	*Colloquial*
maison	house	family home	(a) home-made (b) firm	(a) first-rate (b) tremendous
élément	element	(a) individual (b) component (c) faith (d) principle	element, cell	(a) (at) home (*dans son*)
poire	pear	(a) pear-shaped (b) quality of a pear (juiciness)	(a) switch (b) syringe	(a) sucker (b) face
métier	job occupation trade	(a) skill (b) experience	loom	(a) (man) (b) my line
Zug	pull tug draught	(a) procession (b) feature	(a) platoon (b) groove (weapon) (c) stop (organ)	(a) streak (b) tendency
Pfeife	whistle	tune	pipe (organ)	wash-out

The first thing to say about this diagram is that it is schematic, and that the colloquial meanings are tied to collocations or fixed phrases. Secondly, the technical meanings are often the worst translation traps (take *enjoliveur*, not 'prettifying' but 'hub cap') since you expect technical terms to be monosemous, i.e. have one meaning only – a widespread illusion. (Admittedly, some of the technical terms mentioned are 'familiar alternatives', and others are often compounded with their classifiers, e.g. *Orgelzug, Orgelpfeife*.)

My next point is that most nouns, verbs or adjectives can be used figuratively and therefore can have figurative meanings – the more common the word, the more contagious and accessible the figurative meanings. If we are desperate, we have to test any sentence for a figurative meaning e.g., 'The man loved his garden'. The garden may symbolise privacy, beauty, fertility, simple hard work, sexual bliss, etc.

Other possible solutions to the 'word problem' are that the word may have an archaic or a regional sense (consult appropriate dictionaries), may be used ironically, or in a sense peculiar or private to the writer (idiolect), or it may be misprinted.

But be assured of one thing: the writer must have known what he wanted to say: he would never have written a drop of nonsense in the middle of a sea of sense, and somehow you have to find that sense, by any kind of lateral thinking: misprint, miscopying (*anatomie* for *autonomie*), author's linguistic or technical ignorance, Freudian slip (*prostate craniale*; *craniale* doesn't exist, *crânienne*; fine, but what has a prostate to do with a skull? Skull, head, top? Upper prostate?). You have to force your word (usually it is a word) into sense, you have to at least satisfy yourself at last that there are no other reasonable alternatives, and you have to write a footnote admitting this to be a *lucus a non lucendo*, a light (actually, a grove) because there is no other light, a reduction to absurdity, and so 'not found'.

So far I have been assuming that the word is more or less context-free – and I do think that far more words are more or less context-free than most people imagine. However, the meaning of many words is determined by their collocations, whether they appear in compounded nouns (*maison centrale*, prison; *maison close*, brothel; *maison de culture*, arts centre; *maison de rapport*, apartment block; *maison de repos*, convalescent home; *maison de maître*, family mansion, etc.), in idioms or as an item in a lexical set (e.g., root, *racine*, *Stamm* in a text on linguistics). Very rarely, they can only be clarified by a reference to the adjoining paragraphs or beyond: any mysterious object qualified by 'the' may take you far outside your sentence.

Another general point about translating is that, in principle, since corresponding SL and TL words do not usually have precisely the same semantic range (though many do in cognate languages), you are over- or under-translating most of the time, usually the latter. In fact, since in the majority of texts you are more concerned with the message (function) than with the richness of description, and since the meanings of all but technical words are narrowed down in their context, translation correspondence is usually close. However, we must remember that a great number of words in one language include and overlap in varying degrees of meaning the words they appear most obviously to translate into another language. Thus French words like *silhouette, discontinuité, assurer, descendre, phénomène, évolution, également* are much more common and have a wider semantic range than their cognates in English, and therefore more often than not they are translated by several different more specific words. This illustrates one of the main problems in translation, the enforced shift from generic to specific units or vice versa, sometimes due to overlapping or included meanings, sometimes to notorious lexical gaps in one of the languages, which may be lacking in a generic word for objects or processes (*aménagement*) or in common specific terms for common parts of the body (*nuque, reins,* 'shin', 'knuckle', 'freckle'). Notoriously, there are surprising lexical gaps and virtual duplications (*visage, figure, Meer, See*) in every language, and languages group objects differently (*un fauteuil* is not *une chaise*) – it needs a translator to expose the apparent bits of linguistic chaos in another language (*nipote* is a grandson, a granddaughter, grandchild, nephew, niece). English, apparently the richest language in the world, cannot do better than 'bank', 'funny', 'plane', etc. for denoting very different referents. (Its numerous monosyllables make it the most pun-prone language in Europe.) However, as long as you are sensitised to these lexical facts, you will not find them a problem unless they are used metalingually.

One little item – say, the precise meaning of a *Höhenvergleichtafel*: what is a 'panorama'? Is it the same in German? Can it be a *Kupferstich*? What is the difference between an etching and an engraving? Between *gravieren* and *einschnitzen*? All this, if you have no informant accessible, can take you longer than the 10–15 pages of the text which follow, and you have to be prepared to give all that time to it (but not in an exam). In real life, you have to be ready to take more time over checking one figure, chasing one acronym, or tracing one 'unfindable' word than over translating the whole of the relatively easy and boring piece you find it in.

THE TRANSLATION OF PROPER NAMES (see also p. 214)

You have to look up all proper names you do not know. First, geographical terms. In a modern text, Beijing is no longer Peking; nor is Karl Marx Stadt now Chemnitz; nor is Mutare (Zimbabwe) any longer Umtali; and in 1997 Hong Kong will be Xianggang. *Im Saaletal* is 'in the Saale valley' not 'in Saaletal'. Do not normally call Polish or Czechoslovak towns by their German names: Posen/ Poznań, Breslau/Wrocław, Karlsbad/Karlovy Vary, Teschen/Děčin. (The Polish Minister of Information rightly protested to the West Germans about this habit recently.) Only the English refer to the Channel as theirs. Consider giving classifiers to any town, mountain or river likely to be unknown to the readership. Check the existence of any place name used in a work of fiction: Tonio Kröger's Aarlsgaard does exist, but not in my atlas. Bear in mind and encourage the tendency of place-names to revert to their non-naturalised names (Braunschweig, Hessen, Hannover), but do not overdo it – let Munich remain Munich. Do not take sides on any political disputes about place-names.

Be particularly careful of proper names in medical texts: a drug in one country will be marketed under another brand name in another, or it may merely be a chemical formula such as 'aspirin'. Tests, symptoms, diseases, syndromes, parts of the body are named after one 'scientist' in one language community and a different one, or are given a more general term, in another. Check the spelling of all proper names – this is where misprints are most common. Remember that while English keeps the first names of foreign persons unchanged, French and Italian sometimes arbitrarily translate them, even if they are the names of living people.

In the period between translating and revision, you should not lose sight of the linguistic problems of the text. (All translation problems are finally problems of the target language.) Do not always be searching for synonyms. A change in word order may be the answer (. . . *de nouveaux types d'électrodes indicatrices* – . . . 'new indicative types of electrodes' – i.e. types indicative of future ranges). If it is a fact, not a word, you are searching for – How many casualties at Cassino? – let your mind play over the various types of reference books – or your own memories. I am not denying neurolinguistic, psychological processes in translation, far from it. I am merely saying you cannot analyse or schematise them; they are unconscious, part of the imagination. If you are lucky, when you brood, you find a solution suddenly surfacing.

REVISION

During the final revision stage of translating, you constantly try to pare down your version in the interest of elegance and force, at the same time allowing some redundancy to facilitate reading and ensuring that no substantial sense component is lost. (Another tension – the translator of a demanding text is always on some tight-rope or other, like Nietzsche's *Übermensch*.) This means translating *le pourcentage de grossesses menées à terme* not as 'the percentage of pregnancies brought to a successful conclusion', far less 'pregnancies taken up to term' but perhaps as 'successful pregnancies'; *faire fonctionner* as 'operating' not 'putting into operation'. You are trying to get rid of paraphrase without impairing your text, the reality behind the text or the manner of writing you have preferred (natural, innovative or stale). The virtue of concision is its packed meaning – and the punch it carries. Your text is dependent on another text but, paradoxically again, in communicative translation you have to use a language that comes naturally to you, whilst in semantic translation, you have to empathise with the author (the more you feel with the author, the better you are likely to translate – if you dislike a literary text, better not translate it at all) – and in your empathy you should discover a way of writing which, whilst normally not natural to you, expresses a certain side of you 'naturally' and sincerely. A great translation is also a work of art in its own right, but a good translation, even of a great work, need not be so.

But my last word is this: be accurate. You have no licence to change words that have plain one-to-one translations just because you think they sound better than the original, though there is nothing wrong with it; or because you like synonyms, because you think you ought to change them to show how resourceful you are. Mind particularly your descriptive words: adjectives, adverbs, nouns and verbs of quality. The fact that you are subjected as a translator to so many forces and tensions is no excuse for plain inaccuracy.

'But that's what the author wrote.' Why do you want to change it? You couldn't have a clearer indication that this is what the author would write in the foreign language, if he could. Why do you think he wrote *cigogne* when you translate it as 'migrating bird'? Why did he not write *oiseau migratoire*? Is it because you're into text-linguistics, because your overall text strategies, your proto-typical structures, the global superstructures, the exciting new developments in the broad interdisciplinary field of the science of cognition demand this change? Surely not.

Many translators say you should never translate words, you translate sentences or ideas or messages. I think they are fooling themselves. The SL texts consist of words, that is all that is there, on the page. Finally all you have is words to translate, and you have to account for each of them somewhere in your TL text, sometimes by deliberately not translating them (e.g., words like *schon* and *déjà*), or by compensating for them, because if translated cold you inevitably over-translate them.

In another chapter (Chapter 19) I detail the various points you have to look out for when you revise. Revision is also a technique that you acquire. I suggest you spend on revising 50–70% of the time you took on translating, depending on the difficulty of the text. If you have the time, do a second revision a day or so later. It is difficult to resist making continual 'improvements' in the taste area, and this is harmless provided you make sure that each revised detail does not impair the sentence or the cohesion of the text. If appropriate, the final test should be for naturalness: read the translation aloud to yourself.

CONCLUSION

Thus one person's view of the translating procedure. But there is a caveat (a warning and a proviso). I have tended to assume a demanding and challenging SL text. One can admittedly find, somewhat artificially, translation problems in any text, any metaphor. Unfortunately, there are a great many run-of-the-mill texts that have to be translated which present few challenges once you have mastered their terminology, which carries you through into a series of frankly boring and monotonous successors. They become remotely challenging only if they are poorly written, or you have to skew the readership, i.e. translate for users at a different, usually lower, level of language and/or knowledge of the topic. Many staff translators complain of the wearisome monotony of texts written in a humdrum neutral to informal style, full of facts, low on descriptions, teetering on the edge of cliché; certainly my account of the translating process will appear largely irrelevant to them. Enterprising translators have to appeal to the research departments of their companies for more interesting papers, or themselves recommend important original foreign publications in their field for translation. Others transfer from, say, general administration to the human rights department of their international organisation to find something worthwhile to do.

It is one of the numerous paradoxes of translation that a vast number of texts, far from being 'impossible', as many linguists and men of letters (not usually in agreement) still believe, are in fact easy and tedious and suitable for MAT (machine-aided translation) and even MT (machine translation) but still essential and vital, whilst other texts may be considered as material for a scholar, a researcher and an artist.

I think that, academically, translation can be regarded as scholarship if:

(1) the SL text is challenging and demanding, e.g., if it is concerned with the frontiers of knowledge (science, technology, social sciences) or if it is a literary

or philosophical text written in innovatory or obscure or difficult or ancient language.

(2) the text evidently requires some interpretation, which should be indicated in the translator's preface.

(3) the text requires additional explanation in the form of brief footnotes.

I think translation 'qualifies' as research if:

(1) it requires substantial academic research.

(2) it requires a preface of considerable length, giving evidence of this research and stating the translator's approach to his original. (Bear in mind that all translated books should have translators' prefaces.)

(3) the translated text is accompanied by an apparatus of notes, a glossary and a bibliography.

Translation is most clearly art, when a poem is sensitively translated into a poem. But any deft 'transfusion' of an imaginative piece of writing is artistic, when it conveys the meaning through a happy balance or resolution of some of the tensions in the process.

CHAPTER 4

Language Functions, Text-categories and Text-types

I suggest that all translations are based implicitly on a theory of language (Jakobson, Firth and Wandruzska put it the other way round – they said a theory of language is based on a theory of translation). Thus in some respects (only) any translation is an exercise in applied linguistics. I am taking Bühler's functional theory of language as adapted by Jakobson as the one that is most usefully applied to translating.

According to Bühler, the three main functions of language are the expressive, the informative – he called it 'representation' – and the vocative ('appeal') functions: these are the main purposes of using language.

THE EXPRESSIVE FUNCTION

The core of the expressive function is the mind of the speaker, the writer, the originator of the utterance. He uses the utterance to express his feelings irrespective of any response. For the purposes of translation, I think the characteristic 'expressive' text-types are:

(1) *Serious imaginative literature.* Of the four principal types – lyrical poetry, short stories, novels, plays – lyrical poetry is the most intimate expression, while plays are more evidently addressed to a large audience, which, in the translation, is entitled to some assistance with cultural expressions.

(2) *Authoritative statements.* These are texts of any nature which derive their authority from the high status or the reliability and linguistic competence of their authors. Such texts have the personal 'stamp' of their authors, although they are denotative, not connotative. Typical authoritative statements are political speeches, documents etc., by ministers or party leaders; statutes and legal documents; scientific, philosophical and 'academic' works written by acknowledged authorities.

(3) *Autobiography, essays, personal correspondence.* These are expressive when they are personal effusions, when the readers are a remote background.

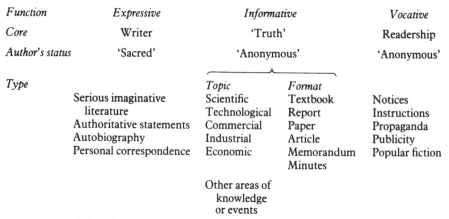

Function	*Expressive*	*Informative*		*Vocative*
Core	Writer	'Truth'		Readership
Author's status	'Sacred'	'Anonymous'		'Anonymous'
Type		*Topic*	*Format*	
	Serious imaginative	Scientific	Textbook	Notices
	literature	Technological	Report	Instructions
	Authoritative statements	Commercial	Paper	Propaganda
	Autobiography	Industrial	Article	Publicity
	Personal correspondence	Economic	Memorandum	Popular fiction
			Minutes	
		Other areas of		
		knowledge		
		or events		

Figure 3. Language functions, text-categories and text-types

It is essential that you, as translator, should be able to distinguish the personal components of these texts: i.e. unusual ('infrequent') collocations; original metaphors; 'untranslatable' words, particularly adjectives of 'quality' that have to be translated one-to-two or -three; unconventional syntax; neologisms; strange words (archaisms, dialect, odd technical terms) – all that is often characterised as 'idiolect' or 'personal dialect' – as opposed to 'ordinary language', i.e. stock idioms and metaphors, common collocations, normal syntax, colloquial expressions and 'phaticisms' – the usual tramlines of language. The personal components constitute the 'expressive' element (they are only a part) of an expressive text, and you should not normalise them in a translation. (See Part II, text no. 3 for a text with expressive passages.)

THE INFORMATIVE FUNCTION

The core of the informative function of language is external situation, the facts of a topic, reality outside language, including reported ideas or theories. For the purposes of translation, typical 'informative' texts are concerned with any topic of knowledge, but texts about literary subjects, as they often express value-judgments, are apt to lean towards 'expressiveness'. The format of an informative text is often standard: a textbook, a technical report, an article in a newspaper or a periodical, a scientific paper, a thesis, minutes or agenda of a meeting.

One normally assumes a modern, non-regional, non-class, non-idiolectal style, with perhaps four points on a scale of language varieties: (1) a formal, non-emotive, technical style for academic papers, characterised in English by passives, present and perfect tenses, literal language, latinised vocabulary, jargon, multi-noun compounds with 'empty' verbs, no metaphors; (2) a neutral or informal style with defined technical terms for textbooks characterised by first person plurals, present tenses, dynamic active verbs, and basic conceptual metaphors; (3) an informal, warm style for popular science or art books (e.g., coffee-table books), characterised by simple grammatical structures, a wide range of vocabulary to accommodate definitions and numerous illustrations, and stock metaphors and a simple vocabulary; (4) a familiar, racy, non-technical style for popular journalism, characterised by surprising metaphors, short sentences, Americanese, unconventional punctuation, adjectives before proper names and colloquialisms. (Note how metaphors can be a yardstick for the formality of a text.) In my experience, English is likely to have a greater variety and distinctiveness in these styles, because it is lexically the product of several language groups (Saxon, Norse, French, Classical), and has been in intimate contact with a wide variety of other languages; being 'carried' over most of the world, it has become the main carrier for technology and has had little authoritative pressure exercised on its growth, apart from a short period in the eighteenth century.

However, note two points: 'informative' texts constitute the vast majority of the staff translator's work in international organisations, multi-nationals, private companies and translation agencies. Secondly, a high proportion of such texts are poorly written and sometimes inaccurate, and it is usually the translator's job to 'correct' their facts and their style (*see* Chapter 18). Thus, in spite of the hoary adages ('translation is impossible', etc.), the majority of translations nowadays are better than their originals – or at least ought to be so.

THE VOCATIVE FUNCTION

The core of the vocative function of language is the readership, the addressee. I use the term 'vocative' in the sense of 'calling upon' the readership to act, think or feel, in fact to 'react' in the way intended by the text (the vocative is the case used for addressing your reader in some inflected languages). This function of language has been given many other names, including 'conative' (denoting effort), 'instrumental', 'operative' and 'pragmatic' (in the sense of used to produce a certain effect on the readership). Note that nowadays vocative texts are more often addressed to a readership than a reader. For the purposes of translation, I take notices, instructions, publicity, propaganda, persuasive writing (requests, cases, theses) and possibly popular fiction, whose purpose is to sell the book/entertain the reader, as the typical 'vocative' text.

The first factor in all vocative texts is the relationship between the writer and the readership, which is realised in various types of socially or personally determined grammatical relations or forms of address: T (*tu, du*) and V (*vous, Sie, usted*) and other variant forms; infinitives, imperatives, subjunctives, indicatives, impersonal, passives; first and/or family names, titles, hypocoristic names; tags, such as 'please', all play their part in determining asymmetrical or symmetrical relationships, relationships of power or equality, command, request or persuasion.

The second factor is that these texts must be written in a language that is immediately comprehensible to the readership. Thus for translation, the linguistic and cultural level of the SL text has to be reviewed before it is given a pragmatic impact. Crudely, *Gardez-vous d'une blessure narcissique*, 'Take pride in your appearance'.

Few texts are purely expressive, informative or vocative: most include all three functions, with an emphasis on one of the three. However, strictly, the expressive function has no place in a vocative or informative text – it is there only unconsciously, as 'underlife'. Most informative texts will either have a vocative thread running through them (it is essential that the translator pick this up), or the vocative function is restricted to a separate section of recommendation, opinion, or value-judgment; a text can hardly be purely informative, i.e. objective. An expressive text will usually carry information; the degree of its vocative component will vary and is a matter of argument among critics and translators, depending partly, at least, on its proportion of 'universal' and 'cultural' components. The epithets 'expressive', 'informative' and 'vocative' are used only to show the emphasis or 'thrust' (*Schwerpunkt*) of a text.

I have proposed three main types of texts, and in the next chapter I shall propose methods of translating them. Consider now Jakobson's three other functions of language: the aesthetic (called by Jakobson the 'poetic'), the phatic and the metalingual.

THE AESTHETIC FUNCTION

This is language designed to please the senses, firstly through its actual or imagined sound, and secondly through its metaphors. The rhythm, balance and contrasts of sentences, clauses and words also play their part. The sound-effects consist of onomatopoeia, alliteration, assonance, rhyme, metre, intonation, stress – some of these play a part in most types of texts: in poetry, nonsense and children's verse and some types of publicity (jingles, TV commercials) they are essential. In many cases it is not possible to 'translate' sound-effects unless one transfers the relevant language units: compensation of some kind is usually possible. In translating expressive texts – in particular, poetry – there is often a conflict between the expressive and the aesthetic function ('truth' and 'beauty') – the poles of ugly literal translation and beautiful free translation.

Descriptive verbs of movement and action, since they describe a manner, are rich in sound effect; e.g. 'race', 'rush', 'scatter', 'mumble', 'gasp', 'grunt', etc., but not hard to translate, unless the word is simply 'missing' in the other language (lexical gap), as this is a universal feature of languages.

In nonsense poetry, the sound-effect is more important than the sense: *Ein Wiesel saß auf einem Kiesel Inmitten Bachgeriesel*. 'A ferret nibbling a carrot in a garret.' 'A weasel perched on an easel within a patch of teasel.' In children's poetry and in the art-for-art literature of the end of the nineteenth century (Gautier, Swinburne, Verlaine, Dowson, etc.) (see Levy, 1969) euphonious 'beauty' precedes 'truth'. In other expressive texts, the expressive precedes the aesthetic function, but if the translation is 'ugly' (cacophony), the purpose of the text is defeated.

Metaphor is the link between the expressive and the aesthetic function. Through images, it is also language's only link with four of the five senses; by producing tokens of smell ('rose', 'fish'), taste ('food'), touch ('fur', 'skin'), sight (all images), as well as the sound ('bird', 'bell') that language consists of, metaphor connects the extra-linguistic reality with the world of the mind through language. Thus original metaphor, being both an expressive and an aesthetic component, has to be preserved intact in translation.

Whilst the preceding four functions may operate throughout a text, the phatic and the metalingual are normally involved in only part of a text.

THE PHATIC FUNCTION

The phatic function of language is used for maintaining friendly contact with the addressee rather than for imparting foreign information. Apart from tone of voice, it usually occurs in the form of standard phrases, or 'phaticisms', e.g. in spoken language, therefore, in dialogue, 'How are you?', 'You know', 'Are you well?', 'Have a good week-end', 'See you tomorrow', 'Lovely to see you', 'Did you have a good Christmas?' and, in English, 'Nasty weather we're having', 'What an awful day', 'Isn't it hot today?' (See Newmark, 1981.) Some phaticisms are 'universal', others (e.g. references to the weather) cultural, and they should be rendered by standard equivalents, which are not literal translations. (References to the weather can be modified by translating with a TL phaticism – *Tu sais, il a fait vilain toute la semaine.*)

In written language, phaticisms attempt to win the confidence and the credulity of the reader: 'of course', 'naturally', 'undoubtedly', 'it is interesting/ important to note that', often flattering the reader: 'it is well known that' . . . Add to these the German modal particles (*ja*, *eben*, *doch*, etc.) and old-fashioned openings and closings of official correspondence (retained in French). The only translation problem I know is whether to delete or over-translate the modal particles, or to tone down phaticisms that verge on obsequiousness (*illustrissimo Signore Rossi*, 'Mr Rossi', etc.)

THE METALINGUAL FUNCTION

Lastly, the metalingual function of language indicates a language's ability to explain, name, and criticise its own features. When these are more or less universal (e.g. 'sentence', 'grammar', 'verb', etc.) – though they may not yet exist in languages which are only spoken or have had little contact with others – there is no translation problem. However, if these items are language-specific, e.g. 'supine', 'ablative', 'illative', 'optative', they have to be translated in accordance with the various relevant contextual factors (nature of readership, importance of item in SL, the SL and TL text, likely recurrences in TL etc.) ranging from detailed explanations, example and translations down to a culturally-neutral third term.

Note also that SL expressions signalling metalingual words, e.g. 'strictly speaking', 'in the true (or full) sense of the word', 'literally', 'so called', 'so to speak', 'by definition', 'sometimes known as', 'as another generation put it', 'can also mean', have to be treated cautiously, as the word following them in the SL would not usually have precisely the same sense if translated one-to-one in the TL. Thus, to get both senses of 'For the last four years, I literally coined money', into French and German: *Ces quatre dernières annees, j'ai frappé des pièces d'argent et j'ai fait des affaires d'or*; *In den letzten vier Jahren habe ich Münzen geprägt und auch viel Geld gescheffelt.* (Ponderous translations.)

I have adopted and adapted the Bühler–Jakobson functions of language operationally as the most convenient way of looking at a text for translation. It is also useful to divide texts by topic into three broad categories: (a) literary; (b) institutional; and (c) scientific – the latter including all fields of science and technology but tending to merge with institutional texts in the area of the social sciences. Literary texts are distinguished from the rest in being more important in their mental and imaginative connotations than their factual denotations.

CHAPTER 5

Translation Methods

INTRODUCTION

The central problem of translating has always been whether to translate literally or freely. The argument has been going on since at least the first century BC. Up to the beginning of the nineteenth century, many writers favoured some kind of 'free' translation: the spirit, not the letter; the sense not the words; the message rather than the form; the matter not the manner. This was the often revolutionary slogan of writers who wanted the truth to be read and understood – Tyndale and Dolet were burned at the stake, Wycliff's works were banned. Then at the turn of the nineteenth century, when the study of cultural anthropology suggested that the linguistic barriers were insuperable and that language was entirely the product of culture, the view that translation was impossible gained some currency, and with it that, if attempted at all, it must be as literal as possible. This view culminated in the statements of the extreme 'literalists' Walter Benjamin and Vladimir Nabokov.

The argument was theoretical: the purpose of the translation, the nature of the readership, the type of text, was not discussed. Too often, writer, translator and reader were implicitly identified with each other. Now the context has changed, but the basic problem remains.

I put it in the form of a flattened V diagram:

SL emphasis	TL emphasis
Word-for-word translation	Adaptation
Literal translation	Free translation
Faithful translation	Idiomatic translation
Semantic translation	Communicative translation

THE METHODS

Word-for-word translation

This is often demonstrated as interlinear translation, with the TL immediately below the SL words. The SL word-order is preserved and the words translated

singly by their most common meanings, out of context. Cultural words are translated literally. The main use of word-for-word translation is either to understand
the mechanics of the source language or to construe a difficult text as a pre-
translation process.

Literal translation

The SL grammatical constructions are converted to their nearest TL equivalents
but the lexical words are again translated singly, out of context. As a pre-translation
process, this indicates the problems to be solved.

Faithful translation

A faithful translation attempts to reproduce the precise contextual meaning of the
original within the constraints of the TL grammatical structures. It 'transfers'
cultural words and preserves the degree of grammatical and lexical 'abnormality'
(deviation from SL norms) in the translation. It attempts to be completely faithful
to the intentions and the text-realisation of the SL writer.

Semantic translation

Semantic translation differs from 'faithful translation' only in as far as it must take
more account of the aesthetic value (that is, the beautiful and natural sound) of the
SL text, compromising on 'meaning' where appropriate so that no assonance,
word-play or repetition jars in the finished version. Further, it may translate less
important cultural words by culturally neutral third or functional terms but not by
cultural equivalents – *une nonne repassant un corporal* may become 'a nun ironing a
corporal cloth' – and it may make other small concessions to the readership. The
distinction between 'faithful' and 'semantic' translation is that the first is uncom-
promising and dogmatic, while the second is more flexible, admits the creative
exception to 100% fidelity and allows for the translator's intuitive empathy with the
original.

Adaptation

This is the 'freest' form of translation. It is used mainly for plays (comedies) and
poetry; the themes, characters, plots are usually preserved, the SL culture converted to the TL culture and the text rewritten. The deplorable practice of having a
play or poem literally translated and then rewritten by an established dramatist or
poet has produced many poor adaptations, but other adaptations have 'rescued'
period plays.

Free translation

Free translation reproduces the matter without the manner, or the content without
the form of the original. Usually it is a paraphrase much longer than the original, a

so-called 'intralingual translation', often prolix and pretentious, and not translation at all.

Idiomatic translation

Idiomatic translation reproduces the 'message' of the original but tends to distort nuances of meaning by preferring colloquialisms and idioms where these do not exist in the original. (Authorities as diverse as Seleskovitch and Stuart Gilbert tend to this form of lively, 'natural' translation.)

Communicative translation

Communicative translation attempts to render the exact contextual meaning of the original in such a way that both content and language are readily acceptable and comprehensible to the readership.

COMMENTS IN THESE METHODS

Commenting on these methods, I should first say that only semantic and communicative translation fulfil the two main aims of translation, which are first, accuracy, and second, economy. (A semantic translation is more likely to be economical than a communicative translation, unless, for the latter, the text is poorly written.) In general, a semantic translation is written at the author's linguistic level, a communicative at the readership's. Semantic translation is used for 'expressive' texts, communicative for 'informative' and 'vocative' texts.

Semantic and communicative translation treat the following items similarly: stock and dead metaphors, normal collocations, technical terms, slang, colloquialisms, standard notices, phaticisms, ordinary language. The expressive components of 'expressive' texts (unusual syntactic structures, collocations, metaphors, words peculiarly used, neologisms) are rendered closely, if not literally, but where they appear in informative and vocative texts, they are normalised or toned down (except in striking advertisements). Cultural components tend to be transferred intact in expressive texts; transferred and explained with culturally neutral terms in informative texts; replaced by cultural equivalents in vocative texts. Badly and/or inaccurately written passages must remain so in translation if they are 'expressive', although the translator should comment on any mistakes of factual or moral truth, if appropriate. Badly and/or inaccurately written passages should be 'corrected' in communicative translation. I refer to 'expressive' as 'sacred' texts; 'informative' and 'vocative', following Jean Delisle, as 'anonymous', since the status of their authors is not important. (There are grey or fuzzy areas in this distinction, as in every aspect of translation.)

So much for the detail, but semantic and communicative translation must also be seen as wholes. Semantic translation is personal and individual, follows the thought processes of the author, tends to over-translate, pursues nuances of meaning, yet aims at concision in order to reproduce pragmatic impact. Communicative translation is social, concentrates on the message and the main force of the text, tends to under-translate, to be simple, clear and brief, and is always written in a natural and resourceful style. A semantic translation is normally inferior to its original, as there is both cognitive and pragmatic loss (Baudelaire's translation of Poe is said to be an exception); a communicative translation is often better than its original. At a pinch, a semantic translation has to interpret, a communicative translation to explain.

Theoretically, communicative translation allows the translator no more freedom than semantic translation. In fact, it does, since the translator is serving a putative large and not well defined readership, whilst in semantic translation, he is following a single well defined authority, i.e. the author of the SL text.

EQUIVALENT EFFECT

It has sometimes been said that the overriding purpose of any translation should be to achieve 'equivalent effect', i.e. to produce the same effect (or one as close as possible) on the readership of the translation as was obtained on the readership of the original. (This is also called the 'equivalent response' principle. Nida calls it 'dynamic equivalence'.) As I see it, 'equivalent effect' is the desirable *result*, rather than the *aim* of any translation, bearing in mind that it is an unlikely result in two cases: (a) if the purpose of the SL text is to affect and the TL translation is to inform (or vice versa); (b) if there is a pronounced cultural gap between the SL and the TL text.

· However, in the communicative translation of vocative texts, equivalent effect is not only desirable, it is essential; it is the criterion by which the effectiveness, and therefore the value, of the translation of notices, instructions, publicity, propaganda, persuasive or eristic writing, and perhaps popular fiction, is to be assessed. The reader's response – to keep off the grass, to buy the soap, to join the Party, to assemble the device – could even be quantified as a percentage rate of the success of the translation.

In informative texts, equivalent effect is desirable only in respect of their (in theory) insignificant emotional impact; it is not possible if SL and TL culture are remote from each other, since normally the cultural items have to be explained by culturally neutral or generic terms, the topic content simplified, SL difficulties clarified. Hopefully, the TL reader reads the text with the same degree of interest as the SL reader, although the impact is different. However, the vocative (persuasive) thread in most informative texts has to be rendered with an eye to the readership, i.e., with an equivalent effect purpose.

In semantic translation, the first problem is that for serious imaginative literature, there are individual readers rather than a readership. Secondly, whilst the reader is not entirely neglected, the translator is essentially trying to render the effect the SL text has on *himself* (to feel with, to empathise with the author), not on any putative readership. Certainly, the more 'universal' the text (consider 'To be or not to be'), the more a broad equivalent effect is possible, since the ideals of the original go beyond any cultural frontiers. The metalingual sound-effects which the translator is trying to reproduce are in fact unlikely to affect the TL reader, with his different sound-system, similarly, but there may be compensation. In any event, the reaction is individual rather than cultural or universal.

However, the more cultural (the more local, the more remote in time and space) a text, the less is equivalent effect even conceivable unless the reader is imaginative, sensitive and steeped in the SL culture. There is no need to discuss again the propriety of 'converting' Keats' 'Season of mists and mellow fruitfulness' or Shakespeare's 'Shall I compare thee to a summer's day?' into languages of countries where the autumns and summers are unpleasant. Cultural concessions (e.g., a shift to a generic term) are possible only where the cultural word is marginal, *not* important for local colour, and has no relevant connotative or symbolic meaning. Thus, in a Bazin text, it is inadequate to translate: *Il est le plus pélican des pères* as 'He is the most devoted of fathers' or 'He is a symbol of paternal love, a pelican.' A compromise version, retaining the cultural element (*pélican*), might be 'He is as devoted as a pelican to his young.' Authoritative statements, being addressed to a readership rather than individual readers, if written in 'public' language should produce equivalent effect: Pericles, Jefferson, Lincoln, Churchill, De Gaulle – the names suggest a universal appeal that asks for a loud and modern echo in translation.

Communicative translation, being set at the reader's level of language and knowledge, is more likely to create equivalent effect than is semantic translation at the writer's level; but a text written some hundred years ago gives the reader of the translation an advantage over the SL reader; the inevitably simplified, under-translated translation in modern language may well have a greater impact than the original. Hence *unser* (our) Shakespeare, as educated Germans used to know his work earlier in the century.

Equivalent effect is an important intuitive principle which could be tested but, as is often the case, the research would not be worth the effort; however, it is usefully applied in reasonable discussion, particularly within the 'skill' (as opposed to the 'truth', the 'art' and the 'taste') area of language. In translating 'I haven't the foggiest idea', (*aucune idée*), would: *Keine blasse Ahnung* or *Nicht die geringste Ahnung* or *Ich habe keinen blassen Schimmer davon* have the closest equivalent effect? (A translation is pre-eminently a matter for *discussion* rather than *fiat*. Too often it is still being imposed as a teacher's 'fair copy' or model. In fact, the simplest sentence – 'The gorgeous girl walked gingerly through the closet' – would, in or in spite of any context, be translated variously by a dozen experts in a dozen different languages.)

I have dealt at length with the 'equivalent effect' principle because it is an important translation concept which has a degree of application to any type of text, but not the same degree of importance.

METHODS AND TEXT-CATEGORIES

Considering the application of the two translation methods (semantic and communicative) to the three text-categories, I suggest that commonly vocative and
informative texts are translated too literally, and expressive texts not literally
enough. Translationese is the bane of tourist material and many public notices
(*toute circulation est interdite de 22 h à 6 h*; *jeglicher Verkehr ist verboten von 22 bis 6
Uhr*; 'all sexual intercourse is forbidden between 10 p.m. and 6 a.m.'). In the UK
the standard of foreign language (FL) publicity and notices is now high but there
are not enough of them. In 'informative' texts, translationese, bad writing and lack
of confidence in the appropriate linguistic register often go hand in hand; the
tendency with familiar-looking but unfamiliar collocations (*station hydrominérale*;
'hydromineral station' – read 'spa') is simply to reproduce them. On the other
hand, the inaccuracy of translated literature has much longer roots: the attempt to
see translation as an exercise in style, to get the 'flavour' or the 'spirit' of the
original; the refusal to translate by any TL word that looks the least bit like the SL
word, or even by the SL word's core meaning (I am talking mainly of adjectives), so
that the translation becomes a sequence of synonyms (grammatical shifts, and
one-word to two- or three-word translations are usually avoided), which distorts its
essence.

In expressive texts, the unit of translation is likely to be small, since words
rather than sentences contain the finest nuances of meaning; further, there are
likely to be fewer stock language units (colloquialisms, stock metaphors and
collocations, etc.) than in other texts. However, any type and length of cliché must
be translated by its TL counterpart, however badly it reflects on the writer.

Note that I group informative and vocative texts together as suitable for
communicative translation. However, further distinctions can be made.

Unless informative texts are badly/inaccurately written, they are translated
more closely than vocative texts. In principle (only!), as they are concerned with
extra-linguistic facts, they consist of third person sentences, non-emotive style,
past tenses. Narrative, a sequence of events, is likely to be neater and closer to
translate than description, which requires the mental perception of adjectives and
images.

The translation of vocative texts immediately involves translation in the
problem of the second person, the social factor which varies in its grammatical and
lexical reflection from one language to another. Further, vocative texts exemplify
the two poles of communicative translation. On the one hand translation by
standard terms and phrases is used mainly for notices: 'transit lounge', *Transithalle*,
salle de transit. On the other hand, there is, in principle, the 'recreative' translation
that might be considered appropriate for publicity and propaganda, since the
situation is more important than the language. In fact, provided there is no cultural
gap, such skilfully written persuasive language is often seen to translate almost
literally.

Scanning the numerous multilingual advertising leaflets available today, I notice: (a) it is hardly possible to say which is the original; (b) how closely they translate each other; (c) the more emotive their language, the more they vary from each other; (d) the variants appear justified. Thus:

Young, fresh and fashionable. *Jung, frisch und modisch. Jeune, frais et élégant.*

Indeed, this is Vanessa. *In der Tat, so können Sie Vanessa beschreiben. Tels sont les qualificatifs de Vanessa.*

This model links up with the latest trends in furniture design. *Dieses Model schliesst bei den letzten Trends im Möbeldesign an. Ce modèle est le dernier cri dans le domaine des meubles design.* The programme exists out of different items. *Das Programm besteht aus verschiedenen Möbeln. Son programme se compose de différents meubles. . . .* which you can combine as you want *. . . die Sie nach eigenem Bedürfnis zusammenstellen können . . . à assembler selon vos besoins . . .* (The three versions reflect the more colloquial style of the English (two phrasal verbs) and the more formal German, as well as English lexical influence ('design', 'trend').)

Where communicative translation of advertisements works so admirably, producing equivalent pragmatic effect, there seems no need to have recourse to 'co-writing', where two writers are given a number of basic facts about one product and instructed to write the most persuasive possible advert in their respective languages.

I should mention that I have been describing methods of translation as products rather than processes, i.e., as they appear in the finished translation.

TRANSLATING

As for the process of translation, it is often dangerous to translate more than a sentence or two before reading the first two or three paragraphs, unless a quick glance through convinces you that the text is going to present few problems. In fact, the more difficult – linguistically, culturally, 'referentially' (i.e., in subject matter) – the text is, the more preliminary work I advise you to do before you start translating a sentence, simply on the ground that one misjudged hunch about a key-word in a text – say, *humoral* in *le bilan humoral* (a fluid balance check-up) or *Laetitia* in *l'actrice, une nouvelle Laetitia* (a Roman actress or an asteroid) – may force you to try to put a wrong construction on a whole paragraph, wasting a lot of time before (if ever) you pull up and realise you are being foolish. This is another way of looking at the word versus sentence conflict that is always coming up. Translate by sentences wherever you can (and always as literally or as closely as you can) whenever you *can* see the wood for the trees or get the general sense, and *then* make sure you have accounted for (which is not the same as translated) each word in the SL text. There are plenty of words, like modal particles, jargon-words or grammatically-bound words, which for good reasons you may decide not to translate. But translate virtually by words first if they are 'technical', whether they are 'linguistic' (*marigot*), or cultural (*sesterce*), or referential (*sessile*) and appear relatively context-free. Later, you have to contextualise them, and be prepared to back-track if you have opted for the wrong technical meaning.

Research is now proceeding on *how* people translate, but there may be many factors (mood, deadline, need for a change of method) which will not be taken into account. Throughout the pre-translation process, you keep a clear image of what is actually happening, if only as a premiss that has to be continuously amended. This applies to poetry as to technical translation. Thus: *Le soleil, sur le sable, ô lutteuse endormie En l'or de tes cheveux chauffe un bain langoureux* (Mallarmé, *Tristesse d'été*) may suggest the sun bathing the golden hair of a sleeping girl lying on the sand struggling (against what?) in languorous heat, and this image has to be kept constantly in parallel with the oblique and elliptical version of it rendered by the language.

OTHER METHODS

As a postscript to this chapter, I add further definitions of translation methods.

(1) *Service translation*, i.e. translation from one's language of habitual use into another language. The term is not widely used, but as the practice is necessary in most countries, a term is required.

(2) *Plain prose translation*. The prose translation of poems and poetic drama initiated by E. V. Rieu for Penguin Books. Usually stanzas become paragraphs, prose punctuation is introduced, original metaphors and SL culture retained, whilst no sound-effects are reproduced. The reader can appreciate the sense of the work without experiencing equivalent effect. Plain prose translations are often published in parallel with their originals, to which, after a 'careful word-for-word comparison', they provide ready and full access.

(3) *Information translation*. This conveys all the information in a non-literary text, sometimes rearranged in a more logical form, sometimes partially summarised, and not in the form of a paraphrase.

(4) *Cognitive translation*. This reproduces the information in a SL text converting the SL grammar to its normal TL transpositions, normally reducing any figurative to literal language. I do not know to what extent this is mainly a theoretical or a useful concept, but as a pre-translation procedure it is appropriate in a difficult, complicated stretch of text. A pragmatic component is added to produce a semantic or a communicative translation.

(5) *Academic translation*. This type of translation, practised in some British universities, reduces an original SL text to an 'elegant' idiomatic educated TL version which follows a (non-existent) literary register. It irons out the expressiveness of a writer with modish colloquialisms. The archetype of this tradition, which is still alive at Oxbridge ('the important thing is to get the *flavour* of the original'), was R. L. Graeme Ritchie, evidently a brilliant teacher and trans-

lator, who was outstandingly more accurate than his imitators. I quote tiny scraps of Ritchie's weaknesses: *La Notre-Dame avanca* – 'The *Notre-Dame* worked her way in'; *La pluie brouilla les objets* – 'The rain obscured everything'; *Cette vie se surpassera par le martyre, et le martyre ne tardera plus* – 'That life was to transcend itself through martyrdom and now martyrdom was not to be long in coming'.

These last two concepts are mine, and only practice can show whether they will be useful as terms of reference in translation.

CHAPTER 6

The Unit of Translation and Discourse Analysis*

INTRODUCTION

Discourse analysis took off as a subject in linguistics about fifteen years ago, partly as an expression of dissatisfaction with sentence-based grammars, possibly also to stress communication rather than the study of language and reference isolated from their users. Discourse analysis can be defined as the analysis of texts beyond and 'above' the sentence – the attempt to find linguistic regularities in discourse. The subject now tends to be swallowed up in text linguistics. Its main concepts are cohesion – the features that bind sentences to each other grammatically and lexically – and coherence – which is the notional and logical unity of a text.

There is at present a confusing tendency for translation theorists to regard the whole text, the basis of discourse analysis, as the unit of translation (UT), which is the opposite of Vinay's and Darbelnet's original concept. Vinay and Darbelnet define the unit of translation as 'the smallest segment of an utterance whose cohesion of signs is such that they must not be separately translated' – in other words, the minimal stretch of language that has to be translated together, as one unit. The argument about the length of the UT, which has been put succinctly by W. Haas, 'as short as is possible, as long as is necessary', is a concrete reflection of the age-old conflict between free and literal translation – the freer the translation, the longer the UT; the more literal the translation, the shorter the UT, the closer to the word, or, in poetry, even to the morpheme. Free translation has always favoured the sentence; literal translation the word. Now, since the rise of text linguistics, free translation has moved from the sentence to the whole text.

It is a futile, unprofitable argument, though it has a certain truth in crudely reflecting two opposing attitudes towards translation. In the last fifteen years the argument has been revived by those who maintain that the only true UT is the whole text. This view has been underpinned by the vast industry in discourse analysis, or text linguistics, which examines a text as a whole in its relations and cohesion at all levels higher than the sentence.

*From *Revue de Phonétique Appliquée*, Vols. 66–8, 1983 (Mons, Belgium). Amended.

Clearly the text cannot be the UT in the 'narrow' sense defined by Vinay and Darbelnet. That would be chaos. The largest quantity of translation in a text is done at the level of the word, the lexical unit, the collocation, the group, the clause and the sentence – rarely the paragraph, never the text – probably in that order. The text can rather be described as the ultimate court of appeal; every stretch at every level of the translation has to conform to the unity of the text, its integrating properties, what Delisle calls its 'textual organicity', if such exists (often it does not).

The general properties of a text have often been described. These are the tone, the intention of the text, your own intention as a translator, the type of the text, the quality of the writing, the permanent features of the writer (dialect, sociolect, period, sex, age, etc.), the situation linked to the readership, the degree of formality, generality or technicality, and emotional tone – say the register and the pragmatic features. The three typical reader-types are: (a) the expert (in the SL text culture and/or the subject of discourse); (b) the educated layman; (c) the ignoramus – in the culture and/or the topic, not to mention their degree of interest in the topic.

My own view of texts derives from Bühler's functional theory of language: I categorise all texts as expressive *or* informative *or* vocative, each with a basic translator's loyalty to the SL writer, *or* the 'truth', the facts of the matter *or* the readership respectively. The functions represent a dominant emphasis, not a total content; for instance, an informative text may close by changing to vocative for its recommendations, and if it is 'anonymous' in Delisle's sense, its expressive element (all texts have expressive elements) can be eliminated by the translator. For example: *L'avantage de ces médicaments est pourtant obéré par ses inconvénients* – 'The advantages of these drugs, however, are outweighed by their disadvantages.'

Expressive texts, which I call 'sacred' texts, are normally translated at the author's level; informative and vocative at the readership's.

The other aspects of text linguistics affecting a translation are: (a) notional; (b) lexical and grammatical; (c) relating to punctuation.

COHERENCE

The more cohesive, the more formalised a text, the more information it, as a unit, affords the translator. Consider first its genre. A Greek or seventeenth-century French tragedy; the agenda or minutes of a well-organised meeting; a recipe, a marriage service or a ceremony – all these compel the translator to follow either SL or TL practice as closely as possible. Similarly, if a narrative has a formulaic opening ('Once upon a time') and a formulaic close ('They all lived happily ever after') the translator has to find standard phrases if they exist. Other stereotypes – weather reports, surveys, enquiries, official forms, medical articles – may have standard forms, a house-style. Recent work on conversations of all kinds, stemming from Grice's implicatures and co-operative principle, tends rather optimistically to suggest that these run on tramlines which could act as pointers in the course of translation.

For a seventeenth-century French tragedy, the translator has a remarkable quantity of pre-information: the unities of time, place and action; a small number of aristocratic characters, each with their less well-born confidants or *gouverneurs*; a lexicon of less than 2000 'noble', abstract words; various stichomythia sequences; alexandrine couplets, which she may want to turn to blank verse; other lines that parallel and echo each other; restricted length, about 1800 lines equally divided into five acts; a serious tone and an unhappy ending usually (not always) marked by a death followed by a brief explanatory epilogue, bringing the survivors back to normality, as in *Hamlet* or *Don Giovanni*.

Next, consider the structure of the text. Notionally, this may consist of: a thesis, an antithesis and a synthesis; an introduction, an entry into the subject, aspects and examples, a conclusion; a setting, a complication, a resolution, an evaluation; a definition of the argument of the title, the pros and cons, and the conclusion; a build-up, a climax, and a denouement; a retrospect, an exposition, a prospect. It may be useful to the translator to note deviations from these and other standard structures. Further, the structure is marked concretely by certain pointers; e.g. chapters, headings, sub-headings, paragraph lengths, and you should consider if these as such will be appropriate in the translation setting, and will conform to its house-style.

TITLES

If the SL text title adequately describes the content, and is brief, then leave it. *Un siècle de courtisans* – 'An age of Courtisans' – is fine. But a sub-title such as *Période de décadence morale et spirituelle* may not suit the English house-style (for instance, we do not use sub-titles in newspapers – only occasional superscriptions), so delete it. Further, truncate the title if it begins with *Un cas de . . .* or *A propos de notions nouvelles sur . . .* Or highlight the main point: 'Candida Septicaemias: the use of amphotericin B', where the French had some unwieldy sentence-like title: *Un nouveau cas de septicémie à Candida albicans provoquée par les cathéters de perfusion veineuse – guérison par l'amphotéricine B*. Don't, like Sean O'Casey, call a book on the modern English theatre 'The Flying Wasp': it is misleading. Translating fiction titles is a separate problem. The title should sound attractive, allusive, suggestive, even if it is a proper name, and should usually bear some relation to the original, if only for identification. Malraux's *La Condition Humaine* was rightly changed from *Storm in Shanghai* to *Man's Estate* (*The Human Condition* would have been even better!), but usually retranslations should not have new titles. Heinrich Mann's *Der Untertan* could have been *The Underling*, but *Man of Straw* is all right. *Days of Hope* is more inviting than *L'espoir*. Scott-Moncrieff's Proust titles, *Cities of the Plain*, *Within a Budding Grove*, *The Sweet Cheat Gone*, *Remembrance of Things Past* for *Sodome et Gomorrhe*, *A l'ombre des Jeunes Filles en fleur*, *La Fugitive*, *A la Recherche du Temps Retrouvé*, are models of translation as transformation.

I distinguish between 'descriptive titles', which describe the topic of the text, and 'allusive titles', which have some kind of referential or figurative relationship to the topic. For serious imaginative literature, I think a descriptive title should be 'literally' kept (*Madame Bovary* could only be *Madame Bovary*), and an allusive title literally or where necessary, imaginatively preserved, as in the Proust examples quoted – it seems a pity that Grillparzer's *Des Meeres und der Liebe Wellen* had to be translated by the descriptive title, *Hero and Leander*, rather than by *The Waves of the Sea and of Love*.

For non-literary texts, there is always a case for replacing allusive by descriptive titles, particularly if the allusive title is idiomatic or culturally bound. Thus, to take imaginary examples, there is a case for translating 'The Impasse', 'Who's that knocking at the door?' or 'King Canute again' by 'Syria's policy towards Lebanon', if that is the subject of the text.

DIALOGUE COHESION

One is apt to neglect the spoken language as part of a separate theory of interpretation. This is mistaken, as translators are concerned with recordings of many kinds, particularly surveys, as well as the dialogue of drama and fiction.

Cohesion is closer in the give and take of dialogue and speech than in any other form of text. Here the main cohesive factor is the question, which may be a disguised command, request, plea, invitation (i.e. grammatically a statement or a command or a question) and where the forms of address are determined by factors of kinship and intimacy, and, regrettably, class, sex and age. Apart from transposing the structure of the sentence (e.g. 'Could you come?' might become *Tu peux venir?* or *Bitte komm*), each language has opening gambits semantically reserved for this exchange, e.g.:

'I wish you'd come'	*Ich hoffe du kommst*
'I wish you could'	*Si seulement tu pouvais*
'I wish you'd stop talking'	*Tu ne peux donc pas te taire?*
'Would you care to'	*Voulez-vous bien*
'Would you mind'	*Ça ne te fait rien si*
'I wonder if you'	*Je ne sais pas si tu*
'See if you can'	*Versuch's vielleicht kannst du*
'I want you to'	*Ich möchte, daß du*
'If you'd just come here'	*Bitte komm her*
'See what happens if'	*Du weisst was geschieht wenn*

Similarly, each language has marking words that signal a break or end of a subject, such as 'Right', 'Well', 'Good', 'Fine', 'Now', 'I see' (*Ach so, Parfait, C'est vrai*), and the internationalism 'O.K.'

Lastly, there are the tags that are used to keep a flagging conversation going: 'isn't it', 'see', 'you know', which require a standard response.

The translator has to bear in mind the main differences between speech and dialogue: speech has virtually no punctuation ('The sentence is virtually irrelevant in speech': Sinclair *et al.*, 1975), is diffuse, and leaves semantic gaps filled by gesture and paralingual features.

PUNCTUATION

Punctuation can be potent, but is so easily overlooked that I advise translators to make a separate comparative punctuation check on their version and the original. The succession of French dashes – to indicate enumerations a, b, c, or 1, 2, 3, or dialogue inverted commas (rarer in French than in English), or parenthesis (often translated by brackets) is obvious. The use of semi-colons to indicate a number of simultaneous events or activities, not isolated or important enough to be punctuated by full stops or exclamation marks, is probably more frequent in French and Italian than in English. The translator has to make a conscious decision whether to drop or retain them. E. W. Baldick, translating *L'Education sentimentale*, often drops them and unnecessarily connects the sentences (in the name of good old smoothness and naturalness), which, this being a 'sacred' text, is a pity. However, perhaps this is a triviality? My question-mark here indicates irony (I do not think it is a triviality), rather than doubt, scepticism or enquiry. Again, a colon may be made more explicit and improved, being translated as 'namely' or 'which includes', and profuse exclamation marks may signal frustration, emotionalism or limited powers of self-expression.

Punctuation is an essential aspect of discourse analysis, since it gives a semantic indication of the relationship between sentences and clauses, which may vary according to languages: e.g. French suspension points indicate a pause, where in English they indicate the omission of a passage; exclamation marks in German are used for drawing attention, for emotive effects and emphasis, for titles of notices (but no longer for 'Dear Mary', in letters) and may be doubled; semi-colons indicate cohesion between sentences; French tends to use commas as conjunctions.

SOUND-EFFECTS

Further, sound-effects, even at the level beyond the sentence, should be taken into account, not only in poetry, but in jingles, where succulent s's can sometimes be transferred, or in realistic narrative, such as *All Quiet on the Western Front*, where the continual repetition of sounds and syllables, *zer-* and *ver-* words and interjections has a powerful effect. Thus: *Granaten, Gasschwaden und Tankflotillen – zerstampfen, zerfressen, Tod . . . Würgen, Verbrennen, Tod* – 'Shells, gas-clouds and flotillas of tanks – shattering, corroding, death, . . . Scalding, choking, death' (trans. A. W. Wheen, 1931). Here the translator has to some extent extended the sound, as he considered this effect to be more important than the meaning of *würgen* and *verbrennen*.

COHESION

Next we consider the relations between sentences. The most common forms these take are connectives denoting addition, contradiction, contrast, result, etc. These connectives are tricky when they are polysemous, since they may have meanings contradicting each other, e.g. *cependant* ('in the meantime', 'nevertheless'), *inversement*, *par contre* ('however', 'on the other hand'), *d'autre part* ('moreover', 'on the other hand'), *d'ailleurs* ('besides', 'however'), *toujours, encore* ('always', 'nevertheless'), *aussi* ('therefore', 'consequently', 'also'), *tout en* + present participle ('whilst', 'although', etc.); cf. 'still' *pertanto* (It.), *vse* (R), *zhe* (R), 'why' ('for what reason', 'for what purpose', 'on what ground'), 'so that', *dès lors*, ('from then on', 'that being the case', 'consequently'), *en effet*.

German notably uses modal connectives (*mots-charnières*) such as *aber, also, denn, doch, schliesslich, eben, eigentlich, einfach, etwa, gerade, halt, ja, mal, nun, schon, vielleicht, so überhaupt, bitte, bestimmt* – all these in talk three times as often as in newspapers and six times as often as in 'literature' (Helbig). Normally, these words can only be over-translated and therefore they are often rightly and deliberately omitted in translation: their purpose is partly phatic, i.e. they are used partly to maintain the reader's or listener's interest, usually with the *nuance* that the accompanying information is just a reminder, they should know it already.

Note here English's tendency to turn SL complex into co-ordinate sentences on the lines of *Si tu marches, je cours*, 'You can walk but I'll run.'

REFERENTIAL SYNONYMS

Sentences cohere through the use of referential synonyms, which may be lexical, pronominal or general. Thus referential synonyms, as in *J'ai acheté l'Huma: ce journal m'intéressait*, may have to be clarified: 'I bought *Humanité*. The paper interested me.' Note also familiar alternatives as referential synonyms, such as 'The Emerald Isle', 'John Bull's Other Country', 'the land of the shamrock' or 'of St Patrick' (cf. 'Hibernian', 'Milesian'), or 'Napoleon', 'the Emperor', 'Boney', '*le Petit Caporal*', 'the Bastard', 'he' in more or less consecutive sentences; SL pronouns and deictics including *le premier, le second* (cf. 'the former', 'the latter') are often replaced by English nouns, since the range of some English pronouns, ('it', 'they', 'this one') is much wider than in languages with nouns split between two or three genders. An example of mistranslation of pronouns is in the Authorised Version, Isaiah 37, 36: 'Then the angel of the Lord went forth and smote in the camp of the Assyrians a hundred and four score and five thousand. And when they arose early in the morning, behold, they were all dead.' Today's English Version: 'An Angel of the Lord went to the Assyrian camp and killed 185,000 soldiers. At dawn the next day, there they lay, all dead.'

Note *tale* (It.), *tel* (Fr.) are also used as pronoun synonyms. Lastly, words at all degrees of generality can be used to connect sentences, from general words ('thing', 'object', 'case', 'affair' (cf. *Vetsh* (Cz.) *Makropoulos*), *machin, truc, phénomène*, *élément*, 'business', *faccenda*, *delo* (R), through 'hypernyms' (superordinate nouns) ('horse') and 'hyponyms' ('foal') to proper name, nickname, familiar alternative, pronoun.

In many cases, all three types of referential synonym are used to avoid repetition rather than to supply new information (which, in any event, is incidental, thematic, and not part of the sentence's message). Whilst the translator must reproduce the new information, he should not be afraid of repetition, in particular of repeating the most specific term or the proper name to avoid any ambiguity.

ENUMERATORS

Enumerators ('enumerative conjuncts') also act as connectors between sentences. Numerical adverbs are usually straightforward, although *zunächst* can mean 'for the time being' as well as 'first', *enfin* has five distinct senses, words like *à la fin*, *somme toute*, *alors*, *dann*, 'next', 'then', 'primarily', *allora* have various senses, and double enumerators ('on the one hand . . . on the other', etc.) may oscillate between enumeration and contrast. *Unter andern* may have to be cunningly translated ('include'), and 'or' is too often ambiguous.

OTHER CONNECTIVES

Linguistic synonyms are also used as a cohesive device to avoid repetition, particularly in a reinforcing sentence. Thus (Dressler, 1973): *Die Linguistik kann man zu den progressiven Wissenschaften zählen. Die Sprachwissenschaft ist ein Element des Fortschritts.* The second sentence is almost redundant, but it emphasises (social) progress whilst the first denotes academic progressiveness, or buoyancy in a head-count; *Sprachwissenschaft*, which in this context (not always) is identical in meaning with *Linguistik*, could be translated as 'the subject' or 'the discipline'. (Outside a context, the 'Classical' member of a couplet of German synonyms is often more 'modern' and voguish, being closer to English and French, as a reaction against the old purist pedantry.)

Words more or less vaguely expressing analogy, e.g. 'similarly', 'likewise', *également*, 'also', *de même*, 'so', 'parallel', 'correspondingly', 'equally', are also used as connectives. Notoriously, *également* usually means 'also', and it is the degree of analogy which the translator often finds difficulty in establishing.

FUNCTIONAL SENTENCE PERSPECTIVE

Functional sentence perspective (FSP), the Prague School's enormous contribution to linguistics which is now spearheaded by Jan Firbas (who, like me, is from Brno, not Prague), links the study of discourse, sentence and emphasis. It is intimately related to translation problems. FSP examines the arrangement of the elements of a sentence in the light of its linguistic, situational and cultural context, determining its function within the paragraph and the text. What is known, or may be inferred, or is the starting-point of a communication (the communicative basis) is to be regarded as the *theme* of a sentence; the elements which convey the new piece of information (the communicative nucleus) is the *rheme*. Rheme in English is often signalled by an indefinite article, a determiner, a specific term, such as 'Robert Smith'; theme by a definite article, a determiner, or a generic term, such as 'Smith'. A further distinction in English between 'Robert Smith' and 'Smith' may be that the first is not known, the second is well known; or the first is used to distinguish one of a larger number of Smiths. Russian obligatorily and Italian stylistically distinguish rheme by word-order, thus *E arrivato uno dei mei amici* ('one of my friends arrived') imposing pragmatic communicative dynamism (CD) on the last word of the sentence, which is the rheme's natural position.

Elements that belong neither to theme nor rheme are *transitional*. The thematic elements are communicatively less dynamic, therefore carry a smaller amount of CD than the rhematic elements.

Normally one proceeds from the known to the unknown: one begins with the theme, and therefore the new elements with the highest degree of CD come last in a sentence: e.g. 'He met a frightening lion.' However, every language has various phonetic, lexicogrammatical and punctuation (italics or inverted commas) devices for highlighting important information: e.g. *C'est X qui*, any unusual change in word order, *eben*, 'precisely', 'in fact', 'himself', 'only', 'merely', 'just', 'actually', 'really', 'truly', and any emphasis in any language can therefore be switched to any part of the sentence. In the normal theme–rheme, or subject–verb–complement sentence, the CD will be on the complement or the last word. If, however, any component of a sentence is 'abnormally' put at the head of the sentence, that component will carry a heavy CD as part of the rheme, engulfing the theme, and this affective procedure must be shown in translation, thus: 'He came down', *Il descendit, Er kam herunter*: 'Down he came', *C'est jusqu'au fond qu'il tomba, Und da fiel er herunter*.

Firbas's 'communicative dynamism' indicates the importance of correctly preserving emphasis in translation. There is always at least an argument for retaining a theme–rheme or rheme–theme order at the sacrifice of syntax and even lexis. The translator has to reconcile the functional, semantic (cognitive and stylistic) and syntactic aspects of each sentence. Crudely, take the sentence 'He was then allowed to leave.' Translate this into French and you have a choice:

(1) *Puis, il lui fut permis de partir.*
(2) *Puis, on lui permit de partir.*
(3) *Puis, il fut autorisé de partir.*
(4) *Puis, il reçut la permission de partir.*

We may perhaps assume that: cognitively, 1 comes closest to the English; stylistically, 2 comes closest; functionally, 3 comes closest, whilst 4 is a possible compromise. The translator therefore has to establish his priorities, which he can do only by considering the text as a whole.

Both French and German have a tendency to put adverbials (prepositional phrases) in the first position even when they are rhematic:

> *En silence ils longèrent encore deux pâtés de maisons* – They walked the next two blocks in silence – *Schweigend gingen sie an den nächsten Blocks entlang.*

> *Derrière ses lunettes, son visage rond était encore enfantin* – Her round face was still childish behind her glasses – *Hinter ihrer Brille war ihr rundes Gesicht noch kindisch* (adapted from Guillemin-Flescher, 1981). (Cf. *In diesen Gebieten nimmt das Saarland eine besondere Stellung* – The Saarland occupies a special position in these areas (adapted from Wilss, 1982).)

German has a tendency to start complex sentences with thematic subordinate clauses, which are finally completed by a brief rhematic main clause; English reverses this sequence for the sake of clarity and because, unlike German, it is not used to waiting so long for the main verb: *Alles, was er ihr erzählte darüber . . . war ihr schon bekannt* – 'She already knew . . . everything he told her about this.'

Thus in considering the functional, semantic and syntactic aspects of a sentence, the translator may have to weigh the writer's functional purposes against the particular language's word-order tendencies (*not* rules).

One of Firbas's most important perceptions is to point out that the nominalisation of the verb has gone further in English than it has in other languages. (I believe this is a general trend due to reification, materialism, emphasis on objects rather than activities, etc.) In particular, when a SL verb appears as rheme it is likely to be translated in English as empty verb + verbal noun: *elle rit* – 'she gave a laugh'; *elle les entrevit* – 'she caught a glimpse of them' to mark what Nida (1975) calls a particularised event. However the tendency to use verb-nouns as jargon, illustrated in Kenneth Hudson's 'The conversion operation is of limited duration', i.e. 'It doesn't take long to convert the equipment' (Hudson, 1979), which has gone far in English and German, has to be resisted by the translator of any informative text, unless it is an authoritative text where the form has to be reproduced (i.e. a 'sacred' text). For this reason, there is a tension between actualisation (verb), emphasis and jargon in the translation of, say, the sentence *La cuisine française apprécie depuis longtemps la saveur délicate de l'écrevisse* (from Guillemin-Flescher, 1981):

(1) 'The delicate flavour of crayfish has long been appreciated in French cooking.' (Actualisation.)
(2) 'With its delicate flavour, the crayfish has long found favour in French cuisine.' (Emphasis on French cuisine.) (Emphasis on 'favour' can be increased by putting 'In French cuisine' at the head of the sentence.)
(3) 'With its delicate flavour, the crayfish has long found appreciation in French cooking.' (Jargon.)

Further aspects of FSP which are of interest to a translator are the various devices for heightening or frustrating expectation, which may differ in two languages. Thus in the sentence: 'There was an uproar in the next room. A girl broke a vase' (Palkova and Palek; Dressler, 1981) the translator may want to show whether the second event is the explanation or the consequence of the first one. Longacre (Dressler, 1981) has pointed out that climax or 'peak' may be attained through tense shifts (e.g. from past to historical present), which is more common in French than in English, or from transition from indirect to direct speech (probably common in many languages).

The presence of an 'expectancy chain' ('He killed, cooked and . . . it'; 'he was hoping to succeed but he . . .') is more helpful to the interpreter than to the translator, unless the gap is filled by a neologism, which can then more easily be deciphered.

CONTRASTS

Climax or focus can also be marked by a *negative–positive* sequence, where the negative is likely to introduce an opposite or a heightened meaning. Again, this may be useful in assessing neologisms, or unfindable words (I define these as words whose meaning, for any reason whatsoever, escapes you): thus, 'not so much self-confidence as triumphalism'; *pas un bikini mais un tanga*; 'it wasn't conviction, it was mere tokenism'.

Less frequently, the contrast is from positive to negative, the latter being signalled as exceptional: *Le sous-marin a une forme parfaitement hydrodynamique; seul le gouvernail fait saillie*. The contrast here is between 'smooth' and 'uneven' (Delisle, 1981).

Contrasts or oppositions are one of the most powerful cohesive factors in discourse. When they introduce clauses (*d'une part . . . d'autre part*, etc.) there is no problem, except to bear in mind that in non-literary texts, *si* (F) or *se* (It.) usually translate as 'whilst', 'whereas', or 'although' rather than 'if'. However, contrasts between objects or actions are just as common. Take De Gaulle's *La diplomatie, sous des conventions de forme, ne connaît que les réalités*, where the main contrast between *forme* and *les réalités* may well be strengthened: 'Diplomacy, behind some conventions of form (purely formal conventions), recognises only realities.' Or later: *tant que nous étions dépourvus, nous pouvions émouvoir les hommes; nous touchions peu les services*. The oppositions between (a) *émouvoir* and *touchions peu* and (b) *les hommes* and *les services* indicate their meanings: 'As long as we were destitute, we could stir men's emotions but we had no effect on government departments.' Again, *Mais aujourd'hui, l'unité française renaissante, cela pèse et cela compte*. Here there is balance rather than contrast, and as above the shift from SL verb to English empty verb plus verbal noun strengthens the balance: 'But today, as French unity is reviving, that counts and carries weight'. (Note again that 'carries' is an 'empty' or 'dummy' verb, and English monosyllabic verbs ('weigh') easily convert to monosyllabic nouns ('weight').)

Other types of contrast are normally signalled by comparatives and superlatives. However, in some languages, notably German and Italian (not, according to pedants, in French), the comparative may be absolute as well as relative (e.g. *grösserer* may be 'fairly large' as well as 'larger than something previously mentioned'); note that in English a comparison is implied, but need not be explicit – 'the larger towns'. Comparatives, superlatives and 'analogues' – 'likewise', 'respectiveley', 'related', 'kindred', 'comparable' (with what ?), 'respective', 'so' ('just like') – are sometimes used as cohesive devices, and are occasionally so obscure that you may have to look for their reference objects in a previous paragraph; these devices are all 'anaphoric' (looking backward). 'Cataphoric' devices (looking forward) are rarer (colons, 'the following', 'viz.', 'i.e.', 'later', 'subsequent', 'as undermentioned', *dans le chapitre qui suit, nous y consacrerons une prochaine étude*) and are often difficult to translate naturally.

Rhetorical questions, which are more common in many other languages than in English, and should frequently be translated into statements, are anaphoric or cataphoric, since they are often used to summarise an argument, or to introduce a fresh subject (as well as to emphasise a statement): *Est-ce à dire que l'efficacité chimique du composé sera supérieure? Rien n'est moins certain, et* . . . – 'In no sense are we implying that this drug is chemically more effective than the remainder of the group.'

Note here that implicit comparatives such as *majeur, mineur, inférieur, supérieur*, even *proche, lointain*, may function as anaphoric connectives that require a case supplement – this is where discourse analysis links with case-grammar.

Sentences are joined to each other by substitutions ('I do', 'I am', 'I think so', 'the same for me', 'I must', etc.) combined with ellipses ('I have –' '– been swimming'). These are usually mechanical and therefore an aspect of comparative linguistics, not translation theory.

General words such as 'structure', 'system', 'balance', 'organisation', 'list', 'catalogue', 'anthology', 'chrestomathia', may be used to group sentences together, e.g., in a passage beginning: 'As to structure . . . .'.

The above has been an attempt to show to what extent a whole text can be regarded as a unit of translation, and what more or less practical indications you, as translator, can derive from this concept. These indications are, I think, appreciable but limited. The mass of translation uses the text as a unit only when there are apparently insuperable problems at the level of the collocation, clause or sentence level. This is a ripple theory of translation. Text as unit has 'naturally' come into prominence because of current emphasis on communicative competence and language, where units of translation become longer, as in notices and instructions; the larger quantity of writing is perhaps descriptive, where there is less emphasis on communication and UTs are smaller.

THE LOWER UNITS OF TRANSLATION

If we include chapter or section under 'text' (but allowing that text may also be one word or one sentence), the next lower unit is the paragraph, which is Nietzsche's unit of thought (and mine). Typical paragraph schemes: (a) start with a generalisation and then produce two or three examples, illustrations, pieces of evidence to support it; (b) introduce and relate an event and give the result; (c) introduce and describe an object or brief scene. In informative texts, you may want to regroup sentences in accordance with such a typical scheme but you have to bear house-styles in mind. Generally, German paragraphs are longer than English; a German paragraph can often be split into several English paragraphs.

The sentence is the 'natural' unit of translation, just as it is the natural unit of comprehension and recorded thought. Within a sentence, transpositions, clause rearrangements, recasting are common, provided that FSP is not infringed, and that there is a good reason for them. On the other hand, unless a sentence is too long, it is unusual to divide it. If it is unusually short, it is likely to be for a special effect. Needless to say, if long sentences are a part of a writer's style in an expressive text, they have to be preserved. Not uncommonly, a French relative clause is hived off into a separate sentence, when it is active rather than descriptive: e.g. *Vos amis sont là qui vous attendent* – 'Your friends are over there. They're waiting for you' (Grévisse, p. 1041; other examples in Guillemin-Flescher, 1981, pp. 339–40). This is an exceptional, well recognised procedure. More commonly, the French relative clause is replaced by a present participle. Normally, by the time you have started working, you translate sentence by sentence, and you will consciously be looking at the larger units – paragraphs and text – only, for example

(1) When you have difficulties with connectives, e.g. *Quelques-uns, vers la fin, s'y endormirent et ronflèrent. Mais, au café, tout se ranime* (*Madame Bovary*). Gerard Hopkins translated: 'When the feast was *nearing its end*, some of them fell asleep and snored, though they woke up again, when coffee *appeared*'. This translation is lexically fairly accurate; the force of the connective is slightly weakened by the fusion of the two sentences, but I think this is a good translation. It is usually justified to fill the case-gaps of nouns like 'beginning', 'middle' and 'end'.
(2) When you are not happy about the sentence as a unit.
(3) When you start revising your version.

Within the sentence, there are five possible sub-units of translation. One of them, the morpheme, the smallest unit of meaning, need not be taken seriously, except in the cases of prefixes such as 'post-', 'inter-' or suffixes such as '-ism' when they have no direct TL equivalent in the word context (but see Catford, 1975, p. 76, who offers: *J'ai laissé mes lunettes sur la table* – 'I've left my glasses on the table'). Two sub-units, the clause and the group, are grammatical; the other two, the collocation and the word (including the idiom and the compound, which is a congealed collocation), are lexical. When you translate, you have to be looking at the grammatical (the general factors of time, mood, space, logic, agreement) and the lexical (the details) at the same time, making sure that FSP is preserved where important. It is not possible to give the one nor the other sub-unit priority, since they all have to be considered, where they exist. (A sentence may be a clause without a phrase or a collocation, consisting only of words.) The more expressive or 'sacred' the text, the more attention you will give to the precise contextual meaning of each word, possibly to the detriment of the message or the communicative value of a text: *Le père de V. Hugo était une espèce de soudard rugueux* (Ionesco), 'Hugo's *father was a kind of rough and rugged old trooper*' (*the difficulty being rugeueux –* 'rough', of a surface) – therefore the more authoritative the text, the smaller the unit of translation. In contrast, when a stretch of language is standardised, it becomes the UT, whether it is as long as a proverb: *Pierre qui roule n'amasse pas mousse _ Wer rastet, der rostet* – 'A rolling stone gathers no moss', or as short as a collocation: *un refus catégorique*, which may however (a fact neglected by Vinay and Darbelnet) have many versions: 'a flat/categorical/blunt denial/refusal', etc.; *diamétralement opposés* – 'diametrically opposite/opposed', 'poles apart'; *subir un échec* – 'suffer/have/undergo a setback/defeat/failure/hiccup'. Note that the most common collocations are: (1) adjective plus noun; (2) adverb plus adjective or adverb; (3) verb plus object, as above.

There are well recognised ways of translating or transposing clauses and grammatical phrases which are set out in one-language grammars and refined in contrastive grammars and books on translation. Many of them invite the choice of converting grammar to lexis (e.g. a verb becomes a noun or an adverb) or turning a clause to a phrase or even a word, e.g. *Dès son lever* – 'as soon as he gets up'; *Au café* – 'when the coffee arrives'. It is useful for a translator to have such transpositions set out in manuals. There is however usually a choice of translations. Grammar always has more alternative forms, is more flexible, than lexis, just as the more general words ('affair', 'thing', 'quality', 'occasion') have more synonyms than the most specific ('oxygen-freezing mixture'). The choice is narrowed when, say, a clause with its lexical constituents is placed within a text, since it becomes determined by a situation, but again the situation may open up other choices. Thus, the phrase out of context *Les ciseaux à la main, l'air mal assuré* suggesting: 'Scissors in hand, looking unsteady, doubtful' (etc.) could become, when contextualised, *Il était debout, les ciseaux à la main, l'air mal assuré* – 'He stood, holding the scissors uncertainly', although in the original *l'air mal assuré* is not necessarily related to *les ciseaux à la main*. (The example illustrates not only Quine's notorious 'indeterminacy of translation', but also the semantic indeterminacy of much language.)

CONCLUSION

I have tried to show that all lengths of language can, at different moments and also simultaneously, be used as units of translation in the course of the translation activity; each length has a functional contribution to make, which can be sum-marised as lexical for the word and the collocation; grammatical (Vinay and Darbelnet's *agencement*) for the group and clause; notional for the sentence, the paragraph and the text (Vinay and Darbelnet's *message*). Further I have tried to show that, operatively, most translation is done at the level of the smaller units (word and clause), leaving the larger units to 'work' (*jouer*) automatically, until a difficulty occurs and until revision starts; further that in an expressive or authori-tative text, there is a certain extra stress on the word; in an informative text, on the collocation and the group; in the vocative or pragmatic section of a text (the part intended to make the readers react), on the sentence and the text as a unit. Finally, although much of this chapter is devoted to text as unit of translation. I think its importance has been recently exaggerated, in particular by writers such as Wilss, Holmes and Neubert who hardly discuss the practical applications of this concept, and also by Delisle who does. To me the unit of translation is a sliding scale, responding according to other varying factors, and (still) ultimately a little unsatisfactory.

CHAPTER **7**

Literal Translation

INTRODUCTION

The present excessive emphasis in linguistics on discourse analysis is resulting in the corresponding idea in translation theory that the only unit of translation is the text, and that almost any deviation from literal translation can be justified in any place by appealing to the text as an overriding authority. The prevailing orthodoxy is leading to the rejection of literal translation as a legitimate translation procedure. Thus Neubert (1983) states that one word of an SL text and a TL word in the translation rarely correspond semantically, and grammatically hardly ever.

In the following three French sentences (about 75 words) and their English translation (68 words), every French content-word except *taux* has its English lexical counterpart, all with a corresponding grammatical function. Only about five function words have no one-to-one correspondents.

> *Les autres pays ont augmenté leurs dépenses publiques relatives à l'enseignement supérieur plus que la Grande-Bretagne pendant les années 1968–1970. (Le taux moyen d'accroissement annuel des dépenses relatives à l'enseignement supérieur est 24,71 en France, 18,07 au Japon, 28,09 en Suède, mais seulement 8,12 en Grande-Bretagne.) Mais notre pourcentage du PNB consacré aux dépenses dans l'enseignement supérieur est quand même plus grand que celui de presque tous nos voisins.*

The other countries have increased their public expenditure relative to higher education more than Great Britain in the years 1968–70. (The average annual increase in expenditure relative to higher education is 24.71 in France, 18.07 in Japan, 28.09 in Sweden, but only 8.12 in Great Britain.) But our percentage of GNP devoted to expenditure on higher education is nevertheless greater than that of almost all our neighbours.

I do not think the French translation could be improved on, although one or two variants in the 'taste' area are always available. But about 90% of these three sentences are literally translated – which is perhaps exceptional, but not so surprising in this type of text. My thesis, however, is that literal translation is correct and must not be avoided, if it secures referential and pragmatic equivalence to the original.

The meaning of many SL verbs is covered in English by a Romance and a rather less formal phrasal verb, which is likely to be Germanic. Your choice as translator will depend both on the object with which the verb is collocated and on the register of the passage. Thus in *derrière lui un garçon distribuait pommes rissolées et petits pois*, the verb *distribuait* is more likely to be 'was giving out' (fried potatoes and peas) than 'was distributing' which sounds, except in some idiolects, like a deliberate (formal) act, or 'was doling out', which betrays a translator's mania for colloquialisms. However, I would not use the most natural 'was serving', since this, by the back-translation test, would be *servait*. Note that other collocations also offer alternatives: for *vivres*, 'distribute' or 'share out'; *courrier*, 'deliver' or 'hand out'; *ordres*, 'give' or 'deal out'; *cartes*, 'deal' or 'deal out'; *argent*, 'distribute' or 'hand round'; *rôle*, 'assign' or 'give out'. Whilst the second alternatives in the above examples are not literal translations in my definition, they all appear to be at variance with Neubert's proposition.

VARIETIES OF CLOSE TRANSLATION

It may be useful to distinguish literal from word-for-word and one-to-one translation. Word-for-word translation transfers SL grammar and word order, as well as the primary meanings of all the SL words, into the translation, and it is normally effective only for brief simple neutral sentences: 'He works in the house – now', *il travaille dans la maison maintenant*. In one-to-one translation, a broader form of translation, each SL word has a corresponding TL word, but their primary (isolated) meanings may differ. Thus in *passer un examen* – 'take an exam', the two verb couplets can be said to correspond with each other, but, out of context, they are not semantic equivalents. Since one-to-one translation normally respects collocational meanings, which are the most powerful contextual influence on translation, it is more common than word-for-word translation. Literal translation goes beyond one-to-one translation in including, say, *le courage*, *der Mut* and 'courage' as literal equivalents; it is particularly applicable to languages that do not have definite and/or indefinite articles.

Literal translation ranges from one word to one word ('hall', *Saal, salle, sala, zal*) through group to group (*un beau jardin*, 'a beautiful garden', *ein schöner Garten*), collocation to collocation ('make a speech', *faire un discours*), clause to clause ('when that was done', *quand cela fut fait*), to sentence to sentence ('The man was in the street.' *L'homme était dans la rue*.). The longer the unit, the rarer the one-to-one. Further, single-word metaphors ('ray of hope', *rayon d'espoir*), extended plural-word metaphors ('force someone's hand', *forcer la main à quelqu'un*) and proverbs ('all that glitters is not gold', *tout ce qui brille n'est pas or*), illustrate a second figurative semantic scale. I extend literal translation to correspondences such as *un bilan sanguin*, 'a blood check' and *après sa sortie*, 'after going out' (but *après son départ*, 'after his departure'), since it can be flexible with grammar whilst it keeps the same 'extra-contextual' lexis. Thus, 'literally', *arbre* is 'tree' not 'shaft', but words like *aufheben, einstellen, Anlage* have no literal translation. Here, as in many other cases, my definitions are 'operational' to suit translation discussion (rather than theory), not 'rigorous' or 'exhaustive' (and so on) to suit linguistics.

I believe literal translation to be the basic translation procedure, both in communicative and semantic translation, in that translation starts from there. However, above the word level, literal translation becomes increasingly difficult. When there is any kind of translation problem, literal translation is normally (not always) out of the question. It is what one is trying to get away from, yet one sometimes comes back to it with a sigh; partly because one has got used to the sound of what at first seemed so strange and unnatural; beware of this. *Une tentation cuisante*: can you get nearer than a 'painful' or an 'intense' temptation? 'Burning temptation' is the nearest, it is still not literal. Literal translation above the word level is the only correct procedure if the SL and TL meaning correspond, or correspond more closely than any alternative; that means that the referent and the pragmatic effect are equivalent, i.e. that the words not only refer to the same 'thing' but have similar associations (*Mama*, 'mum'; *le prof*, 'the prof') and appear to be equally frequent in this type of text; further, that the meaning of the SL unit is not affected by its context in such a way that the meaning of the TL unit does not correspond to it. Normally, the more specific or technical a word, the less it is likely to be affected by context. Further, a common object will usually have a one-to-one literal translation if there is cultural overlap, though most languages have strange lexical gaps (e.g. 'fingers', 'waist', 'knuckles', 'shins'). A term for a common object sometimes has other common senses ('bank', 'peace') – so that language, particularly in English with its monosyllables, appears inefficient.

THE TRANSLATION OF POETRY

The translation of poetry is the field where most emphasis is normally put on the creation of a new independent poem, and where literal translation is usually condemned. Thus Rose Marilyn Gaddis, in her stimulating paper on Walter Benjamin (1982) demonstrating Stefan George's superiority over Benjamin as a translator of Baudelaire's *Recueillement*, states that 'Benjamin's German translation goes into literal English more easily than George's, and is not far removed semantically from a literal plain prose English translation of the original' and 'Whereas Benjamin is working with the word, George works with a larger prosodic unit.'

I agree that George is the better translator – in my experience, the greatest of all translators of poetry – but what I want to demonstrate is that he is more literal in his translation of the words as well as the structures. Compare George's title *Sammlung* with Benjamin's *Vorbereitung*: Benjamin's is way out, George's is materially and figuratively close. Compare the two opening lines:

> *Sois sage O ma douleur, et tiens-toi plus tranquille* (Baudelaire)
> *Sei ruhig, O mein leid, und klage schwächer* (George)
> *Gemach mein Schmerz und rege du dich minder* (Benjamin)

> *Tu réclamais le Soir; il descend; le voici:* (Baudelaire)
> *Du riefst den abend nieder, sieh er kam!* (George)
> *Der Abend den du anriefst sinkt und glückt* (Benjamin)

Both lexically and grammatically, George's openings are nearer to Baudelaire than Benjamin's: even *ruhig* is closer to *sage* than is *gemach*. Again compare George's:

> *Dem einen bringt er ruh, dem anderen gram*
> *(Aux uns portant la paix, aux autres le souci)*

with Benjamin's:

> *Die jenen friedlich macht und den bedrückt*

George's:

> *Mein leid, gib mir die hand von ihnen fern*
> *(Ma Douleur donne-moi la main; viens par ici)*

with Benjamin's:

> *Gib mir die Hand mein Schmerz lass uns entrückt*

and finally George's:
> *Horch, teure! horch! die nacht die leise schreitet!*
> *(Entends, ma chère, entends la douce Nuit qui marche)*

with Benjamin's:

> *Vernimm vernimm sie doch die süsse Nacht die schreitet.*

The word- and clause-order correspondence in George and Baudelaire is striking.

Purely lexically, George has *der sterblichen* for *des Mortels* (Benjamin: *der Menschenkinder*); *gemeiner* for *vile* (*taub*); *toten* for *défuntes* (*alten*); *verblichenen* for *surannées* (no word); *Reue* for *Regret* (*Verzicht!*); *wassern* for *eaux* (*Flut!*); *sterben* for *moribond* (nothing); *langes* for *long* (nothing).

Reading George's translations, I am constantly impressed by his attempts at literalness, the fact that he abandons literalness only when he has to. Similarly, Leyris's Hopkins is a miracle of literal translation; the strength of Michael Hamburger's translation of Celan's *Corona* is in its closeness, and he has it easier since he is not constrained by rhyme or metre. Inevitably, when I look more closely at a good translation of poetry, I find many points of divergence, and what appeared to me a literal translation and attractive for that reason (the truth, not the cosmetic) is not one. For me, a translation can be inaccurate, it can never be too literal. (The reason why *destiné à* is not normally translated as 'destined for' is not that the latter is too literal, but because *destiné à* is: (a) current; (b) a loose connective; and 'destined for' is: (a) heavy; (b) fateful; (c) not common.)

If translation is to be regarded – if only partially – as 'scientific', it has to: (a) reduce its options to the taste area; (b) in claiming accuracy and economy as its main aims, reject both the open choices and the random paraphrasing of free translation; (c) eliminate the universal negative connotations of and prejudices against literal translation.

Ordinary or conversational language however must always be translated by ordinary or conversational language, and this is rarely literal translation. *Quand il pénétra dans l'Hôtel Mâtignon, il dit: 'Avec nous, c'est le peuple qui entre ici.'* ('When he entered the Hotel Matignon, he said: "With us, it's the people taking over here."')

FAITHFUL AND FALSE FRIENDS

However, my main point is that we must not be afraid of literal translation, or, in particular, of using a TL word which looks the same or nearly the same as the SL word. At school and university I was told I must never do this, but 'theatre' is *théâtre* is *Theater* is *teatro* is *teatr*; only in Czech is it *divadlo* (the same applies to 'music', where the Czech is *hudba*). The translation of objects and movements is usually more literal than that of qualities and ways of moving. Many common adjectives of feeling cut up meaning in their own way, so that we cannot trust a transparent translation of 'sincere', 'loyal', 'trivial', 'important', 'truculent', 'brutal'; only one or two like 'excellent' and 'marvellous' are usually transparent. And again, the more general and abstract words ('phenomenon', 'element', 'affair') may or may not be translated transparently; there is often a shift at that abstract level (*qualité* as 'property') but the translation is still usually one-to-one. In general, there are more faithful friends than *faux amis*, and we must not hesitate to use them, since any other translation is usually wrong. This presupposes that, in context, the readership of O and T have similar interest and language levels. Otherwise the translation may well be different.

Many theorists believe that translation is more a process of explanation, interpretation and reformulation of ideas than a transformation of words; that the role of language is secondary, it is merely a vector or carrier of thoughts. Consequently, everything is translatable, and linguistic difficulties do not exist. This attitude, which slightly caricatures the Seleskovitch School (ESIT, Paris), is the opposite of the one stating that translation is impossible because all or most words have different meanings in different languages, i.e. all words are culture-specific and, to boot, each language has its peculiar grammar. My position is that everything is translatable up to a point, but that there are often enormous difficulties.

WORDS IN THEIR CONTEXT

All the same, we do translate words, because there is nothing else to translate; there are only the words on the page; there is nothing else there. We do not translate isolated words, we translate words all *more* or *less* (and sometimes less rather than more, but never not at all) bound by their syntactic, collocational, situational, cultural and individual idiolectal contexts. That is one way of looking at translation, which suggests it is basically lexical. This is not so. The basic thought-carrying element of language is its grammar. But since the grammar is expressed only in words, we have to get the words right. The words must stretch and give only if the thought is threatened.

I am not making any plea for literal or one-to-one translation, since, if it is translationese (and there is far too much translationese published), it is wrong. But the re-creative part of translation is often exaggerated, and the literal part underestimated, particularly in literary translation, but also in other types of texts which have nothing linguistically wrong with them, which are competently written.

Take the following extracts from an advertisement by Bendicks Ltd, where we might expect the widest divergences:

(1A) 'B are a unique confection, often copied, never equalled.'
(1B) *B sont de confection unique, souvent imités mais jamais égalés,*
(1C) *I cioccolatini B sono un prodotto senza eguale spesso imitato, mai eguagliato.*
(1D) *B ist ein einzigartiger Konfekt, der oft nachgeahmt aber nie nachgemacht worden ist.*

(2A) 'Blended together they provide a very distinctive and widely appreciated example of the chocolatier's art.'
(2B) *Ce mélange est l'exemple très distingué et largement apprécié de l'art du chocolatier.*
(2C) *La loro fusione è un perfetto esempio dell'arte distintiva e vastamente apprezzata del cioccolatiere.*
(2D) *– ein ausgezeichnetes und weithin geschätztes Beispiel fachlichen Könnens.*

One notices first how close these translations are; and they could even be closer, being in some cases elegant (and unnecessary) variations on the original, which is presumably English (e.g., *mais* in 1B; *senza eguale* in 1C, which is blurred by *mai eguagliato*). Secondly, syntactical changes in the translation appear to be precipitated by the lack of a suitable word for 'blend'. Again, as German cannot risk *chocolatier* (a pity), it has recourse to the more generic *fachlich* ('professional'). German also introduces an effective word-play (*nachgeahmt, nachgemacht*) which alters and improves the sense of the English. (*Nachmachen* means both 'to make up' and 'to copy'; there is word-play with *nachahmen*.)

ELEGANT VARIATIONS

Elegant variations on literal or one-to-one translation are common, and sometimes satisfy the translator's understandable wish to write in a style or phrase that is entirely natural to him. More often, however, they are irritating to the critic, introduced to exhibit the translator's flair for colloquialisms or synonymy, and, even when insignificant, unnecessary. They are not justified in semantic or even communicative translation. They are a temptation (and an indulgence) for any translator.

Literal translation may appear tedious, but there is satisfaction in weighing it against this or that more elegant version and finding it more accurate and economical. Thus the first sentence of Bendicks' advert:

> Bendicks of Mayfair have established a reputation respected throughout the world for the manufacture of chocolate confectionery of the highest quality.

> '*Bendicks of Mayfair*' ont établi leur réputation, reconnue dans le monde entier, pour la confection de chocolats de la plus haute qualité.

The translation is lexically and grammatically literal, but for 'confectionery', which has to be changed and is satisfactorily conflated with 'manufacture', and the two unnecessary elegant variations, *leur* and *reconnue*.

BACK-TRANSLATION TEST (BTT)

The validity of literal translation can sometimes be established by the back-translation test: e.g. (crudely) a 'black frame' should translate back centrally as *un cadre noir, ein schwarzer Rahmen*, etc. The back-translation test is not valid in the case of SL or TL lexical gaps: thus 'a murky street', 'a bright vision' (or *une personne maladive*) will not translate back satisfactorily. But 'the literary dictates of his time' will never translate back satisfactorily into *les modes littéraires de son temps*.

Note also that the figurative element in language militates against literal translation when it is a cultural or a stock metaphor, but favours literal translation when it is universal and/or original.

ACCEPTED TRANSLATION

Some transparent institutional terms are translated literally in at least Western European languages even though the TL cultural equivalents have widely different functions: thus 'President', 'Senate', 'Prefect', 'Chancellor', 'Mayor'. Note also that concept-words such as 'radicalism' or 'realism' are translated literally and often misleadingly, as their 'local' connotations are often different. Any 'core' denotative meaning is swamped by the connotative pragmatic meaning. The terms are normally so important in their relation to the TL culture that a literal translation rather than transference is indicated – a translated word more than a transferred one is incorporated at once into the target language. However, for new institutional terms, a translator must be careful about translating the terms directly into the TL, if they already exist but have quite different functions in the TL culture.

CONSTRAINTS ON LITERAL TRANSLATION

I am not suggesting that any more or less context-free SL word must always be translated one-to-one or literally by its 'usual' TL equivalent. The SL word may: (a) be used more frequently (within the register); (b) have a wider semantic range than the corresponding TL word. Thus *hardiesse* may translate as 'effrontery' (pejorative) as well as 'daring' (positive, honorific) depending on the context. But *la plaine* which appears almost to coincide in frequency and semantic range with 'the plain' will always translate as 'plain', unless it is the alternative spelling of *la plane* ('plane').

If a perfectly natural SL unit produces a clumsy literal translation, e.g. *il ne parvenait pas à se dégager de sa surprise* as 'he wasn't succeeding in freeing himself from his surprise', then the translation is 'wrong', however expressive the rest of the SL text ('he was unable to rid himself of his feeling of surprise', 'he couldn't overcome his surprise').

'Ordinary language', which in English is usually descriptive language, not colloquial but neutral, is equally appropriate in written and spoken language, marked by phrasal verbs, familiar alternatives (such as 'bloke', 'kids', 'cash', 'job', 'make love'), empty verbs and verb-nouns ('make his way to'), and can hardly ever be translated literally.

NATURAL TRANSLATION

However, there are all kinds of insidious resistances to literal translation. You may feel it is not translation, it is mechanical, it is automatic, it is humdrum, it is not clever. You have been told at school not to practise it. It does not enrich your knowledge either of the source or of the target language. It is too easy. We have to resist these arguments. Apart from translationese (i.e. inaccurate translation) the only valid argument against what I might find an acceptable literal translation of an ordinary language unit is that you find it unnatural. Take *l'heure est venue* or *les maisons basses*: if you insist you would not normally say 'the hour has come', only 'the time has come'; not 'the low houses', only 'the squat or low-lying houses', I would suspect you were deluding yourself, but I believe that, except for an expressive text, you should write in a manner natural to yourself, a manner that expresses your own sense of good style. This is yet another of the tensions within translation. In fact, by repeating several times to yourself a slightly 'unnatural' unit of language, or by saying it in a soft tone of voice, you can sometimes make it sound more natural, and convince yourself it is a good translation. If it still remains unnatural to you, you should avoid it. In this sense, the argument in favour of a translation having the impress of a translator's own way of writing has precedence over the principle of literal translation.

Note that it is sometimes advisable to retreat from literal translation when faced with SL general words for which there are no 'satisfactory' one-to-one TL equivalents even though one is over-translating. Thus *Darstellungen* is more common and concrete than 'representations', and, in the context, 'drawings', 'pictures' or 'diagrams' may be quite suitable.

A further point. One can say that, in the human view, all objects are symbols and all words are either representations or symbols of objects. In this sense, literal translation can go either way. Commonly, *atropinique* can mean, literally, 'made of atropin' or 'atropin-like'; *brûlure*, a 'burn' or 'a burn-like sensation'. Less commonly, *Die Apfelsine fällt mir ein* may literally mean 'The orange' (previously mentioned) or 'The idea of the orange occurs to me'.

RE-CREATIVE TRANSLATION

Literal translation is the first step in translation, and a good translator abandons a literal version only when it is plainly inexact or, in the case of a vocative or informative text, badly written. A bad translator will always do his best to avoid translating word for word. Re-creative translation – 'contextual re-creation' as Delisle (1981) calls it – which means, roughly, translating the thoughts behind the words, sometimes between the words, or translating the sub-text, is a procedure which some authorities and translation teachers regard as the heart or the central issue of translation ('get a far away as possible from the words'). The truth is the opposite: 'interpret the sense, not the words' is, to my mind, the translator's last resource; an essential resource, certainly, and a touchstone of his linguistic sensitivity and creativity, not to mention his alertness and perspicacity, when words mislead. Further, contextual re-creation is likely to be more common in interpretation, if delegates are speaking off the cuff, than in written language translation, where words are more carefully measured and perhaps closer to thought. But most translation is not creative in this sense. You have to like struggling with words before you reach the longer passages.

In recent years, London has, in its notices and advertisements, become a trilingual often a quadrilingual (you add Dutch) city. Coming so late to reality, the British Transport Board has profited from others' mistakes and has done well. One of the most striking things about the adverts (of all things) has been how close to each other they are, how near to literal translation:

> *Que ce soit votre première ou votre cinquantième visite en Grande-Bretagne, parions que, avant la fin de la journée, vous n'aurez pas manqué de remarquer mille curiosités nouvelles, typiques du pays et de ses habitants.*

> *Ob Du Großbritannien zum ersten oder zum fünfzigsten Mal besuchst, wetten wir, daß Du jeden Tag immer noch neue Besonderheiten bei Land und Leuten entdeckst.*

LITERARY TRANSLATION

It is ironical that modern literary translators, reacting against a stiff and literary style, a 'periphrastic study in a worn-out poetical fashion', as T. S. Eliot put it in *East Coker*, should neglect 'the intolerable wrestle with words and meanings', should continually pursue what is to them more natural, more colloquial, more easy, more relaxed, than the original, which was not particularly relaxed anyway, for example, translating *il faisait chaud* as 'it was a blazing hot afternoon'; *le soleil incendie les maisons trop sèches*, 'the sun bakes the houses bone-dry'; *d'aspect tranquille* as 'a smug and placid air'; *un lieu neutre* as 'a negative place'. What is the reason for this? Certainly not the translators' deficient knowledge of French (ignorance of German is more common); they are often bilingual, perhaps anxious to transfer their own colloquial, easy, non-academic, non-bogus French to their English translation. One reason, then, is their relish for racy, earthy, idiomatic English, which is in flagrant contrast with a neutral original.

THE SUB-TEXT

Another reason may be the search for the 'hidden agenda', the pursuit of the sub-text, the awareness that when, for instance, the Mayor in Ibsen's *An Enemy of the People* says: 'We have our splendid new Baths. Mark my words! The prosperity of the town will come to depend more and more on the Baths. No doubt about it', he is expressing his belief in progress and the established order, which he will support even when he learns that it is corrupt, rather than just praising the new baths.

Michael Meyer (1974) has made much of the concept of the 'sub-text', what is implied but not said, the meaning behind the meaning. 'Ibsen', he writes, 'is a supreme master of the sub-text; almost all his main characters are deeply inhibited people, and at certain crises they are brought to bay with what they fear, and talk evasively, saying one thing but meaning another. To an intelligent reader, the true meaning behind the meaning is clear, and the translator must word the sentence in such a way that the sub-text is equally clear in English.'

The above statement is in fact a plea for accuracy, and the implication is that the translator should not go beyond the words of the original by promoting the sub-text to the status of the text. Meyer complains of a previous version of *Little Eyolf* that the translator 'had repeatedly got the literal meaning and missed the real point, translated the text but missed the sub-text'; however, it suggests to me that this translator, like the legendary William Archer, had gone wrong not so much in being too literal (unless he had *misunderstood* metaphors, idioms, colloquial language, phaticisms, cultural references) as in translating Norwegian 'ordinary' language by cumbersome, outdated, bookish language (slightly outdated language is usually comic anyway). Certainly Meyer's own merit as a translator is in his economy rather than his accuracy. (These are to my mind the main purposes of a translation, but accuracy should come first.) One small example: Archer: 'Yes, you remember. Won't you be good enough to give him a friendly talking to and perhaps you can make some impression on him.' Meyer: 'You remember? Perhaps you'd give him a friendly talking to – that might have some effect.'

Thus the tautness of dialogue. The dramatist can say in five lines what the novelist needs a page for, as Terence Rattigan said to Meyer.

The concept of the sub-text is a useful variant term for the function or the intention of a text, the thin thread which the translator has to pursue throughout his work. But the concept is dangerous and misleading if the sub-text starts to obtrude on the text; put differently, if the description, or the surface text, is partially or wholly replaced by the function, the deep structure of the text, the symbol by its meaning, and so on. You cannot normally translate 'When his father died his mother couldn't afford to send him to Eton any more' by *Als sein Vater starb, konnte seine Mutter es sich nicht mehr leisten, ihn auf eine der teuren Privatschulen zu schicken* (Hönig and Kussmaul, 1982). Now, I am not suggesting that a literal translation – transferring Eton without stating its function – is adequate for an average German readership, though for an educated one it should be enough. But Eton is an essential element of the translation, and Eton's function (the most prestigious school in the UK) is inadequately stated. Thus sub-text as a reason for embroidering on the original will not stand. If someone says one thing while he means another, that is a psychological feature that has to be cleanly translated; it must be equally inhibited or concealed in the translation; it may or may not be culturally induced, but, linguistically, the translation is not affected, must not be tampered with.

THE NOTION OF THE 'NO-EQUIVALENT' WORD

The difficulties of literal translation are often highlighted not so much by linguistic or referential context as by the context of a cultural tradition. Bagehot wrote about 130 years ago that 'Language is the tradition of nations . . . people repeat phrases inculcated by their fathers, true in the time of their fathers but now no longer true.'

If you consider Faust's famous struggle to translate the word *logos*, a word that is virtually context-free, and therefore has to be translated for itself

(Weinrich's notorious slogan 'Words are untranslatable, texts can always be translated' – see his brilliant book *Linguistik der Lüge* – is salutary but sometimes the reverse of the truth), how Faust moves hesitantly and subjectively from *Wort* ('word'), *Sinn* ('sense', 'meaning', 'thought'), *Kraft* ('strength', 'power', 'force') to finally *Tat* ('deed', 'fact', 'action', 'activity') and making his own comments quite independently of the Greek or the referential truth ('I can't possibly rate the Word as highly as that – I must translate it differently, if only my mind will make it clear to me, so I'll write "sense", "meaning" and I have to think carefully, I'll have to think that line out again, not be over-hasty, can it be "sense" which makes and produces everything, I'll write "force" ("strength", "power") but as I write that, something is warning me I can't stay with that, so I can safely write "deed", "act", "action"') – all this illustrates a painful struggle with four key words, one of which, *Kraft* according to Gadamer (1976), is conditioned, not by its context in the play or the New Testament, but by its past – its connection with Newtonian physics and its development (integration) in the German public consciousness by Ottinger and Herder: 'the concept of force was made comprehensible on the basis of the living experience of force. As this integration occurred, the technical concept grew into the German language and was individualized to the point of becoming untranslatable.'

To write off as 'untranslatable' a word whose meaning cannot be rendered literally and precisely by another word is absurd, particularly when it could at least be better delineated by componential analysis into four or five words, though as a footnote, not in the text of the play. Looking at translation in an ideal sense, Gadamer has pointed out that 'no translation can replace the original . . . the translator's task is never to copy what is said, but to place himself in the direction of what is said (i.e. in its meaning) in order to carry over what is to be said into the direction of his own saying'. Again, this reliance on the *vouloir-dire* and the significance of what the SL text deliberately left unsaid can be dangerous, and applies only to the most difficult texts, where some kind of interpretation and hermeneutics are essential if the translator is to be active, to 'become again the one saying the text'. Here the moment of period and time, as well as the translator's personality, the judgments he has made in the course of his emotional and intellectual development, the pre-judgments (*Vorurteile*) and preconceptions with which he meets a particular problem (after a year, he will translate the same text in a different way: is this chance or personal change?) – all this is important when one considers translating texts that appear to be on the borders of language and thought, and the struggle is with grammar as well as words, the nuances of mood (modals), and time (tense) and duration (aspect).

But in the vast majority of cases, Gadamer is not going to help the translator at all. His statement 'No translation is as understandable as the original' is misleading. Many translations have been and are a good, simple introduction, a lead-in into the original – particularly translations of languages such as German with an artificial word-order inflicted on them by their scribes, their *clercs*, i.e. the in fact non-SVO (subject–verb–object) languages, which postpone the lexical elements of their verbs to the end of the proposition. However, Gadamer uses his statement 'the most inclusive meaning of what's said comes to language only in the original saying and slips away in all subsequent saying and speaking' as an argument against literal translation. 'Hence the translator's task must never be to copy what is said', which seems dangerous to me, suggesting that the translator has to anticipate changes of meaning into language of the future. In fact, Kant, Hegel, Heidegger and Gadamer are initially more understandable in translation than in the original.

However, where Gadamer is a healthy corrective is in his insistence on the personality of the translator, the translator's state of consciousness and awareness, the limitations of the usually recognised types of context.

THE ROLE OF CONTEXT

My last point, in fact, is that, in translation, the translator indeed has to be aware of all the varieties of contexts – so many it is idle to list them again – but this does not mean that context is the overriding factor in all translation, and has primacy over any rule, theory or primary meaning. Context is omnipresent, but it is relative. It affects technical terms and neologisms less than general words; it permeates a structured text and touches disjointed texts rather lightly. Where a writer deliberately innovates, the translator has to follow him, and blow the context.

A translator with his eye on his readership is likely to under-translate, to use more general words in the interests of clarity, simplicity and sometimes brevity, which makes him 'omit' to translate words altogether. (A translator has to account for every SL word, not to translate it.) Under-translation is justified if an informative text is deficient in clarity. It is not justified if it is unnecessary and is a mere retreat from a literal translation. You must not write down to your reader.

A good literal translation must be effective in its own right. If it shows SL interference, that must be by the translator's conscious decision. Some mild translationese in a tourist brochure has a gentle charm, like the local colour of a transferred word. 'New means of creative work ripened and brought fruit later.' The translator unconscious of SL interference is always at fault. The less context-bound the words (e.g. lists, technical terms, original metaphors, 'unacceptable' collocations), the more likely a literal translation – whilst the more standard are the collocations, colloquialisms, idioms, stock metaphors, the less likely is a literal translation. Inevitably, there is a proper place for literal translation as a procedure in all good translations.

Half the misunderstanding about translation in Britain is due to the fact that so many teachers tell their pupils to avoid translating an SL word by a similar-looking TL word whenever possible. Thus the pupils expand their TL vocabulary and distort their translations.

CHAPTER 8

The Other Translation Procedures

While translation methods relate to whole texts, translation procedures are used for sentences and the smaller units of language. Since literal translation is the most important of the procedures, we have discussed it in a separate chapter (Chapter 7). We shall now discuss the other procedures, whose use always depends on a variety of contextual factors. We shall not discuss here the special procedures for metaphor and metalanguage.

TRANSFERENCE

Transference (*emprunt*, loan word, transcription) is the process of transferring a SL word to a TL text as a translation procedure. It is the same as Catford's transference, and includes transliteration, which relates to the conversion of different alphabets: e.g. Russian (Cyrillic), Greek, Arabic, Chinese, etc. into English. The word then becomes a 'loan word'. Some authorities deny that this is a translation procedure, but no other term is appropriate if a translator decides to use an SL word for his text, say for English and the relevant language, *décor, ambiance, Schadenfreude*; the French diplomatic words: *coup d'état, détente, coup, attentat, démarche*; *dachshund, samovar, dacha*, or for German *Image, Job*, 'last but not least'. However, when the translator has to decide whether or not to transfer a word unfamiliar in the target language, which in principle should be a SL cultural word whose referent is peculiar to the SL culture (see Chapter 9), then he usually complements it with a second translation procedure – the two procedures in harness are referred to as a 'couplet'. Generally, only cultural 'objects' or concepts related to a small group or cult should be transferred; the vogue for transferring so called 'national characteristics' (*Gemütlichkeit, machismo, dolce vita*) should be abandoned. Needless to say, in principle, the names of SL objects, inventions, devices, processes to be imported into the TL community should be creatively, preferably 'authoritatively', translated, if they are neologisms, although brand names have to be transferred. It is not the translator's job to assist any SL advertiser's financial, national or personal prestige interests. At the same time, one cannot be rigid or dogmatic. The media, the experts, will be transferring words whether the translators like it or not. Perhaps when the translator's professional status is raised, they will not be transferring so many.

The following are normally transferred: names of all living (except the Pope and one or two royals) and most dead people; geographical and topographical names including newly independent countries such as (le) Zaire, Malawi, unless they already have recognised translations (see *Naturalisation* below); names of periodicals and newspapers; titles of as yet untranslated literary works, plays, films; names of private companies and institutions; names of public or nationalised institutions, unless they have recognised translations; street names, addresses, etc. (*rue Thaibaut*; 'in the Rue Thaibaut').

In all the above cases, a similar type of readership is assumed and, where appropriate, a culturally-neutral TL third term, i.e. a functional equivalent, should be added.

In regional novels and essays (and advertisements, e.g., gîtes), cultural words are often transferred to give local colour, to attract the reader, to give a sense of intimacy between the text and the reader – sometimes the sound or the evoked image appears attractive. These same words have to be finally translated in non-literary texts (e.g. on agriculture, housing) if they are likely to remain in the TL culture and/or the target language.

There are often problems with the translation of 'semi-cultural' words, that is abstract mental words which are associated with a particular period, country or individual e.g., 'maximalism', 'Enlightenment', Sartre's 'nothing-ness' (*néant*) or Heidegger's *Dasein*. In principle, such words should first be translated, with, if necessary, the transferred word and the functional equivalent added in brackets, until you are confident that your readership recognises and understands the word. Unfortunately such terms are often transferred for snob reasons: 'foreign' is posh, the word is untranslatable. But the translator's role is to make people understand ideas (objects are not so important), not to mystify by using vogue-words. Freud's formidable key-terms may have been mistranslated, but at least they *were* translated. The argument in favour of transference is that it shows respect for the SL country's culture. The argument against it is that it is the translator's job to translate, to explain.

NATURALISATION

This procedure succeeds transference and adapts the SL word first to the normal pronunciation, then to the normal morphology (word-forms) of the TL, e.g. *Edimbourgh, humeur, redingote, thatchérisme*. Note, for German, *Performanz, attraktiv, Eskalation*.

CULTURAL EQUIVALENT

This is an approximate translation where a SL cultural word is translated by a TL cultural word; thus *baccalauréat* is translated as '(the French) "A" level', or *Abitur* (*Matura*) as '(the German/Austrian) "A" level'; *Palais Bourbon* as '(the French) Westminster'; *Montecitorio* as '(the Italian) Westminster'; *charcuterie* – 'delicatessen' (now English 'deli'); *notaire* – 'solicitor'. The above are approximate cultural equivalents. Their translation uses are limited, since they are not accurate, but they can be used in general texts, publicity and propaganda, as well as for brief explanation to readers who are ignorant of the relevant SL culture. They have a greater pragmatic impact than culturally neutral terms. Occasionally, they may be purely functionally, hardly descriptively, equivalents, e.g., *le cyclisme*, 'cricket', 'baseball'; 'tea break', *café-pause*; *carte d'identité*, 'car licence'. Functional cultural equivalents are even more restricted in translation, but they may occasionally be used if the term is of little importance in a popular article or popular fiction. They are important in drama, as they can create an immediate effect. 'He met her in the pub' – *Il l' a retrouvée dans le café*. Or again, *vingt mètres derrière lui* – 'twenty yards behind him'. However, the main purpose of the procedure is to support or supplement another translation procedure in a couplet.

FUNCTIONAL EQUIVALENT

This common procedure, applied to cultural words, requires the use of a culture-free word, sometimes with a new specific term; it therefore neutralises or generalises the SL word; and sometimes adds a particular thus: *baccalauréat* – 'French secondary school leaving exam'; *Sejm* – 'Polish parliament'; 'Roget' – *dictionnaire idéologique anglais*.

This procedure, which is a cultural componential analysis, is the most accurate way of translating i.e. deculturalising a cultural word.

A similar procedure is used when a SL technical word has no TL equivalent. Thus the English term 'cot death' translates as *mort subite d'un nourrisson*, although the components 'unexpected' and 'without known reason' are here omitted from the French.

This procedure occupies the middle, sometimes the universal, area between the SL language or culture and the TL language or culture. If practised one to one, it is an under-translation (e.g. *dégringoler* as 'tumble'). If practised one to two, it may be an over-translation. For cultural terms, it is often combined with transference: *taille*, as 'a tax on the common people before the French Revolution, or *taille*'. I refer to the combination of two translation procedures for one unit as a 'couplet'.

DESCRIPTIVE EQUIVALENT

In translation, description sometimes has to be weighed against function. Thus for *machete*, the description is a 'Latin American broad, heavy instrument', the function is 'cutting or aggression'; description and function are combined in 'knife'. *Samurai* is described as 'the Japanese aristocracy from the eleventh to the nineteenth century'; its function was 'to provide officers and administrators'. Description and function are essential elements in explanation and therefore in translation. In translation discussion, function used to be neglected; now it tends to be overplayed.

SYNONYMY

I use the word 'synonym' in the sense of a near TL equivalent to an SL word in a context, where a precise equivalent may or may not exist. This procedure is used for a SL word where there is no clear one-to-one equivalent, and the word is not important in the text, in particular for adjectives or adverbs of quality (which in principle are 'outside' the grammar and less important than other components of a sentence): thus *personne gentille*, 'kind' person; *conte piquant*, 'racy story'; 'awkward' or 'fussy', *difficile*; 'puny effort', *effort faible*. A synonym is only appropriate where literal translation is not possible and because the word is not important enough for componential analysis. Here economy precedes accuracy.

A translator cannot do without synonymy; he has to make do with it as a compromise, in order to translate more important segments of the text, segments of the meaning, more accurately. But unnecessary use of synonyms is a mark of many poor translations.

THROUGH-TRANSLATION

The literal translation of common collocations, names of organisations, the components of compounds (e.g. 'superman', *Übermensch*) and perhaps phrases (*compliments de la saison*, 'compliments of the season'), is known as *calque* or loan translation. I prefer the more transparent term 'through-translation'.

In theory, a translator should not 'initiate' a through-translation. In fact, through-translations in contiguous cultures sometimes fill in useful gaps, and perhaps it is time that 'Good appetite', 'through-compose', 'leading motif', 'relaxation' (for *détente*), 'no longer the youngest', 'birthday child', should finally enter familiar English. The most obvious examples of through-translations are the names of international organisations which often consist of 'universal' words which may be transparent for English and Romance languages, and semantically motivated for Germanic and Slavonic: e.g., EEC, *Communauté Économique Européenne*, *Europäische Wirtschaftsgemeinschaft* (*EWG*, now *EG*); European Cultural Convention, *Convention culturelle européenne*; *groupe d'études*, 'study group' but *Arbeitsgruppe*; 'working party', *commission d'enquête*, *Arbeitsausschuss*.

International organisations are often known by their acronyms, which may remain English and internationalisms (UNESCO, UNRRA, FAO) or French FIT (International Federation of Translators), but more often switch in various languages (ILO, *BIT* (F), *IAO* (G); WHO, *OMS* (F), *WGO* (G); NATO, *OTAN* (F), *NATO* (G)).

Translated brochures, guide-books and tourist material are apt to pullulate with incorrect through-translations: 'highest flourishing', 'programme building', etc., which are evidence of translationese.

Normally, through-translations should be used only when they are already recognised terms.

SHIFTS OR TRANSPOSITIONS

A 'shift' (Catford's term) or 'transposition' (Vinay and Darbelnet) is a translation procedure involving a change in the grammar from SL to TL. One type, the change from singular to plural, e.g. 'furniture'; *des meubles*; 'applause', *des applaudissements*; 'advice', *des conseils*; or in the position of the adjective: *la maison blanche*, 'the white house' is automatic and offers the translator no choice.

A second type of shift is required when an SL grammatical structure does not exist in the TL. Here there are always options. Thus for the neutral adjective as subject, *l'intéressant, c'est que*; *das Interessante ist, daß, l'interessante è che* . . ., there is a choice of at least: 'What is interesting is that . . .', 'The interesting thing is that . . .', 'It's interesting that . . .', 'The interest of the matter is that . . .'. (But for French and Italian, it may be 'valuable' or 'useful' depending on the various contextual factors.) Again the English gerund ('Working with you is a pleasure') offers many choices. The gerund can be translated by verb-noun (*le travail, die Arbeit*), or a subordinate clause ('when, if, etc. I work with you'), with a recast main clause, or, in some languages, a noun-infinitive (e.g. *das Arbeiten*, which is formal style), or an infinitive.

I think the gerund is the most neglected of all translator's transpositions, e.g., *Wenn Humboldt den Auftrag . . . erhielt, so waren das mehreren Faktoren zu danken* – 'Several factors were responsible for Humboldt's receiving the commission'. Note also the English 'do' auxiliary, 'do come': *komm doch* (or *mal*); *viens donc*. French has '*venir de*' plus the infinitive: *il vient de le faire* is usually translated by 'recently' or 'just'. Again, Italian's reflexive infinitives (*per il precisarsi degli effetti negativi*, 'by stating the negative effects', 'when the negative effects are stated'; *il suo espandersi*, 'its expansion', 'the process of its expansion'; *l'esserci imbattuta in un caso*, 'since we have come upon a case', 'the fact that we have come upon a case') offer several choices. German has active or passive participial constructions which are normally translated by adjectival clause or non-finite participial clauses. Thus *Bei jeder sich bietenden Gelegenheit* may be: 'At every opportunity that occurs' or 'At every available opportunity' or 'Whenever the opportunity occurs' or 'At every opportunity' (taking *sich bieten* as an empty verb). Again, *Im Sinn der von der Regierung verfolgten Ziele* (Wilss, 1982) may be 'In accordance with the aims pursued by the government', 'In accordance with the aims which the government are pursuing' or 'in accordance with the government's aims' – the three translations indicate a different degree of emphasis.

The third type of shift is the one where literal translation is grammatically possible but may not accord with natural usage in the TL. Here Vinay and Darbelnet's pioneering book and a host of successors give their preferred translations, but often fail to list alternatives, which may be more suitable in other contexts or may merely be a matter of taste. (Grammar, being more flexible and general than lexis, can normally be more freely handled.)

Thus, for SL verb, TL adverb: *Notre commerce avec l'étranger n'a cessé de s'améliorer*, 'Our foreign trade has improved steadily (continuously)', 'Our foreign trade has shown continuous improvement'; *Il ne tardera pas à rentrer*, 'He will come back soon', 'He'll be back (return) in a moment (shortly)'; *La situation reste critique*, 'The situation is still critical', 'The situation remains critical'.

In other cases Vinay and Darbelnet, sometimes rather arbitrarily, offer one out of many possible translations; there is nothing wrong with this, but they should have stated the fact. The translator is always concerned with questions of currency and probability, and there is a great difference between *Dès son lever*, 'as soon as he gets up', where *lever* shows up an English lexical gap and therefore the translation has a high degree of probability, and *Dès qu'on essaie d'être arbitraire, on est tout de suite aux prises avec des contradictions*, 'Any attempt to be arbitrary at once involves one in inconsistencies', where ten translators might produce ten different versions, and the semi-literal translation: 'As soon as one tries to be arbitrary, one is immediately faced with contradictions' ought, at first sight, to be the most probable. But Vinay and Darbelnet's prejudice against literal translation (admirably discussed in Wilss, 1982) has become notorious and has had a baneful influence on translation teaching if not translation. Incidentally, the last example contains several transpositions in Vinay and Darbelnet's version:

(1) SL verb, TL noun (*essaie*, 'attempt')
(2) SL conjunction, TL indefinite adjective (*dès que*, 'any')
(3) SL clause, TL noun group (*dès qu'on essaie*, 'any attempt')
(4) SL verb group, TL verb (*est aux prises*, 'involves')
(5) SL noun group, TL noun (*des contradictions*, 'inconsistencies')
(6) SL complex sentence, TL simple sentence (etc!)

However, the fact that it is not possible to strictly standardise transpositions in the way that Vinay and Darbelnet do, since so many overlap and convert to lexis (what Catford calls 'level-shifts' e.g., *après sa mort*, 'after she had died'), in no way detracts from their usefulness, and you should become sensitised to their possibilities.

Further, there are a number of standard transpositions from Romance languages to English which are worth noting even though they all have alternative translations:

(1) SL adjective plus adjectival noun, TL adverb plus adjective: *d'une importance exceptionnelle*, 'exceptionally large'
(2) SL prepositional phrase, TL preposition: *au terme de*, 'after' (cf. *dans le cadre de, au niveau de, à l'exception de, au départ de*)

(3) SL adverbial phrase, TL adverb: *d'une manière bourrue*, 'gruffly'
(4) SL noun plus adjective of substance, TL noun plus noun: *la cellule nerveuse*, 'nerve cell'
(5) SL verb of motion, with *en* and present participle of description, TL verb of description plus preposition (Vinay and Darbelnet's 'criss-cross' transposition): *Il gagna la fenêtre en rampant*, 'He crawled to the window'
(6) SL verb, TL empty verb plus verb-noun: *Il rit*, 'he gave a laugh'
(7) SL noun plus (empty) past participle or adjectival clause (etc.) plus noun, TL noun plus preposition plus noun (the 'house on the hill' construction): *Le complot ourdi contre lui*, 'the plot against him'; *la tour qui se dressait sur la colline*, 'the tower on the hill'
(8) SL participial clause (active and passive), TL adverbial clause or (occasionally) group, as in the following scheme:

SL participial clause (active) *L'unité française renaissante, l'opinion pèsera de nouveau*	→ TL adverbial clause (group) 'As French unity is reviving (with the rebirth of French unity) public opinion will carry weight again'
SL participial clause (active) *Le moment arrivé je serai prêt*	→ TL adverbial clause (or group) 'When the time comes (at the right time) I'll be ready'

The fourth type of transposition is the replacement of a virtual lexical gap by a grammatical structure, e.g. *après sa sortie*, 'after he'd gone out'; *il le cloua au pilori*, 'he pilloried him'; *il atteint le total*, 'it totals'; 'he pioneered this drug', *il a été l'un des pionniers de ce médicament*.

Certain transpositions appear to go beyond linguistic differences and can be regarded as general options available for stylistic consideration. Thus a complex sentence can normally be converted to a co-ordinate sentence, or to two simple sentences: *Si lui est aimable, sa femme est arrogante* – 'He is (may be) very pleasant, but his wife is arrogant' – 'He is pleasant; his wife, however, is arrogant'. This also works the other way round, although some would say that English, influenced by the King James Bible (Hebrew), prefers simple or co-ordinate to complex sentences.

Again many languages appear to be capricious in converting active verbs to animate nouns, thus: 'He is a heavy drinker' – *Il boit sec*; *La tâche d'un exécuteur fidèle d'instructions reçues* – 'The task of someone (one) who faithfully carries out the instructions they (he) have (has) received' (note the attempt to de-sex language); *Une équipe de préleveurs* – 'A staff team to take (blood) samples'.

A group of typical transpositions centre on a Romance-language subject:

(1) *M. Tesnière, grammarien, m'a aidé* 'M. Tesnière (who was) a grammarian, helped me'
(2) *Une fois parti, M. Tesnière* . . . 'once (when) he had left, M. Tesnière . . .'

(3) *Ce livre, intéressant, m'est venu à l'esprit* – 'The book, which was (as it was, though it was) interesting, came to my mind'

(4) *L'homme, qui faisait*. . . – 'The man doing . . .

The last point I want to mention about transpositions is that they illustrate a frequent tension between grammar and stress. To take an example, should you translate *Seine Aussage ist schlechthin unzutreffend* by 'His statement is (a) completely false (one)' or 'There is absolutely no truth in his statement'? My only comment is that too often the word order is changed unnecessarily, and it is sometimes more appropriate to translate with a lexical synonym, retain the word order and forgo the transposition in order to preserve the stress.

Transposition is the only translation procedure concerned with grammar, and most translators make transpositions intuitively. However, it is likely that comparative linguistics research, and analysis of text corpuses and their translations, will uncover a further number of serviceable transpositions for us.

MODULATION

Vinay and Darbelnet coined the term 'modulation' to define 'a variation through a change of viewpoint, of perspective (*éclairage*) and very often of category of thought'. Standard modulations such as *château d'eau*, 'water-tower', are recorded in bilingual dictionaries. Free modulations are used by translators 'when the TL rejects literal translation', which, by Vinay and Darbelnet's criteria, means virtually always. Further, modulations are divided into eleven rather random categories, whilst the – in my opinion – only important one, the 'negated contrary' (*sic*), is not discussed.

As I see it, the general concept, since it is a super-ordinate term covering almost everything beyond literal translation, is not useful as it stands. However, the 'negated contrary', which I prefer to call 'positive for double negative' (or 'double negative for positive') is a concrete translation procedure which can be applied in principle to any action (verb) or quality (adjective or adverb):

Il n'a pas hésité – 'He acted at once'
Il n'est pas lâche – 'He is extremely brave'

You will note that the translations are free, and in theory the double negative is not as forceful as the positive; in fact the force of the double negative depends on the tone of voice, and therefore the appropriateness of this modulation must depend on its formulation and the context.

In the few cases where there is a lexical gap in an opposition (e.g. 'shallow'; *peu profond*), this modulation is virtually mandatory. In all other sentences the procedure is potentially available, but you should only use it when the translation is not natural unless you do so. Thus 'minor' collocated with, say, 'detail' seems to call for a translation such as *sans importance, unbedeutend*, although *petit, klein*, etc., remain as alternatives. Again, 'it will not seem unlikely that' is perhaps best translated as *il est fort probable que* . . . In other cases, the procedure is merely a 'candidate' for use, e.g. 'He made it plain to him' – *il ne le lui cacha pas, il le lui fit comprendre*; 'Men will not always die quietly' (J. M. Keynes) – *Les hommes ne mourront pas toujours sans se plaindre*; 'no mean city' – *cité qui n'est pas sans importance*; 'no mean performer on the violin' – *il joue supérieurement du violon.*

Vinay and Darbelnet's second modulation procedure, 'part for the whole', is rather misleadingly described; it consists of what I call familiar alternatives, viz. *le 14 juillet* (*fête nationale*); *l'homme du 18 juin* (*De Gaulle*); *la fille aînée de l'Eglise* (France); 'Athens of the North' (Edinburgh).

The other modulation procedures are: (a) abstract for concrete ('sleep in the open', *dormir à la belle étoile*); (b) cause for effect ('You're quite a stranger', *On ne vous voit plus*); (c) one part for another ('from cover to cover', *de la première à la dernière page*); (d) reversal of terms (*lebensgefährlich, danger de mort*; *n'appelez pas du bas de l'escalier*, 'don't call up the stairs'; *assurance-maladie*, 'health insurance'); (e) active for passive; (f) space for time ('as this in itself (space) presented a difficulty', *'cela présentant déjà* (time) *une difficulté*); (g) intervals and limits; (h) change of symbols.

Of these procedures, 'active for passive' (and vice versa) is a common transposition, mandatory when no passive exists, advisable where, say, a reflexive is normally preferred to a passive, as in the Romance languages. Reversal of terms (Nida's 'conversive' terms) is also a distinct procedure, usually optional for making language sound natural: 'buy/sell', 'lend/borrow', *hauteur d'eau*/'depth of water'; for English 'loan' there are alternatives in other languages and *créance* translates 'claim' as 'credit' or 'debt' depending on the point of view.

You will note that though I think Vinay's and Darbelnet's categorisation of modulation unconvincing, their abundant translation examples are always stimulating.

RECOGNISED TRANSLATION

You should normally use the official or the generally accepted translation of any institutional term. If appropriate, you can gloss it and, in doing so, indirectly show your disagreement with this official version. Thus *Mitbestimmung* (in management) has to be translated first as 'co-determination'; *Rechtsstaat* as 'constitutional state'. Personally I think 'co-determination' is a poor translation of *Mitbestimmung* though it has the virtue of distinctiveness and brevity. (Compare the plainer but clumsier 'employers' and workers' joint management'.) But it is now too late to change the term to 'workers' participation', and if you did so in any official or serious informative text, you would cause confusion. Similarly, when translating Gay-Lussac's *Volumengesetz der Gase* it is no good giving it your own title or even a brief explanation; nothing but the accepted term ('law of combining volumes') will do.

TRANSLATION LABEL

This is a provisional translation, usually of a new institutional term, which should be made in inverted commas, which can later be discreetly withdrawn. It could be done through literal translation, thus: 'heritage language', *Erbschaftssprache*, *langue d'héritage*.

COMPENSATION

This is said to occur when loss of meaning, sound-effect, metaphor or pragmatic effect in one part of a sentence is compensated in another part, or in a contiguous sentence.

COMPONENTIAL ANALYSIS (see Chapter 11)

This is the splitting up of a lexical unit into its sense components, often one-to-two, -three or -four translations.

REDUCTION AND EXPANSION

These are rather imprecise translation procedures, which you practise intuitively in some cases, *ad hoc* in others. However, for each there is at least one shift which you may like to bear in mind, particularly in poorly written texts:

(1) SL adjective of substance plus general noun, TL noun: *atteintes inflammatoires et infectieuses*, 'inflammations and infections'; *science linguistique* (etc.), 'linguistics'.
(2) For expansion, a not uncommon shift, often neglected, is SL adjective, English TL adverb plus past participle, or present participle plus object: *cheveux égaux*, 'evenly cut hair'; *belebend*, 'life-giving'.

PARAPHRASE

This is an amplification or explanation of the meaning of a segment of the text. It is used in an 'anonymous' text when it is poorly written, or has important implications and omissions.

OTHER PROCEDURES

Vinay and Darbelnet also give:

(1) *Equivalence*, an unfortunately named term implying approximate equivalence, accounting for the same situation in different terms. Judging from Vinay and

Darbelnet's examples, they are simply referring to notices, familiar alternatives, phrases and idioms – in other words, different ways of rendering the clichés and standard aspects of language, e.g. 'The story so far', *Résumé des chapîtres précédents*.

(2) *Adaptation*: use of a recognised equivalent between two situations. This is a matter of cultural equivalence, such as 'Dear Sir' translated as *Monsieur*; 'Yours ever' as *Amitiés*.

Both the above illuminate what sometimes happens in the process of translating, but they are not usable procedures.

As I see it, there are about fourteen procedures within a certain range of probability which are useful to the translator.

COUPLETS

Couplets, triplets, quadruplets combine two, three or four of the above-mentioned procedures respectively for dealing with a single problem. They are particularly common for cultural words, if transference is combined with a functional or a cultural equivalent. You can describe them as two or more bites at one cherry.

Quadruplets are only used for metalingual words: thus, if you translate the sentence: 'The nominal-*ing* clause, a participial clause, occurs in the subject position', apart from a more or less literal translation of 'nominal-*ing* clause', you might also: (a) transfer it; (b) explain, in an adjectival clause, that the present participle is used as a kind of gerund in English; (c) produce a translation label; (d) give an example, with TL literal and functional translations!

You will note my reluctance to list 'paraphrase' as a translation procedure, since the word is often used to describe free translation. If it is used in the sense of 'the minimal recasting of an ambiguous or obscure sentence, in order to clarify it', I accept it.

NOTES, ADDITIONS, GLOSSES

Lastly, here are some suggestions about 'Notes' (when and when not to use them) or supplying additional information in a translation.

The additional information a translator may have to add to his version is normally cultural (accounting for difference between SL and TL culture), technical (relating to the topic) or linguistic (explaining wayward use of words), and is dependent on the requirement of his, as opposed to the original, readership. In expressive texts, such information can normally only be given outside the version, although brief 'concessions' for minor cultural details can be made to the reader, e.g. perhaps by translating Hemingway's 'at Handley's' by *dans le bar Handley*, *in der Handley Bar*, etc. In vocative texts, TL information tends to replace rather than supplement SL information. Thus if you translate 'you can pay for ceramic tiles under a convenient credit purchase scheme' the latter term may be 'translated' by the more precise 'long-term payment facility'.

Additional information in the translation may take various forms:

(1) Within the text

    (a) As an alternative to the translated word: e.g., *la gabelle* becomes 'the *gabelle*, or salt-tax'.

    (b) As an adjectival clause: e.g., *la taille* becomes '*la taille*, which was the old levy raised in feudal times from the civilian population'.

    (c) As a noun in apposition: e.g., *les traites* becomes 'the *traites*, customs dues . . . .'.

    (d) As a participial group: e.g., *l'octroi* becomes '*l'octroi*, taxes imposed on food stuffs and wine entering the town'.

    (e) In brackets, often for a literal translation of a transferred word: e.g. *das Kombinat* becomes 'the *kombinat* (a "combine" or "trust")'.

    (f) In parentheses, the longest form of addition: e.g., *aides* becomes '*aides* – these are excise dues on such things as drinks, tobacco, iron, precious metals and leather – were imposed in the eighteenth century'.

    (g) Classifier: e.g., *Speyer*, 'the city of Speyer, in West Germany'.

Round brackets should include material that is part of the translation. Use square brackets to make corrections of material or moral fact where appropriate within the text.

Where possible, the additional information should be inserted within the text, since this does not interrupt the reader's flow of attention – translators tend to neglect this method too often. However, its disadvantage is that it blurs the distinction between the text and the translator's contribution, and it cannot be used for lengthy additions.

(2) Notes at bottom of page.

(3) Notes at end of chapter.

(4) Notes or glossary at end of book.

The remaining methods (2–4) are placed in order of preference, but notes at the bottom of the page become a nuisance when they are too lengthy and numerous; notes at the back of the book should be referenced with the book page numbers at the top – too often I find myself reading a note belonging to the wrong chapter. Notes at the end of the chapter are often irritating if the chapters are long since they take too long to find.

Normally, any information you find in a reference book should not be used to replace any statement or stretch of the text (unless the text does not correspond to the facts) but only to supplement the text, where you think the readers are likely to find it inadequate, incomplete, or obscure. Thus I think it misguided to translate say *La drépanocytose s'individualise par une anomalie particulière de l'hémoglobine* by 'Sickle-cell disease is distinguished by the fact that one amino-acid in the bent chain of the haemoglobin is out of place'. The emphasis of the text-sentence on 'particular abnormality' is lost, and the new information, accurate as it is, is unnecessary and is given later in the SL text. Certainly encyclopaedia articles often give information that reads like a paraphrase of the technical text that is being translated, but the corresponding key-terms, not whole sentences, should be 'lifted' from them. Similarly, when you consult an expert, be careful not to let him, with a professional flourish, rewrite the whole text for you, even if he produces a better text. His explanations and interpretations also have to be at least related to, if not (literally?) subjected to, a close translation of your text.

If you are translating an important book, you should not hesitate to write a preface and notes to discuss the usage and meanings of the author's terms, particularly where you sacrificed accuracy for economy in the translation, or where there is ambiguity in the text. In the case of a scholarly work, there is no reason why the reader should not be aware of the translator's informed assistance both in the work and the comment. The artistic illusion of your non-existence is unnecessary.

CHAPTER **9**

Translation and Culture

DEFINITIONS

I define culture as the way of life and its manifestations that are peculiar to a community that uses a particular language as its means of expression. More specifically, I distinguish 'cultural' from 'universal' and 'personal' language. 'Die', 'live', 'star', 'swim' and even almost virtually ubiquitous artefacts like 'mirror' and 'table' are universals -- usually there is no translation problem there. 'Monsoon', 'steppe', 'dacha', 'tagliatelle' are cultural words – there will be a translation problem unless there is cultural overlap between the source and the target language (and its readership). Universal words such as 'breakfast', 'embrace', 'pile' often cover the universal function, but not the cultural description of the referent. And if I express myself in a personal way – 'you're *weaving* (creating conversation) as usual', 'his "underlife" (personal qualities and private life) is evident in that poem', 'he's a *monologger*' (never finishes the sentence) – I use personal, not immediately social, language, what is often called idiolect, and there is normally a translation problem.

All these are broad and fuzzy distinctions. You can have several cultures (and sub-cultures) within one language: *Jause* ('Austrian' tea), *Jugendweihe* (GDR – 'coming out' ceremony for twelve-year-olds), *Beamter* (Austria, Switzerland, FRG – but not GDR) are all cultural words which may need translation within German. However dialect words are not cultural words if they designate universals (e.g., 'loch', 'moors'), any more than the notorious *pain, vin, Gemütlichkeit*, 'privacy', *insouciance*, which are admittedly overladen with cultural connotations. And, when a speech community focuses its attention on a particular topic (this is usually called 'cultural focus'), it spawns a plethora of words to designate its special language or terminology – the English on sport, notably the crazy cricket words ('a maiden over', 'silly mid-on', 'howzzat'), the French on wines and cheeses, the Germans on sausages, Spaniards on bull-fighting, Arabs on camels, Eskimos, notoriously, on snow, English and French on sex in mutual recrimination; many cultures have their words for cheap liquor for the poor and desperate: 'vodka', 'grappa', 'slivovitz', 'sake', 'Schnaps' and, in the past (because too dear now), 'gin'. Frequently where there is cultural focus, there is a translation problem due to the cultural 'gap' or 'distance' between the source and target languages.

Note that operationally I do not regard language as a component or feature of culture. If it were so, translation would be impossible. Language does however contain all kinds of cultural deposits, in the grammar (genders of inanimate nouns), forms of address (like *Sie, usted*) as well as the lexis ('the sun sets') which are not taken account of in universals either in consciousness or translation. Further, the more specific a language becomes for natural phenomena (e.g., flora and fauna) the more it becomes embedded in cultural features, and therefore creates translation problems. Which is worrying, since it is notorious that the translation of the most general words (particularly of morals and feelings, as Tytler noted in 1790) – love, temperance, temper, right, wrong – is usually harder than that of specific words.

Most 'cultural' words are easy to detect, since they are associated with a particular language and cannot be literally translated, but many cultural customs are described in ordinary language ('topping out a building', 'time, gentlemen, please', 'mud in your eye'), where literal translation would distort the meaning and a translation may include an appropriate descriptive–functional equivalent. Cultural objects may be referred to by a relatively culture-free generic term or classifier (e.g., 'tea') plus the various additions in different cultures, and you have to account for these additions ('rum', 'lemon', 'milk', 'biscuits', 'cake', other courses, various times of day) which may appear in the course of the SL text.

CULTURAL CATEGORIES

However, in this chapter I shall be discussing the translation of 'foreign' cultural words in the narrow sense. Adapting Nida, I shall categorise them and offer some typical examples:

(1) *Ecology*
Flora, fauna, winds, plains, hills: 'honeysuckle', 'downs', 'sirocco', 'tundra', 'pampas', *tabuleiros* (low plateau), 'plateau', *selva* (tropical rain forest), 'savanna', 'paddy field'
(2) *Material culture* (artefacts)
  (a) Food: 'zabaglione', 'sake', *Kaiserschmarren*
  (b) Clothes: 'anorak', *kanga* (Africa), *sarong* (South Seas), *dhoti* (India)
  (c) Houses and towns: *kampong, bourg, bourgade*, 'chalet', 'low-rise', 'tower'
  (d) Transport: 'bike', 'rickshaw', 'Moulton', *cabriolet*, 'tilbury', *calèche*
(3) *Social culture* – work and leisure
ajah, amah, condottiere, biwa, sithar, raga, 'reggae', 'rock'
(4) *Organisations, customs, activities, procedures, concepts*
  (a) Political and administrative
  (b) Religious: *dharma, karma*, 'temple'
  (c) Artistic
(5) *Gestures and habits*
'Cock a snook', 'spitting'

GENERAL CONSIDERATIONS

A few general considerations govern the translation of all cultural words. First, your ultimate consideration should be recognition of the cultural achievements referred to in the SL text, and respect for all foreign countries and their cultures. Two translation procedures which are at opposite ends of the scale are normally available; transference, which, usually in literary texts, offers local colour and atmosphere, and in specialist texts enables the readership (some of whom may be more or less familiar with the SL) to identify the referent – particularly a name or a concept – in other texts (or conversations) without difficulty. However, transference, though it is brief and concise, blocks comprehension, it emphasises the culture and excludes the message, does not communicate; some would say it is not a translation procedure at all. At the other end, there is componential analysis, the most accurate translation procedure, which excludes the culture and highlights the message. Componential analysis is based on a component common to the SL and the TL, say in the case of *dacha*, 'house', *dom*, to which you add the extra contextual distinguishing components ('for the wealthy', 'summer residence'; cf. *maison secondaire*). Inevitably, a componential analysis is not as economical and has not the pragmatic impact of the original. Lastly, the translator of a cultural word, which is always less context-bound than ordinary language, has to bear in mind both the motivation and the cultural specialist (in relation to the text's topic) and linguistic level of the readership.

ECOLOGY

Geographical features can be normally distinguished from other cultural terms in that they are usually value-free, politically and commercially. Nevertheless, their diffusion depends on the importance of their country of origin as well as their degree of specificity. Thus 'plateau' is not perceived as a cultural word, and has long been adopted in Russian, German and English, but translated in Spanish and usually Italian (*mesa, altipiano*). Many countries have 'local' words for plains – 'prairies', 'steppes', 'tundras', 'pampas', 'savannahs', 'llanos', *campos, páramos*, 'bush', 'veld' – all with strong elements of local colour. Their familiarity is a function of the importance and geographical or political proximity of their countries. All these words would normally be transferred, with the addition of a brief culture-free third term where necessary in the text. This applies too to the 'technical' *tabuleiros* (Brazilian low plateau) if one assumes that the SL writer would not mention them if he does not attach importance to them.

The same criteria apply to other ecological features, unless they are important commercially – consider 'pomelo', 'avocado', 'guava', 'kumquat', 'mango', 'passion fruit', 'tamarind – when they become more or less a lexical item in the 'importing' TL (but note 'passion fruit', *passiflore, Passionsfrucht*) – and may be subject to naturalisation: *mangue, tamarin, avocat* (Sp. *aguacate*) particularly, as here, in French.

Nida has pointed out that certain ecological features – the seasons, rain, hills of various sizes (cultural words: 'down', 'moor', *kop*, 'dune') – where they are irregular or unknown may not be understood denotatively or figuratively, in translation. However, here, television will soon be a worldwide clarifying force.

MATERIAL CULTURE

Food is for many the most sensitive and important expression of national culture; food terms are subject to the widest variety of translation procedures. Various settings: menus – straight, multilingual, glossed; cookbooks, food guides; tourist brochures; journalism increasingly contain foreign food terms. Whilst commercial and prestige interests remain strong, the unnecessary use of French words (even though they originated as such, after the Norman invasion, 900 years ago) is still prevalent for prestige reasons (or simply to demonstrate that the chef is French, or that the recipe is French, or because a combination such as 'Foyot veal chops with Périgueux sauce' is clumsy). Certainly it is strange that the generic words *hors d'oeuvre, entrée, entremets* hold out, particularly as all three are ambiguous: 'salad mixture' *or* 'starter'; 'first' *or* 'main course'; 'light course between two heavy courses' *or* 'dessert' (respectively). In principle, one can recommend translation for words with recognised one-to-one equivalents and transference, plus a neutral term, for the rest (e.g., 'the pasta dish' – cannelloni) – for the general readership.

In fact, all French dishes can remain in French if they are explained in the recipes. Consistency for a text and the requirements of the client here precede other circumstances.

For English, other food terms are in a different category. Macaroni came over in 1600, spaghetti in 1880, ravioli and pizza are current; many other Italian and Greek terms may have to be explained. Food terms have normally been transferred, only the French making continuous efforts to naturalise them (*rosbif, choucroute*).

Traditionally, upper-class men's clothes are English and women's French (note 'slip', 'bra') but national costumes when distinctive are not translated, e.g., *sari, kimono, yukala, dirndl,* 'jeans' (which is an internationalism, and an American symbol like 'coke'), *kaftan, jubbah.*

Clothes as cultural terms may be sufficiently explained for TL general readers if the generic noun or classifier is added: e.g., 'shintigin trousers' or 'basque skirt', or again, if the particular is of no interest, the generic word can simply replace it. However, it has to be borne in mind that the function of the generic clothes terms is approximately constant, indicating the part of the body that is covered, but the description varies depending on climate and material used.

Again, many language communities have a typical house which for general purposes remains untranslated: *palazzo* (large house); *hôtel* (large house); 'chalet', 'bungalow', *hacienda, pandal, posada, pension.* French shows cultural focus on towns (being until 50 years ago a country of small towns) by having *ville, bourg* and *bourgade* (cf. *borgo, borgata, paese*) which have no corresponding translations into English. French has 'exported' *salon* to German and has 'imported' *living* or *living room.*

Transport is dominated by American and the car, a female pet in English, a 'bus', a 'motor', a 'crate', a sacred symbol in many countries of sacred private property. American English has 26 words for the car. The system has spawned new features with their neologisms: 'lay-by', 'roundabout' ('traffic circle'), 'fly-over', 'interchange' (*échangeur*). There are many vogue-words produced not only by innovations but by the salesman's talk, and many anglicisms. In fiction, the names of various carriages (*calèche, cabriolet,* 'tilbury', 'landau', 'coupé', 'phaeton') are often used to provide local colour and to connote prestige; in text books on transport, an accurate description has to be appended to the transferred word. Now, the names of planes and cars are often near-internationalisms for educated(?) readerships: '747', '727', 'DC-10', 'jumbo jet', 'Mini', 'Metro', 'Ford', 'BMW', 'Volvo'.

Notoriously the species of flora and fauna are local and cultural, and are not translated unless they appear in the SL and TL environment ('red admiral', *vulcain, Admiral*). For technical texts, the Latin botanical and zoological classifications can be used as an international language, e.g., 'common snail', *helix aspersa.*

SOCIAL CULTURE

In considering social culture one has to distinguish between denotative and connotative problems of translation. Thus *charcuterie, droguerie, patisserie, chapellerie, chocolaterie, Konditorei* hardly exist in anglophone countries. There is rarely a translation problem, since the words can be transferred, have approximate one-to-one translation or can be functionally defined, 'pork-butcher', 'hardware', 'cake' or 'hat' or 'chocolate' 'shop', 'cake shop with café'. Whilst many trades are swallowed up in super- and hypermarkets and shopping centres and precincts (*centre commercial, zone piétonniere, Einkaufszentrum*) crafts may revive. As a translation problem, this contrasts with the connotative difficulties of words like: 'the people'; 'the common people'; 'the masses'; 'the working class' *la classe ouvrière*; 'the proletariat'; 'the working classes'; 'the hoi polloi' ('the plebs'); *les gens du commun; la plèbe*; 'the lower orders'; *classes inférieures*. Note that archaisms such as the last expressions can still be used ironically, or humorously, therefore put in inverted commas, that 'the working class' still has some political resonance in Western Europe amongst the left, and even more so in Eastern Europe; though it may disappear in the tertiary sector, 'proletariat' was always used mainly for its emotive effect, and now can hardly be used seriously, since the majorities in developed countries are property-owning. 'The masses' and 'the people' can be used positively and negatively, but again are more rarely used. 'The masses' have become swallowed up in collocations such as 'mass media' and 'mass market'. Ironically, the referent of these terms is no longer poor, a toiler or a factory worker. The poor remain the out-of-work minority. The political terms have been replaced by *la base, die Basis*, 'the rank and file', 'the grass roots', the bottom of the bureaucracies.

The obvious cultural words that denote leisure activities in Europe are the national games with their lexical sets: cricket, bull-fighting, *boule, pétanque*, hockey. To these must be added the largely English non-team games: tennis, snooker, squash, badminton, fives, and a large number of card-games, the gambling games and their lexical sets being French in casinos.

SOCIAL ORGANISATION – POLITICAL AND ADMINISTRATIVE

The political and social life of a country is reflected in its institutional terms. Where the title of a head of state ('President', 'Prime Minister', 'King') or the name of a parliament (*Assemblée Nationale, Camera dei Deputati* or 'Senate') are 'transparent', that is, made up of 'international' or easily translated morphemes, they are through-translated ('National Assembly', 'Chamber of Deputies'). Where the name of a parliament is not 'readily' translatable (*Bundestag; Storting* (Norway); *Sejm* (Poland); *Riksdag* (Sweden); *Eduskunta* (Finland); *Knesset* (Israel), it has a recognised official translation for administrative documents (e.g., 'German Federal Parliament' for *Bundestag*, 'Council of Constituent States' for *Bundesrat*) but is often transferred for an educated readership (e.g., *Bundestag*) and glossed for a general readership ('West German Parliament'). A government inner circle is usually designated as a 'cabinet' or a 'council of ministers' and may informally be referred to by the name of the capital city. Some ministries and other political institutions and parties may also be referred to by their familiar alternative terms, i.e., the name of the building – *Elysée, Hôtel Matignon, Palais Bourbon*, 'Pentagon', 'White House', *Montecitorio*, 'Westminster' – or the streets – 'Whitehall', 'Via delle Botteghe Oscure' (Italian Communist Party), '(10) Downing Street' – where they are housed.

Names of ministries are usually literally translated, provided they are appropriately descriptive. Therefore 'Treasury' becomes 'Finance Ministry'; 'Home Office', 'Ministry of the Interior'; 'attorney-general', 'chief justice', or the appropriate cultural equivalent; 'Defence Ministry', 'Ministry of National Defence'. Translations such as 'Social Domain' and 'Exchange Domain' (Guinea) should be replaced by 'Social Affairs' and 'Trade'.

When a public body has a 'transparent' name, say, *Electricité de France* or *Les Postes et Télécommunications*, the translation depends on the 'setting': in official documents, and in serious publications such as textbooks, the title is transferred and, where appropriate, literally translated. Informally, it could be translated by a cultural equivalent, e.g., 'the French Electricity Board' or 'the Postal Services'.

Where a public body or organisation has an 'opaque' name – say, *Maison de la*

Culture, 'British Council', 'National Trust', 'Arts Council', *Goethe-Institut*, 'Privy Council' – the translator has first to establish whether there is a recognised translation and secondly whether it will be understood by the readership and is appropriate in the setting; if not, in a formal informative text, the name should be transferred, and a functional, culture-free equivalent given (*Maison de la Culture*, 'arts centre'); such an equivalent may have to extend over a word-group: 'National Trust', *organisation chargée de la conservation des monuments et parcs nationaux (britanniques)*; in some cases, a cultural equivalent may be adequate: 'British Council', *Alliance française*, *Goethe-Institut*, but in all doubtful cases, the functional equivalent is preferable, e.g., 'national organisation responsible for promoting English language and British culture abroad'; the description (e.g., the composition and manner of appointment of the body) should only be added if the readership requires it; a literal translation or neologism must be avoided. If the informative text is informal or colloquial, it may not be necessary to transfer the organisation's name. The cultural (or, if this is non-existent, the functional) equivalent may be sufficient. For impact and for neatness, but not for accuracy, a TL cultural equivalent of an SL cultural term is always more effective than a culturally free functional equivalent but it may be particularly misleading for legal terms, depending on the context. ' "A" level' for the *bac* has all the warmth of a metaphor, but there are wide differences.

One assumes that any series of local government institutions and posts should be transferred when the terms are unique (*région, département, arrondissement, canton, commune*) and consistency is required. 'Mayor', *maire, Bürgermeister, sindaco* translate each other, although their functions differ. *Giunta* ('junta') is usually transferred though, being an executive body usually elected from a larger council, 'board' is the nearest English equivalent; this becomes *junte* in French, though used only for non-French institutions. Ironically, the caution about *faux amis* applies to 'dictionary' rather than 'encyclopaedia' words. Thus, 'prefect', 'secretary' and *Conseil d'Etat (consiglio di stato)* but not 'tribunal' tend to translate each other, although their functions differ.

The intertranslatability of single words with Graeco-Latin morphemes extends through political parties to political concepts. Within the frame of right, centre and left, about twenty words make up the names of most of the political parties of Europe, East and West. Whilst concepts such as 'liberalism' and 'radicalism' each have a hazy common core of meaning, they are strongly affected by the political tradition of their countries, not to mention the confusion of ideas that either identify or polarise socialism and communism. Here the translator may have to explain wide conceptual differences (e.g., 'the Italian Liberal Party is right wing', 'the British – left of centre'; 'the French right is liberal').

In general, the more serious and expert the readership, particularly of textbooks, reports and academic papers, the greater the requirement for transference – not only of cultural and institutional terms, but of titles, addresses and words used in a special sense. In such cases, you have to bear in mind that the readership may be more or less acquainted with the source language, may only be reading your translation as they have no access to the original, may wish to contact the writer of the SL text, to consult his other works, to write to the editor or publisher of the original. Within the limits of comprehension, the more that is transferred and the less that is translated, then the closer the sophisticated reader can get to the sense of the original – this is why, when any important word is being used in a special or a delicate sense in a serious text, a serious translator, after attempting a translation, will add the SL word in brackets, signalling his inability to find the right TL word and inviting the reader to envisage the gap mentally (e.g., any translation of Heidegger, Husserl, Gramsci). No wonder Mounin wrote that the only pity about a translation is that it is not the original. A translator's basic job is to translate and then, if he finds his translation inadequate, to help the reader to move a little nearer to the meaning.

Historical terms

Up to now I have been discussing the translation of modern institutional terms. In the case of historical institutional terms, say, *procureur-général*, *le Grand Siècle*, *l'Ancien Régime*, *Siècle des Lumières*, *Anschluss*, *Kulturkampf*, *intendant*, *ispravnik*, *zemstvo*, *obshchina*, *duma*, the first principle is not to translate them, whether the translation makes sense (is 'transparent') or not (is 'opaque'), unless they have generally accepted translations. In academic texts and educated writing, they are usually (e.g., all the above except *Siècle des Lumières*, 'the Age of Enlightenment') transferred, with, where appropriate, a functional or descriptive term with as much descriptive detail as is required. In popular texts, the transferred word can be replaced by the functional or descriptive term.

International terms

International institutional terms usually have recognised translations which are in fact through-translations, and are now generally known by their acronyms; thus 'WHO', *OMS* (*Organisation Mondiale de la Santé*), *WGO* (*Weltgesundheitsorganisation*); ILO, *BIT* (*Bureau International du Travail*), *IAA* (*Internationales Arbeitsamt*). In other cases, the English acronym prevails and becomes a quasi-internationalism, not always resisted in French ('UNESCO', 'FAO', 'UNRRA', 'UNICEF').

Ironically, whilst there is a uniquely platitudinous international vocabulary of Marxism and communism which offers translation problems only in the case of a few writers like Gramsci, the only international communist organisations are CMEA (Council for Mutual Economic Assistance – Comecon), the Warsaw Pact, which appears to have no official organisation, and the International Bank for Economic Co-operation (*Internationale Bank für wirtschaftliche Zusammenarbeit – IBWZ*). The others – WFTU (World Federation of Trade Unions – German *WGB*) and World Peace Council (German *RWF*) etc. – appear to have fallen into decline.

Religious terms

In religious language, the proselytising activities of Christianity, particularly the Catholic Church and the Baptists, are reflected in manifold translation (*Saint-Siège, Päpstlicher Stuhl*). The language of the other world religions tends to be transferred when it becomes of TL interest, the commonest words being naturalised ('Pharisees'). American Bible scholars and linguists have been particularly exercised by cultural connotation due to the translation of similes of fruit and husbandry into languages where they are inappropriate.

Artistic terms

The translation of artistic terms referring to movements, processes and organisations generally depends on the putative knowledge of the readership. For educated readers, 'opaque', names such as 'the Leipzig *Gewandhaus*' and 'the Amsterdam *Concertgebouw*' are transferred, 'the Dresden *Staatskapelle*' hovers between transference and 'state orchestra'; 'transparent' names ('the Berlin', 'the Vienna', 'the London' philharmonic orchestras, etc.) are translated. Names of buildings, museums, theatres, opera houses, are likely to be transferred as well as translated, since they form part of street plans and addresses. Many terms in art and music remain Italian, but French in ballet (e.g., *fouetté, pas de deux*). *Art nouveau* in English and French becomes *Jugendstil* in German and *stile liberty* in Italian. The *Bauhaus* and *Neue Sachlichkeit* (sometimes 'New Objectivity'), being opaque, are transferred but the various -isms are naturalised, (but usually *tachisme*) even though 'Fauvism' is opaque. Such terms tend to transference when they are regarded as *faits de civilisation*, i.e., cultural features, and to naturalisation if their universality is accepted.

GESTURES AND HABITS

For 'gestures and habits' there is a distinction between description and function which can be made where necessary in ambiguous cases: thus, if people smile a little when someone dies, do a slow hand-clap to express warm appreciation, spit as a blessing, nod to dissent or shake their head to assent, kiss their finger tips to greet or to praise, give a thumbs-up to signal OK, all of which occur in some cultures and not in others.

Summarising the translation of cultural words and institutional terms, I suggest that here, more than in any other translation problems, the most appropriate solution depends not so much on the collocations or the linguistic or situational context (though these have their place) as on the readership (of whom the three types – expert, educated generalist, and uninformed – will usually require three different translations) and on the setting. I have attempted to indicate the alternatives below.

SUMMARY OF PROCEDURES

A Culture

Way of life and its manifestations peculiar to one speech community.

(1) *Ecology*
   Animals, plants, local winds, mountains, plains, ice, etc.
(2) *Material culture* (artefacts)
   Food, clothes, housing, transport and communications
(3) *Social culture* – work and leisure
(4) *Organisations, customs, ideas* –
   Political, social, legal, religious, artistic
(5) *Gestures and habits* (often described in 'non-cultural' language)

Contrast: universals, i.e. general aspects of nature and humans and their physical and mental activities; numbers and dimensions

Distinguish: cultural focus, distance (or gap) and overlap

B Frame of reference

Contextual factors

(1) Purpose of text
(2) Motivation and cultural, technical and linguistic level of readership
(3) Importance of referent in SL text
(4) Setting (does recognised translation exist?)
(5) Recency of word/referent
(6) Future of referent

Translation procedures

 (1) Transference
 (2) Cultural equivalent
 (3) Neutralisation (i.e. functional or descriptive equivalent)
 (4) Literal translation
 (5) Label
 (6) Naturalisation
 (7) Componential analysis
 (8) Deletion (of redundant stretches of language in non-authoritative texts, especially metaphors and intensifiers)
 (9) Couplet
(10) Accepted standard translation
(11) Paraphrase, gloss, notes, etc.
(12) Classifier

CHAPTER 10

The Translation of Metaphors

DEFINITIONS

Whilst the central problem of translation is the overall choice of a translation method for a text, the most important particular problem is the translation of metaphor. By metaphor, I mean any figurative expression: the transferred sense of a physical word (*naître* as 'to originate', its most common meaning); the personification of an abstraction ('modesty forbids me' – *en toute modestie je ne peux pas*); the application of a word or collocation to what it does not literally denote, i.e., to describe one thing in terms of another. All polysemous words (a 'heavy' heart) and most English phrasal verbs ('put off', *dissuader*, *troubler* etc.) are potentially metaphorical. Metaphors may be 'single' – viz. one-word – or 'extended' (a collocation, an idiom, a sentence, a proverb, an allegory, a complete imaginative text).

So much for the substance. The purpose of metaphor is basically twofold: its referential purpose is to describe a mental process or state, a concept, a person, an object, a quality or an action more comprehensively and concisely than is possible in literal or physical language; its pragmatic purpose, which is simultaneous, is to appeal to the senses, to interest, to clarify 'graphically', to please, to delight, to surprise. The first purpose is cognitive, the second aesthetic. In a good metaphor, the two purposes fuse like (and are parallel with) content and form; the referential purpose is likely to dominate in a textbook, the aesthetic often reinforced by sound-effect in an advertisement, popular journalism, an art-for-art's sake work or a pop song: 'Those stars make towers on vowels' ('Saxophone Song', Kate Bush) – *tours sur foules?*, *Turm auf Spur?* – you have to bear this in mind, when opting for sense or image. Metaphor, both purposes, always involves illusion; like a lie where you are pretending to be someone you are not, a metaphor is a kind of deception, often used to conceal an intention ('Cruise trundling amicably in the English lanes' – *The Economist*).

Note also that metaphor incidentally demonstrates a resemblance, a common semantic area between two or more or less similar things – the image and the object. This I see first as a process not, as is often stated, as a function. The consequence of a surprising metaphor (a 'papery' cheek? – thin, white, flimsy, frail, feeble, cowardly?) may be the recognition of a resemblance, but that is not its purpose.

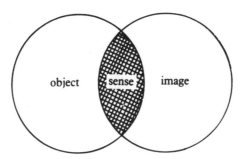

Figure 4. The translation of metaphor

Note that one of the problems in understanding and translating an original or an adapted and, to a lesser extent, a stock metaphor is to decide how much space to allot to the criss-crossed area of sense, and further to determine whether this area is: (a) positive *or* negative; (b) connotative *or* denotative. Thus in the sentence: 'Kissinger: A TV *portrait* featuring a Metternich of today', it is not clear whether 'Metternich' refers to: (a) Metternich's career as a European statesman; (b) his craftiness (negative); (c) his shrewdness (positive); (d), less likely, his autocratic nature. (This may be clarified in the subsequent sentences.) Here, broadly, the translator has the choice of: (a) a literal translation, leaving the onus of comprehension on the (educated) reader; (b) transferring 'Metternich' and adding the preferred interpretation, e.g. 'a statesman of Metternich's cunning'; (c) for a readership that knows nothing of Metternich, translating simply as 'a cunning (world) statesman'.

I use the following terminology for discussing metaphors:

Image: the picture conjured up by the metaphor, which may be *universal* (a 'glassy' stare), *cultural* (a 'beery' face), or *individual* (a 'papery' cheek); 'her continual "forgive me" was another professional deformation' (of a Catholic). *Object:* what is described or qualified by the metaphor, e.g., 'P.J.' in 'P.J. was binding up his wounds'. *Sense:* the literal meaning of the metaphor; the resemblance or the semantic area overlapping object and image; usually this consists of more than one sense component – otherwise literal language would do. Thus, 'save up for a rainy day' – time of need, financial shortage, gloom, worry, etc., – *une poire pour la soif, Notpfennig zurücklegen.* Note that these metaphors are hardly expressive. Usually the more original the metaphor, the richer it is in sense components. *Metaphor:* the figurative word used, which may be one-word, or 'extended' over any stretch of language from a collocation to the whole text. *Metonym:* a one-word image which replaces the 'object'. It may be a cliché metaphor ('crown' as monarchy), recently standardised ('juggernaut', *masto-*

donte) or original ('sink' as hold-all receptacle). Metonym includes synecdoche (i.e., part for whole, or whole for part) e.g., 'bottom' (boat) or 'army' (one solider). Many technical terms such as *arbre, tour, métier, élément, pile, chien* are metonyms.

Symbol: a type of cultural metonymn where a material object represents a concept – thus 'grapes' as fertility or sacrifice.

Usually cultural metaphors are harder to translate than universal or personal metaphors. I see language not primarily as a deposit expressing a culture but as a medium for expressing universals and personality as well.

TRANSLATING METAPHORS

Whenever you meet a sentence that is grammatical but does not appear to make sense, you have to test its apparently nonsensical element for a possible metaphorical meaning, even if the writing is faulty, since it is unlikely that anyone, in an otherwise sensible text, is suddenly going to write deliberate nonsense. Thus, if you are faced with, say, *L'après-midi, la pluie tue toujours les vitres*, you first test for a misprint. If it is an authoritative or expressive text, you translate 'In the afternoons, the rain always kills the window-panes', and perhaps leave interpretation for a footnote. But if it is an anonymous text, you must make an attempt: 'In the afternoons, the rain darkens/muffles/blocks the light from the window-panes.' You cannot avoid this, you have to make sense of everything. Usually, only the more common words have connotations but, at a pinch, any word can be a metaphor, and its sense has to be teased out by matching its primary meaning against its linguistic, situational and cultural contexts.

TYPES OF METAPHOR

I distinguish six types of metaphor: dead, cliché, stock, adapted, recent and original, and discuss them in relation to their contextual factors and translation procedures.

Dead metaphors

Dead metaphors, viz. metaphors where one is hardly conscious of the image, frequently relate to universal terms of space and time, the main part of the body, general ecological features and the main human activities: for English, words such as: 'space', 'field', 'line', 'top', 'bottom', 'foot', 'mouth', 'arm', 'circle', 'drop', 'fall', 'rise'. They are particularly used graphically for concepts and for the language of science to clarify or define. Normally dead metaphors are not difficult to translate, but they often defy literal translation, and therefore offer choices.

Thus, for '(in the) field' of human knowledge, French has *domaine* or *sphère*, German *Bereich* or *Gebiet*, Russian *oblast'*. For 'at the bottom of the hill', French has *au fond de la colline* but German only *am Fuß des Bergs*. Some simple artefacts such as 'bridge', 'chain', 'link', also act as dead metaphors in some contexts, and these are often translated literally. Lastly, common words may attain a narrow technical sense in certain contexts: e.g., 'dog', 'fin', 'element', 'jack', *arbre* ('shaft'), *plage* ('bracket'), *métier* ('loom'), *Mutter* ('nut'). These are just as surprising in all foreign languages, and are particularly insidious and irritating if they make half-sense when used in their primary sense. Remember Belloc's advice, which one cannot take serioulsy even though it has a certain truth: look up every word, particularly the words you think you know – and now I will add to Belloc: first in a monolingual, then in a bilingual encyclopaedic dictionary, bearing in mind the rather general tendency in many languages to 'decapitalise' (remove the capital letters from) institutional terms.

Note that in English, at least, dead metaphors can be livened up, sometimes into metonyms, by conversion to phrasal words ('drop out', 'weigh up') and this must be accounted for in the translation (*marginal, mettre en balance*).

Cliché metaphors

I define cliché metaphors as metaphors that have perhaps temporarily outlived their usefulness, that are used as a substitute for clear thought, often emotively, but without corresponding to the facts of the matter. Take the passage: 'The County School will in effect become not a *backwater* but a *break through* in educational development which will *set trends* for the future. In this its *traditions* will help and it *may well* become *a jewel in the crown* of the county's education.' This is an extract from a specious editorial, therefore a vocative text, and in translation (say for a private client), the series of clichés have to be retained (*mare stagnante, percée, donnera le ton, joyau de la couronne, traditions*, not to mention the tell-tale *en effect* for 'well') in all their hideousness; if this were part of a political speech or any authoritative statement, the same translation procedures would be appropriate.

However, a translator should get rid of clichés of any kind (collocations as well as metaphors), when they are used in an 'anonymous' text, viz. an informative text where only facts or theories are sacred and, by agreement with the SL author, in public notices, instructions, propaganda or publicity, where the translator is trying to obtain an optimum reaction from the readership. Here there is a choice between reducing the cliché metaphor to sense or replacing it with a less tarnished metaphor: 'a politician *who has made his mark*' – *ein profilierter* (vogue-word) *Politiker; politicien qui s'est fait un nom, qui s'est imposé*. For an expression such as 'use up every ounce of energy', 'at the end of the day', 'not in a month of Sundays', there are many possible solutions, not excluding the reduction of the metaphors to simple and more effective sense: *tendre ses dernières énergies, définitivement, en nulle occasion* and you have to consider economy as well as the nature of the text. Bear in mind that a cultural equivalent, if it is well understood (say 'every *ounce* of energy'), is likely to have a stronger emotional impact than a functional (culture-free, third term) equivalent (*grain d'énergie*). If in doubt, I always reduce a cliché metaphor or simile to sense or at least to dead metaphor: 'rapier-like wit' – *esprit mordant, acerbe*.

Cliché and stock metaphors overlap, and it is up to you to distinguish them, since for informative (i.e., the majority of) texts, the distinction may be important. Note that the many translation decisions which are made at the margin of a translation principle such as this one are likely to be intuitive. The distinction between 'cliché' and 'stock' may even lie in the linguistic context of the same metaphor.

Stock or standard metaphors

I define a stock metaphor as an established metaphor which in an informal context is an efficient and concise method of covering a physical and/or mental situation both referentially and pragmatically – a stock metaphor has a certain emotional warmth – and which is not deadened by overuse. (You may have noticed that I personally dislike stock metaphors, stock collocations and phaticisms, but I have to admit that they keep the world and society going – they 'oil the wheels' (*mettre de l'huile dans les rouages, schmieren den Karren, die Dinge erleichtern*).)

Stock metaphors are sometimes tricky to translate, since their apparent equivalents may be out of date or affected or used by a different social class or age group. You should not use a stock metaphor that does not come naturally to you. Personally I would not use: 'he's in a giving humour' (*il est en veine de générosité*); 'he's a man of good appearance' (*il présente bien*); 'he's on the eve of getting married' (*il est à la veille de se marier*). All these are in the Harrap dictionary but they have not 'the implications of utterance' (J. R. Firth) for me; but if they have to you, use them.

The first and most satisfying procedure for translating a stock metaphor is to reproduce the same image in the TL, provided it has comparable frequency and currency in the appropriate TL register, e.g. 'keep the pot boiling', *faire bouillir la marmite* ('earn a living', 'keep something going'); *jeter un jour nouveau sur*, 'throw a new light on'. This is rare for extended metaphors (but probably more common for English-German than English-French), more common for single 'universal' metaphors, such as 'wooden face', *visage de bois, hölzernes Gesicht*; 'rise', 'drop in prices': *la montée, la baisse des prix, die Preissteigerung, -rückgang*. Note, for instance, that the metaphor 'in store' can be translated as *en réserve* in many but not all collocations, and in even fewer as *auf Lager haben* (*eine Überraschung auf Lager haben*).

Symbols or metonyms can be transferred provided there is culture overlap: 'hawks and doves', *faucons et colombes, Falken und Tauben*; this applies to many other animals, although the correspondence is not perfect: a dragon is maleficent in the West, beneficent in the Far East. The main senses are symbolised by their organs, plus the palate (*le palais, der Gaumen*), for taste; non-cultural proverbs may transfer their images: 'all that glitters isn't gold'; *alles ist nicht Gold was glänzt*; *tout ce qui brille n'est pas or*.

But a more common procedure for translating stock metaphors is to replace the SL image with another established TL image, if one exists that is equally frequent within the register. Such one-word metaphors are rare: 'a drain on resources', *saignée de ressources*, *unsere Mittel belasten* (all these are rather inaccurate); 'spice', *sel*. Extended stock metaphors, however, often change their images, particularly when they are embedded in proverbs, which are often cultural, e.g. 'that upset the applecart'; *ça a tout fichu par terre*; *das hat alles über den Haufen geworfen*. These examples are characteristic of translated stock metaphors, in that the equivalence is far from accurate: the English denotes an upset balance or harmony and is between informal and colloquial; the French stresses general disorder and, being more colloquial, has the stronger emotional impact; the German has the same sense as the French, but is casual and cool in comparison.

When the metaphors derive from the same topic, equivalence is closer: 'hold all the cards'; *alle Trümpfe in der Hand halten* (cf. *avoir tous les atouts dans son jeu*). Note that the French and German are stronger than the English, which can keep the same image: 'hold all the trumps'.

English's typical cultural source of metaphor may be cricket – 'keep a straight bat', 'draw stumps', 'knock for six', 'bowl out', 'bowl over', 'on a good/sticky wicket', 'that's not cricket' (cf. 'fair play'; 'fair'); 'I'm stumped'; 'field a question'. Note that all these metaphors are rather mild and educated middle-class, and you normally have to resist the temptation to translate them too colloquially and strongly. 'Fair play' has gone into many European languages, which represents a weakness of foreign translators (in principle, non-cultural terms such as qualities of character should not be transferred) – but 'fair' is only transferred to German, Czech and Dutch.

A stock metaphor can only be translated exactly if the image is transferred within a correspondingly acceptable and established collocation (e.g. 'widen the gulf between them', *élargir le gouffre entre eux*, *die Kluft erweitern*). As soon as you produce a new image, however acceptable the TL metaphor, there is a degree of change of meaning and usually of tone. Thus, *des tas de nourriture* may be a precise equivalent of 'heaps of food'; 'tons of food' or 'loads of food' may be adequately rendered by *des tas de nourriture*, *un tas de nourriture*, but 'loads' is heavier than 'heaps', as is 'tons' than 'loads'. (Much depends on the imagined tone of voice.) These additional components cannot be economically rendered within the collocation (*grand tas* would not help, as there is no reference criterion for *grand*), so there is a choice between compensation elsewhere in the linguistic context and intermitting or under-translating. When you translate there is always the danger of pursuing a particular too far, accreting superfluous meaning, and so the whole thing gets out of balance. Everything is possible, even the reproduction of the sound-effects, but at the cost of economy.

The same caveat applies to the third and obvious translation procedure for stock metaphors, reducing to sense or literal language: not only will components of sense be missing or added, but the emotive or pragmatic impact will be impaired or lost. Thus the metaphor: 'I can read him like a book' has an immediacy which is lacking even in *ich kann ihn wie in einem Buch lesen* ('I can read him as in a book'), which weakens half the metaphor into a simile; *je sais, je devine tout ce qu'il pense* merely generalises the meaning – it should be preceded by *à son aspect, à son air* – and the emphasis is transferred from the completeness of the reading to the comprehensiveness of the knowledge. Even though the English metaphor is standard, it still has the surprising element of a good metaphor, and the French version is prosaic in comparison. Again, 'a sunny smile' could be translated as *un sourire radieux* which is itself almost a metaphor, or *un sourire épanoui*, but neither translation has the warmth, brightness, attractiveness of the English metaphor. The 'delicacy' or degree and depth of detail entered into in the componential analysis of a stock metaphor will depend on the importance you give it in the context. Maybe a synonym will do: *Notre but n'est pas de faire de la Pologne un foyer de conflits*: 'It isn't our purpose to make Poland into a centre (source, focus) of conflict.' For a metaphor such as *visiblement englué dans la toile d'araignée des compromis et des accommodements*, you may wish to keep the vividness of 'visibly ensnared in the spider's web of compromises and accommodation', but, if in an informative text this is too flowery and obtrusive, it could be modified or reduced to 'clearly hampered by the tangle of compromise he is exposed to'. Or again, *il a claqué les portes du PCE* may just be a familiar alternative to 'he left the Spanish Communist Party' or 'he slammed the door on', 'he refused to listen to', 'he rebuffed'. The meaning of a word such as *claquer* can be explicated referentially ('left abruptly, finally, decisively') or pragmatically ('with a bang, vehemently, with a snap'), extra-contextually or contextually, again depending on consider-ations of referential accuracy or pragamatic economy.

Further, you have to bear in mind that reducing a stock metaphor to sense may clarify, demystify, make honest a somewhat tendentious statement. Some-times it is possible to do this naturally, where the TL has no metaphorical equivalent for a SL political euphemism: 'In spite of many redundancies, the industry continues to flourish – *Malgré les licenciements (Entlassungen), la mise en chômage de nombreux employés, cette industrie n'en est pas moins en plein essor.* Stock metaphors are the reverse of plain speaking about any controversial subject or whatever is taboo in a particular culture. They cluster around death, sex, excretion, war, unemployment. They are the handiest means of disguising the truth of physical fact. Inevitably, a stock metaphor such as *disparaître (si je venais à disparaître,* 'if I were to die') becomes harsher when reduced to sense.

Stock cultural metaphors can sometimes be translated by retaining the metaphor (or converting it to simile), and adding the sense. This is a compromise procedure, which keeps some of the metaphor's emotive (and cultural) effect for the 'expert', whilst other readers who would not understand the metaphor are given an explanation. Thus *il a une mémoire d'éléphant* – 'He never forgets – like an elephant.' *Il marche à pas de tortue* – 'He's as slow as a tortoise.' *Il a l'esprit rabelaisien* – 'He has a ribald, Rabelaisian wit.' The procedure (sometimes referred to as the 'Mozart method', since it is intended to satisfy both the connoisseur and the less learned), is particularly appropriate for eponymous stock or original metaphor, e.g. *un adjectif hugolesque* – a 'resounding' ('lugubrious' etc., depending on context) 'adjective, such as Victor Hugo might have used'. When an eponymous metaphor becomes too recherché, or the image is classical and likely to be unfamiliar to a younger educated generation, the metaphor may be reduced to sense (*victoire à la Pyrrhus*, 'ruinous victory'; *c'est un Crésus*, 'a wealthy man'; *le benjamin*, 'the youngest son') but this depends on the importance of the image in the SL and correspondingly the TL context.

Stock metaphors in 'anonymous' texts may be omitted if they are redundant. I see no point in his 'sharp, razor-edge wit' (*esprit mordant*).

Translation of sense by stock metaphor is more common in literary texts, where it is not justified, than in non-literary texts, where it may be so, particularly in the transfer from a rather formal to a less formal variety of language, or in an attempt to enliven the style of an informative text. Expressions like *das ist hier einschlägig* can be translated as 'that's the point here'; *er verschob es, das zu tun*, 'he puts off doing that' – here the metaphors are dead rather than stock; *man muß betonen daß* – 'one must highlight the fact that . . .'

This procedure may be better applied to verbs than to nouns or adjectives since these metaphorical variants ('tackle', 'deal with', 'see', 'go into', 'take up', 'look into' (a subject)) are often less obtrusive than other types of metaphors.

Adapted metaphors

In translation, an adapted stock metaphor should, where possible, be translated by an equivalent adapted metaphor, particularly in a text as 'sacred' as one by Reagan (if it were translated literally, it might be incomprehensible). Thus, 'the ball is a little in their court' – *c'est peut-être à eux de jouer*; 'sow division' – *semer la division* (which is in fact normal and natural). In other cases, one has to reduce to sense: 'get them in the door' – *les introduire (faire le premier pas?)*; 'outsell the pants off our competitors' – *épuiser nos produits et nos concurrents* (?). The special difficulty with these 'sacred' texts is that one knows they are not written by their author so one is tempted to translate more smartly than the original.

There are various degrees of adapted stock metaphors ('almost carrying coals to Newcastle' – *presque porter de l'eau à la rivière*; 'pouring Goldwater on the missiles' – *Goldwater se montre peu enthousiaste pour les engins*) but since their sense is normally clear the translation should 'err' on the side of caution and comprehension.

Recent metaphors

By recent metaphor, I mean a metaphorical neologism, often 'anonymously' coined, which has spread rapidly in the SL. When this designates a recently current object or process, it is a metonym. Otherwise it may be a new metaphor designating one of a number of 'prototypical' qualities that continually 'renew' themselves in language, e.g., fashionable ('in', 'with it', *dans le vent*); good ('groovy', *sensass*; *fab*); drunk ('pissed', *cuit*); without money ('skint', *sans le rond*); stupid ('spastic', 'spasmoid'); having sex ('doing a line'); having an orgasm ('making it', 'coming'); woman chaser ('womaniser'); policeman ('fuzz', *flic*).

Recent metaphors designating new objects or processes are treated like other neologisms, with particular reference to the 'exportability' of the referent and the level of language of the metaphor. A recent neologism, 'head-hunting', being 'transparent', can be through-translated (*chasse aux têtes*), provided its sense (recruiting managers, sometimes covertly, from various companies) is clear to the readership. Again 'greenback', a familiar alternative for a US currency note, has probably only recently come into British English, and is translated 'straight'. 'Walkman', a trade name, should be decommercialised, if possible (*transistor portatif*).

Original metaphors

We must now consider original metaphors, created or quoted by the SL writer. In principle, in authoritative and expressive texts, these should be translated literally, whether they are universal, cultural or obscurely subjective. I set this up as a principle, since original metaphors (in the widest sense): (a) contain the core of an important writer's message, his personality, his comment on life, and though they may have a more or a less cultural element, these have to be transferred neat; (b) such metaphors are a source of enrichment for the target language. Tieck and Schlegel's translations of Shakespeare's great plays have given German many original expressins, but many more metaphors could have been transferred. Take Wilfred Owen's 'We wise who with a thought besmirch Blood over all our soul' ('Insensibility') and Gunter Böhnke's translation: *Wir weisen, die mit einem Gedanken Blutbesudeln unsere Seele*, whatever this means, the translator can only follow the original lexically since the metre will not quite let the grammar be reproduced – the metaphor is virtually a literal rendering, and the readers of each version are faced with virtually the same difficulties of interpretation. However, if an original cultural metaphor appears to you to be a little obscure and not very important, you can sometimes replace it with a descriptive metaphor or reduce it to sense. Evelyn Waugh's 'Oxford, a place in Lyonnesse' could be 'Oxford, lost in the mythology of a remote, vanished region' (or even, 'in Atlantis').

Finally, I consider the problem of original or bizarre metaphors in 'anonymous' non-literary texts. The argument in favour of literal translation is that the metaphor will retain the interest of the readership; the argument against is that the metaphor may jar with the style of the text. Thus in an economics text, *Quelque séduisante que puisse être une méthode, c'est à la façon dont elle mord sur le réel qu'il la faut juger* (Lecerf) – 'However attractive a working method may be, it must be judged by its bite in real life' is not far from the manner of *The Economist* (or *Spiegel*). The metaphor could be modified by 'its impact on reality' or reduced to sense by 'its practical effect'. It seems to me that one has to make some kind of general decision here, depending on the number and variety of such metaphors in the whole text. Again, a typical *Guardian* editorial starts, under the title 'Good

Faith amid the Frothings', 'and on the second day, the squealing (sic) of brakes was loud in the land . . . The National Coal Board had gone about as far as it could go.' Such metaphorical exuberance would hardly be possible in another European language, and, unless the purpose of a translation were to demonstrate this exuberance ('a ton of enforced silence was dumped on Mr. Eaton . . . window of opportunity . . . dribbling offers, and trickling talks . . . Kinnock scrambles out from under' – all in the first paragraph), the metaphors should be modified or eliminated: 'The NCB suddenly issued no more statements . . . Mr. Eaton made no more statements . . . An opportunity . . . Insignificant offers . . . Slow talks . . . Mr. Kinnock emerges' – but a great deal of the sense as well as all the picturesqueness, flavour and sound-effect of the original would be lost. (The connection between metaphor and sound-effects, more often than not sacrificed in translation, is close; metaphor can summon the other three senses only visually.)

Original or odd metaphors in most informative texts are open to a variety of translation procedures, depending, usually, on whether the translator wants to emphasise the sense or the image. The choice of procedures in expressive or authoritative texts is much narrower, as is usual in semantic translation.

Nevertheless, in principle, unless a literal translation 'works' or is mandatory, the translation of any metaphor is the epitome of all translation, in that it always offers choices in the direction either of sense or of an image, or a modification of one, or a combination of both, as I have shown, and depending, as always, on the contextual factors, not least on the importance of the metaphor within the text.

CHAPTER **11**

The Use of Componential Analysis in Translation

INTRODUCTION

Componential analysis (CA) in translation is not the same as componential analysis in linguistics; in linguistics it means analysing or splitting up the various senses of a word into sense-components which may or may not be universals; in translation, the basic process is to compare a SL word with a TL word which has a similar meaning, but is not an obvious one-to-one equivalent, by demonstrating first their common and then their differing sense components. Normally the SL word has a more specific meaning than the TL word, and the translator has to add one or two TL sense components to the corresponding TL word in order to produce a closer approximation of meaning: thus, sometimes:

stürzen	= 'to fall' (+ suddenly + heavily + refers to an important person or entity)
élancé	= 'slender' (+ long + elegant + refers to object)
portière	= 'door' (+ of railway carriage or car, therefore with window)
pruneau	= 'bullet' (+ slang)
pleurs	= 'tears' (+ 'refined' style)
'gawky'	= '*gauche* (+ *maladroit* + *plaisant*)

The sense components of a lexical unit may be referential and/or pragmatic. Comprehensively, a SL word may be distinguished from a TL word on the one hand in the composition, shape, size and function of its referent; on the other in its cultural context and connotations, as well as in its currency, period, social class usage and its degree of formality, emotional tone, generality or technicality and, finally, in the pragmatic effect of its sound composition, e.g., onomatopoeia or repetitive phonemes or suggestive symbolical consonantal clusters.

A word like 'chair' (*chaise, Stuhl*) has only referential components, being pragmatically 'neutral'; but 'jolly' in 'jolly good' is mainly pragmatic, a slight, middle-class intensifier, which can only be over-translated in French (*drôlement*)

114

and under-translated in German (*ganz, vielleicht*) – both languages missing the connotation of social class.

Sense components have been variously called semantic features or semes. (Do not confuse a seme with a single complete sense of a word, which you can call a sememe if you like.) Any SL and TL word pair that you are analysing will show some common and some distinguishing or diagnostic components. Many words also have supplementary, figurative or technical components which become diagnostic in certain contexts; thus for 'mule' – 'stubborn', 'obstinate'. In 'spinning machine' the technical replaces the other components. The more common components are sometimes contrasted at two ends of a scale: e.g. '± young', '± long', '± loud', etc. They are then grouped in the category 'dimension', e.g., 'age', 'length', 'sound', etc. or, rather artificially, '± having legs', '± made of wool', etc. In translation, the polar '±' distinction is only useful when a SL lexical set is being distinguished through componential analysis:

	Material (silk/cotton, etc.)	Length	Finish	Softness
velvet	+	−		
plush	+	+		+
velours	+		+	

In CA, the various single senses (sememes) of a word have to be analysed separately, although such senses are usually related.

A translator may find an extra-contextual componential analysis useful, either if the relevant SL word is more or less context-free, or to establish the semantic limits of a SL word (*fastueux* will stretch to 'luxurious', perhaps, but not to 'lavish'). More commonly, he will analyse a word contextually, thereby dealing only with one *sense* of the word, and thereby restricting its TL sense-components. Normally, he carries out a CA only on a word of some significance in the TL text which cannot adequately be translated one to one. If the word is not important, he will normally make do with a TL synonym (e.g., 'kind', *gentil, gütig*, etc.).

CAs in linguistics are often presented as tree diagrams (for single words), matrix diagrams or scalar diagrams. In translation, matrix diagrams are useful for SL lexical sets and scalar diagrams for SL lexical series, but most CAs can be presented as equations (as above) or performed mentally. Parallel tree diagrams are useful in showing up lexical gaps. (See Figures 5–8.)

If one thinks of translation as an ordered rearrangement of sense components that are common to two language communities (such a definition can hardly be challenged) then the value of CA in identifying these components becomes clear. Further, CA attempts to go far beyond bilingual dictionaries; all CAs are based on

(1)

English	**German**	**French**
hillock		*coteau*
	Hügel	
hill		*colline*
	Berg	
mountain		*montagne*

(2)

English	**German**	**French**
hamlet	*Weiler*	*hameau*
village	*Dorf*	*village* *bourgade* *bourg*
town	*Stadt*	*ville*
city	*Grosstadt*	*grande ville*
	Stadt mit Bischofssitz	*ville épiscopale*

(3)

German	**English**	**French**
Ton	tone	*ton*
Laut	sound	*son*
Schall		
Klang		
Geräusch	noise	*bruit*
Lärm (coll.)	din (coll.)	*vacarme* (coll.)

Figure 5. Scalar diagrams

Ton = sound ($\pm$ human, $-$ vibration, $-$ loud, $-$ long)
Laut = sound ($+$ human, $-$ vibration, $-$ loud, $-$ long)
Schall = sound ($-$ human, $+$ vibration, $+$ loud, $+$ long)
Klang = sound ($-$ human, $+$ vibration, $+$ loud, $+$ long)

(N.B. This equation diagram is intuitive, not analytical.)

Figure 6. Equation diagram

(Pottier)

	Distinctive semes					
	for sitting in	*on legs*	*for one person*	*with back*	*with arms*	*wood or metal material*
canapé	+	+	−	+	±	+
fauteuil	+	+	+	+	+	+
chaise	+	+	+	+	−	+
tabouret	+	+	+	−	−	+
siège (generic term)	+	+	±	±	±	±
pouf	+	−	+	−	−	−

Figure 7. Matrix diagram

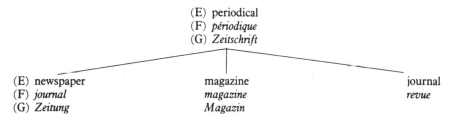

(N.B. Thus for 'journal', German is wissenschaftliche Zeitschrift.)

Figure 8. Parallel tree diagram

SL monolingual dictionaries, the evidence of SL informants, and the translator's understanding of his own language. *The only purpose of CA in translation is to achieve the greatest possible accuracy*, inevitably at the expense of economy. However, it is a technique that is more precise and limiting than paraphrase *or* definition. In practice, you are picking out characteristics in their order of importance.

LEXICAL WORDS

The first and most obvious use of CA is in handling words that denote combinations of qualities, or combinations of actions and qualities, that appear to show up a lexical gap in the target language: English words such as 'quaint', 'gawky', 'murky', 'loiter', 'hop', 'sleazy', 'dingy'; French words like *rêche, renâcler, bourru, relais, filière, braderie, bricoleur, moche*; German words like *düster, bunt, knapp, schroff, pochen, knistern, Prunk*. (These are my 'untranslatable' words in the sense that they have no obvious one-to-one translations.)

Note that many of these words tend to be etymologically obscure or at least unrelated to any corresponding words in other languages; a minority, however, like *trivial, pensum* are 'false' cognates. Indeed, there are many SL words that can profitably be analysed componentially in relation *to* their TL cognates, but only in context. The present tendency is for these words to converge in meaning (*contrôler, harmonisation*, 'protocol'), and CA may be useful in distinguishing them contextually. In other cases, the SL word shares a common component with a non-cognate TL word, whilst the sense of the TL's cognate word may provide an SL distinctive (or supplementary) component: Thus, *actuel*, 'present day' ('actual' or 'topical').

Although these *faux amis* are not cultural words, one is tempted to transfer them in translation, as many of them appear to have an individual feel to them. Nevertheless, as they express universal characteristics, they have to be translated, not transferred.

Note that the pragmatic effect of sound composition particularly applies to German (and probably Russian) words, since the language has such a strong physical element: thus the extra-contextual differences between *klopfen, pochen* and 'knock' are to some extent a matter of sound – *pochen* is also less current than *klopfen*. In some contexts the difference between a loud and a soft knock could be expressed by *klopfen* and *pochen* (tap) – but this is partly a subjective judgment.

As my first examples of the main use of CA, I take *blafard*, 'murky' and *mise au point*, which in some contexts are not adequately translated one to one.

Blafard is normally translated as 'pale' (in 'refined' contexts 'pallid' or 'wan') and collocated rather narrowly with *teint, teinte, couleur, aube*. Its supplementary components are: (1) 'faint'; (2) 'almost faded'; (3) 'unpleasant'; (4) 'insipid'. Where the word is significant, 'pale', 'faint', or 'unpleasantly pale' may be an appropriate translation, collocated perhaps with *teinte*.

Mise au point has a wide semantic range ('focusing', 'correction', 'perfection', 'explanation', 'completion', 'adjustment', 'regulation', etc.) but its most common sense, as in *mise au point d'un produit, d'un procédé, d'une invention* appears to be not much more than 'production'. However, in a sentence such as *il annonca la mise au point d'un procédé, permettant de produire le virus en quantités importantes*, the value of *mise au point* could be reflected in 'he stated that a process for manufacturing the *virus in large quantities had been finally developed*'. Thus the manufacturing stages as well as the final production in *mise au point* can be brought out.

Many dictionaries, even the best, monolingual as well as bilingual, tend to enumerate synonyms rather than state the semantic components of a word. Thus for 'cringe', the Collins dictionaries give *ramper, s'humilier; kriechen, katzbuckeln*: 'cringe' combines behaviour ('draw back', 'bow down') with an emotion ('servility', 'cowardice', 'timidity') which is always negative – therefore neutral translations such as *reculer, zurückweichen, schaudern, zurückschrecken* miss the point.

Many words of quality or description appear to have two fairly evenly divided components when out of context – thus *rêche*: 'harsh' and 'bitter'; *épanoui*: 'radiant' and 'serene'; *bunt*: 'bright' and 'many-coloured'; *düster*: 'dark' and 'sinister'; *Prunk*: 'magnificence' and 'display'; 'bustle': *hereineilen* and *geschäftig* – but in collocation one or other component is likely to predominate so that the addition of another component in the translation depends on the importance of the word in the text.

The pragmatic component of many words consists primarily in their positive or negative connotations: thus *maigre, paperasserie, befremden, entfremden, orgueilleux, brutal* have to be shown as negative in translation. 'Favour' (verb), *promouvoir, fördern* are positive, but *favoriser* is neutral; *systématique* is often negative in French ('dogmatic', 'doctrinaire'), 'systematic' usually positive in English. *Phantasievoll* may be negative, as 'fanciful' ('unreliable') or positive, as 'imaginative'.

Degrees of formality can be noted as pragmatic components when they have no TL equivalents: thus *frangin, frangine* (colloquial); '(tiny) tot' (familiar); *bouffer* (verb of 'nosh' or 'grub').

My final example of an 'untranslatable' word is 'murky'. Out of context, the components are: 'dark', 'cloudy', 'drizzly', 'fuzzy', 'rainy', 'dirty', 'unclear', 'impenetrable', 'thick', 'heavy', 'gloomy', always with a negative connotation. ('Hell is *murky*', *Macbeth*, V.I.38.) In context, 'murky' collocates easily with 'sky' (*ciel brouillé et sombre; dunkler finsterer Himmel*); 'alley' (*ruelle sale et noire; schmutzige, dunkle, Gasse*); water (*eau trouble et salie*); 'atmosphere' (*atmosphère obscure, fuligineuse*); 'past' (*réputation, passé obscur et ténébreux*); 'fog' (*brouillard opaque et sombre; dunkler, undurchsichtiger Nebel*). The choice of French and German components are merely a proposal. It may be influenced not so much by the referential and pragmatic meaning of the total text, which does not usually affect a recognised collocation, but by previous choice of words (avoiding repetitions) and considerations of euphony. Further, the meaning of 'murky' is partly in the taste area, and therefore translators may choose various translation components, since the word is out of reach of any back-translation test.

CULTURAL WORDS

The second use of a componential analysis is in translating cultural (and institutional) words that the readership is unlikely to understand; whether the CA is accompanied by an accepted translation (which must be used in all but the most informal texts), transference, functional equivalent, cultural equivalent and so on will depend, firstly, on the particular text-type; secondly, on the requirements of the readership or the client, who may also disregard the usual characteristics of the text-type; and thirdly, on the importance of the cultural word in the text. The above considerations will affect the degree of detail (the delicacy) of the CA, but normally you should include at least one descriptive and one functional component;

thus *gîtes*: 'rural lodgings in France let to tourists'; *Konditorei*: 'coffee shop serving and selling cakes and pastries'; 'British Council': 'official organisation promoting English language and culture overseas'; 'Arts Council': 'national organisation subsidising the arts in UK'; *giunta*, 'municipal/town council in Italy'; *rédacteur à la préfecture*, 'French departmental official responsible for drafting legal documents.'

Further, in principle, the components in each example are recursive or unlimited, although in a steeply descending order of significance. This applies equally to stock as to original metaphor; thus 'worn-out' (*usé*) as a metaphor could be analysed as: 'long in existence, frequently used, no longer useful' with supplementary components 'banal, boring, consisting of common words, used by trite speakers' and so on; in *Zeit ist Geld*, 'time is money', the components of 'money' are infinite but decreasingly significant: (a) precious; (b) concrete; (c) measurable; (d) can depreciate.

SYNONYMS

CA can be used to differentiate SL synonyms in context. Frequently, such synonyms (e.g., 'worship and adore') are used for emphasis only, and can be translated by using a verb with an adverb or adverbial group as an intensifier, e.g., *adorare con fervore*; *aufs innigste anbeten*; *adorer avec ferveur*. Further, object-synonyms are coupled in a few set phrases such as 'let and hindrance', 'will and testament', 'goods and chattels', 'freedom and liberty' (in English coupling Romance and Germanic words) where a parallel coupling in translation would normally be unnecessary. However, when synonyms are coupled by an innovative writer, the translator has to attempt a parallel coupling. Thus in *Les courants marins relient ou enchaînent ce roc à la côte du Languedoc* (P. Valéry, *Inspirations méditerranéennes*, adapted): 'The sea currents link and chain this rock to the Languedoc coast', it seems that *enchaîner* both contrasts with and reinforces *relier* to impose a strong physical impact, although *enchaîner* is a high-frequency word in many contexts and normally has not this force. Similarly, a translator may be compelled to make a distinction between lexical sets such as 'appreciate and value' (*apprécier et priser*), 'assess and evalute (*estimer et évaluer*), 'esteem and prize' (*estimer et priser*), etc., although the distinction would have a considerable element of subjectiveness:

	Personal enjoyment	High regard	Objective	Report	Approximation
appreciate	+	+	+	−	−
value	+	+	+	−	−
assess	−	−	+	+	+
evaluate	−	−	+	+	−
esteem	−	+	+	−	−
prize	+	+	−	−	−

SETS AND SERIES

Fourthly, CA can be used to distinguish the meanings of SL cultural sets or series, when their TL 'equivalents', even if they have transparently similar names, have widely different functional and or descriptive (substantive) components. This goes back to the origins of CA which was concerned with kinship terms which, being more numerous in developing than in industrialised societies, are most conveniently described through CA. A detailed CA establishes, for instance, that a *fauteuil* is not a *chaise*, 'brown' is not usually *brun*, German has no satisfactory equivalent for 'cattle'.

I take as an example of a cultural set (which, unlike a 'series', is unordered) the various forms of French bread:

	Length	*Thickness*	*Oblong*	*Roundness*	*Regional currency*
baguette	+	−	−	−	
ficelle	(+)	=	−	−	
flûte	+	−	−	−	
gros	+ +	+	+	−	
miche	+	+	−	+	
boule	+		−	+	(army)

The translator can 'read off' the components, with 'loaf' as the classifier, coupled or not with the transferred word. Similar sets can be drawn up for many artefacts, e.g., beers, cheeses, nails, windows, shirts, colours.

Universal or cultural series or hierarchies are all amenable to CA – kinship terms, ranks, hierarchies, local government administrative units (e.g., *région*, *département*, *arrondissement*, *canton*, *commune*). You will find a non-serious table of English meals on the next page.

CONCEPTUAL TERMS

CA, together with case-grammar (see Chapter 12), is useful in analysing conceptual terms. Take 'liberalism', with its obvious component of freedom of the individual, which may have further components at every point of the political spectrum, as well as moral and/or intellectual attitudes depending on the relevant national and group culture – often the slipperiest word in any language. Note that if a concept-word becomes a key word, i.e., if it is central to a professional non-literary text, it may be useful to analyse the concept componentially in a footnote at its first mention, scrupulously repeating the word at all later citations. Thus Gramsci's *egemonia* could be translated as 'hegemony, in the sense of cultural leadership and consensus exercised by the intellectuals over a country's institutions, comple-

	Time	*Class*	*Area*	*Content*
breakfast				
'Great British'	up to 9.30 a.m.	WC	UK	tea, coffee, cereal, bacon and eggs
Continental	up to 9.30 a.m.	MC	UK	tea, coffee, toast
coffee break (elevenses)	10–11 a.m.	all	UK	coffee, biscuits
brunch	11 a.m.–12.30 p.m.	–	N. America	hot meal
lunch	1–2 p.m.	UMC	UK	hot meal
dinner	1–2 p.m.	WC children	UK	hot meal
luncheon	1–2 p.m.	nobility	UK	hot meal
snap	1–2 p.m.	WC	N. England	packed lunch
tea break	3–4 p.m.		UK	tea, biscuits
tea	4–5 p.m.	MC	UK	tea, bread, jam, cake
(high) tea	6–7 p.m.	WC	N. England	main meal
supper	8–11 p.m.		UK	light meal
dinner	8–9 p.m.	UMC	UK	main meal

MC, middle class; UMC, upper-middle class; WC, working class.

Note also: 'brekkers' (children); 'brakky' (Australian); 'dindins' (infants' lunch, UMC); 'ploughman's lunch' (simple pub lunch of bread, pickles and cheese and beer); 'fork lunch' (cold buffet, standing); 'wedding breakfast' (ceremonial meal after wedding, with champagne); 'harvest supper' (meal in church hall, after harvest time); 'funeral meal' (referred to in Anglo-Irish as a 'wake'); 'Christmas dinner' (1 – 3 pm; traditionally turkey plus Christmas pudding – rich, steamed, with suet, dried fruit, spices, brandy butter).

CA versions for Jamaican meal terms and an indication of United States meal terms can be found in Robbins Burling's *Man's Many Voices*.

Figure 9. Meals diagram

mented or contrasted with political leadership and control'. Here CA and definition or lexicography appear to coincide; CA for the translator, however, is normally based on analysing the difference between an SL word and its closest one-to-one TL approximation.

NEOLOGISMS

Further, CA is useful in translating neologisms, whether these are new words naming newly invented or imported objects or processes, or new expressions that suddenly fill one of the innumerable gaps in a language's resources for handling human thought and feeling at some level of formality. In each category, it is a question of arranging components in order of importance.

In the first category, consider *Waldsterben*, a German neologism relating to death of forests due to pollution; although the causal component is not in the

German term, it is desirable that it appear in the translation; 'forest destruction' is misleading, 'forest acid death' may establish itself, depending on the future of 'acid rain'. In the case of new objects, the SL word is likely to be a trademark, and CA could only be used as a gloss: thus, '*Magnashield*, a double-glazed patio door retaining warmth'.

In the second category, the CA of a new idiom such as 'get your act together' demonstrates four components: (1) concerted preparation; (2) ensuring effective action; (3) implication of previous disarray; (4) pragmatic informality. The translator is left with the problem of transferring the first two components, if not the third, into the TL. (Unfortunately bilingual dictionaries do not give equivalents that are on a different level of formality.) A CA that records pragmatic meaning will ensure that the translator does not merely transfer the denotative meaning of neologisms such as a 'downer' (sedative), a 'wet' (moderate Tory critic of Mrs Thatcher) or a 'ligger' (life-long freeloader).

WORDS AS MYTHS

Lastly, perhaps, CA is used for the words that have become symbols of untranslatability and cultural consciousness, the Frenchman's 'bread', the English 'cricket', the American 'baseball', the Italian *pasta*, the Russian *kvass*, etc. When such 'opponents' of translation as Robert Graves, Ortega y Gasset and Paul Valéry talked about the 'impossibility' of translating *pain* as 'bread', *vin* as 'wine' and so on, they were conscious of the gap in feeling and connotation between the SL and the TL word, which they considered to be unbridgeable. But in fact the explanation is the translation. An ordered account of the cultural difference between two words with the same referent but different pragmatic components is offered by CA, rather than two separate definitions. Thus the translator, faced, say, with the different definitions of 'capitalism' given in the UK and the Soviet editions of the Oxford *Student's Dictionary of Current English*, may first note the common substantive or descriptive component – 'private ownership of the means of production' – and the distinguishing functional components – UK: 'basis of a system of society offering freedom to operate or manage property for profit in competitive conditions'; Soviet: 'basis of the exploitation of man by man'.

In fact there is nothing specifically English or Soviet about either of these perfectly 'legitimate' definitions of the internationalism 'capitalism', but where appropriate it is the translator's duty to show which sense such words have in the SL text, and CA offers the most pertinent, economical and necessary comprehensive method of making this distinction.

CONCLUSION

I have briefly reviewed seven uses of CA in translation. I see it as a flexible but orderly method of bridging the numerous lexical gaps, both linguistic and cultural, between one language and another. Needless to say it will never do it perfectly. In its fight against under-translation (use of synonymy) it will tend to over-translate. In its striving for accuracy, it will tend to sacrifice economy and therefore the pragmatic impact, which may well be sold short. (However, it is likely to be more economical than paraphrase or definition.) Operationally, it rests on the existence of universals and cultural overlaps, as does all translation, but theoretically, it does not attempt to enter that field of philosophical and linguistic controversy. Many will regard it as no more than common sense, but I hope I have shown you, by demonstrating the various approaches and techniques, that there is more to it than that.

CHAPTER 12

The Application of Case Grammar to Translation

INTRODUCTION

Grammar is the skeleton of a text; vocabulary, or, in a restricted sense, lexis, is its flesh; and collocations, the tendons that connect the one to the other. Grammar gives you the general and main facts about a text: statements, questions, requests, purpose, reason, condition, time, place, doubt, feeling, certainty. Grammar indicates who does what to whom, why, where, when, how. Lexis is narrower and sharper; it describes objects (animate, inanimate, abstract), actions (processes and states) and qualities; or, roughly, nouns, verbs, adjectives and adverbs. Grammar indicates the relations between them, for instance through prepositions of time and place or through the shorthand of pronouns.

There is a grey area between grammar and lexis: prepositional phrases like *au sein de* ('within'), *au niveau de*, *al livello di* ('in' or 'at'), semi-verbs like *venir de* ('just'), *se borner à* ('merely'), *ne cesser de* ('always'), 'he used to' (*habituellement*), *je peux* ('perhaps') hover between the two, though they only translate each other approximately. Halliday wrote that lexis begins where grammar ends, but I think they partly overlap, like most polar concepts in translation. Natural word-order is an aspect of grammar, but odd (or 'marked') word-order is used for emphasis or stress, which can also be indicated by lexis, e.g., such words as 'precisely', 'itself', 'actual', 'even', 'undoubtedly', and the superlatives of adjectives, and punctuation (italics, capital letters, inverted commas).

As translators, we are interested in grammar only as a transmitter of meaning. Therefore Bloomfieldian or 'structuralist' grammar, stretching as far as and including Zellig Harris, is of little interest to us, since it excludes meaning, and the grammars of Saussure and Chomsky, since they deal with *langue* and 'competence' rather than *parole* and 'performance' respectively, i.e., with the principles of language rather than with authentic texts, are, as I see it, not very helpful; one can build a theory round the transition from a SL surface through a universal deep to a TL surface structure, but it often becomes an academic exercise. Nida's applications of transformational grammar, however, notably in *Exploring Semantic*

Structures, clarify the subtleties of English in an insightful way, and prompt good translations. Since Chomsky, linguistics with its emphasis on discourse analysis and sociolinguistics has moved closer to 'real' utterances, and some linguists have 'semanticised' or given fresh and closer meanings to many grammatical concepts, such as the cases. Yet most writers on translation who use case grammar are only concerned with the normal sequence of, say, participants, process and circumstance, in each language, contrasting the different valencies in each case, thus:

> *La maison se détache sur un fond vert* – The house stands out against a green background – *Das Haus hebt sich von einem grünen Hintergrund ab.*

I regard this as useful, but as a feature of contrastive linguistics rather than translation theory.

In this chapter I propose to show how knowledge of some aspects of case grammar* may be useful to the translator and therefore constitutes a part of translation theory. Since case grammar centres upon the relationship between the verb and its satellites or partners, I shall discuss the translation of verbs, in particular missing verbs, first; next I shall specify the case-partners that are closely associated with the verb; and finally I shall go into the semantic relationships that are 'freely' associated with the verb, and therefore often called 'circumstantial'.

THE TRANSLATION OF MISSING VERBS, I.E., VERBAL FORCE

I define case grammar as a method of analysing a sentence, a clause, or a verbless compound in a manner that demonstrates the central position of the verb or the word that has verbal force within the word sequence; this word may be an adjective – 'responsible', an adverb – 'responsibly', a noun – 'responsibility', a collective noun – 'group' (consisting of whom?), a common noun – e.g., 'wind' in 'windmill' (the wind propels the mill) or 'factory' in 'toy factory', or an adverbial in a verbless sentence where a verb is implied, e.g.

> *So Helmut Schmidt* – 'As Helmut Schmidt stated'
> *Darauf Kienast* – 'Kienast replied'
> *Raus (Dehors)* – 'Get out'
> *Herein* – 'Come in'.

Further, the verb may be implied in an idiomatic phrase with a nominalisation as in: *D'où la mise au point d'un dépistage systématique* – 'For this reason a unit has been set up to screen patients systematically', or in a cry or an exclamation mark

---

* I prefer the term 'case grammar' to 'valency theory' and to Tesnière's version of dependency grammar, since it is transparent. However, any elements from whatever provenance that are useful as translation tools will be incorporated into my own version of an extended case grammar.

such as Käthe Kollwitz's *Brot*: 'We want bread', or it may be implied in a vivid nominal and adverbial style, as in *Der Untertan*, where Heinrich Mann uses verbless sentences in succession as a device which would hardly be correspondingly effective in an English translation, thus:

> *Und gefällig schrie das Häuflein mit. Diederich aber, ein Sprung in den Einspanner und los, hinterdrein . . .* – The little crowd obligingly echoed Diederich's cry but he, jumping into the one-horse carriage, started off in pursuit.

(Note that here *Sprung*, *los* and *hinterdrein* have each been transposed into verbs.) Again:

> *Der Wagen entrollte dem Tor, und Diederich: Es lebe der Kaiser!* – The carriage bowled through the gateway and Diederich cried out: 'Long live the Kaiser!'

Finally a suspicious individual behind a pillar is seen concealing papers . . .

> *Da aber Diederich! Wie den Sturm und mit Kriegsgeschrei sah man ihn über den Platz tosen.*

The first three words could be translated as: 'But Diederich was waiting for him', 'But Diederich did for him', 'Diederich however suddenly appeared.' The official (anonymous?) translation is: 'This was Diederich's opportunity.'

In all these instances, the translator has a wide semantic choice if he wishes to supply a verb, since stylistically the source language text in omitting the verb is attempting to give a rather general impression of sudden, strong action. Obviously, the selection is finally limited by the context, but contexts (unlike explicit words) often exercise a wide rather than a close semantic constraint. When a verb is omitted it is inevitably semantically underdetermined, but given its importance the translator must supply it, if he decides that the reasons for its omission, which may be syntactical, stylistic or pragmatic, do not apply in the target language.

Whilst I have shown that, in a number of cases, an English translation has to supply a finite verb that is missing in the SL text, there are many more examples where the 'communicative dynamism' of a SL verb shifts to an English verb-noun or gerund, normally retaining its case-partners. (This trend of the English verb has been demonstrated by Firbas in a number of papers.) Thus we find in the same paragraph of an OECD brochure on *Refus de vendre*: *faire respecter des prix de revente imposés* – '*enforcing observance* of fixed retail prices'; *qui vise à empêcher que ne soient tournées les interdictions* – '*whose object is* to prevent the evasion of the prohibitions'; *pour inciter à s'y conformer* – 'to enforce *compliance* with them'; *estime la Cour Suprême* – 'in the Supreme Court's view'. Similarly in translating *l'inflation s'augmente* the rheme carries more weight when translated with nominals as 'there is a rise in inflation' or 'inflation is on the increase' than with a verbal construction as 'inflation is increasing'. Here the implied case-partners ('inflation of prices, money', etc. and reflexive pronoun for 'increasing') need not be expressed in the translation. Lastly a stretch of language such as *en vue d'inciter à adopter un comportement qui* . . . – 'for the purpose of inducing *other companies* to adopt conduct which . . .' illustrates the need to supply a case-partner as well as the English trend towards the gerund.

Passing from 'missing' verbs to word groups, clauses, sentences, it is fairly obvious that clauses such as 'It's my hope, my belief, a matter for regret that' become *j'espère que*, or *ich hoffe daß*, *je crois que* or *ich glaube daß*, *je regrette (c'est regrettable)* or *ich bedaure (es ist bedauerlich)*. Contrariwise: *Die Schüsse auf den amerikanischen Präsidenten Reagan* requires a verb in English or French: 'The shots (which were) fired at (which hit) President Reagan' – *Les coups tirés sur le Président Reagan*. More usually, the noun plus preposition plus noun construction for English ('the house on the hill') requires a verb (adjectival clause or past participle) in French, whilst the indirect object plus adjective plus noun construction in German: *der ihnen fremde Staatsmann* – 'the statesman whom they don't know, who is strange to them' – requires a relative clause in English or French. Lastly the translation of a phrase such as *l'effort des hommes sur le monde extérieur* requires an infinitive ('to affect, to influence'): 'man's attempt to influence the external world', or a verb–noun collocation ('to make his mark on') but the words supplied would be semantically limited by the rest of the sentence. Note also that English shows a remarkable difference between standard forms, which require the use of a verb, and non-standard forms which are often verbless just like the German standard forms; thus the standard forms are *er will heraus* – 'he wants to get out of here'; *ich bin gerade dabei* – 'I'm just doing it' and the non-standard form is 'I want out'.

In French the startling effect of a missing verb to connect the agent case with the complement is embedded in the historical infinitive, e.g., *Et lui de partir*. An initial *autre* may also introduce a dramatic effect: *Autre arrêt dont les motifs ont des résonances capitales* – 'The following is another decision where the motives involved had important repercussions.' More commonly, a verb 'derived' from one of the case-partners and the context is simply omitted, but normally 'restored' in English, thus: *Et quelques lignes après* . . . – 'A few lines later, he stated . . .' (Marks of suspension, more common in French, induce a verb in the English translation.) A further case of significant punctuation is the following:*

> *Trimmer: Stau des Beschnittmaterials, dadurch schräge Weiterführung des Produkts*
> → *Stau, etwa 4% aller Stopper*

> Trimmer: build-up of guillotine waste *made* the copies move on skew, *causing* jamming, approx. 4% of all stoppages.

In other contexts in this piece, '→' was translated by nominal or verbal constructions such as 'and as a result', 'which means that', 'which results in'.

---

* I gratefully acknowledge the help of David Harvey and Harold Leyrer in supplying examples.

Note that it is not difficult to 'derive' missing verbs from statements since, in contrast to nouns, the number of basic verbs is limited. The number of nouns (i.e., objects) is infinite, but new verbs can only be created on the basis of combining a few fundamental human actions with new objects; the vast majority of verbs consist of one or more of a few meaning components ('semantic primitives') such as 'cause to', 'become', 'change', 'use', 'supply' combined with an object or quality. In the sentence: 'First a flower, then a rose, then a dog rose', the translator would find no difficulty in supplying the missing verbs in the context. (Note also that whilst some languages have no common verbs to indicate inanimate possession, others may cover the sense with a genitive case, and others require a more formal verb: thus 'conditions for the lots and graves in the cemetery' may become *les conditions de concession des lots et des fosses que détient le cimetière*.)

I take the above set of examples as representative of the most important aspect of the case grammar application, where the translator supplies a verb. Obviously he will do so more readily if he is translating 'communicatively' than 'semantically', but when the stylistic effect of verb omission cannot be reproduced in the target language, as in the Heinrich Mann examples, he has to intervene 'semantically'.

THE TRANSLATION OF CASE-GAPS

A more common, if perhaps less important, aspect of case grammar applies to case-gaps in the SL text. Take the following sentence: *Le profit ne peut provenir qu d'un progrès (même mineur) ou d'un effort pour résoudre une carence ou une inadaptation* (see Lécuyer, 1978). I take this as an example of a sentence (characteristic of modern technical jargon) that includes five apparently incomplete verbal nouns: in the event, one might want to know who makes the profit, the progress and the effort; what is lacking, and who is failing to adapt to what. There are in fact several 'missing' or 'empty' case-partners for each verbal noun, whose specific content may or may not be clarified in the larger context. One might assume the following translation: 'Profit can come only from the progress that *a company has achieved* (even if it is only on a small scale) or from the effort *it has made* to make up for a shortage *in supply* or for a failure to adapt *to the economy*.' The only point I am trying to establish here is not whether I have filled in the gaps correctly, but that most translators (or general readers) would think it desirable that at least some of the gaps were filled in. If this is accepted, I consider first the degree of importance of such gaps, and secondly their nature.

Extending Helbig's (1969) three case-partners (mandatory, optional, 'free indications' (*freie Angaben*)), I define four main categories of case-gaps, which represent different points on a scale, and may overlap: (1) mandatory; (2) implied; (3) optional; and (4) supplementary.

Mandatory case-gap filling

This is basically syntactical. Here the translator automatically fills in the case-gap, *either* because the syntax of the TL requires it, for example:

SL I do	TL *Je le fais* (or *je l'aime* etc.)
SL *Gib her*	TL Give *it* me
SL I give up	TL *j'y renonce*; *ich verzichte darauf*
SL *Et de ramener le chat à l'ambassade*	TL And *they brought the cat back to the embassy*

or because a sentence in the SL text is ambiguous or otherwise linguistically defective:

SL *Die Verhandlungen wurden abgebrochen und berichtet*	TL It was reported that negotiations had broken down

Implied case-gaps

These constitute the most important category for a translator: basically this is a semantic category, but there is often a syntactic compulsion to fill in the gap. Thus on the one hand SL words such as 'growth' – *croissance*; 'claim' – *revendication*; 'distribution' – *répartition*; 'investment' – *placement, Anlage*, have strong implications of economy, wages, wealth and capital respectively, but it may be unnecessary to fill them in. A medical or geological text, however, may have to be clarified: *Les défauts d'apport et les troubles d'absorption* may refer to deficient intake and difficulties in absorbing protein; *exagération des fuites et des dégradations digestives* refers to increased losses and degradation of albumin in the digestive tract; *une fissure initiale aussitôt injectée* (note the past participle *injectée* instead of the more common verbal noun *injection*) – 'an initial fissure in the earth's crust into which magma is immediately injected'.

Two isolated types of implied categories are associated with verbs for 'to happen' and 'to behave'. 'To happen' normally implies a time and/or a place and a translator would have to supply this detail if it is lacking in the SL text. 'To behave' implies a manner of behaviour. If this is not stated in the SL text (e.g., 'Did you behave?' – *Hast Du Dich benommen?*) it may have to be supplied in the TL text: *Tu t'est bien comporté? Tu t'est bien conduit?*

Verbs of duration, living, staying, sitting, standing, existing, and putting, all implying place, form a similar category; here the 'case-partner' is virtually mandatory. 'He went on and on' requires an additional expression of time in the TL. This category is often expressed by a reflexive verb in Romance languages (*se tenir, se dérouler*).

Two other case relations, accounted for in traditional grammar by the genitive case, but not usually accounted for in case grammar, are not infrequently implied: (a) *la croûte*, translated as 'the Earth's crust' and 'la crête', the 'ridge crest', where the case-gap represents the whole to which the named term refers; (b) *le groupe*, translated as the 'student group', 'the group of students', or *la rougeole*, referring to a particular form of measles, where the missing partner gives a more specific form to the named term, which is collective or generic. The relation between the two nouns is equative ('consists of', 'belongs to'); this type of verb appears to play no part in Tesnière (1965), Fillmore (1968) or Halliday (1973), who do not attempt to 'semanticise' the genitive case, but the translator has to account for the relation (e.g. in 'father', 'president', 'place').

Many case grammars find no place for the genitive or possessive case and its many 'variants', all of them alternate meanings of this case or say the preposition 'of' – subjective, objective, associative ('my brother's firm'), quantitative ('pint of milk'), constitutive ('rod of iron'), equative ('City of London'). Since valency theory posits the dependency of all cases on the verb, it does not include the semantic value of the genitive, which 'grammatically' is dependent on its noun; in deep structure, however, it is dependent on a verb and no longer exists as a genitive (e.g. 'the architect's house' = 'the house built/owned/mentioned by the architect'). The above remarks also apply to the single- or multi-noun compounds which, in English and German, replace the 'noun plus of plus noun' group in many combinations.

Clearly the translator is much concerned with SL genitive case-gaps. Frequently, nouns after objects have to be added after collective nouns such as 'group', 'party', 'number', 'variety', 'range', etc. In a French medical text, elliptical expressions such as *les séries, le fibrinogène, la paroi, une chaleur locale* are best expanded to 'patient groups', 'the fibrinogen method', 'vessel wall', 'a localised area of heat'.

Optional case-partners

These are semantic and stylistic. The translator is at liberty to supply them or not as he wishes. This is partly a pragmatic decision, partly a decision dictated by reasons of exhaustiveness or style. A satisfactory example would require a large context. One could select from verbs such as 'hinder', 'protect', 'threaten', 'prevent', 'appoint', 'supply', 'give', etc. all of which have a mandatory direct object (objective? goal? patient?) partner, and one or two other partners which may be mentioned, implied or omitted in another part of the text. Take the sentence: *Der Ausschuß ernannte Herrn Schmidt* – 'the committee appointed Herr Schmidt': the nature of the appointment (e.g. *zum Vorsitzenden, zum Professor, zum Konsul*) is probably implied in the text, and the translator could supply it if it is not clear in the immediate context. Other case-partners such as time, place and duration of the appointment, the number of other candidates and the purpose of the appointment (e.g., to teach what subject where?) are optional, provided they are stated elsewhere in the text.

Supplementary information (Helbig's 'free indications')

This is 'referential'. It consists of additional information, not given in the text, but which the translator chooses to supply from his knowledge of the situation and the cultural context. Thus if the drink 'tea' were to be culturally explained, it would be given supplementary partners (milk or lemon or rum with cake, etc.) in the translation. Such supplementary information need not be given in 'case' form, though.

VARIOUS TYPES OF CASE-PARTNER

I now propose to enumerate and briefly discuss the various types of case-partner. In the last 50 years some linguists have proposed that grammatical terms such as 'nominative', 'vocative' and 'subject', 'object', etc., should be restricted to their syntactic functions, and that a set of semantic case-functions should be determined. Thus we have (among many others) Brinkmann's 'identity, alterity, finality'; Fillmore's and Halliday's (respectively) 'agentive' or 'actor'; 'instrumental' or 'instrument'; 'dative' or 'recipient'; 'factitive' or 'resultant'; 'locative' or 'place'; 'objective', 'patient', or 'goal'; 'benefactive' or 'beneficiary'. The designations are clumsy and incomplete, and Fillmore, at least, has already changed them. I think a translator cannot restrict himself to such a small number of 'gaps', nor is he confronted with the subtleties of the 'factitive' compared with the 'objective'. Faced with an incomplete verb or verbal noun or adjective, he may have to consider (in a possible order of priority) say: who does what, why, to whom, with what, how, when, where? or more delicately: for what purpose does who do what to whom with what instrument, for what reason, on what ground, in what manner, at what time, at what place? There are of course other gaps that tend to be confined to particular sets of verbs: 'against what' ('protest'); 'in favour of what' ('vote'); 'to or from what place' ('go'); 'for how long' ('last'); 'away from what' ('run'); 'under what' ('cover'), etc.

It is possible that such a scheme is too general for a translator to handle. Following on Fillmore (1977), one could suggest particular case-frames for particular types of verbs. Thus for 'protect': who protects what (whom) with what, against whom (or what) (agent–patient–instrument–adversary); here in a SL text, the agent and patient are mandatory, the instrument is implied (it may also be the agent), but the adversary ought to be clear: i.e., the TL reader has a right to have the adversary supplied. Similarly, in what Fillmore calls a 'commercial event', if X bought a dozen roses from H for five dollars, or X paid five dollars for a dozen roses, or H sold X a dozen roses for five dollars, at least two verb-partners are mandatory in all cases, the other two may be required and, in the TL context, both the location and time of the purchase and the value of the money may be relevant. (These being Tesnière's 'circumstantial' rather than 'actant' constituents.)

Lastly, in a group of 'hospitality' verbs, say, 'invite', 'welcome', 'bid', 'ask', the TL reader must know who invites whom to what (the latter the SL text need not supply 'syntactically' in the sentence, but should have elsewhere in the paragraph), and probably has a right to know when and where, and, if the occasion is out of the ordinary, why: thus there are two mandatory, one implied and two or three optional case-gaps to be filled in.

I take the essential to be 'Who does what for what purpose to whom?', the purpose being the link between the relevant sentence and its predecessor and successor, which the translator may have to supply if it is missing in the SL text. The remaining gaps are filled by the 'actants', the more important partners, in Tesnière's terms. The main actant (always animate) is sometimes missing, for instance:

> *Ce temps chaud invite à la paresse* – In this weather I feel lazy

> *Il est de bon ton dans les milieux dits modérés de prétendre que* (Thiel, 1980) – In politically moderate circles it is good form (*for people*) to maintain that – *In gemäßigten Kreisen, behauptet man gern*

> Because we could not control the adults, the reaction was to take it out on our children – *Weil wir die Erwachsenen nich an die Hand nehmen konnten, reagierten wir, indem wir unseren Ärger an den Kindern ausließen*

> *Der Schluß auf Radium war zwingend* – We concluded that it must be radium.

In the above and other cases, the translator may feel that the subject should be manifestly expressed, although it would not be difficult to reproduce the rather impersonal SL original.

As I see it, the most common missing case-partner is the direct object, in semantic terms, the thing directly affected. In Romance languages there is a long series of verbs: *pousser, persuader, obliger, inciter, empêcher, défendre, engager, inviter, forcer*, etc., without an object that take *de* or *à* with the infinitive, where the translator has two standard alternatives. Thus for *Une publicité tapageuse incite à acheter des marchandises même inutiles* he can supply the subject: 'Encouraged by obtrusive advertising, *we* buy goods, even unnecessary ones' – or leave it implied: 'Goods that may well be unnecessary are bought (*by people*) as a result of loud and showy advertising.' In both examples, the original implied object becomes the agent ('we', 'by people') in the translation.

However, the most obvious example of an implied or optional object follows a verbal noun. The vogue for verbal nouns, an encouragement to jargon, appears to invite the omission of an object as something everyone ought to know. Thus in the following passage:

> *Plus nos sociétés sont préoccupées de bien-être, plus elles tendent à projeter l'aspiration égalitaire . . . elles réduisent les écarts économiques . . . l'exigence en ce domaine n'a jamais été aussi ardente.*

> (R. Aron).

Here the object of *aspiration* is 'swallowed' in the adjective: 'aspiration for equality'; the object of *écarts* is implied: 'gaps in income groups'; *exigence* has an implied subject as well as an object: 'people's expectations'. The very fact that all verbal nouns have in principle four meanings – take, e.g., 'establishment': an

active process (in establishing something), a passive process (what is being established), the concrete result (establishment as an institution) and, additionally,
often the place and personnel involved (for instance a group of people having
institutional authority) – facilitates both the omission of the relevant case-partners
and the quick accretion of new associated meanings (cf., 'intervention',
'indexation', *derivazione*, 'subsidiary of firm'). There is a further tendency to omit
either subject or object cases when a verbal noun is in a genitive relation with
another noun: e.g., 'the creation of the world', 'the Spirit of Promise', 'the day of
the preparation', 'the baptism of repentance', 'the remission of sins', etc.; all these
Biblical phrases, Nida (1974) implies, require amplification, e.g., 'God forgives'
('remits the people's sins'), in translation. Even an apparently concrete noun like
'grace' in fact implies an action ('show grace to people'). Thus a verb as well as an
additional case-partner has to be supplied by the translator.

Finally, the vertiginously increasing types of multi-noun compound which
delete the 'of' also have missing case-partners, e.g., 'keyboard computer'
(computer which receives input from the keyboard) or 'cathode ray tube visual
display unit', but since these are standardised terms they are more likely to remain
intact when translated or transcribed in translation.

Note that the semantically more restricted alternatives to the verbal noun,
the gerund (e.g., 'establishing the company') and the verb-noun ('the chasing of
the hunters'), do not exist in some non-English languages and will normally require
a supplied subject (impersonal, implied) in translation: e.g., 'establishing the
company will be difficult' – *il sera difficile d'établir la société* – *Wir werden die
Gesellschaft nur unter Schwierigkeiten gründen.*

Comment is hardly required on Tesnière's third actant (for whose benefit or
detriment the action takes place); it is normally stated or implied in verbs such as
'grant', 'accord', 'harm', 'injure' and may have to be supplied. The subject and the
direct object positions are the two basic case-positions; the third, the indirect object
position, occupied by an (animate) 'recipient' (Halliday), is either stated or implied
in a large number of verbs, headed by 'offer', 'allow', 'teach', 'ask', 'show' –
Tesnière's trivalent verbs. Note that a third actant appears much more commonly
when the verb is in the active voice, 'he gave (showed, offered) her a book', than in
the two possible passive forms: 'She was given (shown, offered) a book by him'; 'a
book was given (shown, offered) her by him'. The agent ('by him') appears as an
artificial appanage and a locative case is perhaps implied, e.g., 'She was given a
book at the prize-giving.'

CONTRAST AND CHOICE IN TRANSLATION

There are two aspects of translation, the contrastive mechanical, and the possible
empty positions. Tesnière regards trivalent verbs as 'dangerous' as they are constructed differently in different languages, and naively states there is an 83%
possibility of error in translation. His own example contrasts the case-switches of

enseigner: j'enseigne la grammaire aux enfants with the Russian versions; German *lehren* and *unterrichten* provide two additional different examples. However Tesnière lists about 60 verbs of 'saying and giving' and most of these have similar constructions in the West European languages. Notable exceptions are the trivalent verbs where the third actant is the loser not the recipient ('hide from', 'borrow from', 'remove from', 'take from', etc.) but remains in the recipient's case in some languages. Many languages also provide alternative constructions for a small set of trivalent verbs: 'supply', 'provide', 'paint', 'daub', 'splash', 'smear', 'load', 'cover', 'cut', 'fill' – e.g., 'supply him with it', 'supply it to him'.

Fillmore (1977) in his second paper on case grammar discusses the alternative constructions of a few of these verbs: e.g., (a) 'I loaded the truck with hay'; (b) 'I loaded hay onto the truck'; pointing out that in (a) but not in (b) one assumes that the truck was filled as a result of the action. The same distinction can be made in German, using two verbs (*beladen, laden*).

The translator would normally fill in gaps for trivalent verbs only if the SL text required clarification. Thus in the sentence *Cette répartition nouvelle ne risque-t-elle pas de provoquer de violentes réactions de la part des groupes économiques au détriment de qui elle s'effectue*, the concept of 'income' needs filling out since it is not referred to in the previous sentence: 'Undoubtedly this new distribution *of income amongst the nation's economic groups* may provoke violent reactions from the ones it prejudices.' The example incidentally illustrates the main use of case grammar in translation: nouns, adjectives, infinitives and gerunds are more likely to require filling out than verbs in their tense forms. The other cases mentioned which are 'circumstants' in Tesnière's sense – instrument, time, place, manner, origin, result – become more or less implied, if not mandatory, depending on the type of verb used – thus 'strike' (with an instrument), 'lie' (place), 'wait' (time), 'act' (manner), 'arise from' (origin), 'end in' (result), the latter often indicated by a colon. Otherwise, such 'circumstantial' cases are optional or supplementary.

SOME RELATED ISSUES

Sequencing a sentence

I take 'purpose' to be a special case, the overriding factor for the translator sequencing his sentences. I take it that in any informative text, the purpose should be foregrounded; thus *C'est un travail comparatif, portant sur des critères essentiellement cliniques visant à mettre en évidence l'incidence des thromboses veineuses profondes* may become '*The purpose* of this comparative study, which is based mainly on clinical criteria, is to demonstrate the incidence of deep venous thromboses', whilst, in subsequent sentences, the value of the connectors keeps the purpose in the forefront.

In particular the translator may have to determine whether each sentence is an addition, a detail, an example, a contrast, an opposition, a reservation, an aside, an afterthought, a consequence, etc. To some extent the sequence is indicated by the connectors, which may each have a variety, indeed a contrariety of meaning (e.g., *d'autre part:* 'moreover', 'on the other hand'; *enfin:* 'indeed', 'in short', 'finally'). Further, to some extent the sequence is based on the following tentative sentence sequence:

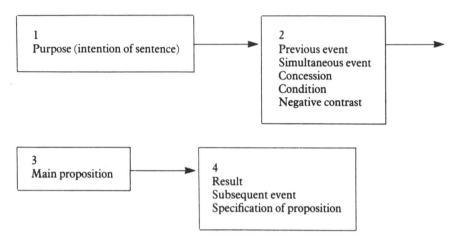

Here all the subordinate clauses take the place of verb-partners. Whilst the above is the logical sequence, the purpose or function of a sentence is so often latent or obscure that the translator may have to foreground it by putting it in the first place. There are variations in many languages: it is common to put 'purpose' before 'proposition' if the subject remains the same – *Pour faire cela . . . il faut* – and after the proposition if the subject changes – *Je le fais pour qu'il le sache.* The proposition will come first if, instead of being a statement, it is a command, wish or question. The more inflected a language, the easier it is to change the word-order to emphasise the meaning. In this area, case-partner and concept tend to identify and case grammar and discourse analysis to merge.

CASE-PARTNERS OF ADJECTIVES AND NOUNS

I next consider the case-forming or combination potential (Helbig's *Fügungspotenz*) of the adjective. There are a large number of adjectives formed from verbs that imply case-partners; they are distinguished from present participles in denoting qualities or roles rather than single actions, obvious examples are *responsable*, *verantwortlich* (for), 'protective' (against), 'decisive', 'anticipatory', etc. Translators frequently prefer to supply the missing partner.

Secondly, there is a group of 'equative' adjectives, often used with equative or copula verbs, which all signal a similar or identical object which is implied: 'different', 'equal', 'similar', 'same', 'analogous', 'other' 'alike', 'parallel', 'equivalent', 'identical', 'imitative', etc. They usually refer to the previous, occasionally the subsequent, sentence, therefore functioning as connectives, where the problem is often whether the reference is specific or general.

Thirdly, I note a type of adjective whose meaning is clarified only in context. Thus in *Une thrombose veineuse ne sera symptomatique que*, *symptomatique* could mean 'produce symptoms' or 'be a symptom' but is clarified as the former after *si les veines profondes sont oblitérées* ('if the veins are blocked'). Again, *Les symptômes sont variables d'aspect* may mean 'The symptoms vary from case to case' or 'The symptoms vary in appearance.' Again *Les couleurs unies ne sont pas limitatives pour des quantités de 1,000 (mouchoirs)*, poorly written as it is, since it is not clear what is being limited, may be 'Quantities of 1,000 handkerchieves are not restricted to plain colours' or, less likely, 'Plain colours can be ordered in quantities of more than 1,000.'

Next I note certain adjectives which have implicit case-partners: thus 'greedy' (food), *âpre* (profit), *acharné* (struggle), unless another case-partner is stated. Others such as *bewandert, eingestellt* are incomplete without a case-relation (e.g., in *Geographie, rechts,* respectively). Many other adjectives directly or indirectly related to verbs ('tired', 'experienced', *müde*, 'ready', 'worse', 'better', 'guilty', *ledig,* 'bitter') offer alternatives: without partners, they either have a general sense (a state of quality) or they have an implied case-partner stating the reason for their condition, which the translator may feel obliged to supply.

Nouns formed from adjectives ('width', 'breadth', etc.) and even more so nouns formed from verbal adjectives ('availability', 'translatability', 'dependability', 'incompatibility') present no special problems. The latter type is often transposed as a routine dejargonising process, which incidentally restores a case-partner, e.g., *Sa fiabilité est hors de doute* – 'We can certainly rely on him.' A problem may also arise from vagueness or bad writing in the text. Thus *Ainsi le profit n'est prélevé sur personne mais seulement sur la masse des inefficacités ambiantes* could be translated as 'Profit is not derived from any one person but only from all the ineffective mechanisms in à given environment.' Here I think there is a case-relationship between *inefficacités* and an implied genitive *mécanismes*; *ambiantes* covers both an adjectival clause or a locative case, depending on the translator's perspective (cf. *l'entreprise déficitaire,* 'the company which shows a debt').

It should be noted that case-relations extend beyond implied nouns or pronouns to clauses within or outside the sentence. Common sections of sentences such as *Er bestand darauf, il y pensa* are likely to require filling in with clauses rather than the lame 'it', 'that', 'this', which, in English, is often less precise than in more inflected languages. Thus concepts are in case-relationship with each other.

The verb as a central element in keeping 'communicative dynamism'

Given that, in case grammar, the verb is the central element in a clause, it inevitably has a directive role in allotting emphasis ('communicative dynamism'; see Firbas,

1972) to the most important component in a sentence. Thus in an extract from a medical piece on haemorrhoids, *Une douleur sourde plus ou moins localisable à la pression: abcès possible*, the directive verb is replaced by the colon and the attention is drawn to the abscess. The semantic subject of this sentence is the abscess, so that a translation could read 'A possible abscess is indicated by a dull pain' etc., which would however emphasise the pain and weaken the force of the verb, as the passive voice always does. The translation therefore has to retain the French word-order and use an equative verb, which always stresses its complement: 'A dull pain which can be detected (depending on the amount of pressure applied) may be indicative of an abscess.' Here the adjective *possible* forms the other element of the verb in translation, i.e. 'may'. Similarly, *Une douleur crampoïde . . . est une proctalgie fugace* – 'A cramp-like pain *may be regarded* as spasmodic proctalgia.' Thus the word-order of a sentence is influenced by the logical order (SVO etc.), the grammar of the language and its contextual stresses (as in FSP, discussed in Chapter 6) but the translator's priority is to reproduce the same degrees of communicative dynamism as on the corresponding nuclei of his text as given in the original.

A REMARK ON TESNIÈRE

It may appear surprising that, in spite of various references to Tesnière, I have made little use of his remarkable 40-page chapter on *métataxe*, which was a pioneering study on the relation between case grammar and translation (1959); he defines his *métataxes* as 'deep translations which have to be rethought rather than applied mechanically'. The fact is that his 13 types of translation process illustrate the differences between the relevant SL and TL constructions rather than any particular translation problems; therefore they are instances of contrastive linguistics, rather than of translation theory. Further, in the style of Malblanc (and before him of Vinay and Darbelnet) he tends to be dogmatic in setting out equivalents, ignoring alternatives, e.g., *Seien Sie so gut und geben Sie mir das Buch* – 'Be so kind and give me the book' – *Ayez la bonté de me donner le livre*, and to use rather odd German to prove his points (*Der ist im Stande und erwürgt mich*). He wrongly claims there is no French equivalent for *heraus* (*dehors*). He could have made his point with *herein* (*entrez*)! That said, Tesnière's chapter is brilliant and stimulating; his translation principle governing the passage from parataxis ('beg and beseech', in fact *orare atque obsecrare*) to hypotaxis (*prier ardemment*) goes beyond contrastive linguistics towards translation theory.

CONCLUSION

In a previous paper (Newmark, 1982) I stated that whilst componential analysis is indispensable in lexicography, it has applications to translation. I have now come to think that the role and use of componential analysis in translation is much more important than at the time I wrote the paper. I now believe that whilst case grammar has an indispensable role in advanced foreign language teaching (and should influence lexicography), it also has applications to translation either 'mechanically', in the contrast between the way two languages manipulate their cases, or creatively, in the detection of various missing verbs or cases in the relevant text. However, case grammar's function is only to sensitise the translator to these gaps and, in doing so, sometimes to compel him to abandon jargon constructions in non-authoritative texts, and it may well be said that a translator who writes well and sensitively will intuitively perceive these gaps without knowing anything about case grammar. Admitting this, admitting also that componential analysis is of greater use to the translator, I remain with the suspicion that the systematic knowledge that case grammar offers is more satisfying than intuitive perception, and that a case grammar hypothesis that is combined with Helbig's insights is going to be a more practical instrument for the translator than any variety of transformational grammar or Nida's configurations and kernels (which however, handle the genitive in a similarly useful way) or other grammars succeeding each other at breakneck speed, or any reductions to a logical language.

CHAPTER **13**

The Translation of Neologisms

INTRODUCTION

Neologisms are perhaps the non-literary and the professional translator's biggest problem. New objects and processes are continually created in technology. New ideas and variations on feelings come from the media. Terms from the social sciences, slang, dialect coming into the mainstream of language, transferred words, make up the rest. A few years ago, 300 'new' words were said to be counted in four successive numbers of the French weekly, *L'Express*. It has been stated that each language acquires 3000 new words annually. In fact, neologisms cannot be accurately quantified, since so many hover between acceptance and oblivion and many are short-lived, individual creations. What is obvious is that their number is increasing steeply and as we become more language- as well as self-conscious, articles, books and specialist and general dictionaries devoted to them appear more commonly. Since they usually arise first in a response to a particular need, a majority of them have a single meaning and can therefore be translated out of context, but many of them soon acquire new (and sometimes lose the old) meanings in the TL.

   Neologisms can be defined as newly coined lexical units or existing lexical units that acquire a new sense. Unless they are opaque, obscure and possibly cacophonous (compare 'yum' with 'yuck'; Strachey's 'parapraxis' for 'Freudian slip' (*Fehlleistung*, 'faulty achievement') and 'cathexis' for *Besetzung* (psychic 'occupation' or 'possession' are obvious alternative translations), neologisms usually attract and please everyone, but purists are so attached to Graeco-Latin conventions(oncethere was a fuss about oracy) that they jib at so-called violations of English grammar ('Who did you get it from?'). Unlike the French, the English have no basis from which to attack new words. Most people like neologisms, and so the media and commercial interests exploit this liking. Multinationals, with their ingenious advertising, make efforts to convert their brand names (Coke, Tipp-Ex, Tesa, Bic, Schweppes, etc.) into eponyms (i.e., any word derived from a proper noun, including acronyms) and in appropriate cases you have to resist this attempt when you translate.

   I propose to review twelve types of neologism (see frame of reference, p.150) and discuss the translation of particular instances by way of the appropriate contextual factors.

OLD WORDS WITH NEW SENSES

Take first existing words with new senses. These do not normally refer to new objects or processes, and therefore are rarely technological. However *créneau*, which started as a metaphor as *créneau de vente* (therefore it is a 'pseudo-neologism') can normally be translated technically as 'market outlet' or informally as 'a range of demand for a particular type of product', depending on the type of readership, of which I envisage three types: (1) expert; (2) educated generalist, who may require extra explanations of the topic or the SL culture; (3) the ignorant, who may need linguistic as well as technical (in relation to the topic of the text) and cultural explanations at various levels. Thus there is rarely a single correct translation of a SL neologism, any more than of any other SL item, however independent the item is of the linguistic context. Take the new sense of 'scene' which is dependent on the possessive adjective, 'my', 'his', 'their' . . . – *mon genre. Bavure* in its new, 1960 sense is defined as 'a more or less serious but always irritating regrettable consequence of any act' and translated in the Collins as an 'unfortunate administrative mistake (euphemism).' Any further sense component can come only from the context (e.g., 'disastrous blunder' for the police shooting an innocent man).

Le Petit Termophile (November 1983) points out that *refoulement* is used in English as 'return of refugees' but may also mean 'refusal of entry', 'deportation' – it is a loose term, dependent on its context. In psychology it is translated as 'repression', and may have to be explained as a technical psychoanalytical term.

The term 'gay' appears to have been deliberately used by homosexuals to emphasise their normality. It is no longer slang – translations such as *pédale, schwul* or *homo* will not do. Possibly when homosexuality loses all its negative connotations, there will be no need for this sense of 'gay' but it is likely to stay – it has gone into French and German as *gay*. You cannot go back in language – a colloquial term is not usually replaced by a formal term.

Take now the term 'wet' in the sense of '(relatively) left-wing Tory opponent of Mrs Thatcher's policies'. Since this term seems unlikely to acquire permanence, or to be important in any TL culture, any initial one-to-one translation is misguided, and the translator has to select the appropriate functional and descriptive TL sense components as economically as possible in the context, possibly adding a negative component (*Waschlappen, nouille, lavette*) where the origin is germane. You cannot standardise the translation of a neologism when its future is in doubt.

If 'urban renewal' is tending to be limited to houses, *réhabilitation* (*Renovierung*) may be appropriate. Consider also *mouvance* – 'sphere of influence'; 'sophisticated' ('technically expert, of a person') – *expert, spécialisé; langue de bois* – 'heavy, bureaucratic language'; *composteur* – 'ticket-punching machine'; *passeur* – 'trafficker in illegal immigrants.'

To sum up, old words with new senses tend to be non-cultural and non-technical. They are usually translated either by a word that already exists in the TL, or by a brief functional or descriptive term. Note the vogue for popularising technical terms: 'exponential' *en hausse rapide*; 'parameter' *facteur permanent* – many of these transfer rapidly in the West. Existing collocations with new senses are a translator's trap: usually these are 'normal' descriptive terms which suddenly become technical terms; their meaning sometimes hides innocently behind a more general or figurative meaning; thus 'high-speed train' – *TGV* (*train de grande vitesse*), 'advanced passenger train'; 'community physician'; 'quality control' (theory of probability applied to sampling) – *contrôle de qualité* – *Qualitätskontrolle*; 'sleeping policeman' – *ralentisseur*; 'listed building' – *monument classé* or *historique*; 'open marriage'; 'open shop' – *atelier ouvert aux non-syndiqués* – German *Open Shop*; 'unsocial hours' – *Stunden außerhalb der normalen Arbeitszeit*; 'token woman' (single woman representative on committee of men) – *femme symbolique*; 'high-rise' – *tour* – *Hochhaus*; 'low-rise' – *maison basse*; 'real time' (computers) – *Echtzeit* – *en temps réel*; 'ring fence' (British tax term).

Existing collocations with new senses may be cultural or non-cultural; if the referent (concept or object) exists in the TL, there is usually a recognised translation or through-translation. If the concept does not exist (e.g., 'tug-of-love') or the TL speakers are not yet aware of it, an economical descriptive equivalent has to be given. There is also the possibility of devising a new collocation ('*lutte d'amour parental*') in inverted commas, which can later be slyly withdrawn.

Translators also have to be aware of the reverse tendency, which is to use 'technical' collocations such as 'critical mass' or 'specific gravity' in a generalised sense – this often leads to jargon which can be 'corrected' in the translation of informative texts.

NEW COINAGES

It is a well known hypothesis that there is no such thing as a brand new word; if a word does not derive from various morphemes then it is more or less phonaesthetic or synaesthetic. All sounds or phonemes are phonaesthetic, have some kind of meaning. Nevertheless the etymology of many words, in particular dialect words, is not known and can hardly be related to meaningful sounds.

The best known exception to the hypothesis is the internationalism 'quark', coined by James Joyce in *Finnegan's Wake* (the word exists in German with another sense), a fundamental particle in physics. The computer term 'byte', sometimes spelt 'bite', is also an internationalism, the origin of the 'y' being obscure. Both these words have phonaesthetic qualities – quark is humorously related to 'quack'.

Nowadays, the main new coinages are brand or trade names ('Bisto', 'Bacardi', 'Schweppes' (onomatopoeic), 'Persil', 'Oxo') and these are usually transferred unless the product is marketed in the TL culture under another name; or the proper name may be replaced by a functional or generic term, if the trade name has no cultural or identifying significance. Thus *Revlon* may be translated by a selection of various components ('Revlon', 'lipstick', 'fashionable American').

In principle, in fiction, any kind of neologism should be recreated; if it is a derived word it should be replaced by the same or equivalent morphemes; if it is also phonaesthetic, it should be given phonemes producing analogous sound-effects. For this reason, in principle, the neologisms in *Finnegan's Wake* or *Ulysses* ('tautaulogically' – *totalogiquement*; 'riverrun' – *courrive*; 'from over the short sea' – *d'oultre la manche mer*; 'to wielderfight his penisolate war' – *pour reluivreferre sa guerre peniseulte*) must be re-created systematically and ingeniously, always however with the principle of equivalent naturalness in mind, whether relating to morphology (roots and inflexion) or sound (alliteration, onomatopoeia, assonance).

Thus the title of Hervé Bazin's novel *Le Matrimoine*, a neologism symbolising all that is the concern of the women in marriage, the 'lioness's share', is not easily translated. In principle, an English neologism deriving from accepted morphemes should be created. 'Matrimone' is a possibility, but it does not fill a natural gap in English as *Matrimoine* (cf. *patrimoine*) does in French. The best I can do is to revive or deform a rare word: 'The Matriarchate' or 'The Matriarchacy' (Liselotte de Vaal, a Dutch translator, has suggested 'Matrimonia', which is better). Similar problems occur with: *reglousser*: *wiedergacksen* is appropriately natural, but 'recluck' is not; *du surfoncier des combles au tréfoncier des caves* – 'from the top soil of the roof to the very subsoil of the cellars'.

DERIVED WORDS

The great majority of neologisms are words derived by analogy from ancient Greek (increasingly) and Latin morphemes usually with suffixes such as *-ismo*, *-ismus*, *-ija*, etc., naturalised in the appropriate language. In some countries (e.g., pre-War Germany, Arabic-speaking countries) this process has been combatted and through-translation by way of the TL morphemes has been preferred (e.g., 'television' – *Fernsehen*). However, now that this word-forming procedure is employed mainly to designate (non-cultural) scientific and technological rather than cultural institutional terms, the advance of these internationalisms is widespread. Normally, they have naturalised suffixes. Many are listed in *Babel*. Swahili appears to be the main non-European language that 'imports' them.

However, this does not mean that the translator can apply the process automatically. For terms like 'reprography', *gazinière*, *télévidéo*, *monétique*, *télématique*, *conique*, he may have first to assure himself that the neologism is not in competition with another. 'Bionomics' has given way to 'ecology' and 'ergonomics' (second sense) to 'biotechnology'. He has to consult the appropriate ISO (International Standards Organisation) glossary, to find out whether there is already a recognised translation; secondly, whether the referent yet exists in the TL culture; thirdly how important it is, and therefore whether it is worth 'transplanting' at all. If he thinks he is justified in transplanting it (has he the necessary authority?), and he believes himself to be the first translator to do so, he should put it in inverted commas. Thus *réprographie* is important and permanent; *gazinière* is a familiar alternative for *four à gaz*, but note we have 'gas stove', 'oven' or 'cooker' – I expect this last predominates. *Télévidéo* appears to be an earlier version of *vidéo*, which has several meanings ('tape', 'recorder', 'cassette'). Note however that most of these words are virtually context-free.

Monétique is the use of plastic cards to pay for goods and services. This may transplant as 'monetics' ('plastic money'?), but perhaps such a coinage (!) should have the authority of a bank rather than of an individual translator. *Iconique* and *iconographie* (which has other senses) lost out to 'iconology', i.e., the study and interpretation of images. *Télématique* (i.e., telecommunications and data processing) appears to be a later version of *téléinformatique*, the latter existing for a time at least in Common Market English as 'tele-informatics' – the present equivalent may be 'teleprocessing', but 'telematics' is winning out.

I think the translator has to distinguish the serious derived neologisms of industry from the snappy ingenious derived neologisms (blends in particular) created by the media, including the advertisers, which may be short-lived. Thus 'oillionnaire'; 'steelionnaire'; 'daffynition' ('crazy definition') – *définition farfelue*; *Abküfi* (*Abkürzung-Fimmel*, 'mania for abreviations'). Whether they are permanent or not, the translator has to consider their function (advertising? neatness? phonaesthetic quality?) before deciding whether to re-create them in the TL or to translate the completed component of the blends (e.g., 'oil millionaire'). One a week appears in the *Sunday Times*, e.g., 'high concept' for an idea so simple that even the most stupid can grasp it.

Note that medical neologisms (e.g., 'chronopharmacology', 'somatomedin' (a hormone, prostaglandin)), and particularly the approved chemical names of generic drugs can often be reproduced with a naturalised suffix (French *-ite*, English *-itis*; French *-ine*, English *-in*). But bear in mind that Romance languages do this more easily than others, since it is their home territory, and you should not automatically naturalise or adopt a word like *anatomopathologie* (1960).

Occasionally French adds a suffix to a word (*mégoter*, 'quibble') which must be rendered by sense. Again, Romance languages combine two or more academic subjects into a single adjective, thus *médico-chirurgical*, *médico-pédagogique*, etc., in a manner that Shakespeare was already satirising in *Hamlet* (II.2) ('pastoral–comical', 'tragical–historical', 'tragical–comical–historical–pastoral' etc.) Such combinations should normally be separated into two adjectives in the translation (e.g., 'medical and surgical', 'both medical and surgical') but 'physio-' (from physiology), 'physico-' (physics) and 'bio-' are common first components of inter-disciplinary subjects.

In all derived words, you have to distinguish between terms like *écosystème* and *écotone* which have a solid referential basis, and fulfil the conditions of internationalisms, and those like 'ecofreak' and *écotage* (sabotage of ecology), which, whatever their future, do not at present warrant the formation of a TL neologism.

ABBREVIATIONS

Abbreviations have always been a common type of pseudo-neologism, probably more common in French than in English (*fac, philo, sympa, Huma*, 'copter', *Uni*, 'fab', 'video'). Unless they coincide (*prof, bus*) they are written out in the TL.

COLLOCATIONS (see also p. 212)

New collocations (noun compounds or adjective plus noun) are particularly common in the social sciences and in computer language. Thus 'lead time', 'sexual harassment', 'domino effect', *fuite en avant*, 'clawback', 'cold-calling', 'Walkman' (brand name for 'personal stereo'), 'acid rain', 'norm reference testing', 'criterion reference testing', 'rate-capping', 'jetlag', 'lateral thinking', 'wishful thinking', *promotion sociale, aménagement du territoire*, 'machine-readable', 'sunshine industries', 'narrow money', 'graceful degradation', 'hash total', 'go–no-go test' – *Ja–nein Kontrolle* – test oui–non' *Kontrollsumme, total de vérification*.

The above represent varying problems. The computer terms are given their recognised translation – if they do not exist, you have to transfer them (if they appear important) and then add a functional -- descriptive term – you have not the authority to devise your own neologism.

'Sexual harassment' (*assiduités abusives*) is a universal concept, at least in any culture where there is both greater sexual freedom and a powerful women's movement – and I think you are entitled to have a go. For German, I suspect it will come out as *Sexualschikane*, for French, *importunité sexuelle* (but *assiduités abusives* already exists). It will have to be translated by a descriptive term until a TL standard term is formulated. 'Lead time', a term for the time between design and production *or* between ordering and delivery of a product, has at present to be translated in context; 'domino effect', which could be a (political) universal, applying as much to the USSR as to El Salvador or Vietnam, probably has to be explained, unless dominoes are familiar to the TL culture and a literal translation in inverted commas is risked; 'cold-calling' (soliciting on the doorstep) may not last as a term, though the practice will; 'jetlag' may have settled down to *décalage horaire*, but the Germans are likely to transfer it; 'clawback' (retrieval of tax benefits) may not last; 'acid rain', unfortunately a universal, is likely to be literally translated everywhere, since it is 'transparent'; 'sunrise industries' refers to electronics and other 'high-tech' industries, and is likely to be ephemeral, therefore the metaphor can be ignored or reduced to sense; 'Walkman' is a trade name (eponym) and therefore should not be transferred; 'rate-capping' is 'cultura. has no future outside the UK and has to be explained in accordance with the specialist or general requirements of the readership – transference would be superfluous, except for a highly specialised TL readership; 'norm' and 'criterion reference testing' are both recent terms for educational assessment and require explanation until the terms become more widely known; 'machine-readable' – *lecture automatique* is suggested in *Le Petit Termophile* (January 1984); 'narrow money' (money held predominantly for spending), *disponibilités monétaires* (approx.), is contrasted with 'broad money' (for spending and/or as a store of value), *masse monétaire* (*au sens large*); *promotion sociale*, a necessary universal, does not seem to have settled at 'social advancement'; compare 'positive discrimination', *discrimination positive*.

This brief discussion illustrates incidentally the difficulty of translating English collocations which appear arbitrarily to juxtapose nouns with verb-nouns because they indicate the two most significant meaning components, but have varied and sometimes mysterious case-relations. Languages which cannot convert verbs to nouns nor, in the case of the Romance languages at least, suppress prepositions in such a ruthless way, cannot imitate this procedure. For this reason, the English collocations are difficult to translate succinctly, and an acceptable term emerges only when the referent becomes so important (usually as a universal, but occasionally as a feature of the SL culture) that a more or less lengthy functional – descriptive term will no longer do. Note, as a curio, the extraordinary problem of translating the institutional term 'British Council', which affords no clue of its function or its constitution. Not surprisingly, it is often transferred (its West German cultural equivalent is a combination of the Goethe-Institut and Inter Nationes) and then glossed to suit the readership: 'Government institution promoting: (a) knowledge of Britain and English; (b) cultural and scientific relations abroad'.

Non-British collocations are easier to translate as they are made less arbitrarily, but the essence of a collocation is perhaps that at least one of the collocates moves from its primary to a secondary sense, and therefore, for standardised terms, literal translations are usually not possible: *Schattenwirtschaft*, 'parallel economy'; *solution de facilité*, 'easy way out' (but here the register switches to colloquial); *bassin d'emploi*, 'employment (catchment) area'.

EPONYMS (see also p. 198)

Eponyms, in my definition any word derived from a proper name (therefore including toponyms), are a growth industry in Romance languages and a more modest one in the English media. When derived from people's names such words ('Audenesque', 'Keynesian', 'Laurentian', 'Hallidayan', 'Joycean', 'Leavisite') tend to rise and fall depending on the popularity or vogue of their referent and ease of composition. When they refer directly to the person, they are translated without difficulty (e.g., *partisans de Leavis*, *critique littéraire britannique*) but if they refer to the referent's ideas or qualities, the translator may have to add these (*idées favorisant l'économie mixte ou concertée de Keynes*). In Italian, 'Thatcherism' can sometimes (temporarily) be naturalised as *il Thatcherismo* without comment. The 'Fosbury flop', a technical term for a method of high-jumping, can be transferred for specialists and succinctly defined for non-specialists. When derived from objects, eponyms are usually brand names, and can be transferred only when they are equally well known and accepted in the TL (e.g., 'nylon', but 'Durex' is an adhesive tape in Australian English). Such generalised eponyms as 'Parkinson's Law' (work, personnel, etc. expands to fill the time, space, etc. allotted to it), 'Murphy's' or 'Sod's Law' (if something can go wrong, it will) have to be 'reduced' to sense. Brand name eponyms normally have to be translated by denotative terms ('Tipp-Ex' – *blanc pour effacer*; *pointe Bic* – Biro – 'ball point' – *bille*). In general, the translator should curb the use of brand name eponyms. New eponyms deriving from geographical names (the tasteless 'bikini' has not been repeated) appear to be rare – most commonly they originate from the products (wines, cheeses, sausages etc) of the relevant area – in translation the generic term is added until the product is well enough known. Many geographical terms have connotations, the most recent for English being perhaps 'Crichel Down' (bureaucratic obstruction) with further details depending on context. Since such eponyms are also metonyms and therefore lose their 'local habitation' (*Midsummer Night's Dream*) they also lose their 'names' and are translated by their sense.

PHRASAL WORDS

New 'phrasal words' are restricted to English's facility in converting verbs to nouns (e.g., 'work-out', 'trade-off', 'check-out' (darts, supermarkets), 'lookalike', 'thermal cut-out', 'knock-on (domino) effect', 'laid-back', 'sit-in') and are translated by their semantic equivalents (*séance d'entraînement, échange (avantage mutuel), caisse, semblable, disjoncteur, effet de domino, détendu, sit-in, manifestation avec occupation de locaux, grève sur le tas*). Note that phrasal words: (a) are often more economical than their translation; (b) usually occupy the peculiarly English register between 'informal' and 'colloquial', whilst their translations are more formal. They are prolific and have an intrinsic 'built-in' (*ancré*) 'in-group' (*noyau fermé*) 'cachet' ('mark-up', 'upmarket', *marge bénéficiaire, supérieur*). They have more (physical) impact than their Graeco-Latin English or Romance language equivalents.

TRANSFERRED WORDS

Newly transferred words keep only one sense of their foreign nationality; they are the words whose meanings are least dependent on their contexts. (Later, if they are frequently used, they change or develop additional senses, and can sometimes no longer be translated back 'straight' into their languages of origin.) They are likely to be 'media' or 'product' rather than technological neologisms, and, given the power of the media, they may be common to several languages, whether they are cultural or have cultural overlaps (*samizdat, nomenklatura, apparatchik*, cf. *refusnik, apparat*), but have to be given a functional – descriptive equivalent for less sophisticated TL readerships. Newly imported foodstuffs, clothes ('cagoule', 'Adidas', 'Gallini', 'sari', 'Levi', 'Wrangler'), processes ('tandoori'), cultural manifestations ('raga', 'kung fu'), are translated like any other cultural words, therefore usually transferred together with a generic term and the requisite specific detail depending on readership and setting.

ACRONYMS (see also p. 198)

Acronyms are an increasingly common feature of all non-literary texts, for reasons of brevity or euphony, and often to give the referent an artificial prestige to rouse people to find out what the letters stand for. In science the letters are occasionally joined up and become internationalisms ('laser', 'maser'), requiring analysis only for a less educated TL readership. Some enzymes are internationalisms – SGOT, 'SPGT' (cf. 'ACTH' and other important substances). Acronyms are frequently created within special topics and designate products, appliances and processes, depending on their degree of importance; in translation, there is either a standard equivalent term or, if it does not yet exist, a descriptive term. Acronyms for institutions and names of companies are usually transferred. Acronyms are sometimes created or move into common language for referents that have been in existence for a long time, e.g. 'GCHQ'; 'We have to change at TCR' (i.e., Tottenham Court Road) and these are normally 'decoded' in translation. Further, the translator must look out for acronyms created simply for the purpose of one text – difficult to locate if he has to translate only an extract. When acronyms are as important in the SL as in the TL, they may be different in both languages ('MAOI' – monoamine oxidase inhibiters – becomes IMAO in French).

Acronyms for international institutions, which themselves are usually through-translated, usually switch for each language, but some, like 'ASEAN', 'UNESCO', 'FAO', 'CERN', 'ANC', 'UNICEF', 'OPEC' are internationalisms, usually written unpunctuated. When a national political or social organisation, e.g., a political party, becomes important, it is increasingly common to transfer its acronym and translate its name, but this may depend on the interests of the TL readership. Note that if the name of an organisation (and therefore its acronym) is opaque, e.g., 'OU', 'CNAA', it is more important to state its function than to decode the initials. Arabic resists most acronyms and explicates them. SL acronyms are often retained for convenience so that they can be used at other points in the TL text.

PSEUDO-NEOLOGISMS

Lastly, the translator has to beware of pseudo-neologisms where, for instance, a generic word stands in for a specific word, e.g., *rapports (d'engrenage)* – 'gear ratios'; *longitudinaux (ressorts longitudinaux)* – 'longitudinal springs'; *humérale* – 'humeral artery'; *la Charrue* – 'The Plough and the Stars'; *la Trilatérale* – a private political commission with representatives from the USA, Western Europe and Japan.

I have tried to give a comprehensive undogmatic view of how to translate the words that teeter on the edge of language, that may stay, may vanish, depending on the real or artificial needs of their users, many of them not yet 'processed' by language and therefore extra-contextual – others, designating new objects and processes, are assured of their place. And the only generalisation I can make is that the translator should be neither favourable nor unfavourable in his view of new words. His responsibility is to see that the mental and the material world that is inhabited by people should be accurately and, where possible, economically reflected in language. This consideration overrides the rather large number of contextual factors with which this chapter has been concerned.

THE CREATION OF NEOLOGISMS

In non-literary texts, you should not normally create neologisms. You create one only: (a) if you have authority; (b) if you compose it out of readily understood Graeco-Latin morphemes. Say, in a French medical text, you meet the word *floraline* as an item of light diet to be given to typhoid fever patients, and the word is unfindable. There is no point in creating a neologism by transferring the word, since it is likely to be a brand name (owing to its suffix, though the word is not capitalised – the other (unlikely) alternative is that it is a local or regional word) and the product may no longer be on the market. As a translator, your job is to account for (not necessarily translate) every SL word, and you therefore have to guess the word's meaning: the external evidence (i.e., the linguistic and situational contexts) suggests it is a light food or preparation; the internal evidence (the composition of the word) suggests that the product is made of flour (cf. *fleur de farine*: 'fine wheaten flour'). Therefore you may translate *floraline* by 'a light flour preparation', adding a footnote for your client: 'The SL original *floraline* not found. Probably a brand name.'

I finish by discussing the translator's right to create neologisms. Firstly, in a literary text, it is his duty to re-create any neologism he meets on the basis of the SL neologism; in other authoritative texts, he should normally do so. Secondly, when translating a popular advertisement, he can create a neologism, usually with a strong phonaesthetic effect, if it appears to follow the sense of its SL 'counterpart' and is pragmatically effective. Thirdly, he can transfer an SL cultural word, if for one reason or another he thinks it important. If he recreates an SL neologism using the same Graeco-Latin morphemes, he has to assure himself: (a) that no other translation already exists; (b) that both the referent and the neologism are not trivial, and that they are likely to interest the SL readership. He should not transfer SL neologisms, say in computer science, which are evidently recent or devised for the particular SL text (*progiciels, tableurs*). He should acknowledge at least with inverted commas any neologism he creates. The more formal the language, the more conservative he should be in respect of neologisms. In technology, he should not usurp the terminologist, who usually works within a team and is in contact with the ISO.

The more general questions of neologism translation are dependent on language planning, policy and politics. Given the world domination of English, most countries are faced with two forms of English neologisms: (a) Graeco-Latin forms; (b) monosyllable collocations. The first are naturalised in most countries, but have their morpheme components translated in Arabic, Japanese and other Asian languages. The monosyllable collocations are officially resisted in France ('pipe-line' – *oléoduc*). Notably German (contrary to its former practice) and Russian do not resist Graeco-Latin forms, and German has accepted a huge number of English monosyllables and their collocations.

A FRAME OF REFERENCE FOR THE TRANSLATION OF NEOLOGISMS

Type	Contextual factors	Translation procedures
A. *Existing lexical items with new senses*	1. Value and purpose of neolog	1. Transference (with inverted commas)
1. Words	2. Importance of neolog to (a) SL culture; (b) TL culture; (c) general	2. TL neologism (with composites)
2. Collocations		3. TL derived word
B. *New forms*	3. Recency	4. Naturalisation
	4. Frequency	5. Recognised TL translation
1. New coinages	5. Likely duration	
2. Derived words (including blends)	6. Translator's authority	7. Functional term
3. Abbreviations	7. Recognised translation	8. Descriptive term
4. Collocations	8. Existence of referents in TL culture	9. Literal translation
5. Eponyms		10. Translation procedure combinations (couplets etc.)
6. Phrasal words	9. Transparency or opaqueness of neolog	
7. Transferred words (new and old referents)	10. Type of text	11. Through-translation
8. Acronyms (new and old referents)	11. Readership	12. Internationalism
9. Pseudo-neologisms	12. Setting	
10. Internationalisms	13. Fashion, clique, commercial	
	14. Euphony	
	15. Is neolog in competition with others?	
	16. Is neolog linguistically justified?	
	17. Is neolog likely to become internationalism?	
	18. Is neolog (acronym) being formed for prestige reasons?	
	19. Milieu	
	20. Status and currency of neologism in SL	

CHAPTER 14

Technical Translation

INTRODUCTION

Technical translation is one part of specialised translation; institutional translation, the area of politics, commerce, finance, government etc., is the other. I take technical translation as potentially (but far from actually) non-cultural, therefore 'universal'; the benefits of technology are not confined to one speech community. In principle, the terms should be translated; institutional translation is cultural (so in principle, the terms are transferred, plus or minus) unless concerned with international organisations. For this reason, in general, you translate ILO as *BIT* (F), IAA (G), but you transfer 'RSPCA' in official and formal contexts, but not in informal ones, where 'RSPCA' would become something like *britischer Tierschutzbund, société britannique pour la protection des animaux.*

The profession of translator is co-extensive with the rise of technology, and staff translators in industry (not in international organisations) are usually called technical translators, although institutional and commercial terms are 'umbrella' (*Dach*) components in all technical translation.

Technical translation is primarily distinguished from other forms of translation by terminology, although terminology usually only makes up about 5–10% of a text. Its characteristics, its grammatical features (for English, passives, nominalisations, third persons, empty verbs, present tenses) merge with other varieties of language. Its characteristic format (see Sager, Dungworth and McDonald, 1980 for an excellent review of technical writing) is the technical report, but it also includes instructions, manuals, notices, publicity, which put more emphasis on forms of address and use of the second person.

TECHNICAL STYLE

Further, unless its non-technical language is jazzed up and popularised, it is usually free from emotive language, connotations, sound-effects and original metaphor, if it is well written. French medical texts are often just the contrary, and the translator's job is precisely to eliminate these features. Thus *le triptyque de ce traitement* becomes 'the three stages of this treatment'. Part of a good technical translator's job often consists in rephrasing poorly written language and converting metaphors to sense.

TERMS

However, the central difficulty in technical translation is usually the new terminology. (You should read this chapter in conjunction with the one on neologisms, Chapter 13; some medical terms are listed on p. 288) I think the best approach to an opaquely technical text is to underline what appear to be its key terms when you first read it and then look them up (even if you think you know them – my memory is full of words I half know or do not know) in the micro of the *Encyclopaedia Britannica* and the relevant Penguin.

Even then, the main problem is likely to be that of some technical neologisms in the source language which are relatively context-free, and appear only once. If they are context-bound, you are more likely to understand them by gradually eliminating the less likely versions. But if, in an article on alcoholic cirrhosis, *un cocktail hépatique toujours appliqué et toujours discuté* is stated to be a fairly common form of treatment, without further details, you can translate it only as 'a drug mixture which is still administered and still much debated', simply verifying that drugs (diuretics) are sometimes used as part of the treatment for cirrhosis.

Contrary to popular belief, even BSI (British Standards Institution) standardised terms may have more than one meaning in one field, as well as in two or more fields (thus 'ply' (of paper), *feuille*; 'ply' (of board), *contre-plaqué*). In the same field, to 'sort (out)' may mean 'to examine individually' (*examiner*) or 'to separate' (*trier*). However, the purpose of any new standardisation is always to establish a single one-to-one relationship between a referent and its name. The less important the referent, the more likely the relationship is to hold. As soon as the 'currency' of the referent increases (owing to more frequent use, greater importance, etc.) its name is likely to acquire figurative senses.

Concept-words are notorious for their different meanings in various technologies (*Kraft* – 'force', 'power', 'strength', 'thrust'; *capacité* – 'capacity', 'capacitance', etc.; see, for instance, many other examples in Maillot, 1969). Other terms have various senses when variously collocated (e.g., *puits de mine* – 'mineshaft'; *puits à ciel ouvert* – 'opencast mine'; *puits perdu* – 'cesspool'; *puits artésien* – 'artesian well'; *puissance fiscale* – 'engine rating'; *puissance de feu* – 'fire-power').

VARIETIES OF TECHNICAL STYLE

Experts will argue as strongly in this field as in any other about the names for the tools actually used 'on the job', 'at the grass roots', the 'nitty gritty'. Paepcke (1975) has in fact usefully distinguished four varieties of technical language: (1) scientific, e.g., *chambre de congélation*; (2) workshop level, e.g., *compartiment réfrigérateur*; (3) everyday usage level, e.g., *congélateur* – 'deep-freeze'; (4) publicity/sales, e.g., *freezer* (as a French word). However, a scale like this one is likely to be valid only for one or two terms in a few fields. Based on medical vocabulary, I suggest the following levels:

(1) *Academic.* This includes transferred Latin and Greek words associated with academic papers, e.g., 'phlegmasia alba dolens'.
(2) *Professional.* Formal terms used by experts, e.g., 'epidemic parotitis', 'varicella', 'scarlatina', 'tetanus'.
(3) *Popular.* Layman vocabulary, which may include familiar alternative terms, e.g., 'mumps', 'chicken-pox', 'scarlet fever', 'stroke', 'lockjaw'.

However, these are general categories to which it is often arbitrary to assign one or another term. In some areas, the nomenclature is clouded by additional obsolete, obsolescent or regional terms (note the chaos of Elsevier multilingual dictionaries, which are useful for reference rather than for translating). There is a frequent tendency to name a product by its latest trademark – thus 'bic' supplants 'biro'. Further, eponyms identify a discovery or an invention by the name of whoever is associated with it, which is not recognised by another country in its language; thus (of thousands of examples) the lesser pancreas is also known as Willis's or Winslow's pancreas, but only in English.

TECHNICAL AND DESCRIPTIVE TERMS

A further problem is the distinction between technical and descriptive terms. The original SL writer may use a descriptive term for a technical object for three reasons:

(1) the object is new, and has not yet got a name;
(2) the descriptive term is being used as a familiar alternative, to avoid repetition;
(3) the descriptive term is being used to make a contrast with another one.

Normally, you should translate technical and descriptive terms by their counterparts and, in particular, resist the temptation of translating a descriptive by a technical term for the purpose of showing off your knowledge, thereby sacrificing the linguistic force of the SL descriptive term. However, if the SL descriptive term is being used either because of the SL writer's ignorance or negligence, or because the appropriate technical term does not exist in the SL, and in particular if an object strange to the SL but not to the TL culture is being referred to, then you are justified in translating a descriptive by a technical term. If one translates 'The submarine's surface is perfectly smooth, with the forward diving planes, rear rudder and radio and sonar bubbles as the only protrusions' by *On a donné au sous-marin une forme parfaitement hydrodynamique; seuls les ailerons de plongée, le gouvernail et les dômes longeant la radio et le sonar font saillie*, one is unnecessarily translating the descriptive term ('smooth surface' – i.e., *surface lisse*) by a technical term (*forme hydrodynamique*), and eliminating the TL linguistic contrast between *lisse* and *hydrodynamique*. (See Delisle, 1982.)

Professional technical translators have a tendency to make a mystique out of their craft by rejecting any descriptive term where a TL technical term exists; a technical term (standardised language) is always more precise (narrower in semantic range) than a descriptive term (non-standardised language). It is often insisted that one must use only words that miners at the coalface, teachers at the board (!), farmers presumably at the grass roots would use – incidentally the mystique tends to ignore any distinction between the spoken and written language, which goes against good translation.

But what if the original uses descriptive terms? Take a piece on machining schedules: *Dans ce cas il est très rentable d'utiliser les machines courantes . . . sans rien créer mais en prévoyant en détail leur adaptation et leur montage. Les machines courantes* could be translated as 'general-purpose machines' in anticipation of *leur adaptation et leur montage*. In this translation, the semi-technical term 'general-purpose' replaces the descriptive *courantes* of the original. More likely, *courantes* is in contrast with *sans rien créer*, and could be translated by the descriptive terms 'standard', 'normal', or 'currently in use'.

Whilst the technical term may be a translator's find (*trouvaille*) and will help to acclimatise the professional reader, it is I think mistaken to invariably prefer it, bearing in mind that the descriptive term in the SL text may serve other communicative purposes. In cases where the piece is technical and there is clear evidence (as there often is) that the descriptive, the more general and generic term is probably only being used because the narrower technical term is rare or lacking in the SL, the use of the technical term in the TL text is certainly preferable.

Conversely, where an SL technical term has no known TL equivalent, a descriptive term should be used. What to do with *dismicrobismo murino*? 'Microbism' being 'a state of infestation with microbes', the *dis-* (English: dys-) appears redundant. If one cannot risk 'murine microbism', a descriptive term such as 'acute infestation by microbes, due to rat fleas' is safer. Again *rideau de terre*, a technical term for a bank separating two terraced fields, is translated as a 'ridge' in La Durie's *Montaillou*. Little is lost in the context.

BEGINNING TECHNICAL TRANSLATION

I think that the basic technology is engineering and the basic branch of engineering is mechanical; if you want to become a technical translator, that is where you start. However, you should not specialise at the start, but, as in any post-graduate translation course, get as much practice as possible in a range of technologies, in particular the ones that are thriving (*de pointe*), which, at present, means computer applications in the spectrum of commerce (particularly the tertiary sector) and industry. Again, bear in mind that you are more interested in understanding the description, the function and the effect of a concept such as entropy rather than in learning laws, particularly axioms, theorems, theories, systems in some of which entropy is involved. In a sense, you are learning the language rather than the content of the subject, but, when I say of the terms that the function is as important as the description, and always easier to grasp, I am in fact bringing you back to the application of the laws and principles. When you translate a text, you have to be able to stand back and understand roughly what is happening in real life, not just, or as well as, convincing yourself that the sentence you have just translated makes sense linguistically. You mustn't write the technical equivalent of: 'The King of France is dead'; there must be a thread of action running through the passage which you can grasp at any time. Even though much scientific and technological language and terminology can be translated 'literally' and in newer subjects contains an increasing number of internationalisms and fewer false friends, you have to check the present validity in the register and dialect (viz. usually British or American English) of the terms you use. But here again, there are priorities. Technical terms that appear on the periphery of a text, say relatively context-free in a list or a foot note, are not as important as those that are central; their nomenclature can be checked without detailed reference to their function or the description. In a word, to translate a text you do not have to be an expert in its technology or its topic; but you have to understand that text and temporarily know the vocabulary it uses.

In science, the language is concept-centred; in technology it is object-centred: in, say, production engineering, you have to learn the basic vocabulary with the translations – e.g. 'lathe', 'clutch', 'clamp', 'bolt', 'mill', 'shaft', 'crank', etc. – in diagrams as in the *Wüster* and Oxford Illustrated dictionaries and obtain a clear idea of outline, composition, function and result, as well as learn the action verbs with which they normally collocate: *une came tourne* – 'a cam rotates'.

TRANSLATION METHOD

Both text and translation are 'thing-bound'. According to Barbara Folkart (1984) 'the latitude which the translator enjoys is subject only to the constraints of register, and possibly, textual cohesion.' This statement is questionable since the SL text is also the basis of the translation, however much the translation departs from it: (a) owing to its different natural usage; (b) if it has to be referentially more explicit than the original – in particular in the case of gerunds and verb-nouns, where case-partners may have to be supplied in the TL text (see Chapter 12). Thus Folkart's example: *un dispositif de fixation d'un pignon d'entraînement des organes de distribution* becomes: 'a device with a pinion attached to it, driving the machine parts which distribute the fuel mixture to the cylinders' (my translation); in such an example, the case-partners have to be supplied referentially; in other contexts, they can be 'recovered' from the previous sentence.

It is notable that whilst Folkart recommends a 'thing-bound' approach which appears at times to be independent of the SL text, her examples are close translations modified by: (a) TL syntactic constraints; (b) appropriate explanatory reference. The point is that when a thing or a situation is 'pinned' down in a (SL) text, particularly a well-written one, it becomes precisely described. If a translator tries to set out from the object or situation, forgetting the SL verbal details, it is going to be an inaccurate translation. 'Co-writing', in which two or more copywriters are given the description and function of a product and asked to apply them (in an advert) to local conditions, temperaments, sense of humour in various differing examples (e.g., Telecom adverts for phoning home), is fine, but any 'common' message is better translated.

When you approach a technical text (it should be useful to you at this point to refer to p. 161) you read it first to understand it (underline difficult words) and then to assess its nature (proportion of persuasion to information), its degree of formality, its intention (attitude to its topic), the possible cultural and professional differences between your readership and the original one. Next, you should give your translation the framework of a recognised house-style, either the format of a technical report adopted by your client, or, if you are translating an article or a paper, the house-style of the relevant periodical or journal.

You have to translate or transfer or, if not, account for *everything*, every word, every figure, letter, every punctuation mark. You always transfer the name of the publication, a periodical. You translate its reference ('Vol.1., No.5') and date, and the general heading or superscript (*Mise au point*, *Rappel Médical*, *Travaux et Originaux Mémoire*, could become 'Medicine Today', 'Medical Review', 'Papers and Originals', 'Original Research Paper' respectively) using the standard formulae of the corresponding English periodical. For authors, delete the *par* or *von*, reproduce names and qualifications, and transfer the place of the author's appointment (e.g., *Ecole des Hautes Etudes* is not normally to be translated) – the reader may want to write to the author. However, you can translate and transferred word in a footnote, if the house-style permits, if you think the clients or readership would find it particularly useful, particularly if it is not a 'transparent' word.

THE TITLE

Normally, as a translator, you are entitled to 'change' the title of your text. All titles are either descriptive or allusive; in a non-literary text, a descriptive title that succinctly names the subject and states its purpose is appropriate. (Allusive titles are suitable for some imaginative literature and popular journalism, and may have to be changed.)

The advantage of the title of a scientific article is that it normally states the subject, but not always the purpose or intention of the process described. Thus it is more (or at least as) important to know that *scintillation* (see Chapter Appendix) is used for the purpose of detecting radio-activity in an organ or an organism than that it consists of minute flashes of light emitted from a phosphor crystal measured by a scintillation counter. It is usually a recall of the purpose of an operation rather than the minutiae of its stages described in an article which makes it coherent and logical for the reader.

The title of the SL article is often too long by English standards and, in the title of the extract quoted in the Chapter Appendix, *en biologie* (for 'organic substances') could be omitted. Again, the 'general' word *utilisation* is best slightly shifted in translation to 'application' – simply on the ground that 'utilisation' is more commonly applied to substances than processes – general words are not uncommonly 'shifted' in this way. *Intéret* is one of several terms common in medical texts (cf. *altération, appareillage, dosage, biologique*) which have at least two possible TL translations, of which the one that transparently resembles the English is the less likely version: thus *intéret* is here 'value' or 'importance'; *appareillage* is 'preparation', not 'matching'; *dosage* is 'measurement' or 'quantity determination', not 'dose' (a *faux ami*); *altération* is usually 'deterioration', not 'alteration'; *biologique* is often 'organic' (samples), 'laboratory', rather than 'biological'. The last important point on the title is that it has a transparent collocation, *scintillation liquide* (cf. in the text *solution scintillante* which sounds like a beautiful phrase from Valéry's *Cimetière Marin*) and the article has *impulsions erratiques, rayonnements cosmiques et telluriques, le proche ultra-violet* which have to be checked. All except *scintillation, scintillante* are mercifully through-translations. (In this case there is no difficulty as several of the titles in the bibliography give 'liquid scintillation'.) I remind you that bibliography titles are reliable whilst the so-called translated abstracts at the end of French, not German, papers are often merely risible rubbish:

> However, there is a classical notion which did not change: the % of good results decreases as the original accident becomes older . . . When treated precociously there is more than 80% chance of success, which may be spectacular as it is still rather rare.

Misleading adjective plus noun collocations for standardised terms are one of the most common sources of error in technical translation. In non-standardised language, transparent or motivated verb plus object, or subject plus verb collocations, can be equally misleading. But this can lead to professional deformation. There is nothing wrong with *qualende Insekten* as 'tormenting insects' even if you have never heard of 'tormenting insects'. It is a descriptive, not a technical term.

The last element in the superscription of medical articles consists of the names of the authors and the addresses of their places of work. All these are usually transferred except in cases: (1) where a 'title' (*Pr., Chefarzt, Privatdozent, Primarius*) has a recognised common translation equivalent ('Prof.', 'Physician in charge of department', 'Head of clinic', 'Unestablished university lecturer' (Austrian)); (2) where the name of a city is currently 'naturalised' (note for instance the strange 'English' version Basle) and where the name of the institution is so opaque (though motivated; German example, *Nervenheilanstalt*) that a translation couplet, i.e., transference plus a semantic translation ('hospital for nervous

diseases'), might be useful to the reader. Names of countries are also translated.
The professional reader can therefore write to the author if he wishes.

GOING THROUGH THE TEXT (see Appendix)

You should then read the article through and underline all words and structures
that appear to contain problems. These may include:

(1) Unfamiliar apparently transparent words with Greek or Latin morphemes. In
this extract, for instance, *radioéléments, leucine, photomultiplicateurs, photocathode, radioluminescence* have to be checked, since translators of technical
texts must not reproduce neologisms (unless they admit it with inverted
commas, if not in a footnote) – occasionally a detachable prefix such as anti-,
pre- or post- can be risked. For chemical terms, suffixes have to be checked. In
the above list *photomultiplicateurs* becomes 'photomultiplier'; 'scintillator' is
correct but the usual word is 'scintillation counter'.

(2) Figures and symbols. These have to be checked for TL equivalence and order –
the innumeracy of some arts graduates can be gathered by the fact that initially
they simply copy figures and symbols unthinkingly into their versions.

(3) Words of the type: *représenter* ('is'), *résider* ('lies'), *porter le nom de, phénomène,
au sein même de, dans le cadre de* – semi-empty words which are likely to be
reduced to 'is' or 'in', etc., in the TL version.

(4) Verbs such as *faciliter, permettre de* (and *inciter, obliger, empêcher, pousser*) which
more often than not require a recasting of the TL sentence: e.g., 'organic
samples and a sophisticated equipment have to be prepared for this technique',
or, 'with the help of this technique which is relatively recent various forms of
metabolism can be investigated', or 'using this technique various forms of
metabolism can be investigated'.

(5) 'Pun words' such as *traitement* ('processing of results'), *si* ('whereas'), *séduisant*
('attractive': 'This counting technique has its attractions but its application is
extremely difficult'); even *coïncidence* which here is the appropriate technical
term in English and French, and *mesure* – 'measuring' or 'measurement' rather
than 'measure' or 'moderation'.

You can then translate sentence by sentence, making grammatical shifts to
form natural language: *émetteurs*, 'which emit'; deleting 'empty' past participles
(*disposé, situé*); *relativement récente*, 'which is relatively recent' – note the
parenthetical or contrastive sense of the enclosing commas: the main thrust is
always on loosening up the syntax in a natural way; on bringing in the English
gerund that all foreign languages lack; on finding a more natural word order; even
on finding the right jargon-word ('low-level', *faible énergie*) but avoiding the jargon
that consists of adding -isation, -bilisation, -ualise, -ality, -ility, -atise, -ivism,
-fiable, -tialism, -ism, -istic, -isticity, -istically, -tionism, -ology, -ibility, to every
noun or verb; on noting all the verbs, here *posséder, contenir, apparaître*, in other

texts *représenter*, *faire état de*, which are often simply rendered by the hold-all English copulas 'to be' or 'to have'. You note that verb-nouns such as *par la détection, par le dosage, dans la suppression de* go straight into English gerunds ('by detecting', 'by determining', 'by eliminating'). Is there any difference between *apparaît d'une manière discontinue* and 'is discontinuous'? You note the obvious modulation: 'without difficulty', an oddity, because more often it is a French adverbial phrase that is translated by an English adverb. You note again the unique French preposition *par*, unique because it appears to have more semantic power than the other French prepositions, and is often translated by 'due to', 'by means of'. One reduces the Latin *quasitotalité* to the Germanic 'almost all', getting rid of more jargon.

Strangely enough, this piece is well written. It has none of the excitement of the weird metaphors (*la revanche de Guignol sur le gendarme*, 'the little man's revenge against authority') and idiosyncratic idiolect (*frappé au même coin de l'interposition*, 'are characteristically placed between') which characterise so many non-literary French texts.

(You will find much of what I have to say about the process of revising your version set out in greater detail in Chapter 19.)

In a technical translation you can be as bold and free in recasting grammar (cutting up sentences, transposing clauses, converting verbs to nouns, etc.) as in any other type of informative or vocative text, provided the original is defective. Here particularly you, who are a professional writer, should produce a better text than the writer of the original, who is not. However, with the terminology take no risks; play for safety.

As a technical translator you vary your format in relation to your customer. If he wants a 'cover-to-cover' translation, you normally keep the house-style of the original. If you translate for a publication, you adopt its house-style, and you should peruse its back-numbers to see what this is. A publication such as the *British Medical Journal* has a 'marked' house-style, including rather pronounced use of passives ('examinations are done', 'a decision was required'), restrained double-noun compounds ('endoscopy plan'), frequent use of suffixed or non-suffixed deverbals collocated with equative verbs or (the 16 Basic English operators) all-purpose verbs (e.g., 'the answer is', 'the outcome was', 'take action', 'have effect', 'medication was given', 'management was changed'), occasional use of 'we' – I note particularly the features that may be transposed ('shifted') in translation.

Lexically, the main characteristic of technical language is its actual richness and its potential infinity – there are always unnamed bones and rocks. In many areas of science, Graeco-Latin terms are used for classification purposes, and in translation they serve as internationalisms, and can be used as functional equivalents when a SL term for a natural object (flora, fauna, new minerals are named by an international committee of nomenclature) is missing in the TL, since the referent is not known in the TL environment – so a nymphalid butterfly such as a 'white admiral' can be translated as *Limenitis camilla*, a 'red admiral' as *Vanessa atalanta*, a gypsy moth as *Lymantria dispar* (cf. beetles, plants, trees) – but an *amorican* gypsy moth is a *Porthetria dispar*. You ensure equivalent level of register by transferring standardised Latin and/or Greek terms and by translating SL Graeco-Latin terms by English Graeco-Latin terms, unless/until the words are so frequent that they have a more common Germanic variant ('bleeding', 'heart failure', 'stroke', 'chicken-pox', 'mumps'), where you also bear in mind that English with its phrasal verbs and nouns, and monosyllables, tends to use a more informal style of its own than Romance languages and, in particular, German.

CONCLUSION

Perhaps inevitably a technical translation is so varied in topic and often diverse in register, and so badly written, that it is not easy to make helpful generalisations about it. It is the writing that is closest to material reality, furthest from the psyche! It spills over into diagrams, graphs, illustrations, photographs, figures, formulae, equations, schemes, references, bibliographies, plans – it is amazing how translators brought up on translation exams at school and university sometimes fail to scan these eagerly, particularly the bibliographies, which often translate the keywords for you. In fact, bibliographies and diagrams are the first things you should look at. Whilst I think it is absurd to maintain that the SL formulation of the text is 'relatively unimportant, and not necessarily just if it is poorly written', Folkart's statement (like many absurd ones) is a timely corrective to superficial translations, not necessarily translationese, an encouragement to greater explicitness (filling the case-gaps) than you find in the original.

My last point is obvious. Technology being an explosion, escalating exponentially, ongoing, this is the field, on the frontier of knowledge, where you have to be most up to date. Data banks, terminology bureaux, informants, the latest editions of all text- and reference books – nothing else will do; tell your client/employer or your librarian that you have to have these available where possible. Do not hesitate to ring relevant firms and ask for their research or their information departments. If you get a chance, go on or press for refresher courses and visits to research conferences, a tour of plants and factories. (The story of the technical translator unaware that the process/appliance he was dealing with was being demonstrated next door/on the floor above has, like the Eskimos' snow, many variants.)

However, I end as I started. Terminology makes up perhaps 5–10% of a text. The rest is 'language', usually a natural style of language; and here you normally find an authoritative text aspires to such a style; if it does not, you gently convert it to natural and elegant language – the writer will be grateful to you. So write it well.

APPENDIX: SAMPLE TEXT

Mise au point

Utilisation et intérêt de la scintillation liquide en biologie

R. Le Net, J. Fabre et *P. Serres*

La scintillation en milieu liquide représente l'une des méthodes le plus couramment employées pour détecter et compter les radioéléments émetteurs de particules bêta de faible énergie. Cette technique, relativement récente (1950), nécessite une préparation des échantillons biologiques et un appareillage complexes ainsi qu'un traitement approprié des résultats. Elle a toutefois permis d'explorer différents métabolismes par la détection et le dosage des molécules marquées à l'aide d'élèments radioactifs bêta aussi essentiels que l'hydrogène (H), le carbone (^{14}C), le soufre (^{35}S) ou le calcium (^{45}Ca). Des études sur l'eau [2], la leucine [9] et des médicaments [14] marqués ont ainsi démontré l'intérêt de cette méthode dans le cadre de recherches biologiques.

1. GÉNÉRALITÉS SUR LA SCINTILLATION EN MILIEU LIQUIDE

Un scintillateur liquide possède la propriété d'émettre, lorsqu'il est exposé à des rayonnements nucléaires ionisants, des photons lumineux situés dans le proche ultraviolet. Cette luminescence ou radioluminescence porte le nom de scintillation lorsqu'elle apparaît d'une manière discontinue [3]. La propriété de ce phénomène est utilisée pour les mesures de radioactivité d'éléments introduits au sein même de la solution.

Pour cette mesure la solution scintillante, contenant le radioisotope émetteur de particules bêta, est placée dans une fiole disposée entre deux photomultiplicateurs. Ceux-ci, par leur photocathode, détectent les scintillations lumineuses apparues au sein même de la solution et transmettent leurs réponses sous la forme d'impulsions électriques à un système de coïncidence. Ce système permet d'éliminer la plupart des impulsions erratiques liées à l'imperfection de l'électronique et aux rayonnement cosmiques et telluriques.

L'un des avantages essentiels de cette technique de comptage réside dans la suppression de l'auto-absorption du rayonnement bêta, très gênante lorsque les radioéléments ont une énergie faible. De plus, les particules bêta sont facilement diffusées par la matière. La mise en solution des échantillons radioactifs permet d'éviter ces pertes de comptage. La quasitotalité des émissions bêta est donc utilisée à produire des scintillations.

Si cette technique de comptage est séduisante, sa mise en oeuvre est très délicate. L'introduction d'échantillons radioactifs dans le détecteur liquide nécessite . . .

(*Rev. Méd. Toulouse*, 1974, pp. 1755–1769)

CHAPTER 15

The Translation of Serious Literature and Authoritative Statements

INTRODUCTION

Theorists sometimes maintain that cognitive translation (the transfer of cold information) is perfectly possible and may be possibly perfect – it is the hard core, the invariant factor; the only snag comes when: (a) there is an emphasis on the form as well as the content of the message or; (b) there is a cultural gap between SL and TL readers (different ways of thinking or feeling, material objects) or there is a tricky pragmatic relation, i.e. between on the one hand the writer and on the other the translator and/or reader. There is a certain truth in these generalisations, though they miss one point, that the adequacy of a translation basically depends on the degree of difficulty, complexity, obscurity of the whole passage, rather than the one or the other aspect. Further, any passage that stresses SL form can be perfectly explained and therefore over-translated into the TL, though it will not have the naked impact of the original. However, if one must make generalisations, I can say that normally the translation of serious literature and authoritative statements is the most testing type of translation, because the first, basic articulation of meaning (the word) is as important as the second (the sentence or, in poetry, the line) and the effort to make word, sentence and text cohere requires continuous compromise and readjustment.

Bühler's expressive function of language, where content and form are on the whole equally and indissolubly important, informs two broad text-categories: serious imaginative literature and authoritative statements of any kind, whether political, scientific, philosophical or legal.

The two categories have obvious differences: (a) authoritative statements are more openly addressed to a readership than is literature; (b) literature is allegorical in some degree; authoritative statements are often literal and denotative and figurative only in exceptional passages, as in broad popular appeals ('islands' amongst the literal language), such as 'The wind of change is blowing' – *Un grand courant d'air souffle* (both stock metaphors); 'I have nothing to offer but blood, toil, tears and sweat' (Churchill, 13 May 1940) – *Je n'ai à vous offrir que du sang, de la sueur, du travail, des larmes* (figurative language, but these are symbols, to be understood literally as well as figuratively); 'the underbelly of the Axis' (Churchill, January 1943) – *le bas-ventre de l'Axe* – not *le point vulnérable* (an original metaphor). Further, the element of self-expression in authoritative statements is only incidental but the translator has to pay the same respect to bizarreries of idiolect as in fantastic literature: *La France y voit un renfort décisif de notre latinité à l'avantage de tous les hommes* – 'France sees it as a decisive strengthening of our Latinity benefiting all men' (De Gaulle).

A further generalisation for the translator: literature broadly runs along a four-point scale from lyrical poetry through the short story and the novel to drama.

POETRY

Poetry is the most personal and concentrated of the four forms, no redundancy, no phatic language, where, as a unit, the word has greater importance than in any other type of text. And again, if the word is the first unit of meaning, the second is not the sentence or the proposition, but usually the line, thereby again demonstrating a unique double concentration of units. Thus in:

> . . . But Man, proud man
> Drest in a little brief authority,
> Most ignorant of what he's most assured
> His glassy essence, like an angry ape,
> Plays such fantastic tricks before high heaven
> As make the angels weep . . .
>
> (Shakespeare, *Measure for Measure*, II.II.117)

the integrity of both the lexical units and the lines has to be preserved within a context of: (a) corresponding punctuation, which essentially reproduces the tone of the original; and (b) accurate translation of metaphor. Consider Tieck's version:

> . . . *doch der Mensch, der stolze Mensch,*
> *In kleine kurze Majestät gekleidet,*
> *Vergessend, was am mind'sten zu bezweifeln,*
> *Sein gläsern Element – wie zorn'ge Affen,*
> *Spielt solchen Wahnsinn gaukelnd vor dem Himmel,*
> *Daß Engel weinen . . .*
>
> (trans. Tieck and Schlegel, *Maß für Maß*)

Here the word – and line – units have been preserved with the punctuation; the image 'plays such fantastic tricks' becomes 'plays such madness, conjuring' but the other images are preserved, whilst 'most ignorant of' becomes 'forgetting' and the positive 'most assured' becomes the double negative 'least to be doubted', which is a common modulation. The greatest and unnecessary loss here is the 'fantastic tricks' metaphor. Original metaphor is the controlling element in all creative language, evoking through a visual image – even abstract images such as justice or mercy become people or objects – not only sight but the four other senses (e.g., fur as touch, food as taste, flowers as smell, bells or birds as sound) as well as the concomitant human qualities, good or evil, pleasure or pain, that these images (sensory, sensuous, sensual, sensitive, perhaps even sensational, to liven up language) can produce. Poetry presents the thing in order to convey the feeling, in particular, and however concrete the language, each represents something else – a feeling, a behaviour, a view of life as well as itself. Original metaphors the translator has to reproduce scrupulously, even if they are likely to cause cultural shock. Shakespeare's 'Shall I compare thee to a summer's day' (Sonnet 18), as Neubert has commented, will leave Arabic or Eskimo readers cold, but the Arabic or Eskimo reader must make the effort to fine out the truth of the simile, which is at least half-revealed in the next line: 'Thou art more lovely and more temperate'. A cultural metaphor (e.g., the technical term '(Summer's) lease') is not so important.

The translator can boldly transfer the image of any metaphor where it is known in the TL culture. But for lines such as Walter de la Mare's:

> And even the thought of her when she is far
> Narcissus is, and they the waters are
> > (*Reflections*)

or Kingsley Amis':

> Should poets bicycle-pump the heart
> Or squash it flat?
> (*Something Nasty in the Bookshop*)

faced with literal translations in cultures where Narcissus and the bicycle-pump are not known, the reader is not so much culturally shocked as baffled. In such poems there is a case for creating a culturally equivalent TL metaphor, or converting the SL metaphor to sense or, where there is space, adding sense to the metaphor; but if the translator regards the metaphor as important, it is his duty to carry it across to launch it on the target language and its culture.

Whilst I think that all images have universal, cultural and personal sources, the translator of poetry cannot make any concession to the reader such as transferring the foreign culture to a native equivalent. If autumn in China is the season not of Keats's 'mists and mellow fruitfulness' but of high clear skies and transparent waters, and the sound of clothes laundered for the cold weather pounded on the washing blocks, then the reader must simply accept this background and, if he wants to feel it, repeated reading is more likely to make it his possession than are detailed background, explanation of allusions and so on. Nevertheless, the European must be aware that, for the Chinese culture, jade is not jade-coloured but white ('jade snow', 'jade beads', 'jade moon'), that comparisons with eyebrows assume the custom of painting women's eyebrows green, that the phoenix has no myth of resurrection, that dragons are close and kindly, that cypresses suggest grave-yards, as in the West (see Graham, *Poems of the Late T'ang*).

The transition from Chinese to English culture is made easier because all the images mentioned are not unfamiliar to an English reader. The difficulty comes when and if local flowers and grasses are used as metaphors.

I am sceptical about the idea that a translator of poetry is primarily communicating – that he is, to his readers in the conventional definition of communicative translation, trying to create the same effect on the target language readers as was created by the poet on his own readers; his main endeavour is to 'translate' the effect the poem made on *himself*. A translator can hardly achieve even a parallel effect in poetry – the two languages, since all their resources are being used here as in no other literary or non-literary medium, are, at their widest, poles apart. Syntax, lexis, sound, culture, but not image, clash with each other. Valéry wrote: 'My aim is *not* literary. It is not to produce an effect on others so much as on myself – the *Self* in so far as it may be treated as a work . . . of the mind. I am not interested in writing poetry without a view to its function.'

Compare John Cairncross, who was not trying to disprove that French, or poetry, or French poetry, or Racine, was untranslatable, or to present Racine to his English readers, or to present his English readers with Racine, but set about translating simply because the English words started forming themselves in his ear, and so he quotes Racine again: *Ce que j'ai fait, Abner, j'ai cru le devoir faire* – 'What I have done, Abner, I had to do' (*Athalie*, 1.467), which is itself an echo of γεγραφα, γεγραφα – Pontius Pilate's 'What I have written I have written'. Take it or leave it.

Now I think that in most examples of poetry translation, the translator first decides to choose a TL poetic form (viz. sonnet, ballad, quatrain, blank verse etc.) as close as possible to that of the SL. Although the rhyming scheme is part of the form, its precise order may have to be dropped. Secondly, he will reproduce the figurative meaning, the concrete images of the poem. Lastly the setting, the thought-words, often the various techniques of sound-effect which produce the individual impact I have mentioned have to be worked in at later stages during the rewriting (as Beaugrande has stated in his fine translation of Rilke). Emotionally, different sounds create different meanings, based not on the sounds of nature, nor on the seductive noises in the streams and the forests, but on the common sounds of the human throat: *Sein oder nicht sein – das ist hier die Frage* appears to have a ring of confidence and challenge in it which is foreign to Hamlet's character – is it the redoubled *ei* sound? – that opens up the whole question of the universal symbolism of sounds. All this plangency, this openness is missing in 'To be or not to be – that is the question' which is almost a word-for-word translation, though the German *hier* – 'that is here the question' – appears to underline the challenge which is not in Shakespeare. The fact is that, however good as a translation, its meaning will differ in many ways from the original – it will, in Borrow's phrase, be a mere echo of the original, not through Gogol's glass pane – and it will have its own independent strength. A successfully translated poem is always another poem.

Whether a translator gives priority to content or manner, and, within manner, what aspect – metre, rhyme, sound, structure – is to have priority, must depend not only on the values of the particular poem, but also on the translator's theory of poetry. Therefore no general theory of poetic translation is possible and all a translation theorist can do is to draw attention to the variety of possibilities and point to successful practice, unless he rashly wants to incorporate his theory of translation into his own theory of poetry. Deliberately or intuitively, the translator has to decide whether the expressive or the aesthetic function of language in a poem or in one place in a poem is more important. Crudely this renews Keats's argument concerning Truth and Beauty: 'Beauty is Truth, Truth, Beauty – that is all you know, and all you need to know', when he maintains that they define and are equivalent to each other, as well as the later argument between art as a criticism of life (Matthew Arnold) and art for art's sake (Théophile Gautier) which character-ised two French poetic movements as well as much turn-of-the-century literature – 'All art is useless', wrote Oscar Wilde, whose own art belies the statement. Clearly Keats, who was not thinking of translation, oversimplified the argument. If Truth stands for the literal translation and Beauty for the elegant version in the trans-lator's idiom, Truth is ugly and Beauty is always a lie. 'That's life', many would say. But a translation theorist would point out that both these versions, the literal and the elegant poem, would normally be equally unsatisfactory as translations of a poem or of anything else. Some fusion, some approximation, between the expres-sive and the aesthetic function of language is required, where in any event the personal language of the poet which deviates from the norms of the source language is likely to deviate even more from those of the target language. Thus Karl Kraus complained that Stefan George, by 'doing violence' to the English sense of Shakespeare's sonnets and to German verbal and grammatical usage, had produced 'a unique abortion'! But, in my belief, George is the closest and most successful of all translators.

Thus:

> *Lebwohl! zu teuer ist dein besitz für mich*
> *Und du weißt wohl wie schwer du bist zu kaufen*
> *Der freibrief deines werts entbindet dich*
> *Mein recht auf dich ist völlig abgelaufen.*

which is:

> Farewell! too dear is your possession for me
> And you well know how hard you are to buy
> The charter of your worth releases you
> My claim to you has fully run its course.

which becomes:

> Farewell! thou art too dear for my possessing,
> And like enough thou know'st thy estimate:
> The Charter of thy worth gives thee releasing;
> My bonds in thee are all determinate.
> (Sonnet 87)

George's translation is notable for its tautness and flexibility, and particularly for its emphasis on the corresponding theme-words ('dear', 'charter', 'releasing', 'bonds', 'determinate'). Where he is unable to reach Shakespeare is in the polysemy of 'estimate', 'releasing', 'bonds', and 'determinate', and thus he restricts the meaning of the quatrain – and above all in the splendid logical statement of Shakespeare's opening with its communicative dynamism on 'possessing', where George is forced into an inversion.

Angus Graham, in his discussion on the translation of Chinese poetry, says that the element in poetry which travels best is concrete imagery. A crib or trot of Chinese such as:

> Kuang Heng write-frankly memorial.
> Success slight Liu Hsiang transmit classic.
> Plan miss.

could be rewritten as:

> A disdained K'uang Heng, as a critic of policy,
> As promoter of learning, a Liu Hsiang who failed.

Here the poet is miserably contrasting his failures with the success of two statesmen, but contrast this with:

> Tartar horn tug North wind,
> Thistle Gate whiter than water
> Sky, hold-in-mouth Koknor Road
> Wall top moon thousand mile

I note that, even in a *Times Literary Supplement* review, Erich Segal comments on most translators 'metarophobia', their unease in the presence of metaphor. Pindar speaks of man being *skias onar* – 'the dream of a shadow' but Richmond Lattimore turns it round to the conventional 'shadow of a dream'. According to Aeschylus, Prometheus *stole* the *anthos/pyros*, the 'blossom of fire', but according to half the translators he merely 'plucked the blossom'.

'*Dichten* equals *condensare*', as Ezra Pound wrote in *ABC of Reading*, mistakenly thinking that *dichten* is related to *dicht* ('dense' or 'thick'), but stating a truth. Original poetry itself has no redundancy, no phatic language, but the translator usually needs a little extra space, he relies on redundancy in over-translating, say, *veule* as 'flabby' or 'weak and soft' and here he is often hemmed in by the metre. Racine's wonderful line *Le jour n'est pas plus pur que le fond de mon coeur* may become: 'My heart is candid as the light of day' (Dillon) or: 'The daylight is not purer than my heart' (Cairncross) and whilst the second translation is closer and more successful, it cannot match the fullness and softness of the original; the alliteration, the monosyllables, the repeated r's, the emotive *fond* are missing.

I have said that original metaphors have to be translated accurately, even if in the target language culture the image is strange and the sense it conveys may only be guessed. *Und jener, der 'du' zu ihm sagte träumt mit ihm: Wir* (Celan, *In Memoriam Paul Eluard*): 'And he who addressed him as "thou" will dream with him: We.' The translator Michael Hamburger has to use 'thou', although the connotations of friendship and love – what I would call *le plaisir de te tutoyer* – will be lost on the reader of the translation or perhaps soon on the reader of the original, now that the intimate *du, tu* has been taken over by the Left and all the under-thirties. *Le plaisir de te tutoyer* has almost gone, unless you are old, but so, thankfully, has *das erste Du stammelte auf ihren keuschen Lippen.*

Sound-effects are bound to come last for the translator, except for lovely minor poetry such as Swinburne's. Inevitably, he must try to do something about them and, if not, compensate, either by putting them elsewhere or substituting another sound. German, the *Brudersprache* to English, often finds its adjectives and nouns – *fremde Frau*, 'alien woman'; *laue Luft*, 'tepid air' – unreproduced, but longer alliterations.

> *Und schwölle mit und schauerte und triefte*
> (G. Benn, *Untergrundbahn*)

can usually find a modest, suggestive equivalence:

> To swell in unison and stream and shudder
> (trans. M. Hamburger)

John Weightman has stated that French poetry is untranslatable into English. I cannot accept this. Firstly, because a lot of French poetry (Villon, Rimbaud, Valéry) has been more or less successfully translated into English; secondly because although there are obvious minuses – the syntactical differences; the huge English vocabulary compared with the small French vocabulary, so that many French words appear to be generic words covering many English specific words that themselves lack a generic word (e.g., *humide, mouillé*: 'humid, damp, dank, moist, wet, clammy, undried'; *noir*: 'black, dark, dim, dull, dusky, deep, gloomy, murky'), making French 'abstract' and intellectual whilst English is concrete and real – yet, in the actual particular of a text, English has infinite creative resources, English has the disyllables as well as the monosyllables, English in the eighteenth century got close to all the so-called French properties and, given empathy, given sympathy, there is no reason why, one day, even Racine should not find his inadequate but challenging English translator.

John Cairncross sets out three considerations for the translation of Racine: (1) the translator must adopt ten-syllable blank verse; (2) Racine must be translated accurately; (3) Racine's verse is particularly difficult owing to his capacity of evoking music from the most unpromising material – I could think of more.

Hippolyte's confession of love – I would not call it that, it is too restless and feverish – to Aricie (*Phèdre*, ll.524-60) is often considered to be *précieux*, i.e., affected, conventional, too polished, sophisticated, class-bound, with too many stock metaphors, but for me they have always been Racine's most beautiful lines, crystallising the neurotic exposed mental and nervous obsession which is the essence of the Racine characater. Taking the critical lines 539-48, it appears to me that in any modern version, the language must be kept modern and formal, the polar oppositions (*fuir, trouver, suivre, éviter, lumière, ombre*) retained, the stresses and repetitions preserved, the image of the hunted, haunted animal (Hippolyte) kept clear, and some attempt made to keep the simple language, the soft sounds with occasional alliteration.

Consider first the version of John Caircross. In general it is accurate, though a new image is unnecessarily created ('Cut from my moorings by a surging swell') and some oppositions blurred:

> Present I flee you, absent you are near
>
> *Présente je vous fuis – absente, je vous trouve*

and the stresses often changed. The translation, written in 1945, has a few old-fashioned phrases: 'in thrall', 'a single blow has quelled'. With all this, lines such as

> Before you stands a pitiable prince . . .
> Who, pitying the shipwrecks of the weak . . .
> Deep in the woods, your image follows me.
>
> *Dans le fond des forêts votre image me suit*
>
> The light of day, the shadows of the night.
>
> *La lumière du jour, les ombres de la nuit.*

(the latter a one-to-one translation)

> Everything conjures up the charms I flee
> I seek but cannot find myself again –
>
> *Maintenant je me cherche, et ne me trouve plus*

(note the unusual number of French monosyllables) are close to the original and successful.

George Dillon, like Cairncross, uses blank verse, and prefers formal accuracy to musicality. His translation is closer than Cairncross's, so that lexical inaccuracies such as 'surprise' for *trouble* and 'hurt' for *déchirer* are disconcerting, as is the weak line: 'Your image moves with me in the deep forests' (the alliteration is compensatory). Some stresses and contrasts are more clearly rendered than Cairncross's:

> With you and with myself, vainly I strive
> (l.541)

> All summon to my eyes what I avoid
>   (1.545)
> I seek myself and find myself no more
>   (1.548)

(the latter the most successful line) – such lines show how simply and precisely Racine can be translated. Both Dillon and Cairncross hit on the same translation for line 544 and there are occasions where one or two lines of Dillon's could improve Cairncross's rather better overall version; Dillon's

> Only my deep sighs echo in the wood;
> My idle couriers have forgotten my voice.

is better than Cairncross's

> My idle steeds no longer know my voice
> And only to my cries the woods resound.

(I do not know why Caircross has reversed the lines.)

Robert Lowell's 'imitation' of *Phèdre* is another matter. These rhymed pentameters attempt to explicate the image of the speech:

> Six months now, bounding like a wounded stag
> I've tried to shake this poisoned dart, and drag
> Myself to safety from your eyes that blind
> When present, and when absent leave behind
> Volleys of burning arrows in my mind.

I do not know how such lines would strike a reader or spectator new to *Phèdre*. For myself, with Racine's images burned into my mind, I find them unsatisfying, because, like Hippolyte, I am continuously looking for and failing to find even the simplest images which Lowell would have had no difficulty in retaining or re-capturing. In fact I find the greatest loss in Racine translations is the resonance of the only 1800 words that are used in the twelve plays.

THE SHORT STORY/NOVEL

From a translator's point of view, the short story is, of literary forms, the second most difficult, but here he is released from the obvious constraints of poetry – metre and rhyme – whilst the varieties of sound-effect are likely to play a minor role. Further, since the line is no longer a unit of meaning, he can spread himself a little – his version is likely to be somewhat longer than the original though, always, the shorter the better. He can supply cultural glosses within the text – not, as in poetry or drama, delete or banish them to some note or glossary: *L'ascenseur ne fonctionnait pas, en raison des économies de courant* – 'With the war-time electricity cuts, the lift wasn't working.'

Since formal and thematic concentration and unity may distinguish the short story from the novel, the translator has to be careful to preserve certain cohesive effects.

I use Thomas Mann's *Tonio Kröger* to illustrate two types of key-words I propose to define: leitmotifs are peculiar to a short story, characterising a character or a situation. When they are repeated, they should be appropriately foregrounded and repeated in the translation: *Zigeuner im grünen Wagen* – 'gypsies in green wagons' for the artists; *die Blonden und Blauäugigen* – 'the blond and blue-eyed ones' for the ordinary people; *die Feldblume im Knopfloch* – 'the wild flowers in his buttonhole' for the respectable bourgeois Knaak with his *gedämpfte Stimme* – 'muffled or subdued voice', or for Magdalena: the clumsy ones, *die immer hinfallen* – 'who always fall down'. Descriptive leitmotifs were used in Romantic short stories before Wagner invented the term, e.g., in Gotthelf's *Dark Spider*, *giftig glotzend* – 'gaping poisonously', where the alliteration is moderately compensated. As dialogue becomes more important in fiction, certain phrases become attached to characters (Grev's billiard remarks in *The Cherry Orchard*, the numerous tags for Dickens's characters, Holden Coulfield's 'phoney', Esmé's 'extremely' in Salinger (now it is 'totally' for anyone) and these have to be foregrounded.

The second type of key-word is the word or phrase that typifies the writer rather than the particular text: *sich verirren, jagen, beirrt, nämlich, beengen* and all the *Beamte* words may be said to typify Kafka, as powerful verbs like *entraîner, épier, agir, frémir, exiger, grelotter, tressaillir, obséder* may typify Mauriac. Some of these words go into a ready one-to-one translation into English, and get their connotational significance from repetition and context (situational and linguistic) which can more or less be reproduced by the translator. Words like *jagen* and *entraîner* are difficult: *jagen* suggests 'hectic chase' and *entraîner* (*Quelle force m'entraîne?*), 'impel irresistibly'.

For key-words, translators have to assess their texts critically; they have to decide which lexical units are central, and have the more important function, and which are peripheral, so that the relative gains and losses in a translation may correspond to their assessment. (I realise that many translators will claim they do all this intuitively, by instinct, or by common sense, and they do not need translation theory to make them aware of relative importance.)

There is no advantage in making generalisations about the translation of serious novels. The obvious problems: the relative importance of the SL culture and the author's moral purpose to the reader – it may be exemplified in the translation of proper names; of the SL conventions and the author's idiolect; the translation of dialect; the distinction between personal style, literary convention of period and/or movement; and the norms of the SL – these problems have to be settled for each text.

The signal importance of the translation of some novels has been the introduction of a new vision injecting a different literary style into another language culture, and when one looks at *Weltliteratur* translations in this sense – I think of Proust, Camus, Kafka, Mann, Pavese – it is clear that the translators have often not been bold, which means not literal, enough: these are the million cases where a literal translation is aesthetically not inferior to a free translation, fashionably justified as 'sub-text', formerly the 'spirit' or the 'genius' of the language or the author.

DRAMA

The main purpose of translating a play is normally to have it performed success-fully. Therefore a translator of drama inevitably has to bear the potential spectator in mind though, here again, the better written and more significant the text, the fewer compromises he can make in favour of the reader. Further, he works under certain constraints: unlike the translator of fiction, he cannot gloss, explain puns or ambiguities or cultural references, nor transcribe words for the sake of local colour: his text is dramatic, with emphasis on verbs, rather than descriptive and explana-tory. Michael Meyer, in a little noticed article in *Twentieth Century Studies*, quoting T. Rattigan, states that the spoken word is five times as potent as the written word – what a novelist would say in 30 lines, the playwright must say in five. The arithmetic is faulty and so, I believe, is the sentiment, but it shows that a translation of a play must be concise – it must not be an over-translation.

Meyer makes a distinction between dramatic text and sub-text, the literal meaning and the 'real point': i.e. what is implied but not said, the meaning between the lines. He believes that if a person is questioned on a subject about which he has complex feelings, he will reply evasively (and in a circumlocutory manner). Ibsen's characters say one thing and mean another. The translator must word the sentences in such a way that this, the sub-text, is equally clear in English. Unfortunately, Meyer gives no examples. Normally one would expect a semantic translation of a line, which may be close to a literal translation, to reveal its implications more clearly than a communicative translation, that simply makes the dialogue easy to speak. Lines such as 'Aren't you feeling the cold?' and 'I think your husband is faithful to you' have potential implications of escape and suspicion respectively in any language, provided there is cultural overlap between them. (They would not have the same implication if the climate or the sexual morality respectively differed considerably in the SL and the TL culture.)

Finally a translator of drama in particular must translate into the *modern* target language if he wants his characters to 'live', bearing in mind that the modern language covers a span of, say, 70 years, and that if one character speaks in a bookish or old-fashioned way in the original, written 500 years ago, he must speak in an equally bookish and old-fashioned way in the translation, but as he would today, therefore with a corresponding time-gap – differences of register, social class, education, temperament in particular must be preserved between one character and another. Thus the dialogue remains dramatic, and though the translator cannot forget the potential spectators, he does not make concessions to them. Given the emphasis on linguistic form, and the subtlety of the SL, his version is inevitably inferior but also simpler and a kind of one-sided introduction to the original. Kant is easier to read in French than in German, perhaps even for a German.

Whilst a great play may be translated for the reading public's enjoyment and for scholarly study as well as for performance on stage, the translator should always assume the latter as his main purpose – there should be no difference between an acting and a reading version – and he should look after readers and scholars only in his notes. Nevertheless, he should where possible amplify cultural metaphors, allusions, proper names, in the text itself, rather than replace the allusion with the sense. ('Hyperion to a satyr' becomes 'a sun god to a monster' in Chinese.)

When a play is transferred from the SL to the TL culture it is usually no longer a translation, but an adaptation.

CONCLUSION

Finally in discussing the translation of serious literature, I must make it clear that I am trying to look at the future. There is no question that translators such as Stuart Gilbert, who translated Malraux and Camus into English and Joyce into French, had a quickening effect on translation: possibly reacting against the stiff and literary translation style which so fouled up the translation of Russian literature at the turn of the century. Profoundly influenced by Hemingway who was mainly responsible for bringing fiction closer to normal speech, Gilbert produced a lively enough equivalence: *Aujourd'hui, maman est morte ou peut-être hier, je ne sais pas* becomes 'Mother died today, or maybe yesterday, I can't be sure'; *Je prendrai l'autobus à deux heures et j'arriverai dans l'après-midi.* – 'With the two o'clock bus I should get there well before nightfall' (examples from Camus, *L'Etranger*). You can see that half the time Gilbert is trying to be more colloquial than the original, yet every time he might have said that the further colloquialism was in the sub-text, i.e., implied or implicated in the original. Nevertheless it is hard to see how one can justify translating *Il faisait très chaud* as 'It was a blazing hot afternoon', and there are a thousand other examples of such 'deviations' which show that these translators may have been aiming at 'intuitive truth', an instinctive naturalness (there is no question usually of ignorance, of carelessness, such as is so common in translations from the German) rather than accuracy at any level. I am suggesting that some kind of accuracy must be the only criterion of a good translation in the future – what kind of accuracy depending first on the type and then the particular text that has been translated – and that the word 'sub-text' with its Gricean implications and implicatures can be made to cover a multitude of inaccuracies.

CHAPTER 16

Reference Books and their Uses; Tracing the 'Unfindable' Word

INTRODUCTION

This is the age of reference books. A combination of popular demand and improved information technology (IT) combines to ensure that a greater variety as well as a greater number of these books is continually produced, and can now be updated annually without difficulty (e.g., the *Petit Larousse*). I remind you there are dictionaries of toponyms, symbols, idioms, rare words, phrasal verbs, clichés, euphemisms; good dictionaries are including an increasing number of collocations, but there is still a gap in this area. All these can be useful if you bear in mind their greatest drawback for language-learners as well as for translators: information about the current frequency of the items; further, description is sometimes either confused with function, or function is missing (a knife is for eating, cutting with, as well as a tool with a (usually) metal blade and a handle).

As a translator you have to know *where* as well as *how* to find information. All reference books, however bad, are potentially useful, provided that you know their limitations – which include the date of their publication (so, for German, an old *Muret-Sanders* is good for translating A. von Humboldt). Multilingual dictionaries give few collocations, and therefore are only useful as initial clues to a further search; bilingual dictionaries are indispensable, but they normally require checking in at least two TL monolingual dictionaries and sometimes an SL monolingual dictionary, to check the status (i.e., modern currency, frequency, connotations) of the word. Hilaire Belloc once wrote that the translator should look up every (presumably SL) word, particularly those he is familar with; others say translators should mistrust all dictionaries, sometimes assuming that knowledge of the topic or subject-matter of the text has precedence over questions of equivalence, or that one cannot translate words, only sentences (or texts) – words alone are meaningless.

All these remarks, like most about translation, have a partial truth. Bilingual dictionaries often contain too many 'dictionary words', i.e. words that are rarely used outside dictionaries (maybe 'posology', 'physiological solution', 'compass declination').

It is useful to look up in dictionaries words you have known by their contexts for years, because you often find you have missed an essential component of their core meaning (for 40 years I thought 'mercenary' meant 'mean', for example). In fact the experience gives the lie to Wittgenstein's notorious 'For a large class of cases (though not for all) . . . the meaning of a word is its use in the language', since this is often an excuse for a translator's vagueness and inaccuracy. From context, you often deduce function rather than description, and admittedly function is the first element in meaning and translation. But a fork is essentially an object with between two and four prongs on the end of a handle as well as something to eat with.

RESOURCES

You need firstly a good English dictionary – *Collins English Dictionary*, because it is clear, well arranged and has a high proportion of proper-name head-words. If you can, use also the *Concise Oxford* and Longman's *Dictionary of the English Language* (1984). Secondly, you must have a *Roget*, at least the new Penguin; a thesaurus is essential for: (a) bringing up words from your passive memory; (b) giving you the descriptive words that show up the lexical gaps in the source language; (c) extending your vocabulary.

Thirdly, you should have a large *Webster* (three volumes) within reasonable distance. Often you look up an SL technical term in the English *Webster* before you look it up in an SL monolingual or an SL–TL bilingual dictionary. Find your way round the *EB* (*Encyclopaedia Britannica*); the Micropaedia has a surprisingly large number of dictionary as well as encyclopaedia terms and names. For new words use the two Barnhart *Dictionaries of New English* and the Supplements to the *Oxford English Dictionary*. For word-meanings at various periods, consult the *OED* (but its merger of the old *OED* and the Supplements is bad lexicography). Buy all the Penguin specialist dictionaries (there are over 30) in your field. A modern dictionary of collocations is missing – there is only the great A. Reum's *Dictionary of English Style* (also for French) (1920). For key-words use Bullock and Stallybrass's *Fontana Dictionary of Modern Thought* (also its *Biographical Companion* by Bullock and Woodings), Roger Scruton's *Dictionary of Political Thought*, Raymond Williams's *Key Words* (2nd edition), Edward de Bono's *Word Power*, Antony Flew's *Dictionary of Philosophy* (which also has tables of logic, set theory and formal language symbols). But note that many 'internationalisms' in key-words, not only political ones, have different meanings in other languages (see Newmark, 1982, 1985). For British institutional terms, use the annual *Britain 198-* published by the Central Office of Information (COI); *Whitaker's Almanack* is class-biased but has useful statistics. Consult *Keesing's* for current events. *Payton's Proper Names* (Warne) is brilliant and essential, as is P. Thody and H. Evans, *Faux Amis and Key*

Words (Athlone), for English as well as French. Use Longman's dictionary for phrasal verbs, Brewer's (revised) for sayings, saws and proverbs. For English engineering language, there has been nothing since Scharf's *Engineering and its Language*. For jargon, use Jonathon Green's *Newspeak* and Kenneth Hudson's *Dictionary of Diseased English*.

'UNFINDABLE' WORDS

Tracing apparently 'unfindable' words and phrases can be a difficult and time-consuming task; it is a problem in translation theory which is often considered to lie outside the scope of theoretical or applied linguistics. The translation theorist should, however, propose a frame of reference or guidelines – a non-diagrammatic flow chart – for this task. The purpose of this is to put some order into the translator's search for the meaning of unfindable words.

Types of unfindable word

There may be at least eighteen types of unfindable word in a source language text:

(1) Neologisms, recent and original, including newly coined forms, newly devised phrases, new collocations, compound nouns, new terminology, old words and phrases with new senses, acronyms, abbreviations, blends, eponyms, new combinations of morphemes. Hundreds of these appear every year in non-specialised periodicals and newspapers for an educated readership and many soon disappear. Tens of thousands are devised to form part of specialised vocabularies in every sphere of knowledge.

(2) Dialect, patois and specialised language which is spoken more often than written.

(3) Colloquialisms, slang, taboo words – now usually recorded, but not in all senses ('non-metropolitan' words, e.g. Canadian French (or *joual*, its colloquial form)); words commonly used in, say, remote anglophone areas rather than the UK (e.g. 'kelper').

(4) Third language or target language words waywardly introduced into a SL text.

(5) New or out-of-date geographical and topographical terms and 'rival' alternative names ('Malvinas', 'Azania', etc.).

(6) Names of small villages, districts, streams, hillocks, streets. They may, in novels, be real (e.g. 'Flatbush') or invented, and may or may not have local connotations; street plans may have to be inspected.

(7) Names of obscure persons.

(8) Brand names, names of patented inventions, trademarks – usually signalled by capitalisation and often more or less standard suffixes.

(9) Names of new or unimportant institutions.

(10) Misprints, miscopyings, misspellings, particularly of proper names (people and geographical names) and bizarre transliterations.

(11) SL, TL and third language archaisms.

(12) Unfamiliar connotations and symbolic meanings of words and proper names.

(13) Familiar alternative terms or words.

(14) Code words.

(15) Common words with specific SL or third language cultural senses.

(16) Private language or manifestations of 'underlife'. ('Underlife' is the evidence of the writer's personal qualities or private life which can be indirectly or tangentially deduced from a reading of the SL text.)

(17) Exophoric (or external) reference. The 'unfindable' word may refer to an object or activity mentioned previously, in or not in the SL text.Thus: *Razmishlenya prodolzhajutsja* appears to mean 'My thoughts are still on this matter', but in the context means 'The lectures on (transcendental) meditation are continuing.' Here *razmishlenya*, 'reflections, thoughts, meditations', is the word chosen by the writer to denote, as a 'synecdoche', lectures on transcendental meditation. The absence of definite/indefinite articles adds to the difficulty. The proximity of previous reference to the lectures governs the ease of solution, which requires a lateral approach.

(18) Dictionary words. These are words that are rarely used but have time-honoured places in the dictionary. Thus *spasmophilie*, 'spasmophilia', and 'haemoscope'. A good dictionary refers the reader to more commonly used classifiers or generic words such as 'proneness to spasms' and 'haematoscope'.

Example

> *Dans la réponse inflammatoire, les molécules comprennent en particulier l'histamine, le sérotonine, le système du complexe, groupe complexe de neuf protéines.*

> In the inflammatory response, the chemical substances consist in particular of histamine, serotonin and the complement system, a complex group of nine proteins.

The clumsy repetition of 'complex' suggests that its first mention may be a misprint. It may, however, be mistakenly used by the writer or form part of a local research group's jargon.

Search procedure

In his search for the unfindable word the translator will try at some time or other to consult the SL text writer and, failing that, appropriate technical experts or source language informants who may well disagree with each other. For the purpose of this chapter, I am assuming that this step cannot be taken because the writer is dead or inaccessible, the experts and the informants are unavailable or do not know the answers, or, more likely, there is not sufficient time available. I now attempt to take the reader through a translator's search, often assuming that English is the source language.

Bilingual general and specialised dictionaries may be consulted first; whether or not they produce answers or clues, they must be followed up with careful checks and cross-checks in SL and TL monolingual dictionaries to determine cognitive and pragmatic equivalence as well as the currency of the TL word cited. It may be a 'dictionary' word (or phrase) – i.e. existing only in dictionaries, particularly if the dictionary is written by SL writers. For English, this hunt covers: (1) *Webster's Third New International Dictionary*, the most up-to-date and comprehensive English-language dictionary available which will 'sweep up' many technical terms, new collocations, acronyms, collocations, colloquialisms and foreign words (e.g. *Luftmensch*, Yiddish (not German) for 'dreamer' in the sense of 'Johnny head in air'); (2) the *Oxford English Dictionary* for archaisms and dialect words (cf. *Littré* for French) and its Supplements (ed. R. W. Burchfield), A–G (1972), H–N (1976), O–Sc (1982); (3) the Micropaedia of the *Encyclopaedia Britannica* for proper names, concepts and technical terms; (4) *The Times Atlas of the World* and the *Columbia Lippincott Gazetteer of the World* for geographical terms in various languages; (5) *Collins English Dictionary* for current British English colloquialisms and slang.

Secondly, the translator has to consider the possibility of a misprint, mis-spelling or variant spelling: 'ch', 'c' and 'k' (e.g. 'calli', 'kalli'); 'f', 'ph' and 'th'; 'oe' or 'ae' (and 'e') alternate between British and American English for words derived from classical Greek; 'y', 'u' and 'j' may alternate. Misprints may create mis-leadingly plausible neologisms: 'astrolobe' or 'astropode' for 'astrolabe'; *Kern* may be a 'convincing' misprint for *Keim*. An apparently English word, 'autochemist', may be put into a French SL text as an equivalent of *auto-analyseur* when only 'auto-analyser' is usually acceptable: this provides a further reminder that the translator can take no word for granted, certainly not the existence of a word in his own language, because it appears in an SL text, unless he is already acquainted with it. The translator must be prepared to engage in the lateral thinking and Cloze test techniques (filling in missing letters) which the problem of misprints and mis-spellings presents.

Consider the problem of *Elle avait un uvéakolobrom congénital*. The 'uvea' is clear, but the *kolobrom* has an improbable non-medical suffix. 'If k doesn't work, try c' is a translator's hint, and this produces 'a congenital coloboma of the uvea' (i.e. a fissure of the iris).

The largest number of neologisms are technical terms made up of mor-phemes based on classical Greek and Latin, the meaning of which are listed (as are acronyms) in the body of modern dictionaries. The composites are usually not difficult to elucidate (e.g. 'ambisonics': stereophonic sound coming from all parts of a room). Neologisms are usually created by analogy (e.g. 'terrisphone' or 'endorphine'). Unfortunately there is no English (or German) equivalent to the French periodical *La Banque des Mots* or the *Dictionnaire des Mots Contemporains* (a revised edition of the *Dictionnaire des Mots Nouveaux*) that attempts to keep up with neologisms; the Council of Europe's *Le Petit Termophile* (edited by Martin Weston) and *Verbatim* are the nearest equivalents. The most elusive unfindable words are often one-syllable slang words which may be abbreviations, figurative or onomatopoeic (e.g., 'zonked') but these indications are only clues and require further search.

A general awareness of historical sound-shifts is valuable in tracking the meaning of slang words, even if in doing so the translator invents his own folk etymologies: thus 'lizzers' (social parasites) (g and y).

Unfindable Romance words (e.g. Italian *nictemerale*) should be pursued in modern French dictionaries (*Robert, Lexis, Quilllet-Flammarion, Larousse*) after allowance has been made for changed spelling (*nycthéméral*) – or in *Webster* ('nychthemeral' or 'nycthemeral'). Again, 'panchronic' (in a translation of Saussure's *Cours*) is *panchronique* in *Lexis*.

Lexicographers are only slowly taking into account that French dictionaries must give appropriate value to metropolitan, Canadian, Swiss and Walloon words (note for instance that the Canadianism *crapet* is denotatively 'a fresh water fish' or 'a type of axe', connotatively a 'brat' (cf. *crapaud*); German to FRG, GDR, Austrian and Swiss words (legal terminology is a common source of differences in all states). Cassells was claiming in 1959 that its *Spanish Dictionary* was the first to give the Spanish of Latin America its due place. Arguably, English dictionaries should include more Welsh words (e.g., *fawr*; *Plaid Cymru*); neither *Intershop* nor *Exquisit* (GDR German) are explained in many English or West German reference books on German (*Collins: Intershop*: 'International shop'!).

New compound nouns are particularly prolific in the more recent technologies, and meanings often have to be surmised from their components.

Blends appear in technology for fusing two nouns ('biostatics', 'biostatistics'); frequently they are internationalisms, but others ('stagflation', 'ecocide') may have to be separated out in translation.

Many local dialect (*patois*) words are only now being recorded at a time when they are disappearing, some at the same time as their relevant trades and industries. For English words, *The Language of British Industry* by Peter Wright should be consulted.

A translator should be able to surmise the new sense of many existing words by taking into account the force of analogy, which is both social (conforming) and psychological (association of images). Thus 'thankfully', based on 'hopefully', 'mercifully', etc. is 'fortunately' with sometimes a religious connotation ('thanks be to God'), cf. 'sadly'; 'sophisticated' moves from inanimate ('advanced') to animate to become 'skilled, subtle, resourceful'.

Ephemeral neologisms are a translator's nightmare. In order to extract meaning from the Tory 'wets' of today, it may be necessary 50 years hence to look up the newspaper files to establish that 'wets', meaning 'feeble, foolish, not conforming to type', was used to denote Tory MPs opposing Mrs Thatcher's monetarist policy.

Old words with new senses can often only be detected if the translator is humble enough to check almost every word in his text, since the word or collocation (e.g. 'polytechnic', 'intercity', 'playgroup', 'morphology', 'juggernaut', 'with

it', 'coffee-table book', 'militant', 'activist', 'high-speed train', 'meaningful') may
make perfectly good contextual sense in its old or a slightly figurative as well as its
new sense. New 'institutional' senses of words (e.g. 'listed building') normally have
to be elicited or verified from official sources. New 'linguistic' senses are best
obtained from informants versed in the media and the 'trendy' movements, particularly youth cultures.

Acronyms consisting of the first letters of institutional terms are more prolific
than abbreviations (which are stable), blends (mainly confined to economics and
electronics?) and the first-syllable acronyms which started the craze after the
Russian Revolution (*univermag, sovkom*, etc.). Acronyms are frequently created *ad
hoc* for the purpose of the article in which they appear or for the school of a
particular discipline (FSP, CD, TME) and a translator can therefore waste time
looking for them. Whilst there are an increasing number of general and specialised
(e.g. medical) dictionaries of acronyms, the tendency of standard dictionaries to
put acronyms, as well as abbreviations and proper names (biographical, geographical, Christian), into the body of the book rather than in separate appendices is
encouraging.

Colloquialisms are the most rapidly changing, recurrent and ephemeral form
of neologism, particularly at present with the large-scale influx of formerly taboo
words. How is the translator to guess that, say in a short story, 'Sod the British
Council' may mean 'I'm not going to the British Council as I've got something
better to do'? All the translation theorist can do is to warn.

I define eponyms (idiosyncratically – 'antonomasia' is the orthodox term) as
any word formed from a proper name. Such words, always common in French
(e.g., *Carlopolitain, Giralducien, Giscardisme, limoger*), have more recently pullu-
lated in English (e.g., 'Bennites', 'Thatcherism', 'Hallidayan', 'Audenesque',
'Orwellian', 'Laurentian', 'Leavisite', 'Shavian', 'Parsonian', 'Gramscian'). These
eponyms are not usually transferred to a TL, and are therefore reduced to their
sense (e.g. 'Bennites': 'Supporters of the left-wing Labour MP Tony Benn'). Note
that 'Shavian' may mean 'relating to Shaw', 'like Shaw', 'representing Shaw's
philosophy', 'witty', 'impish', 'ironical'.

Brand names are notoriously turned into eponyms by the people's voice and
clever advertisers, who soon spell them with small letters. In some contexts, a
translator may have to guess a brand name because no linguistic term is current
('sellotape'. 'Tesa', 'bic', 'biro', etc.). How to translate 'She swathed her legs in
Tubigrips'? 'Tube-shaped bandages' is a poor substitute. A brand name is normally
transferred in translation, but there may be a case for adding or replacing it with its
TL equivalent if it exists, particularly in reference to drugs.

SL familiar alternate words (e.g. 'Dizzy', 'Rab', 'the Maid of Orleans', 'the
Sherardian Professor', 'the Gunners') are difficult to locate in standard reference
books. Familiar alternative terms may be linguistic or referential synonyms,
nicknames, former names, abbreviations, colloquialisms, used as informal alternatives to the correct or official name for the referent; in this usage, they have no
other connotations. For example, in the present climate of opinion. 'Salisbury'

could not be regarded as a familiar or informal alternative to 'Harare', but 'Russian' is normally a familiar alternative to 'Soviet'. A translator may not only find it difficult to 'place' a familiar alternative word (since reference books prefer to use 'correct' terms) but also to determine whether it is being used as such rather than with another connotation, which may be literal (e.g. 'a Gaul') or loaded (e.g. 'Königsberg').

Private language or underlife can be detected by obsessive repetitions, way-out or intimate quotations and illustrations, and so on. (I once read a translation theory article in *Fremdsprachen* where all examples appeared to be rather anti-Soviet – I need hardly say it was unique.) Private language sometimes can hardly be distinguished from non-private neologisms – who knows whether Auden's 'dowly days' (contrasted with 'good days') is underlife, or Middle English, or dialect ('dull') or private language? Being in an 'expressive' text, it could be translated by a neologism with a sense connotation based on the form of the words and its context, i.e., *douloureux*. In an informative text, such a word would be regarded as aberrant and normalised in the translation.

In principle, a translator has to find out the reference of any proper name as of any 'dictionary' word, even though he may not make use of his knowledge in his version. *Payton's Proper Names*, *Keesing's Contemporary Archives* and the *Fontana Dictionary of Modern Thought* are invaluable for proper names (as well as for many familiar alternatives). German appears to be unique in making extra difficulties for the translator by capitalising all its nouns as though they were brand drugs. Thus in an extract from the Four-Power Treaty over West Berlin, a reference to *Steinstücken* might have been confused with 'cutting up stones' and could be located as a small West Berlin enclave within East Berlin only by referring to a supplement of the *Großes Brockhaus* encyclopaedia.

The division between 'words' and proper names may be difficult to detect; *le Chêne Vert* may be a farm or a small hamlet or a tree: 'a Smith' may be a member of the Smith family or a person resembling Smith; the tendency to form adjectives or qualities (-ism, -*isme*) from proper names is spreading rapidly from French to English.

Common words with specific SL cultural senses may be generally well known, even notorious (e.g., *sympa*, *mañana*, *domani*, *nichevo*, *molodets*, *moshno*, etc.); they may be confined to a particular topic (e.g., 'peace', 'faith', 'hope', etc. in religious writing); they may also be 'unfindable' if their pragmatic meanings are not easily defined (GDR: *Kollektiv*, *Aktivist*, *parteilich*, *Abgrenzung*, *Diversant*).

Translators have to be particularly wary of: (a) *faux amis*, viz. SL or third-language words that are now TL words which have a different primary or secondary sense in the TL (e.g. *amateur*, 'dilettante'); (b) *amis loyaux*, which have the same sense in TL as in SL; (c) TL words in the SL text which now have a different meaning in the SL – these are more common in French than in German.

Dialect words (regional and class) can often be confused with neologisms and colloquialisms, including swear words, and they may merge with occupational jargon. They may not be 'distinguished' by inverted commas. In English, they are often monosyllables and appear as slight deformations of standard words or as figurative language. English dialect words may be tracked in the *OED*, Wright's vast *English Dialect Dictionary* (1898–1905) and Eric Partridge's *Dictionary of Slang and Unconventional English*. The translation of isolated dialect words depends both on the cognitive and pragmatic purposes for which they were used.

Immigrants are developing new varieties of British English, in particular Pakistani and Jamaican English (see F. G. Cassidy and R. B. Le Page's *Dictionary of Jamaican English*).

Unfamiliar connotations and symbolic meanings of words or proper names in a SL text may be universal (birth, sex, death, food, shelter), cultural or personal to the SL writer. When not covered by a modern dictionary such as *Collins* (1978), they may be found in the *Dictionary of Subjects and Symbols in Art* by James Hall (Murray), J. C. Cooper's *Illustrated Encyclopaedia of Traditional Symbols* (Thames and Hudson) or J. E. Cirlot's *Dictionary of Symbols*, E. Lehner's works or *Man and his Symbols* and other works influenced by C. G. Jung. Universal and personal symbols can usually be translated 'straight', but cultural symbols should usually be interpreted as well as translated.

Translation procedure

Whether a third-language or TL word introduced into the SL text is transferred or translated depends on whether it is used for 'expressive' or 'informative' purposes – respectively! A TL word, if appropriately used, would normally be 'returned'.

If the 'unfindable' word is established as a misprint, misspelling, misuse of words, rare spelling, etc., the deviation is normally ignored and the correct word is translated.

If the 'unfindable' word is found as a little-known proper name – a person or a geographical feature – it is normally transferred (or transliterated) with the addition of some generic information (e.g., 'Kocerga, a small town in the Irkutsk region, USSR'; the river Egiyn, in the Lake Baikal region'; 'Snoilsky, a nineteenth-century Swedish poet').

If the word is verified as a neologism, the translator has the choice of various procedures (transference, new coinage, literal translation, general or cultural equivalent, label) depending on various considerations (importance of referent, type of text, nature of readership) – all of which I have previously discussed in Chapter 13 above; see also my *Approaches to Translation* (1981).

When the name of a new or unimportant institution is identified, it is either transferred with a statement of its function and status, or replaced by a generic name, such as 'body', 'committee', 'company', etc., with a statement of its function.

An old 'linguistic' word used in a new sense (e.g., 'jogging', 'kicks) may require componential analysis before translation and therefore may be translated by two or more words. An old 'institutional' word used in a new sense (e.g. *Fachhochschule*, *IUT*, 'polytechnic') may be given an approximate cultural equivalent (as above) or, for a more technical text, be transferred, accompanied by a brief functional definition. (A functional definition explains the purpose of the referent, a descriptive definition states its size, colour, composition.)

The translator can never 'abandon' an unfindable word, must never assume, because it appears to be nonsensical (a non-existent word, or an existing word clearly out of place), that nothing was intended, that it can be ignored. On the contrary, he must finally make some kind of guess at the word he cannot find, some compromise between the most likely contextual meaning of the word (again, a kind of Cloze test technique) and the meaning suggested by the morphology or form of the word, if such exists. Needless to say, he has to append a note stating 'Not found', and giving his reasons for his interpretation of the unfindable word, showing the extremes of the most likely contextual gap and the apparent extra-contextual meaning of the word build up by its component morphemes. If he suspects that a word has been misread by the typist ('miscopied'), he must say so in a note.

In locating and interpreting 'unfindable' words, the translator requires common sense even more than resourcefulness, imagination and 'good connections'. The chase for words, and the sudden relief or satisfaction when the word is found, are amongst the greater attractions of the job.

CHAPTER **17**

Translation Criticism

INTRODUCTION

Translation criticism is an essential link between translation theory and its practice; it is also an enjoyable and instructive exercise, particularly if you are criticising someone else's translation or, even better, two or more translations of the same text. (See Part II, especially Texts 10–13.) You soon become aware not only of the large 'taste area', but that a text may be differently translated, depending on the preferred method of the translator. For example:

> *Cette rue, cette place ressemblent à la rue, à la place d'alors: elles ne sont pas les mêmes, et, les autres, je puis avoir l'impression qu'elles existent encore.*
> (Jacques Borel, *L'Adoration*)

translated by N. Denny as

> Those places look as they did then, but they are not the same; and as for the others, I have the feeling that they still exist.

The point here is not how good this is as a translation or why it was not more closely translated, perhaps into: 'This street, this square are like the street, the square of those times; they are not the same, and as for those others, I may feel that they still exist . . .', but why Mr Denny wanted to make an emotional, dramatic utterance into a calm, natural statement. Thus there are various aspects of translation criticism: you can assess the translation by its standard of referential and pragmatic accuracy, but if this is inappropriate and rather futile, because there is so much to 'correct', you can consider why the translator has apparently transposed or changed the mood so drastically; whether any translator has the right to change *en même temps immobile et comme entré . . . dans une espèce d'éternité* to 'unchanging and fixed in a sort of eternity'. How far is a translator entitled to get away from the words, to devote himself to the message, the sense, the spirit?

I think there are absolute values of accuracy and economy as well as relative values but these absolute values (like translation) must be continually reconsidered and rediscussed in various cultural contexts; they cannot be taken for granted. (This resembles the argument for God.) Up to now, translation has mainly followed the prevailing and sometimes the countervailing ideology of the time: thus classicism (balance, noble expression, Pope), romanticism (richness of folk language, local colour, Tieck, Schlegel), art for art's sake (re-creation, Dowson), scientific realism (transference, James Strachey) all to some extent find their reflection (*Niederschlag*) in translation. The challenge in translation criticism is to state your own principles categorically, but at the same time to elucidate the translator's principles, and even the principles he is reacting against (or following). In this sense, good translation criticism is historical, dialectical, Marxist. In proposing my own two translation methods, 'semantic' and 'communicative', I tend to think of the first as absolute, the second as relative, but I am (pathetically) aware that both methods are to some extent reactions to or against Nida, Nabokov, Rieu and others. Nevertheless I think there is a new element in translation now, as it becomes a profession. The introduction of a 'scientific' method, the testing of any hypothesis or generalisation (itself arising from translation examples) by a series of further data or translation examples, tends not to eliminate but at least to reduce the range of choices, the extremes of ideology in translation. At the grossest level, the evidence of the 'group loyalty factor' so brilliantly detected by Ivars Alksnis in several numbers of *Parallèles* (Geneva), showing the variations of nationalist and sex prejudice in a large number of published translations of novels, would, if it were widely disseminated, make the extremes of ideology, political and even literary, more difficult. Nida's 1964 title to this fine book *Towards a Science of Translating* was prophetic: translation (and translating) is not and never will be a science, but as the discipline that treats (*behandelt*) it advances, translation's scientific frame of reference will be more generally acknowledged.

Translation criticism is an essential component in a translation course: firstly, because it painlessly improves your competence as a translator; secondly, because it expands your knowledge and understanding of your own and the foreign language, as well as perhaps of the topic; thirdly, because, in presenting you with options, it will help you to sort out your ideas about translation. As an academic discipline, translation criticism ought to be the keystone of any course in comparative literature, or literature in translation, and a component of any professional translation course with the appropriate text-types (e.g., legal, engineering etc.) as an exercise for criticism and discussion.

A translation may be evaluated by various authorities (*Instanzen*): (a) the reviser employed by the firm or the translation company; (b) the head of section or of the company (this may be described as 'Quality Control', if translations are sampled; the term is at present being overused and broadened); (c) the client; (d) the professional critic of a translation or the teacher marking one; and (e) finally by the readership of the published work. Ironically, as Nabokov pointed out, many reviewers of translated books neither know the original work nor the foreign language, and judge a translation on its smoothness, naturalness, easy flow, readability and absence of interference, which are often false standards. Why should a translation not sometimes read like one, when the reader knows that is what it is? Here, however, I am assuming that the evaluation, whether in the form of a critique or a graded assessment, is done by way of a comparison between the original and the translation. What is required at the present time is a reconsideration of many of the translations that have most influenced indigenous cultures, of the kind that has been signally performed by Bruno Bettelheim in his criticism of the authorised English version of Freud's work.

PLAN OF CRITICISM

I think any comprehensive criticism of a translation has to cover five topics: (1) a brief analysis of the SL text stressing its intention and its functional aspects; (2) the translator's interpretation of the SL text's purpose, his translation method and the translation's likely readership; (3) a selective but representative detailed comparison of the translation with the original; (4) an evaluation of the translation – (a) in the translator's terms, (b) in the critic's terms; (5) where appropriate, an assessment of the likely place of the translation in the target language culture or discipline.

TEXT ANALYSIS

In your analysis of the SL text, you may include a statement of the author's purpose, that is, the attitude he takes towards the topic; characterisation of the readership; an indication of its category and type. You assess the quality of the language to determine the translator's degree of licence, assuming for example that he can reduce cliché to natural language in informative but not in authoritative texts. You briefly state the topic or themes, but do not précis the text and do not 'plot-monger' (painfully retell the plot).

I suggest you do not discuss the author's life, other works, or general background, *unless* they are referred to in the text – they may help you to understand the text, but they are not likely to affect how you appreciate or assess the translation.

THE TRANSLATOR'S PURPOSE

The second topic, your attempt to see the text from the point of view of this translator, is sometimes overlooked in translation criticism. You may decide that the translator has misinterpreted the author by omitting certain sections of the text – notoriously, the first English translation of Hitler's *Mein Kampf* by Captain E. S. Dugdale contained only about a third of the original, and omitted the most virulent anti-semitic passages. The translator may have decided to deliberately antiquate the narrative and/or the dialogue of his version, e.g., *allora tornò* – 'Eftsoons he turned', to moderate the figurative language of the original or to 'liven up' simple sentences with colloquial and idiomatic phrases: *se tremper hâtivement dans les eaux baptismales européennes à Strasbourg* – 'they are hastily initiated into the work of the Assembly at Strasbourg'. Normally all translations are under-translations, less particularised than the original, notably in its descriptive passages (*elle est bien laide* – 'she is as ugly as sin') rather than its dramatic, and in its mental rather than its physical passages; you have to establish whether the translator has attempted to counteract by over-translating, resulting usually in a text somewhat longer than the original: *Il était bien charpenté* – 'He was well built'. You have to assess to what extent the text has been deculturalised, or transferred to the TL culture: *Jeu ou gentillesse, Luque avait été entreprenant dans la voiture* – 'Whether to be friendly or by design, Luque had not been idle in the car.' In interpreting the translator's intention and procedures, you are here not criticising them but attempting to understand why he has used these procedures. It is all too easy for a reviewer to pounce on a translation's howlers, listing them one after another, triumphantly discovering *faux amis*, wayward and stretched synonyms ('wistful' translated as *triste* or *nachdenklich*), stiff and old-fashioned structures, which, in some situations, may be perfectly natural ('Thus, by the hand of God and man, has the city emerged largely unblemished' – official guide to York)*, anachronistic colloquialisms, literal translations of stock metaphors, and to ignore the fact that translators are vulnerable, that good translations can and do tolerate a number of errors, and that translators who translate in a stiff, old-fashioned, colloquial or racy style that does not square with the original may be doing so deliberately, however misguidedly. If so, it is your job as critic to suggest the reasons. (In a better world, these would be given in the translator's preface.) In any event, here you empathise with the translator, and you distinguish between incompetence (inadequate knowledge of SL and/or topic) and a translation method which may be too idiomatic or too academic for your own tastes but which appears consistent.

COMPARING THE TRANSLATION WITH THE ORIGINAL

Thirdly, you consider how the translator has solved the particular problems of the SL text. You do not take the points successively; you group them selectively under general heads: the title; the structure, including the paragraphing and sentence connectives; shifts; metaphors; cultural words; translationese; proper names; neologisms; 'untranslatable' words; ambiguity; level of language; and, where relevant, meta-language, puns, sound-effect.

This third section of your critique should consist of a discussion of trans-

---

*Note the French translation: *Ainsi, grâce à la nature* [sic] *et aux hommes, la ville est parvenue au 20ᵉ siècle en grande partie intacte*. The translator's ideological interference is perhaps rather more convincing than the English original.

lation problems and not quick recipes for a 'correct' or a better translation. Why, for instance, did the translator within the context prefer 'less intensely' to 'less acutely' or 'with less intensity' for *vivre avec moins d'acuité*? Why did he prefer 'uncharted territory' to *'terra ignota'* for *terra ignota*? (Latin tags more familar to French than to English educated readers?) Why was 'drastic statement' preferred to 'severe judgment' for *jugement sévère*? (It can be justified on the ground that French has no obvious one-to-one translations for 'drastic' or 'statement', and therefore the translator was merely exploiting French lexical gaps; further, *jugement* has a wider semantic range than 'judgment', which would be rather heavy in this context.)

This third section is the heart of the critique; normally it has to be selective since, in principle, any passage that diverges from literal translation in grammar, lexis or 'marked' word order (as well as any deliberate sound-effect) constitutes a problem, offers choices, requires you to justify your preferred solution. Why was *Un historien contemporain écrivait, il y a quelques années, que . . .* changed to 'Some years ago it was remarked by a contemporary historian that . . .' instead of 'A contemporary historian stated, a few years ago, that . . .'? Clearly 'Some years ago' is a more natural, less marked, word order when placed at the head of the sentence rather than in parenthesis, but there seems no good reason for passivising the sentence and replacing *écrivait* with 'remarked'.

THE EVALUATION OF THE TRANSLATION

Fourthly, you assess the referential and pragmatic accuracy of the translation by the tranlator's standards. If the translation is not a clear version of the original, you consider first whether the essential 'invariant' element of the text which consists usually (not always) of its facts or its ideas is adequately represented. However, if the purpose of the text is to sell something, to persuade, to prohibit, to express feeling through the facts and the ideas, to please or to instruct, then this purpose is the keystone of the invariance, which changes from text to text; and this is why any general theory of translation invariance is futile, and I am at least a little sceptical about making a rule of Tytler's 'the complete transcript of the ideas of the original work precedes style and manner of writing' or Nida's 'form is secondary to content' (though I accept that form in translation must be changed to accommodate meaning) given that the keystone of invariance may be expressed as much through words of quality (adjectives, concept-words, and degree) as through words of object and action.

After considering whether the translation is successful in its own terms, you evaluate it by your own standards of referential and pragmatic accuracy. You have to avoid criticising the translator for ignoring translation principles that were not established nor even imagined when he was translating. The main question here is the quality and extent of the semantic deficit in the translation, and whether it is inevitable or due to the translator's deficiencies. Further, you assess the translation also as a piece of writing, independently of its original: if this is an 'anonymous' non-individual text, informative or persuasive, you expect it to be written in a natural manner – neat, elegant and agreeable. If the text is personal and authoritative, you have to assess how well the translator has captured the idiolect of the original, no matter whether it is clichéd, natural or innovative.

THE TRANSLATION'S FUTURE

Finally, in the case of a serious text, say a novel, a poem, or an important book, you assess the work's potential importance within the target language culture. Was it in fact worth translating? What kind of influence will it have on the language, the literature, the ideas in its new milieu? These questions should, in my opinion, be answered in the translator's preface, but the tradition of the translator's anonymity dies hard. This is the translation critic's attempt to 'place' the translation in its unfamiliar surroundings.

MARKING A TRANSLATION

I close this chapter with some observations about the difficulties of assessing a translated text. The above scheme has illustrated two possible approaches, the functional and the analytical. The functional is a general approach, the attempt to assess whether the translator has achieved what he attempted to do and where he fell short. This response is in terms of ideas. Details tend to get missed out. To some extent this is a subjective approach, the equivalent, in the case of a teacher grading a script, of 'impression marking', and therefore unreliable.

The analytical approach is detailed. As I see it, it rests on the assumption that a text can be assessed in sections and that just as a bad translation is easier to recognise than a good one, so a mistake is easier to identify than a correct or a felicitous answer. I assume that all translation is partly science, partly craft, partly art, partly a matter of taste. Firstly, science. 'Science' here is a matter of wrong rather than right, and there are two types of 'scientific' mistakes, referential or linguistic. Referential mistakes are about facts, the real world, propositions not words. Statements like 'water is air', 'water is black', 'water breathes', etc. are referential mistakes (though as metaphors they may be profoundly true). Referential mistakes exist in 'fiction' (i.e., creative literature) only when it incorrectly depicts the real world now or in history. They reveal the ignorance of the translator, or worse, of the writer, which the translator has 'copied'. Linguistic mistakes show the translator's ignorance of the foreign language: they may be grammatical or lexical, including words, collocations or idioms.

Referential and linguistic mistakes are marked (or regarded) negatively – a figure deducted from a total for a sentence or a paragraph, or as part of a total deficit. In the real world, referential errors are both more important and potentially more dangerous than linguistic errors, although both in the educational system (many teachers) and amongst laymen they are often ignored or excused – 'after all, that's what the original says, the translator's job is to reproduce it faithfully'. This is misguided. A Dutch translator once told me he was paid three times his normal rate for a translation he never did – he simply pointed out to his client that the (financial) text was full of dangerous errors.

Secondly, translation is a craft or skill. The skill element is the ability to follow or deviate from the appropriate natural usage: pragmatic and persuasive in vocative texts, neat in informative texts, hugging the style of the original in expressive and authoritative texts – you have to distinguish 'right' from odd usage, to gauge degrees of acceptability within a context. You can say 'at present the railways are working on improving their computer links', and whilst you will never get that precise nuance of informality and continuous effort of 'working on' in another language, you will get a servicable equivalent, 'trying to improve'. However, mistakes of usage would be easily identified in a sentence such as 'contemporarily/for the nonce the railroads are operating/functioning/labouring on bettering/beautifying/embellishing their computer liaisons/relations.' These are mistakes of usage, due firstly to an inability to write well, secondly perhaps to misuse of dictionary, thirdly to disregard of *faux amis* (deceptive cognates), fourthly to persistent seeking of one-to-one equivalents; fifthly and mainly to lack of common sense. Where translationese is written by a native SL translator no one is surprised; where it is written by a native TL translator it sounds absurd but is just as common and is due to carelessness coupled with mesmerisation with SL words at the textual level. The idea that translators, particularly of non-literary texts (informative texts), have to write well is far from generally accepted – many believe that, where facts are concerned, style takes second place. But the truth is, it is the style that ensures that the facts are effectively presented – bear in mind, when I think of style, I am not thinking of 'beauty', I am thinking of the fight against expressions like the trade unionist's 'at the end of the day' and the jargon-monger's 'intentionality', 'translationality' and 'integrality'. There is a certain 'plainness' (a unique, 'untranslatable' word with an exceptionally wide semantic span: 'honest, direct, smooth, simple, clear unadorned') about good usage which makes it difficult to regard it as a 'plus' in translation. Whilst mistakes of truth and language are graver than mistakes of usage, it is skilled usage that ensures successful transmission.

Thus far I have described negative factors in assessing translation. The third area, translation as an art, is a positive factor. It is the 'contextual re-creation' described by Jean Delisle, where, for the purpose of interpretation, the translator has to go beyond the text to the sub-text; i.e., what the writer means rather than what he says, or where, for purposes of explanation, he produces an economical exposition of a stretch of language. When *fidélité aux différents bilans* translates neatly as 'adherence to the various schedules'; when *Entgleisung*, used figuratively, becomes 'complication'; when, in a text on electrocardiograms, *Artefakt* is rightly translated by the technical term 'artefact', i.e. an electrocardiogram wave that arises from sources other than that of the heart, e.g., a mechanical defect; when a translator brings out an inference or an implication a little more clearly than in the SL text (say the literal as well as the figurative significance of a metaphor); when *participation* has to be translated as the 'involvement' of the endocrine system to indicate a verb-noun's or a gerund's missing case-partner (or 'referring consultant' is *le médecin-consultant adressant les sujets à la clinique*); when a cultural word is neatly explained ('he enjoyed the bananas and meat in his tapadas snack'); when a sound-effect or a colloquialism in one part of a clause is compensated in another (*pipe mise dans son nez*, 'pipe stuck in his mouth (or gob)') – these can be described as creative translation, a find, a happy or elegant solution. Creative translation usually has the following features: (a) a 'surface' translation is not possible; (b) there are a variety of solutions, and ten good translators will produce this variety; (c) the translation is what the writer meant rather than what he wrote. The solution closest to the original is the best pragmatically, has to be weighed against referential accuracy, and there is no clearly superior version.

If a book on A. von Humboldt starts: *Alexander von Humboldt – ja, warum denn?*, a coarse translation would suggest 'Why write a book about Alexander von Humboldt of all people?' But since the style is more refined, one might try: 'It may appear strange to be writing a book about Alexander von Humboldt', or simply: 'Alexander von Humboldt . . . Yes, but why?' The first version is referentially, the second pragmatically closer. The third is brief and closest. This is creative translation.

The fourth area of translation, that of taste, has to be accepted as a subjective factor. This area stretches from preferences between lexical synonyms to sentences or paragraphs that under- and over-translate in different places, e.g., for *Sa compagne offrait l'image d'une figure admirablement harmonieuse* one has a choice between 'His companion's face presented a picture of admirable harmony' and 'His companion's face was a picture of admirable harmony.' Inevitably, the critic has to allow for his own taste for or bias towards either 'literal' or 'free' translation. The taste area, on the fuzzy perimeter of translation (with science at its centre), renders the concept of an ideal, perfect or correct translation a nonsense, and is itself an essential concept; the consequence is that a sensitive evaluation of a translation is cautious and undogmatic – usually!

You will notice that in my analytical approach to translation criticism, the negative factors of mistakes of truth, language and usage tend to outweigh the positive factors of creative translation, the felicitous renderings that make a translation not only accurate but effective, whether we are discussing an advertisement, or a short story. However, accuracy can also be assessed positively, with marks given for accurate renderings of sentences or paragraphs, and deducted for mistakes; this is called 'positive marking' and is becoming more favoured by examination boards. Being the reverse of negative marking, it often achieves the same result. The paradox is that items of 'creative translation' are likely to receive less credit in positive than in negative marking; since a competent translation of a sentence gets the maximum mark, nothing is left for a 'happy' translation.

QUALITY IN TRANSLATION

The question remains: What is a good translation? What fails? (And what is a bad translator *sans emploi*, as the great Louis Jouvet phrased it inimitably in *Quai des Brumes*?) What is a distinguished translation? 'Often we cannot agree what a particular translation should be like. But can one teach what one does not know?' (Neubert, 1984, p. 69). Rhetorical questions such as: would you employ this man to do your translations? are useful only because they produce an immediate instinctive reaction.

Ultimately standards are relative, however much one tries to base them on criteria rather than norms. A good translation fulfils its intention; in an informative text, it conveys the facts acceptably; in a vocative text, its success is measurable, at least in theory, and therefore the effectiveness of an advertising agency translator can be shown by results; in an authoritative or an expressive text, form is almost as important as content, there is often a tension between the expressive and the aesthetic functions of language and therefore a merely 'adequate' translation may be useful to explain what the text is about (cf. many Penguin Plain Prose translations), but a good translation has to be 'distinguished' and the translator exceptionally sensitive; for me, the exemplar is Andreas Mayor's translation of Proust's *Le Temps retrouvé* – '*Time Regained*'.

In principle, it should be easier to assess a translation than an original text, since it is an imitation. The difficulty lies not so much in knowing or recognising what a good translation is, as in generalising with trite definitions that are little short of truisms, since there are as many types of translations as there are of texts. But the fact that there is a small element of uncertainty and subjectivity in any judgment about a translation eliminates neither the necessity nor the usefulness of translation criticism, as an aid for raising translation standards and for reaching more agreement about the nature of translation.

CHAPTER **18**

Shorter Items

WORDS AND CONTEXT

Many translators say you should never translate words, you translate sentences or ideas or messages. I think they are deceiving themselves. The SL text consists of words, that is all that is there, on the page. Finally all you have is words to translate, and you have to account for each of them somewhere in your TL text, sometimes by deliberately not translating them (e.g. sometimes words like *schon* and *déjà*), or by compensating for them, because if translated cold you inevitably over-translate them, e.g., *Ich bin schon lange fertig* – 'I have been ready for ages'; *1000 francs, c'est déjà mal* – '1000 francs, that's not bad at all'.

I am not suggesting you translate isolated words. You translate words that are more or less linguistically, referentially, culturally and subjectively influenced in their meaning, words conditioned by a certain linguistic, referential, cultural and personal context. The linguistic context may be limited to a collocation (90% of the time, it is no more than that): *un hiver blanc* – 'a white winter' (*blanc* has many other meanings); or it may be as large as a sentence in the case of an extended metaphor or a proverb. And occasionally, a word may be linguistically conditioned by its use beyond the sentence, when it is a concept-word variously repeated or modified or contrasted in other sentences or paragraphs, or again where it is used as a stylistic marker or leitmotif throughout the text.

Secondly, the referential context. This relates to the topic of the text. Often only the topic will nail the meaning of a thousand technical words such as *défilement* ('scrolling'), *stockage* ('storage'), *rechercher* ('search'), *fusionner* ('merge'), *appel* ('calling'), which happen to be related to electronic data processing. However, the number of such words even in an 'opaquely' technical text, i.e., one that is comprehensible only to the relevant expert, does not usually exceed 5–10%.

Thirdly, there is the cultural context, words related to ways of thinking and behaving within a particular language community, and words which may be cultural (e.g., *kuffiah*, an Arabic head-dress) or universal (e.g., 'tea') denoting a specific material cultural object.

Lastly, there is the individual context, the idiolect of the writer, the fact that we all use some words and collocations in a way peculiar to ourselves.

All words are more or less context-bound in their meanings. The least so are the technical words like 'haematology', which is normally 'context-free', unless it is a code-word. Such words bring their contexts with them.

Further most words for common objects and actions are hardly contextually bound if they are 'unmarked', e.g., 'tree', 'chair', 'table'. Only when they are 'marked', i.e., technically used, e.g., *arbre* ('shaft'), *métier* ('loom'), *chaîne* ('radio channel') can they be realistically described as context-bound.

A common mistake is to ignore context. A not uncommon mistake is to make context the excuse for inaccurate translation.

THE TRANSLATION OF DIALECT

It is normally accepted that the literary genres which in translation necessarily suffer varying degrees of loss of meaning are poetry, sonorous prose, texts with a large proportion of word-play or cultural content, and dialect. This does not mean that these genres are unsuitable for translation. Poetry in particular has been superbly and closely (or more freely) translated at various times, resulting in a brilliant fusion of the poet's and the poet–translator's language, and often demonstrating the translator's suggestive and tactful compensatory sound techniques:

> The expense of spirit in a waste of shame
> Is lust in action; and till action, lust
> Is perjured, murd'rous, bloody, full of blame,
> Savage, extreme, rude, cruel, not to trust.
> (Shakespeare, Sonnet 129)

> *Verbrauch von geist in schändlicher verzehr*
> *Ist lust in tat, und bis zur tat, ist lust*
> *Meineidig, mörderisch, blutig, voll unehr,*
> *Wild, tierisch, grausam, roh, des lugs bewusst.*
> (trans. Stefan George)

Some of the sound-effects of prose, advertisements, jingles can be captured or compensated, and puns can usually be partially replaced. In all these cases, the translator has to be aware, not that he is attempting the traditionally impossible – 'poetry is what gets lost in the translation' (R. Frost); even 'bread' and *pain* have completely different meanings (thus Robert Graves who, as Chukovski (1984) pointed out, mutilated Homer) – but that he can have only partial success, and that if he tries to reproduce or compensate for all the sound-effects of his original, he will be 'over-translating' with a vengeance and inevitably mangling the sense. Normally, he reproduces sound-effect here and there, in a minor key, suggestively, tactfully as indeed a small echo of the original since, in a serious poem, the main effect is created by its rhythms, its literal or figurative meaning, and its metre.

I now turn to the translation of dialect, not particularly because you will have to translate it, but because it is sometimes set up as the ultimate impossibility in translation, which it is not.

If dialect appears metalingually, i.e. as an example of language, you normally transfer it, translate it into neutral language, and clarify the reasons why it is cited.

However, when dialect appears in fiction or drama, the problem is different. In my opinion there is no need to replace a coalminer's dialect in Zola with, say, a Welsh coalminer's dialect, and this would only be appropriate, if you yourself were completely at home in Welsh dialect. As a translator, your main job is to decide on the functions of the dialect. Usually, this will be: (a) to show a slang use of language; (b) to stress social class contrasts; and more rarely (c) to indicate local cultural features. Given the decline of dialects in present-day British English, a translation into dialect runs the risk of being antiquated. For the English translator, the most important thing is the ability to use and possibly neologise phrasal verbs and nouns. On the stage, a working-class accent is quite enough to cover apparent distortions like: *Wenn ich bloß wißte, was du meenst* – 'Wish I know what you meant'; a shift to dialect 'tha meant' would not help. But take:

> *Die hat a erscht gar nich mehr in der Tasche, der Hungerleider, verdammte, dahier. In ganzen Kreese muß a sich rumpumpen. Nischte wie Schulden, wo man hinheert. Wie lange werd's dauern, da is a fertig da muß a selber naus aus dem Hause statts daß a andre Leute läßt nausschmeißen.*
> (Gerhard Hauptmann, *Fuhrmann Henschel*; Silesian dialect of the 1860s.)

Here a few dropped h's and missing agreements to suggest uneducated 'peasants' would be ineffective. The important thing is to produce naturally slangy, possibly classless speech in moderation, hinting at the dialect, 'processing' only a small proportion of the SL dialect words:

> He hasn't got a bean any more, the bastard, he's cleaned out, he's near starving. He's scrounging around all the time, you hear that anywhere you go. Don't ask me how long it's going to be before he's bloody skint. Then he'll have to clear out here, instead of chucking other people out.

This is no model, but I am trying to show that I have ignored the 'bad grammar' and 'mispronunciation' (faulty spelling) of the original; these linguistic features are irrelevant in a dialect, which is a self-contained variety of language not a deviation from standard language. The main dialect effect has to be left to the cast.

YOU AND THE COMPUTER

If you have anything to do with computers, it seems to me you are likely to be engaged on one or more of eight tasks:

(1) Pre-editing (Taum?).

(2) Feeding the computer's memory with the relevant lexical and grammatical data before translating.
(3) 'Pressing the buttons', i.e. operating the computer yourself while translating (ITT, ALPS).
(4) Post-editing (Systran, Weidner).
(5) Storing and using ('accessing') terminological data banks.
(6) Research on MT (machine translation).
(7) Outside the field of direct MT, managing terminology databases. Terminologists are in fact in the process of constituting a separate profession.
(8) General use of computers as word-processors (WPs) in editing, searching, replacing and so on, therefore as an aid to your normal 'manual' translation. Note that major employers of staff translators, such as the UN and the Canadian government, regard the ability to use WPs as an essential qualification for translators.

Therefore, if you are not a computer expert, do not get involved in a long spiel on the history of MT, CAT (computer-aided translation), AT (automatic translation), its technical evolution, its future. You know that the computer is useful for translation, in particular for LSPs (languages for special or specific purposes), that at present it can generally hand only 'informative' texts and administrative texts, and that its output needs some kind of editing. MT, like translation, is not only possible, it happens. There is no need for the one-upmanship of sporting the names of the latest models.

If you are working on Systran or Weidner, you will have to do a lot of post-editing; A.-M. Loffler Lorian (1985) offers several examples, e.g., French original: *Les travailleurs ont intérêt à ce que . . .*; computer translation: 'The workers had interest with . . .'; post-edited version: 'It was in the workers' interest that . . .'

Working on computer translations, you will have to get used to the idea of yourself producing two types of translation:

(1) 'Rapid information-translation' (*Rohübersetzung*), i.e., language that may be clumsy, not natural usage, with traces of translationese, but clear, fit for 'internal consumption' and economical compared with human translation.
(2) 'Publication translation', which risks being uneconomical as soon as you think you might just as well have done it all yourself.

Clearly, the more restricted the language and the greater the proportion of standard or technical terms, the more likelihood there is of MT being acceptable. In fact, an important difference between MT and human translation is that the MT user (as opposed to the translator), is likely to want only the information contained in the SL text, set out clearly, and not particularly stylishly, as gist, summary, abstract or 'raw translation'.

Pre-translation is desirable, if you know the lexical and grammatical content already in the computer's memory. Basically, your job is to 'disambiguate', to turn the text into plain English, to reduce metaphors to sense, to replace difficult words with those from the basic vocabulary of the text's LSP. Whether and how well you can do this depends on the time you take – remember MT is a strictly commercial operation in a sense that human translation will probably never be: if it is not cost-effective, if it does not save time and money, it should not be done at all. It was the enormous cost of translation now that 'reversed' ALPAC's famous decision of the '60s that MT had no future.

Pre-editing for an organisation that has had many years' experience in building up its own language-style, an extended version of its house-style, through its journal, minutes of meetings, agendas, reports is easier than a 'blind' approach to a text. Such phrases as 'The Council sees advantage in . . .', put into the store, may tactfully unify a variety of recommendations and directions.

In operating the computer you can be working on an independent or an interactive system (ALPS), where the computer asks you questions to which you feed back the answers.

I have no doubt that unless, as in Meteo (the Canadian weather forecasting system), the computer language consists mainly of standard phrases, the most interesting and important job in MT is post-editing, for which the correction of, say, tourist brochure translationese (or 'interlanguage' in a language-teaching class), which should be a feature of any translation theory course, is a valuable preparation. But usually, you are more likely to be working on a routine informative text written in a neutral style than one that addresses itself specifically to the readership (i.e., a 'vocative' text) or that describes a new process and includes new terms or original use of language.

The emergence of MT in the '50s was not unconnected with the behaviourist phase in linguistics. Improvement in MT will depend on linguistic research in particular language varieties, particularly in the frequency and currency of the various features: grammatical structures, idioms, collocations, metaphors and words; this activity itself requires as much use of computers as the parallel research into the improvement of interactive computer systems.

In general, you can accept MT as a particular translation mode. It has obvious advantages in a particular LSP text, and the 'ease with which words and clauses can be juggled around on the screen of a WP' (Robin Trew, personal communication*) but not on a typewriter or a sheet of paper (though this illustrates the importance of double spacing) is likely to encourage you to be more flexible and less mesmerised when you perform shifts or transpositions. One obvious disadvantage apparently endemic in the computer is the promotion of jargon, in both senses, multi-noun compounds, and unthinking language provoked by a quickly responsive machine that has to be fed in order to justify itself, rather than by the mind.

---

*I am grateful to Robin Trew for his comments on this section.

FUNCTION AND DESCRIPTION

Admitted that a definition of a word without a statement of its function is absurd (e.g., the *COD*'s definitions of 'soda' and 'metaphor'); admitted that, in many cases, particularly in translation, function precedes description – for the majority of people, it is more important to know what the House of Commons, the Arts Council, the GLC, the CNAA *do* than what they consist of, and this emphasis is likely to be reflected in any translation for this purpose – nevertheless a purely functional theory of translation is misguided. Catford's behaviouristic pronouncement that 'SL and TL texts or items are translation equivalents when they are interchangeable in a given situation' is seductive but wrong, since it licenses many kinds of synonymy, paraphrase and grammatical variation, all of which might do the job in a given situation, but would be inaccurate. Hönig and Kussmaul carry the functional theory of translation to its extreme, when they translate 'those double-barrelled names' as 'those proud names' (*jene stolzen Namen*) and 'his mother couldn't afford to send him to Eton any more' as 'his mother couldn't afford to send him to one of the expensive private schools any more' (*seine Mutter konnte es sich nicht mehr leisten, ihn auf eine der teueren Privatschulen zu schicken*). They are right in assuming that, for the TL reader, the functions of 'double-barrelled names' and of 'Eton' are more important than their descriptions in this context but both 'double-barrelled names' and 'Eton' are significant cultural facts and normally the TL reader should not be deprived of them.

Normally function is simpler, more concise, more forceful than substance, and it is tempting for the translator to substitute it for substance and he sometimes does so, but only as a last resort. Usually, a translation has both elements, if it is accurate, and even if description supplies only the small print. A saw is for cutting with but a description is essential to distinguish it from other tools with the same purpose. The neglect of function (purpose, intention, reason) in the past has already been shown by the evidence from dictionaries, but this is no reason for now ignoring substance. Function is wide and simple and lends itself particularly to communicative translation. Description refines function with detail, and characterises semantic translation. Where a compromise is necessary in the interests of economy, description usually has to give; but even the 'double-barrelled names' could become *die vornehmen zweiwörtigen (zweiteiligen) Zunamen* ('the fashionable two-worded (bipartite) surnames').

THE TRANSLATION OF EPONYMS AND ACRONYMS

Definition

I define an 'eponym' as any word that is identical with or derived from a proper name which gives it a related sense. This definition is operational, and does not tally with the definitions in the standard dictionaries, which differ surprisingly. The original eponym is 'academic', from the academy named after *Akademos*, where Plato taught; this is one of many eponyms where the proper name is no longer 'felt' and is virtually ignored in translation as it is in *limoger* ('dismiss') and in 'boycott' in many European languages. I propose to divide eponyms into three categories, those derived from persons, objects and places.

Persons

In the first category, eponyms denoting objects usually derive from their inventors or discoverers; in translation, the main difficulty is that they may have an alternative name (e.g., 'Humboldt Current' *or* 'Peru current'), the authenticity of the discoverer may be implicitly disputed ('Arnold's fold' – *valvule de Krause*; 'Desnos's disease' – *maladie de Grancher*), or more commonly, replaced by a technical term (*Röntgenographie* – 'radiography'; 'Hutchinson's angioma' – *angiome serpigineux*). In this category, there is a tendency for eponyms to be gradually replaced by descriptive terms ('Davy lamp' – *Grubensicherheitslampe* – *lampe de sécurité* (*de mineur*).

The biggest growth-point in eponyms in many European languages is the conversion of prominent persons' names to adjectives (-ist) and abstract nouns (-ism) denoting either allegiance to or influence of the person, or a conspicuous quality or idea associated with them. This has always been common for French statesmen and writers (not artists or composers) where phrases like *une préciosité giralducienne* ('like Giraudoux's') have a certain vogue. It extends now to statesmen whose name lends itself readily to suffixation – often the eponym declines with the personality's fame (e.g. 'Bennite'). Thus we have 'Thatcherism', 'Scargillism', 'Livingstonian' – Reagan has to make do with 'Reaganomics' (i.e., economic policy) – others are hampered by their names, e.g., Kinnock. Sometimes, mainly in French (*gaullien, gaulliste*), occasionally in English (Marxian, Marxist) a distinction is made between value-free and value-loaded eponyms through the suffixes -ian and -ist respectively (cf. Italian *marxiano, marxista*). Sometimes one eponym, say 'Shakespearean', 'Churchillian', has many potential meanings which can be reduced to one only by considering the collocation and the context.

The main problem in translating eponyms derived from persons is whether the transferred word will be understood; thus the noun or adjective 'Leavisite' is useful in English to summarise certain principles of literary criticism, but it would mean little in most TLs unless these were stated and, usually, related to F. R. Leavis. Such connotations (e.g., for 'Shavian'; wit, irony, social criticism) need recording. In other cases, e.g., Quisling, Casanova, Judas, where not much else is known of the character, the eponym has a single connotative meaning and is often transferred. In such cases, if the readership is unlikely to understand an eponym, footnotes are usually unnecessary, but you have to decide whether it is worth transferring the name as well as the sense, depending on its cultural interest and its likelihood of recurrence or permanence in the TL. In some cases, where the interest of the proper name is purely 'local' and probably temporary, only the contextual sense is translated; in others (Dante, Shakespeare, Goethe), the eponym is naturalised, though the connotation may differ somewhat between the source and the target language.

Objects

In the second category, that of objects, we are firstly discussing brand names which tend to 'monopolise' their referent first in the country of their origin, then internationally, e.g., 'aspirin', 'Formica', 'Walkman', which in translation require additional descriptive terms only if the brand name is not known to the readership. Secondly, you have to consciously resist subliminal publicity for manufacturers of products such as 'Pernod', 'Frigidaire', 'Durex' ('adhesive tape' in Australia), 'Tipp-Ex', 'Velcro', Jiffy bag', 'bic', 'biro', 'Tesa', 'sellotape' (two pairs of cultural equivalents), 'Scotch' (tape and whisky), translating them by a brief descriptive term (which is not always easy) rather than transferring them. Often it is too late. You have to accept TL standard terms, whether they are eponyms or recognised translations; jargon you must fight, either by eliminating it or by slimming it down.

Geographical names

Thirdly, geographical terms are used as eponyms when they have obvious connotations: firstly the towns and villages of Nazi horrors (Belsen, Dachau, Vel'drome, Drancy, Terezen, Oradour), which you should transfer and, where necessary, gloss, since this is basic education. Secondly, beware of idioms such as 'meet your Waterloo' – *faire naufrage*; *il y aura du bruit à Landerneau* – 'it's just tittle-tattle'; 'from here to Timbuktu' – *d'ici jusqu'à Landerneau*. Lastly you should note the increasing metonymic practice, mainly in the media, of referring to governments by the name of their respective capitals or locations and institutions or ministers by their residences or streets ('Whitehall' – the British government; 'the Pentagon' – US military leadership; 'Fleet Street' – the British press).

Acronyms

I define an acronym, again unconventionally, as the initial letters of words that form a group of words used (vertiginously) for denoting an object, institution or procedure. My first point is that one should be wary of wasting time looking for the acronym in the numerous reference-books when it has been specially coined for the text (e.g., of an academic paper) and can be found there. Normally, you should not recreate your own acronyms, except for this purpose. Secondly, there are many 'cultural' reasons why the acronym may or may not be worth transferring (depending on the 'standard' contextual factors, i.e., readership, translation prospects, etc.), but where the function is more important than the description; thus acronyms of political parties are usually transferred, but currently it is more important to know that the RPR claims to be the true Gaullist party than that the acronym stands for *Rassemblement pour la République* or translates (meaninglessly) as 'Rallying for the Republic'. For other aspects of translating acronyms see p. 148.

FAMILIAR ALTERNATIVE TERMS
(From *Lebende Sprachen*)

L'Armorique is 'Armorica' (according to Harrap's Dictionary), *lo Stivale* is 'the Boot', *Hexagone* is 'the Hexagon', *lusitanien* is 'Lusitanian', *helvétique* is 'Helvetian', and many other names, ('Old Reekie', 'Brum', 'Scouse', 'Pompey', 'the Gunners', 'the Hammers', 'Norma Jean') appear to be 'untranslatable' into another language. In fact, there is no translation problem, because familiar, often hypocoristic proper names are simply being used as alternatives by people who are perhaps over-familiar with their 'proper' proper names. The TL reader will not be so familiar with these referents, and is usually given the normal neutral translation: Brittany, Italy, France, Portuguese, Swiss, Edinburgh, Birmingham, Liverpudlian, Portsmouth Football Club (FC), Arsenal (FC), West Ham United (FC), Marilyn Monroe. Such familiar alternatives may be difficult to find in reference books: e.g., 'the Hardy Country' for Dorset, 'GBS' for Shaw, 'the Sage of Königsberg' for Kant, 'Winnie' (forgotten now) for Winston Churchill, 'the Old Lady of Threadneedle Street' for the Bank of England.

Secondly, many synonymous couplets – 'freedom' and 'liberty'; *Objekt* and *Gegenstand*, *Sprachwissenschaft* and *Linguistik*, 'ecology' and 'environment', 'daring' and 'audacity', 'memoirs' and 'autobiography', 'aid' and 'assistance', etc. – are sometimes used as familiar alternatives to each other, and in such a context the translator has to take care not to show their differences in meaning. He often prefers one to the other unconsciously simply because it sounds better in the word group or sentence. *Gesellschaft und Linguistik* sounds better than *Gesellschaft und Sprachwissenschaft*.

Just as individuals have familiar alternative terms for members of their family and close friends (nicknames), so familiar objects and actions are often designated by alternative terms, rather misleadingly referred to as slang ('sixty-nine' or *soixante-neuf* designated as 'vulgar slang' – why?), colloquialisms, vulgar, popular (*français populaire*, etc.) since they are no longer confined to the argot of thieves, beggars, swindlers, rakes, the working classes, etc., but are in general, often affectionate, use. Such words as *mec, nana, môme, fric, boulot*, 'bloke', *Kerl, Kinder* (chaps), 'kids', 'bird', 'tart', 'cash', 'job' have to be translated by neutral terms, if the TL has no corresponding familiar alternative. In my opinion, these words (there are about 200 of them in a language, in my terms) should be introduced early into any foreign- or second-language learning course, but they rarely are. I think they are more important than idioms.

Familiar alternative language is common in journalism and is used more frequently now in more formal varieties of informative writing, particularly in

English and French, with the superficial, not real, dropping of sexual and class taboos. Thus it is a sign of being 'with it' or 'in' for a French local newspaper to use the term *loubard* ('drop-out') coined only in 1973 without even a *soi-disant*. French does not appear to use inverted commas or italics for neologisms or slang out of register as often as English or German. German, being more formal, has possibly fewer familiar alternative terms than English, and perhaps they are more likely to appear in Austrian than in West or East German. (But note *pennen*, *fressen*, etc.)

It is not always easy to distinguish between slang and familar alternative language; the latter is often what used to be regarded as slang whilst a separate category of slang and colloquial language remains on a fragile base.

Translators may have to consider carefully 'the reasons for the use of a familiar alternative term before they translate it. A term like 'cash' or 'lolly' may be used: (a) to avoid unnecessarily emphatic repetition; (b) for phatic reasons, to show warmth/friendliness towards the reader; (c) to break register and shock the reader; (d) to show off, suggesting that the SL writer has special knowledge, belongs to an 'in group'.

Incidentally, establishing the reason may not affect the translation, in particular if the TL language has a satisfactory familiar alternative equivalent (*fric*, but nothing for German except *Kohle* or *Mäuse?*). The relation between the amount of knowledge actually used in a translation and the amount of background and awareness required is often that between the tip and the rest of the iceberg. For instance, the translator has to be aware of the various sound-effects – all sound has meaning – in the SL text (assonance, internal rhyme, rhythmic effect, alliteration, onomatopoeia are more common outside poetry and advertising than is usually thought) but he usually does not do much about it, as it would require metalingual additions, which are a translation procedure. All the reader often sees is the tip of the iceberg of all the knowledge the translator has had to acquire to produce his version.

Familiar alternative terms may originate as *argot* ('underworld' language); as old words, e.g., *helvétique* ('Helvetia' is on the stamp, because it is not German nor Swiss nor Italian – so Latin triumphs again!), put to new uses; as metaphors ('bread', 'lolly', 'grub') that become metonyms; as abbreviations and of course as nicknames, e.g., those extraordinary childish variants on surnames or initials with which the male members of the British upper middle classes in their hateful schools used to try to prove that they did after all have feelings (Dizzy, Smithy, Robbie, Plum, Rab (Butler), F E (Smith), Plum, Nobby, Sonny); as regional dialect words; as professional jargon terms; as straight synonyms.

Familiar alternative language should not be confused with the tendency in language to replace one word by another for the well-known reasons of sense or word change (see Waldron, 1979); thus 'car' replaced 'automobile' to abbreviate an object coming into frequent use; 'hairdresser' replaced 'barber' and 'funeral director', 'undertaker', for reasons of prestige – but these are not in my sense familiar alternatives.

Present and formerly bilingual areas are a ready source of familiar alternative terms, particularly place-names. In specifically diglossia areas (see Ferguson, 1975) the L (low) variety is usually the source, but in my contexts the familiar alternative terms are not being used for the purposes that Ferguson indicates (e.g., 'instructions to servants, waiters, workmen, clerks', etc. – was Ferguson living in this world?). In references to potentially irredentist areas, the translator has to distinguish between politically loaded and familiar alternative references to towns like Brünn, Breslau, Pola, Fiume, etc. (Even now, West German newspapers refer to 'Danzig'. The charitable explanation of this oddity is that the word is being used only as a familiar alternative term to Gdansk, but when a country or town acquires a new name, it should I think be accepted by translators and others as a transferred word, particularly if it is in a politically sensitive area.) Even now many conscious Marxists will not accept that 'Russian' is a familiar alternative to 'Soviet' (you can't say 'a Sovietian') rather than an expression of hostility to the USSR*; similarly, expressions such as 'Eastern bloc', 'Soviet bloc', 'Comecon' as alternatives to 'CMEA (Council for Mutual Economic Assistance) countries'. (This is a huge subject: in some people's minds 'familiar alternatives' are a sentimental fig-leaf covering every type of exploitation; in others' they are an ignorant but genuine expression of warm feelings.) Talking to an 'East German' (another familiar alternative) historian, I innocently referred to *die Tschechei* using it as a familiar alternative; and was reproached for using a politically reactionary and nationalist term, suggesting that Czechoslovakia is an inferior nation.

Note that familiar alternative language is far from being only lexical. Mathiot (1979) distinguishes between the normative ('neutral') and intimate (i.e., 'familiar alternative') method of referring to objects through pronouns revealing sex roles. Thus she quotes: 'Yeah, I finally fixed her up' ('her' is a door); 'He is just a spindly thing, but she's lovely' ('he' and 'she' are plants), etc. Anything from cars (naked women) to ice cream cones and mathematical formulae can be 'upgraded entities' (Mathiot's phrase, not mine), while a thief can become 'it'.

Obviously this is a translation problem, but not an insoluble one. (There are no insoluble translation problems.) The translator may: (a) keep the personalised pronouns; (b) normalise the sentence, regarding the 'familiar alternative' as not important; (c) substitute a familiar alternative noun for the pronoun — say, *der Kerl* for the plant, *die Kleine* for the car, *die Schöne* for the mathematical formula; (d) add explanatory metalingual comment. Context decides.

Further I suspect that many people have familiar alternative syntactic structures (mine are the gerund and the split infinitive) which are slightly off the purists' standard forms. Thus 'I' and 'me', 'we' and 'us', 'she' and 'her' are interchangeable in the spoken language.

Eczema, measles, chickenpox are familar alternatives to dermatitis, rubeola, varicella (jaundice to hepatitis is not) and can often be used as such even in

---

* However, the noun 'a Soviet' is slowly gaining currency. Note also the regrettable absence of a noun or adjective for 'United States', apart from the loaded classifier 'American', in English, French and German, but not Italian (*statounitense*) or Spanish (*estadounidense*).

academic papers though such usage tends to offend medical mystique. Similarly, it would be good to accept 'neither are' as a familiar alternative to 'neither is' which would offend the purists, but would stop discussion of such a trivial matter. (See Crystal (1981) for many other arguments which could be settled by the acceptance of the familiar alternative concept.)

The most important aspect of familiar alternatives is that they should not be inappropriately used: there are many contexts where, in translations only 'neither is . . .', 'I', 'dermatitis', 'Norma Jean', etc., will do, others, where the choice is a matter of taste, the fourth area of translation (after science, skill and art) which it is unprofitable to argue about.

The linguist, whether translator, teacher or lexicographer, has to bear in mind that most familiar alternative words, whilst they are commonly used as strict synonyms of other words, have themselves alternative senses, which should be shown in the dictionary. Thus words like 'Pressburg', 'Stettin', 'Königsberg' are also used for political reasons. In Erica Jong's remarkable poem 'Sylvia Plath is alive in Argentina', 'Norma Jean' denotes not simply 'Marilyn Monroe' but the poor unhappy child from a broken home who became Marilyn Monroe ('Men did them in'). *Armorique* may simply refer to Roman Brittany, and 'kite', 'prang', etc. may have been used as a code to show off, or to establish oneself as a member of a group. All these factors would be recorded in a good comprehensive dictionary or encyclopaedia – I don't distinguish between the two.

Thus familiar alternative language has applications in translation theory, language learning and lexicography; is subject to the vagaries of fashion, but responds to a continuous human linguistic need; is in danger of obscuring and sentimentalising profound issues of social, ethnic and sexual relations, but genuinely encompasses personal relationships. It is, particularly in French and in the informal varieties of language, a powerful and common cohesive feature.

WHEN AND HOW TO IMPROVE A TEXT

I begin by reminding you that you have no right to improve an authoritative text, however wayward, clichéd, quirky, jargonised, tautologous, innovative, unnatural its language may be; you have to pursue the same style, making slight concessions for the different stylistic norms of the target language, but assuming on the whole that the personality of the author is more important than any norms of language. Possibly you make more concessions to the readership when translating non-literary texts (e.g., De Gaulle) than creative writing, since a readership is being specifically addressed. In authoritative texts I assume you make any type of comment (correction of facts, etc.) only in a separate, signed note.

However, here I am discussing 'anonymous' texts: these are mainly informative (but also vocative) texts, where your first loyalty is to the truth or the facts of the matter, and where you assume the author of the original would be only too grateful if you corrected his facts (if necessary) and discreetly improved his style, always making as few modifications as possible.

I propose to list and exemplify some heads under which a translation can 'correct' and therefore be an improvement on the original, but only if the original is defective in its writing or lacking in information essential to the putative reader.

Logical sequence

This is a matter of orderly sequences: in time, in space, and in argument. I take one example from Gowers and Fraser (1977):

> A deduction of tax may be claimed in respect of any person whom the individual maintains at his own expense, and who is (i) a relative of his or his wife and incapacitated by old age or infirmity from maintaining himself or herself or (ii) his or his wife's widowed mother, whether incapacitated or not or (iii) his daughter who is resident with him and upon whose services he is compelled to depend by reasons of old age or infirmity.

I adapt the Gowers and Fraser 'translations':

> If you maintain a relative of yours or your wife's who is unable to work because of old age or infirmity, you can claim a tax deduction. You can also claim a deduction if you maintain your wife's or your old widowed mother, whether she is unable to work or not. If you maintain a daughter who lives with you and has to look after you because you are old or infirm, you can also claim an allowance.

Note here, first, that an informative text had been turned into a vocative text, aiming its effect pragmatically at the reader; secondly, that the logic of cause and effect, or of condition/premiss and result has been three times extrapolated from one long impersonal sentence.

Whether the second version is justified as a model translation of the original depends on the translator's purpose. The main criterion for improvement is the translator's conviction that he is helping the SL writer to get his message or information across without distorting it.

The type of rearrangement made by the English translator of LaDurie's *Montaillou* is logically justified.

> *A un niveau encore inférieur, on trouve la Chapelle de la Vierge: elle est liée à un culte folklorique, issu de rochers à fleur de sol. Le cimetière local flanque ce bas sanctuaire, dédié à la Mère de Dieu.*

is translated as:

> Lower down still, surrounded by the local cemetery, there is a chapel dedicated to the Virgin Mary, though it is also linked to a traditional cult connected with some nearby rocks.

The translator has noted that the 'local cemetery' is incidental and interrupts the current of thought in the original; further that there are two unnecessary sets of referential synonyms: *Vierge* and *Mère de Dieu*; *chapelle* and *bas sanctuaire*. He has put the 'local cemetery' into a subordinate position and, in foregrounding the chapel, has got rid of the referential synonyms. There is no question that this is an improvement on LaDurie, but the question remains whether a translator has a right to improve on LaDurie.

Syntactically weak sentences

It is difficult to find any informative text without its syntactically weak sentence:

> *Nous avons été frappé également par le fait qu'aucun de ces enfants ne présentait de difficultés scolaires isolées ou qui auraient pu être rattachées à des causes simples, par exemple un absentéisme dû à la fréquence plus on moins grande des crises d'asthme ou par exemple des troubles instrumentaux comme une dyslexie ou une dysorthographie.*

We were also impressed by the fact that none of these children had difficulties at school which were isolated or could have been ascribed to simple causes such as absenteeism due to more or less frequent asthma attacks or merely instrumental disorders such as dyslexia or poor spelling.

The syntactical defect here was the lack of equal emphasis on *isolées* and *rattachées*, as well as the examples of absenteeism which tend to weaken the contrast between the negative in this paragraph and the positive that follows.

Idiolect

On the whole the quirks and sports of idiolect are normalised by the translator: in particular, rather exaggerated or exuberant metaphors and extravagant descriptive adjectives.

I suspect that few people can write 500 words without using one or two words in a manner peculiar to themselves: 'This kind of community with its strong family bindings always poses a challenge to outsiders': whether the word 'bindings' is one or a combination of 'units' or 'ties', I think a German translator has to normalise it to *mit ihrem starken Familiensinn* or *familiären Bindungen*.

In some cases, it is not easy to distinguish between poor writing and idiolect (*les signes et présence d'un asthmatique attirent vers la notion d'allergie microbienne*) but the translator does not have to make the distinction, and merely normalises: 'The signs suggest that the patient has a bacterial allergy.'

Again, a specialist may refer to psychotherapy as *une arme à divers volets*; the strained mixed metaphor, however fossilised, has to be reduced to sense, e.g., 'a treatment which can be put to various uses'.

Ambiguity

Ambiguity may be deliberate or unintentional, and a deliberate ambiguity has, if possible, to be retained in the translation, sometimes separating out the two meanings of a homonym. *Le Ministère est responsable de ces difficultés* may in context be translated 'The Ministry has caused these problems and is responsible for their solution.'

An unintentional ambiguity is usually clarified in the context, but the translator has to avoid any possible misunderstandings: 'I did not write that letter because of what you told me' is more likely in any event to be: *En vue de ce que tu m'as dit, je n'ai pas écrit cette lettre.*

Metaphor

In theory, metaphor is only justified in the more popular or journalistic type of informative text, where the reader's interest has to be roused. In fact, as Lakoff and Johnson (1980) have shown, conceptual thinking is impregnated with metaphors which are basic, universal, more or less dead and frequently translated literally (they are 'congruent' metaphors) though the translator is barely aware of the images: e.g., *le culte de l'esprit critique, qui n'est ni un éveilleur d'idées ni un stimulateur de grandes choses; il a toujours le dernier mot.* The entire world of the mind is metaphorical, since it is neither concrete nor literal.

Nevertheless, one can normally assume that an obtrusive metaphor is out of place in any kind of informative text. A translator is bound to be sceptical about translating the opening of an Italian text on the future of the car:

> *Gli sceicchi obbediscono al volere di Allah. Il volere di Allah non può essere altro che buono. Dunque la stretta nell'erogazione del greggio dai pozzi del Golfo Persico non può essere altro che un bene.*

> Sheikhs obey the will of Allah. The will of Allah can only be good. Therefore the scarcity in the supply of crude oil from the wells in the Persian Gulf can only be a blessing.

One is tempted to delete the first two sentences and abbreviate the third.

The basic question about metaphor in informative texts is when and whether one is permitted to convert sense to metaphor and vice versa. Thus in an article on the Parliamentary Assembly of the Council of Europe in its *Courier*, is it legitimate to translate *L'Assemblée ne doit pas craindre de s'affirmer si elle veut renforcer son influence* as 'It has to stick its neck out if it wants to heighten its impact'? *Délicat* as 'touchy'? *S'attaquent à* as 'tackle', *rôle de pionnier* as 'path-breaking', *grouper* as 'pool', *tirer parti de* as 'nurture', *se mettre vaguement au courant* as 'have a nodding acquaintance with', *sous l'autorité coordinatrice* as 'under the co-ordinating eye', *se réunir* as 'meet face to face'?

Instead of dealing separately with each of the above examples, I propose to suggest some general principles: (1) it 'ought' to be unnecessary to translate sense by metaphor in informative texts; (2) original and colloquial metaphors are out of place; (3) the use of cliché metaphors destroys the point of using a metaphor at all; (4) where a metaphor is unobtrusive and blends with the text's register (not 'sticks its neck out'), in particular where it is a semi-technical term (e.g., 'pool'), it is legitimate, in particular if the original literal language is a little tired or clichéd (e.g. *renforcer son influence, se mettre vaguement au courant*). Lastly, if the text is not important, the question is 'academic' only in the literal sense, i.e., in, say, an examination. If you are translating journalism, the alternatives in the previous paragraph are not all that important. Contrariwise, it is justified to convert metaphor to sense, if the metaphor is wayward or conventional. Thus a sentence such as: *Après les hautes sphères dans lesquelles M. Halpern nous a promenés tout à l'heure, il nous faut revenir un peu sur terre, sinon au ras de sol* should be brought down to: 'After the abstractions M. Halpern has been indulging in we must now become a little more realistic and down to earth.' But idioms like *jeter les bases de* ('initiate'), *Sturm in Wasserglas* ('violent argument over a trivial matter'), *adorer la veau d'or* ('devoted to material wealth') are often rendered more literally and less emotively, whilst bizarre metaphors such as *se tremper hâtivement dans les eaux baptismales européennes à Strasbourg* should at least be modified ('they are hastily initiated into the work of the Assembly at Strasbourg') not translated as 'a quick baptism in European waters at their Strasbourg fountain-head', which is the official translation.

Metaphors are particularly picturesque in English sport, arts, criticism, pop music, finance and journalism. For Stock Exchange terms, many metonyms (e.g., 'bull', 'bear', 'gilts', 'equities', 'black', 'red') are often toned down to less striking terms in other languages. In other topics, individual English journalists make their mark on the basis of their 'racy', 'elegant' or 'witty' styles, all of which usually have a basis of metaphor. The translator may have to separately review the whole text to assess the proportion, originality and force of its imagery and consider its appropriateness in the TL text. In mechanical engineering and computer science, the recurrent metonyms (congealed metaphors) present translation rather than translation theory problems.

Redundancy and clichés

The case in favour of eliminating the redundancies of the SL version in translation has been put with a wealth of examples by Duff (1971) which is a refreshing blast in contrast to the stale jargon of translation theory literature. He rightly takes his texts from advertisements, guides, company brochures, hand-outs, trade magazines etc., not from authoritative statements (where the redundancy would have to be reproduced). Redundancies hang particularly loosely round clichés, phatic phrases ('phaticisms') ('naturally', 'of course', 'understandably'), repeated implied superlatives ('basically', 'fundamentally'), prepositional phrases (*au niveau de, dans le cadre de*, 'in view of the fact that'), rhetorical flourishes ('in the long march of history'), abstract terms ('development', 'evolution') and sonorous phrases used for sound-effect ('might and main', 'ways and means').

Normally the translator has to use restraint in excising redundant SL features, confining himself to pruning here and there, since if he goes too far he is sometimes likely to find the whole text redundant.

Slips, misprints, errors, miscopying

Where the translator is certain that the SL writer has made a referential slip, as in *l'arthrite est une inflammation des parois artérielles* or *Pasteur est né en 1722* or a linguistic slip, grammatical or lexical (*er arbeitete bei einem Schreibtisch; Mühle abladen verboten*), he normally corrects the slip (without annotation) in the translation. Again, if there is a SL text misprint, say *in vitro* for *in vivo*, *Keimforschung* for *Kernforschung*, 'Alderman Howard takes a sanguine view of the project. It will cost £200 million and will never pay', or words out of place: 'The Taganka theatre was to death with a private evening to mark the anniversary of his songs' (*Guardian*, 28.7.81) for: 'The Taganka Theatre was to mark the anniversary of his death with a private evening devoted to his songs', he corrects the errors. Again this is automatic and mandatory, and requires no acknowledgment. Be careful also of cases where the typist has been unable to decipher the author's writing (or his cassette voice) and the mistake has just lived on.

If the SL writer has clearly made a mistake, the translator corrects it and, unless the mistake is so obvious that it might as well be a slip, writes a note to explain the error and, if necessary, his reasons for the change, e.g., *Der Bürgerbräu-Putsch von 1923 wurde von Ludendorff angestiftet.*

The translator must, as always, be as careful of proper names, as of dictionary words. Thus in translating Valéry's speech (but this is a 'sacred' not an anonymous text) in honour of Goethe (*Variété*, IV, p. 102): *ce n'est plus la guerre de Louis XV et de Monsieur de Thorane*, it is no good translating 'it is no longer the war of Louis XV and Monsieur de Thorane', since Monsieur de Thorane never existed. Further, *ce n'est plus la guerre* requires a somewhat more idiomatic rendering, e.g., 'Louis XV's and Monsieur de Thorane's war had been over a long time ago'. Goethe mistakenly referred to the king's representative at Grasse, the Comte de Théas Thoranc, as Monsieur de Thorane and Valéry unwittingly perpetuated the mistake. The translator has to point this out, in a footnote, 'preserving' Goethe's and Valéry's mistake, but annotating it.

In principle, the translator's duty is to correct any mistakes of fact in the original and to comment separately on any improbability, particularly on matters of consequence, such as statistics, experimental work, etc., and prejudice. In informative texts, the translator's only loyalty is to the truth.

Jargon

I assume that the translator is entitled to delete, reduce or slim down jargon, by which I mean, mainly, more or less redundant words or words that are semantically too broad for the features they are describing; in particular, more verbal or adjectival nouns. When these have a technical sense (e.g., city 'development') I cannot quarrel with them. But take Gowers's and Frazer's 'untranslatable' piece and I should say that a translator cannot afford himself the luxury of qualifying any stretch of language as untranslatable, unacceptable, deviant):

> To reduce the risk of war requires the closest co-ordination in the employment of their joint resources to underpin these countries' economies in such a manner as to permit the full maintenance of their living standards as well as the adequate development of the necessary measures.

Whatever the 'language', the translator might justifiably reduce this passage, unless it were an authoritative statement, to:

> To reduce the risk of war, resources have to be adequately co-ordinated whilst ensuring that these countries' living standards are secured.

How far the translator can go in reducing the jargon depends on two factors: (a) the degree of authoritativeness of the SL statement (i.e., the less authoritative, the more linguistic changes can be made); (b) the norms of the SL and TL. It is easier to get rid of empty verbs and synthesised words (many originating from the turn of the nineteenth century), which jargon largely consists of – for instance 'in the contemplated eventuality' (i.e., 'if so') or a made-up word like 'basicalisation' – if the TL is a relatively 'intact' language and does not accommodate such words easily. A sentence such as *J'allais déclencher votre agressivité en affirmant que nous étions en retard dans la médecine sur la conceptualisation dans le domaine de l'homme* represents a degree of sophistication which could hardly be transferred into another language – possibly 'when I stated that French psychologists were behind hand in conceptualising psychological medicine I knew I would rouse your hostility'. Good or bad writing is good or bad writing in any language, and nothing exposes the one or the other more tellingly than translation. Jargon in the sense that I am using it is platitudinous or meretricious thought 'dressed' either in the colourless language of bureaucracy (technocracy, chancery language, Marxism, officialese) or in the literary/national tradition of a 'folk', e.g., German philosophical obscurity, or late nineteenth century sensuality and religiosity.

All writing, once its protective local linguistic and cultural carapace has been removed by an accurate translation, is exposed and vulnerable. The following passage is redundant enough in English:

> One of the main objects of a theory is obviously to enable systematic and exhaustive description and explanation of each and every phenomenon regarded as belonging to the sphere it covers; and when a theory does not make it possible to account for all the phenomena recurring in the research field, and considered part of it, the fault is with the theory – and not with the phenomena; and the thing to be done is to revise the theory, not discard the facts which resist being accounted for by its terms.
>
> (Gideon Toury, *In Search of a Theory of Translation*)

Whether the above is itself a piece of translationese I am not qualified to say, though 'enable an explanation' suggests that it is. What is clear is that the phrases that stick out ('regarded as belonging to the sphere it covers', 'obviously', 'considered part of it', 'which resist being accounted for by its terms') are likely to sound even more grotesque in any other language.

The work of Charles Morgan, no longer read in English, is intellectually pretentious enough to sound better in French, whilst Duff (1980) has shown that a writer like Barthes can be killed dead by translation:

> 'Bourgeois ideology can spread over everything. It can without resistance subsume bourgeois theatre, art and humanity under their eternal analogues; it can ex-nominate itself without restraint when there is only one single human nature left.'
>
> (Barthes, *Mythologies*)

Duff asks anxiously why this translation 'sounds wrong', although each word, though difficult, makes sense. I am suggesting there is nothing wrong with the translation: what is 'wrong' is the original, which inevitably sounds nicer and smoother in the French. But nonsense is nonsense in any language, however culturally determined it may be.

Duff also quotes sufficiently from Marxist publications to show that an exceptionally large amount of material emanating presumably from Moscow or the CMEA published in the media of the Soviet bloc and its followers in other countries is both abstract jargon and translationese; although one can reduce the translationese, such as 'The measures adopted to promote science and technology are designed to ensure high and steady growth rates in the economy, especially as regards labour productivity, this being in the best interests of the people', it remains doubtful whether any laundered version is going to mean more (or less) to the reader than the original. But Gorbachev has stated that he will make war on Soviet clichés. (I add a sceptical *sic*.)

Prejudice and the translator's moral responsibilities

The area of informative texts is, as I have said, peculiar in that I think that the translator's (ultimate) responsibility is neither to the reader nor to the writer but to the truth, a bold statement but, given the translator's mistakes with the Hiroshima bomb (alleged), the Ems telegram (he should have checked on Bismarck), the bowdlerisation of the *Mein Kampf* translation, various howlers made by former President Carter's and the Queen's interpreters – and for every significant mistranslation that is discovered there are usually many more that remain covered – one has to be explicit. Not only physical truth, but also moral 'truth', the acknowledgment that people are equally valuable and have equal potential, has to be reaffirmed in the notes if it is violated in the text. The translator mediates between two parties and his job is to eliminate misunderstandings. It appears to me that the extracts that used to be quoted in the *Guardian*'s 'Naked Ape' column every week are as much of an insult to human dignity as any racialist or class or religious or age or sanity propaganda, but the sexism is rarely direct. Obviously a passage such as 'a kitchen is a place which a woman calls her domain, is proud of and enjoys working in' or 'Any office girl could do this job' has to be translated 'neat' but, as I see it, each passage may require a footnote pointing out the prejudice. Eventually this is a matter for a translator's code of ethics. It is always your duty to 'desex' language ('they' for 'he', 'humanity' for 'Man', etc.) tactfully, without being counter-productive.

Conclusion

I am not suggesting that you can be as free as you like with informative texts. I am merely establishing your right, if the original has no stylistic pretensions or is an example of bad writing, to 'select an appropriate style of your own, usually the clearest, most straightforward writing you can muster'. 'If the authors of original texts always observed the principle of clear thinking, it would help. When they do not, the translator must still strive for excellence.' Thus the Quebec Ministry of Information's advice to translators. This is an area of translation texts where certain acceptable styles of language are to be expected, narrower and stricter in the more formal manner of textbooks than in the more figurative writing of journalism.

The fact still remains that every item – words, idioms, structures, emphases – has to be accounted for by the translator, in the sense that he must be able to give reasons for its transference, direct or indirect translation or deletion, if challenged. There is no question of eliminating author or reader in the interest of some 'higher' truth. The translator will adopt the author's register, unless he is translating for a different type of readership in a different type of setting, and he can and must justify modifications to the text only on the basis of its inadequacy in the respects I have discussed.

COLLOCATIONS

In linguistics, a collocation is typically defined as the 'habitual co-occurrence of individual lexical items' (Crystal). For the translator, for whom the collocation is the most important contextual factor collocation, in as far as it usefully affects translation, is considerably narrower; it consits of lexical items that enter mainly into high-frequency grammatical structures, viz.:

(1) Adjective plus noun
    (a) 'heavy labour', *travail musculaire, schwere Arbeit*
    (b) 'runaway (galloping) inflation', *galoppierende Inflation, l'inflation galopante*
    (c) 'economic situation', *situation économique, Konjunkturlage*
    (d) 'inflationary pressure', *pressions (tensions) inflationnistes, Inflationsdruck*
(2) Noun plus noun (i.e., double-noun compound)
    (a) 'nerve cell', *cellule nerveuse, Nervenzelle*
    (b) 'government securities', *effets publics, Staatspapiere (Staatsanleihen)*
    (c) 'eyeball', *globe oculaire, Augapfel*
(3) Verb plus object, which is normally a noun that denotes an action, as in 'read a paper'
    (a) 'pay a visit', *faire une visite, einen Besuch machen (abstatten)*
    (b) 'score (win) a victory', *remporter une victoire, einen Sieg erzielen*

(c) 'read a(n) (academic) paper', *faire une communication, ein Referat halten*
(d) 'attend a lecture', *eine Vorlesung hören* or *besuchen, suivre une conférence*

The above are the most common collocation-types. All three are centred in the noun, the second component (collocate) of the collocation. The translator asks himself: you have *travail musculaire* in French, can you say 'muscular work' in English? A 'cell' is 'nervous' in French, what is it in English? You 'hold a paper' in German, do you 'hold' one in English? Or what are the verbs that collocate normally with 'a door'? Recognising whether or not a collocation is familiar, natural, or just acceptable, is one of the most important problems in translation. As usual there are grey areas and choices: you can 'go on' as well as 'pay' a visit. Note that in (1) and (2) above, English is closer to German than to French. French makes more use of adjectives which stand for objects not qualities (e.g. adjectives for all towns) and does not use double-noun compounds; this particularly in scientific–technical language; in Romance language medical texts, you normally assume that a SL noun plus adjective group, e.g., *radioactivité plasmatique*, is going to be switched round to a noun-plus-noun compound, 'plasma radioactivity', provided the SL adjective is formed from a noun of substance.

A second useful way of approaching collocations in translation is to consider the acceptable collocational ranges of any lexical word. This particularly applies to adjectives of quality, and verbs that describe as well as state an activity; *blême* collocates with 'face' and 'light'; but not normally with objects; *trouble* with looks, emotions, liquids ('cloudy') but not people; *grincer* with doors ('creak'), teeth ('grind' or 'gnash'), metallic objects ('grate') but not with animals; *keusch* with people and their expressions ('pure', 'chaste'), not with objects or foods.

You have to identify unusual SL collocations if you want to render them into similarly unusual TL collocations (for adverts, poetry – not for the average 'anonymous' text).

However, sensitiveness to collocations is most useful when considering SL collocations and relating them to transparent TL collocations. *Maladie grave* is 'serious' or 'severe' rather than 'grave' illness; 'grave condition' is *état inquiétant* rather than *grave*, which is not so grave. *Contester sa gestion* is to 'question' or 'dispute' rather than 'contest his management'.

Translation is sometimes a continual struggle to find appropriate collocations, a process of connecting up appropriate nouns with verbs and verbs with nouns, and, in the second instance, collocating appropriate adjectives to the nouns and adverbs or adverbial groups to the verbs; in the third instance, collocating appropriate connectives or conjunctions (the prepositions are already in the adverbial groups). If grammar is the bones of a text, collocations are the nerves, more subtle and multiple and specific in denoting meaning, and lexis is the flesh.

I have concentrated on the most frequent collocation-types. Where a word normally has only one collocate (e.g., the sounds made by common animals, musical instruments, tools – *miauler, aboyer*), there are few options, and therefore this is a question of contrasted languages rather than a translation problem though the figurative senses of such sounds, which are normally onomatopoeic, offer an alternative interpretation.

There is a smaller range of collocations when one seeks a single item for an uncountable noun: 'cake (piece) of soap', *Stück Seife*, *pain de savon*; 'plot of ground', *lopin de terre*, *Stück Land*; 'pat of butter', *noix*, *motte de beurre*, 'portion of butter' (here 'piece', *Stück*, *pezzo*, *morceau*, but not *pièce* are all-purpose words) or a collective noun for various countables, e.g.:

'flock of sheep', *un troupeau de moutons*, *Schafherde*
'herd of cattle', *un troupeau de bétail*, *eine Herde Rinder*
'set of tools', *assortiment d'outils*, *Werkzeug*
'pack of cards', *jeu de cartes*, *Kartenspiel*

I have listed only the most common collocations. Some verbs, say, *assouvir* ('satisfy', 'appease'), collocate physically with animate (person, patient, hungry wolf), figuratively with abstract (desires, passions, greed, anger, etc.) objects. A few verbs ('work hard', 'deeply regret', 'devoutly hope') and adjectives ('profoundly unnecessary', 'immensely disturbing', 'totally wrong', 'desperately unhappy', etc.) are collocated with adverbs, many of which degenerate into disposable clichés. Some nouns such as *couvercle* can be seen as objects which naturally suggest, prompt, or call for a small range of verbs (*fermer*, *soulever*, *enlever*, *ouvrir*, *ôter*, etc.) *Coûter* goes with *cher* or *peu*. Some words go naturally with idioms.

Collocations should be distinguished from words in a semantic field (colours, ranks, etc.) or from the frame of a topic which, if they are on the same level, do not immediately collocate with each other.

The only systematic dictionaries of collocations that I know are the two superb works by Reum (see Chapter 16). They include synonyms and antonyms, and much other information.

There are various degrees of collocability. Some words such as 'bandy' and 'rancid' may only have one material collocate ('legs', 'butter'), but figuratively they open up more choice (appearance, taste). They are always linked with the concept of naturalness and usage, and become most important in the revision stages of translation.

THE TRANSLATION OF PROPER NAMES

People's names

Normally, people's first and surnames are transferred, thus preserving their nationality, and assuming that their names have no connotations in the text.

There are exceptions: the names of saints and monarchs are sometimes translated, if they are 'transparent', but some French kings (Louis, François) are transferred. The names of popes are translated. Some prominent figures of classical Greece (*Platon* (F), *Thucydide* (F), *Aeschyle* (F), *Sophocle* (F), and Rome (Horace, Livy, *Tite-Live*, *Catulle*) and the Renaissance (*Arioste*, *Le Tasse*, *Le Grec*) are naturalised in the main European languages. (See other examples in Newmark, 1981.) Romance languages often translate the first names of prominent foreigners, if these are transparent. Some Renaissance and eighteenth-century personalities (e.g., Copernicus, Spinoza, Linnaeus (von Linné), Melanchthon, which translates Schwarzerd, his original name) adopted classical names which are then sometimes naturalised – e.g., *Linné*, *Copernic* (F). In some languages, such as Hungarian, surnames precede first names (e.g., Kádar János). Even now there is no standardised transliteration system from Cyrillic, and it is a pity that the Soviet (unlike the Chinese) government has made no recommendations.

There remains the question of names that have connotations in imaginative literature. In comedies, allegories, fairy tales and some children's stories, names are translated (e.g., *Cendrillon*), unless, as in folk tales, nationality is important.

Where both connotations (rendered through sound-effects and/or transparent names) and nationality are significant, I have suggested that the best method is first to translate the word that underlies the SL proper name into the TL, and then to naturalise the translated word back into a new SL proper name – but normally only when the character's name is not yet current amongst an educated TL readership. Thus 'Miss Slowboy' could become *Flaubub* and then 'Flowboob' for German; *Lentgarçon* then 'Longarson' for French; note that the procedure is likely to be more effective, particularly for sound-effect, in German than in French. Michael Holman (1983) has done this effectively with characters from Tolstoy's *Resurrection*: *Nabatov* → 'alarm' → 'Alarmov', 'Toksinsky'; *Toporov* → 'axe' → 'Hackitov', 'Hatchetinsky'; *Khororshavka* → 'pretty' → 'Belle', 'Chi-Chi'.

I list below possible reasons for translating 'Harriet', the name of a chicken in P. G. Wodehouse's *Love among the Chickens*, by 'Laura' in Swedish, and other considerations.

(1) As this is a light novel, there is nothing sacrosanct about the SL proper name.
(2) The name is incongruous and should raise a smile or a laugh.
(3) 'Harriet' is specifically English and connotes an old-fashioned fussiness. (This trait must be checked with the character of the chicken in the novel.)
(4) This connotation would be lost in any TL, and therefore there is a case for adopting a culturally overlapping proper name such as 'Laura'.
(5) Laura is often considered to be a romantic, beautiful, idealised name (connected with Petrarch). Again, incongruous for a chicken.
(6) Any special connotations have to be considered for 'Laura' in Swedish. (However, as a counter-argument, the Mist hairspray was stated to be successful in West Germany, where it means 'filth'!)

(See also Newmark, 1981, p. 71.)

Names of objects

Names of objects as proper names consist of trademarks, brands or proprietaries. They are normally transferred, often coupled with a classifier if the name is not likely to be known to the TL readership: thus, 'Tipp-Ex', *du liquide correcteur Tipp-Ex*; 'Tampax', *un tampon Tampax*; 'Anglepoise lamp', *une lampe de bureau à pièces réglables (Anglepoise)*. You have to ensure you do not become an instrument to promote the advertiser's attempts to make an eponym out of the product's name (unless you are translating the advert). For drugs, you have to consult a pharmacopoeia to check whether the drug is marketed under another name in the TL; it is prudent to add the generic name.

Geographical terms

You have to be up to date in your rendering, to check all terms in the most recent atlas or gazetteer and, where necessary, with the embassies concerned. You have to respect a country's wish to determine its own choice of names for its own geographical features. Some features are sufficiently politically uncontested to remain as they were in English: Belgrade (Beograd), Prague (Praha), Algiers (Al-Djazair), Tunis (Tunus), Tripoli (Tarabulus – Libya and Lebanon); the transliteration of many Egyptian and Middle East towns appears rather wayward and wilful. Note also that Italian names for German and Yugoslav towns can be rather obscure: *Monaco* (Munich), *Agosta* (Augsburg), *Aia* (Aachen), *Colonia* (Cologne), *Treviri* (Trier, Trêves (F)). Note also *Lione* (Lyon) and *Marsiglia* (Marseille). When there is no official line, and perhaps the town lacks an airport (the airlines are keeping 'Nuremberg' going?), you should encourage the trend to revert to the correct name (Livorno, Braunschweig, Hannover) and respect Romania (not Rumania).

Where appropriate, you have to 'educate'. Austerlitz is Slavkov, a town in Czechoslovakia; Auschwitz, the most terrible word in any language, is Oswiecim.

Do not invent new geographical terms: *Saaletal* is 'the Saale valley', not 'Saaletal' nor 'the valley of the Saale'. *Fécampois* is Fécamp (not 'Fecampien') – all French towns, even villages, have adjectival forms, which have to be reduced to the place name.

Note, in general, that 'the works of Mozart' is becoming as (pompous and) obsolescent as 'the books of the boy'. Even professional translators are often mesmerised by *de*, *von*, *di*, etc. into forgetting that 'apostrophe -s' is usage, not 'of plus noun', unless one is talking about Marx, Hodgkiss, Ramuz.

Finally, in an age of misprints, do not trust any proper name that you are not familiar with. An article in *Le Monde* refers to an *université d'été* (political party summer school? summer university?) at 'Sofia-Antipolis' (Alpes-Maritimes). Bulgaria in France? In fact it is Sophia Antipolis, a new industrial and cultural complex, and barely on the map. Again, a German textbook refers to a people of Guyana as the *Akkawau*. In Webster, this is 'acawai', 'akawai', 'acawais' or 'akawais'.

Lastly, distinguish between toponyms as names or items in an address, when they are transferred, and as cultural scenery in an advertising brochure, when at least the classifiers such as 'river', 'plain', 'mountains', 'church', even 'street' can be translated. In a guidebook, the two procedures can be combined in a couplet.

THE TRANSLATION OF PUNS

One makes a pun by using a word (e.g. 'tit'), or two words with the same sound ('piece'/'peace'), or a group of words with the same sound (*personne alitée/personnalité*) in their two possible senses, usually for the purpose of arousing laughter or amusement, and sometimes also to concentrate meaning. Puns are most common in English and Chinese, since they are most easily made with monosyllables.

Puns are most easily translated if they are based on Graeco-latinisms that have near-equivalents in the source and target languages, particularly if they simply contrast the material and the figurative sense of the word; thus there would be no difficulty in translating both senses of words like *point, animal, infernal*, if a pun were made on them in French and, again, the material and figurative sense of a word often corresponds with one-to-one equivalents, such as 'sleep', 'die', 'be born'. Further, animals (pig, ape, mouse) and colours *sometimes* have the corresponding double meanings.

If the purpose of the pun is merely to raise laughter, it can sometimes be 'compensated' by another pun on a word with a different but associated meaning. This is done in the translation of *Astérix* into many languages, and requires exceptional ingenuity.

Puns made by punning poets are most difficult to translate, since they are limited by metre. Often, the pun simply has to be sacrificed.

However, when the two senses of the pun are more important than the medium, they can sometimes be translated by reproducing the two senses in an incongruous way; thus '*dans le panneau*' referring to a misleading signboard system introduced into a city (*panneau* – (a) 'a sign board', *panneau indicateur*; (b) 'a trap', *tomber dans le panneau*) could be translated as 'the signboard mess'.

Finally, where a pun is used in a SL text to illustrate a language, or a slip of the tongue, or the sense is more important than the witticism, it has to be transferred, translated (in both senses) and usually explained. (See Newmark, 1981, pp. 106–7.)

The translation of puns is of marginal importance and of irresistible interest.

THE TRANSLATION OF WEIGHTS, MEASURES, QUANTITIES AND CURRENCIES

The translation of units of the metric system and others (say the Russian *verst*) will depend on their setting and the implied readership. Thus in translating newspaper and periodical articles into English, they are normally converted to the (so-called) Imperial system, i.e., miles, pints, pounds, etc. In translating specialised articles, professional magazines, etc., they are usually transferred (i.e., the metric system is retained) but for cookery articles they are both transferred and converted to the Imperial system.

For fiction, the decision whether to convert or transfer depends on the importance of retaining local colour. Unless there are strong arguments (e.g., time in a period novel, as well as region), I suggest you convert to miles, pounds, acres, gallons, etc. You have to take care not to confuse long and metric tons (tonnes) when accuracy is important. Note that 'billion', formerly 10^{12}, now usually means a thousand million (10^9); 'milliard' (10^6) is no longer used.

When approximate figures are given in the SL text, translate with correspondingly approximate figures (thus 10 km would be 6 miles, not 6.214 miles). Note that figures like *trois dizaines*, *trois douzaines*, etc. can be translated by '(about) three dozen' or 'between thirty and forty', etc. depending on which sounds more natural.

SI units should be used in all scientific translations and supplementarily, where approppriate, in others.

Non-English currency is usually transferred when English is the TL. 'Crowns' are tending to revert to *krone* (Danish, Norwegian) or *kčs* (Czechoslovak). The British pound usually has a standard translation.

AMBIGUITY

I take 'ambiguity' in the sense of a stretch of SL text, normally a word or a syntactic structure, having apparently more than one meaning, in or in spite of its context; 'vagueness' or 'obscurity' can usually be reduced to ambiguity. I am not here discussing the deliberate ambiguities of puns or *double-entendres*.

Grammatical ambiguity

If a sentence is syntactically ambiguous within its context, it must be poorly written. All the notorious ambiguous sentences and groups ('the shooting of the hunters', 'John's book', 'slow neutrons and protons', 'flying planes can be dangerous') as well as less obvious ones ('modern language teaching', 'considering my ignorance', 'What he performed at first was of no interest' (i.e. ambiguously placed adverbs), 'the larger or largest towns' (absolute or relative comparatives or superlatives), 'the house was shut, (state or event), 'summer students' group' (any multiple-noun compound)) – all these can be disambiguated if the context is reasonably informative. You have to become intensively and selectively sensitised to the common syntactical ambiguities of the languages you are translating from. These ambiguities are rather more common in English than in, say, the Romance languages, since English has fewer grammatical inflections (accidence). Note also the tendency of all languages to use many present and past participles independently as adjectives with a slightly different stative meaning and so to give rise to ambiguities (e.g., *perdu*, 'lost', 'ruined'; *désolé*, 'sorry', 'distressed'; 'striking' (two senses); and many German past participles which have independent meanings).

Note that grammatical or functional words are themselves a common source of ambiguity. Common prepositions often have many senses (e.g., *dans*, *à*, *unter*, *gegen*, *um*). It is sometimes notoriously difficult to identify the referents of pronouns. Connectives usually have widely differing senses (e.g., *aber*). Most phrasal verbs but not so many phrasal nouns have at least two meanings.

Lexical ambiguity

Lexical ambiguity is both more common and more difficult to clear up than grammatical ambiguity. Words may have anything from one sense to say 30 (e.g., *Anlage*) and the senses may be close to or remote (as in puns) from each other. Sometimes a word has two senses which are both equally effective (pragmatically and referentially) in the relevant stretch of language, e.g., *contrôler*, to 'verify' or 'direct'; sometimes, as in the case of the metaphorical and the literal sense of a word, you may translate with both senses in mind.

Again, it may not be clear whether *un rein énervé* refers to an 'irritated kidney' or, using *énervé* in its obsolete sense, an 'injured' or 'damaged kidney'.

Pragmatic ambiguity

We all know that 'There's a bull in the field' may 'mean' 'Let's get out', but since these types of pragmatic signals are similar in all languages, provided they are relatively culture-free, a literal translation may well be pertinent. We have perhaps been told too often (e.g., Seleskovitch, 1985) that 'I just came from New York' will translate as *J'en viens*, *Je rentre à peine de New York*, *Je débarque*, *Je suis New Yorkais* depending on the prompting sentence ('Would you like to go to New York?', 'Would you like to go to Boston today?' 'Why do you seem/look so out of place?' respectively), but not often enough that it might be translated as *Je viens d'arriver de New York* after the rather more obvious question: 'Where have you come from now?'

Pragmatic ambiguity is inevitably more common in written than in spoken language, since it arises when the tone or the emphasis in an SL sentence is not clear; e.g., in *On conçoit bien le nombre élevé des protéines différentes qui peuvent être finalement produits par de telles combinaisons*, I suggest that the meaning of *on conçoit bien* may stretch from 'clearly one can understand' to 'one can't possibly imagine', depending on the tone of the text. Again, the emphasis of a sentence such as 'I'm working here today', can only be perceived, if at all, from its context, although italics for one word would help. In the 1985 Eurovision Song Contest, the sense of 'Goodnight' was widely understood as 'Hello' or 'Goodbye', the time of day being irrelevant.

Cultural ambiguity

In principle, cultural terms should not be ambiguous, as they refer to particular features of a single culture. However, ambiguity may arise if the function or the substance of a cultural feature changes at a point of time and the term remains whilst the period background is not clear in the SL text. Further, many cultural and concept-words that are near-internationalisms in many languages have different as well as common sense-components and it may not be clear whether they are being used in the normal SL or in another language's sense: e.g., 'queen', 'prime minister', 'senate', 'province', 'region', or again 'liberalism', 'anarchism', 'poverty', 'idealism'.

Idiolectal ambiguity

You have to bear in mind that most people use some words in a sense that is peculiar to themselves, often because they have heard them used in many situations but have never looked them up in a dictionary, or because they feel a lexical gap in their language or thought and fill it with an inappropriate word. (Some think 'jesuitical' means 'turning a criticism to one's own advantage' rather than 'casuis-tical'.) Wittgenstein's statement 'The meaning of a word is its use in the language' is sometimes right, sometimes wrong, but it is good advice to a translator if he can establish the sense in which a misused word is meant from its context, and translate it accordingly. (If the text is authoritative, he has to add a footnote to explain the correction he has made.)

Referential ambiguity

In a sense all ambiguity is referential, since it prompts two or more images of the reality the translator is trying to describe. Here, however, I have in mind the ambiguous use of proper names in an SL text, e.g., if a person, a town or a patented product is not unmistakably identified.

Metaphorical ambiguity

You can find ambiguities in most sentences if you try hard enough – that is the nature of language, the inadequate and loose dress of thought. The only too obvious advice I can give you is to translate the most probable sense, and to put the less probable sense in a footnote if you judge this sense to be important. Otherwise sensitise yourself to the most common sets of ambiguities in your foreign languages – in translation, you rarely make the same mistake twice, particularly if it is a bad one. There is nothing so educative as making a howler.

CHAPTER 19

Revision Hints
for Exams and Deadlines

(1) I assume that in a translation exam for professional purposes, you can bring in reference books with you, and that reference books are provided. This is realistic, and if it does not happen, you should make a fuss. Therefore you should bring in: *Collins English Dictionary*, the best monolingual SL dictionary, one bilingual dictionary, and *Roget*.

(2) Say you have three hours for a test: you should develop a technique that allows 15 minutes for translational analysis, 2 hours 10 minutes for translating, and 35 minutes for revision, and check the time every half hour.

(3) Write double space and leave gaps between paragraphs. This gives you more space for corrections. Do not do a rough copy except for difficult passages.

(4) Underline all words you intend to look up. Look them up in batches.

(5) Look up all words not familiar to you, and, in SL monolingual dictionaries, any words that look like English words.

(6) You should check any word you look up in a bilingual dictionary in at least one SL and one TL monolingual dictionary. Further, look up all technical words or collocations (SL or TL) in the English *Collins* and the *Webster*, where you may find the words you fail to find in the bilingual dictionaries, e.g., *kermès*.

(7) Look up all proper names. You may have to 'classify' geographical terms and historical names as part of your translation. But looking up is usually the 'iceberg' rather than the 'tip'.

(8) Do not spend excessive time on words that defeat you. Translate them provisionally according to their derivational and/or analogical sense. Then edge the meaning nearer to what makes most sense in the context.

(9) Translate easier sentences and paragraphs first, including the last paragraph if appropriate. Do not leave the paper half finished.

(10) Spend relatively more time on sentences which you think you have a fair chance of getting right, therefore which you have to work on.

(11) Make sense, or at least do not write nonsense, unless you know the passage is ironical or is purposely irrational. Do not reproduce dictionary translations that are obviously wrong in the context. Do not get mesmerised by the SL text.

(12) There are two basic articulations of meaning – those of words and those of sentences. Usually, the meanings of words cannot be stretched beyond certain limits. But when a culture looks at an object in a different way (*château d'eau* – 'water tower'), one word is replaced rather than translated by another. The meaning of sentences must cohere with those of the previous and the following sentences, then the paragraph, then the text.

(13) Your translations have to be referentially and pragmatically accurate. Withdraw from literal translation when you become inaccurate for these reasons only.

(14) Grammar is more flexible than lexis. You can sometimes make a translation natural by using an alternative structure, converting a clause into a group, a verb into a noun. SL words that won't go into one TL word may go into two.

(15) Make use of all the time available. If you have the time, revise separately for accuracy, naturalness (usage), collocations, sentence connectives (logic), punctuation (correspondence or divergence from original), word-order.

(16) It is essential to read your version without looking at the original, paying particular attention to unfamiliar adjective-plus-noun collocations.

(17) Correspondingly, compare your version closely with the original at least to make sure you've not omitted any word, sentence or paragraph. You have to account for the meaning (function) of every SL word, but you don't always have to translate it.

(18) Play for safety with terminology, but be bold with twisted syntax.

(19) Do not replace the dictionary with the encyclopaedia. Do not replace/ translate explanations in the TL text with TL encyclopaedia explanations. Do not translate a technical term by a descriptive term (which is usually wider), unless the technical term does not exist in the TL. Contrariwise, do not translate a descriptive term by a technical term, but this is occasionally justified provided: (a) the technical term does not exist in the SL; (b) the descriptive term is not being used to make a 'linguistic' contrast; (c) an expert assures you that the TL technical term would be better understood.

(20) Always consider the use of couplets for translating institutional and cultural terms and recherché metaphors, for the purpose of informing expert and uninformed readers. (Experts may require a transference, educated readers a functional equivalent, uninformed readers a cultural equivalent.)

(21) The more context-free a word, the more it is likely to be used in its primary (most frequent) meaning.

(22) Write well and naturally, unless the SL text is 'sacred' or linguistically banal or innovatory. In that event, follow the banalities or innovations of your SL text.

(23) Finally, fill in all gaps, guided by your contextual understanding of the piece. Do not write alternative translations.

(24) Normally, write your own note only:

    (a) when you have translated a word you have not located. Write 'not found' and, if appropriate, briefly justify your translation.

(b) if there is a factual mistake in the text which you have corrected.

(c) possibly, if there is a substantial ambiguity in the text, where the second version would make almost equally good sense.

(25) Be suspicious of and particularly careful with easy (looking) texts. Examiners have to differentiate. Scaled marking can magnify mistakes.

(26) Unless you detest pencils, use pencils first and write over with ballpoints.

(27) Remember the marker will note linguistic and referential mistakes of accuracy as well as pragmatic mistakes of usage. Usage is almost as important as accuracy.

(28) There is no such thing as a correct or perfect or ideal translation of a challenging text. Ten first-rate translators may well produce ten different, more or less equally good translations of a complicated sentence. The area of taste in a translation remains, after the area of science, skill and art. So take courage.

(29) If you are working for an employer or a client and you fix your own deadline allow for at least a two-day gap between your main revision and your final reading, so that you can return to your version and see it in a different light. You may have to spend more time pursuing one word than on the whole of the rest of the piece.

All these hints are my own, not objective, not subjective, for you if you prefer to react against.

CHAPTER **20**

By Way of a Conclusion

Why can translation be so horrible? Firstly, because originals can be so monotonous, consisting of different statistics incorporated in similar formats, styles and
registers, important perhaps, but grey, dreary, tediously long, numerous, recurrent, boring, the occupational scourge of the staff translator. Secondly, because
you are so vulnerable – slips, howlers, ghastly knowledge gaps, SL word mesmi-
risation, all take their toll, all humiliate. Consolation: you do not usually make the
same mistake twice in translation: either you have 'taken the strain' by trying to
think of a word for a long time, or the horror of the careless mistake is so great, or
you look the word up after an exam where you are not allowed to use reference
books (such exams should not exist) – you always remember it, it does not recur,
you truly learn from your mistakes. In my case, that is what my translation theory
writing is about – going over the steps leading to mistakes and ensuring they do not
happen again. Thirdly, translating an authoritative text, thinking you could put it
better but are not allowed to. You are unable to stretch the SL words beyond their
meanings. Fourthly, sometimes, the being a 'shadow', the lack of credit, the
belonging to a new, often unacknowledged, profession, and the slanders: 'all you
need for your job is a dictionary'; 'one day when all are bi- or trilingual, go-
betweens like you will become unnecessary'; 'parasites'; 'always second best: after
the job is done, fetch the translator'.

Why can translating be so enjoyable and satisfying? Firstly, because you are
explaining something. It may be to other people and understanding between
peoples, entente, détente, health or education, or social advance may depend on it.
Or it may be your own pleasure when you are learning to understand someone by
taking the impact of a personality through words, to pursue the subtleties of ideas,
empathise with one person, and you are translating for yourself, not for any reader.
Secondly, because it is a continual chase, often devious and lateral, after words and
facts, since, though the element of luck is important, success depends entirely on
you, and what relief if it comes – the joy of finally finding a word in a book after
hours of searching on the shelves and in your mind. Thirdly, because it is never-
ending, because you can always improve it, because it gives you a tactile feeling and
relish for words as well as the rhythms of sentences read aloud to yourself.
Fourthly, the challenge, the wager, the isolation – often you write on behalf of an

224

author you do not know to readers you never meet, who may be educated all-rounders or ignorant; they may be like an identikit or as diverse as humanity. Fifthly, the joy of the find, the happy concise stretch of language, when you feel you have written just what the author wanted to but did not. Sixthly, the sense, when you are translating some novel or biography, that you are identifying not only with the author, but with the main character, and incidentally with someone dear to you who appears to embody him.

'Splendours and miseries of translation': thus Ortega y Gasset, following Balzac who so described courtesans. This struggle with a text which may now be EEC legislation, or a patent, as well as the vagaries of a capricious and complicated mind, is still essentially personal. What is now clear is that whilst this struggle always embraces some minor defects, it must be mainly successful – it is too important to be anything else (Thomas Mann pointed out that reading the Russian classics was a major factor in his education, though the translations were very weak (quoted by Chukovsky, 1984)). And this is why all the statements about the impossibility of translation (Quine taken up by Frawley and his fellows, Benjamin by Derrida and Derrida by Graham (1985) and his group) are silly: what they are doing is dismissing the possibility of perfect translation. Translation is enjoyable as a process, not as a state. Only a state is perfect.

PART II

Methods

Introductory Note

The thirteen texts that follow are material for four types of exercise: (a) a translational analysis of a source language text; (b) translations of the same text to illustrate the difference between 'semantic' and 'communicative' translation as methods; (c) translations with commentaries; (d) examples of translation criticism. Both topic and register of the thirteen texts are varied.

No attempt has been made to treat these texts in a uniform way. Commentaries can always be written either in the order that the problems appear, or the examples can be grouped under heads such as grammar, metaphor, proper names, and so on. Each text presents rather similar types of problems, but their degree of importance, and the way they are solved (they are always solved) differ.

In no sense are these workings to be regarded as models, fair copies or paradigms. They are simply the way I handled the problems a year ago – next year I would be handling them slightly differently. They are to be regarded as hints and suggestions of working methods both for students and teachers, to be helpful as preparation for classes and exams. The text analysis serves first to sensitise you to problems (all deviations from literal translation are problems and present choices, including the return to literal translation after smoother options have been abandoned); the writing of 'communicative' and 'semantic' versions is a useful training in writing a variety of stylistic registers as opposed to a text that retains either every originality or oddity or every crudity or banality of the original. Translation commentaries and criticisms are creative as well as critical and when you criticise a translation solution, you inevitably feel prompted to produce a better one, even when you feel your thought, your comprehension, is like a prisoner within your language.

The texts here are deliberately mixed. Text 1 (from *The Economist*), Text 5 (on the French Socialist Party— and Text 13 (on the FRG) are the 'least' authoritative – in principle, what the authors thought is not as important as the texts' effective expression. In the medical texts, the facts are vital, and they must also be persuasively presented. Proust, Waugh and De Gaulle are authoritative, and you have to be faithful to them. But in the case of Proust, you are listening to an interior voice, and I do not think any reader is as important as yourself as receptor; while De Gaulle addresses the French, his readers, you have also to be aware of this

229

relationship. Waugh writes beautifully, but his attitude and his themes are often trivial, so you may consider making cultural concessions to your readers, explaining a local or period custom, if you can do it elegantly.

I am exceptionally grateful to Dr David James for his painstaking and expert comments on my draft treatments of the three medical texts (Texts 2, 7 and 8).

Power Needs Clear Eyes

A great power knows it is dangerous to be seen to flinch, because its assorted enemies around the world take new heart and its friends' knees knock. A great power also knows that if it sets out on an adventure without seeing precisely what it needs to do, and how to do it, it can get into bad trouble. In
5 Grenada, President Reagan this week rejected the flinch and moved in to achieve a clearly identified, and achievable, objective. In much more important Lebanon, he is still between the rock and the hard place. The bombings in Beirut which killed about 300 American and French soldiers on Sunday morning make it plain that the United States went into Lebanon last
10 year with fine general intentions but without, after the first few weeks, either a clear plan of action or the military strength needed to carry out one possible clear plan of action.

    The relatively easy business in Grenada, like Britain's difficult business in the Falklands last year, had a straightforward objective: the defeat and
15 removal of a fairly small number of men who had shot their way into local power. The operation in Lebanon has no such simplicity. The four-country force, of which America's marines are the core, was originally intended to be a cordon between the Israeli army on the outskirts of Beirut and the shambles within the city. But then the Israelis pulled back from the edge of Beirut and
20 the marines, having sailed away and hurriedly sailed back again, found themselves supervising a mishmash of very different purposes.

    Part of the new job, admirably done by the Italians, was to protect the surviving Palestinians in the refugee camps of southern Beirut. The rest of the multinational force slid, inexorably, into politics. The French were there
25 to demonstrate that Lebanon was still a French interest. The tiny British unit was there to hold an American little finger. The American contingent last month used naval gunfire to save the Maronite Christian militia and the Lebanese army from defeat by the Druzes in the hills above Beirut. But the Americans have also been trying to persuade the minority Maronites to give
30 up some of the majority of Lebanese political power they have held since

Source: *The Economist*, 29 October 1983.

1943. It is sometimes necessary to protect a man with one arm while removing his trousers with the other, but it is not easy to explain to the people watching on television: or to the man himself.

The phrases used by the spokesmen to justify the American presence in
35 Lebanon – 'restoring peace' and 're-creating the Lebanese state' – are bland words for commendable objectives, but only a rough and ready description of the complexity they conceal. The Americans need to lean back, remember what their interests in the Middle East are, and then apply these interests to the problem they face in Lebanon.

GENERAL PROBLEMS

Intention: To state the aims and complexities of US policy in the Lebanon, and contrast them with Syria's aims.
Type of Text: Informative.
Readership: Educated English readership with good general knowledge of topic.
'Setting': Journal with wide political and economic interests.
Language: Educated, informal, with wide variety of metaphors and colloquialisms. Well written. Warm in tone.
Intention of translator: To translate the text accurately and economically to an an educated Arabic readership of a similar journal, or for a client. There are no problems of culture transfer.
Method: Communicative, at level of readership.

SOME PARTICULAR PROBLEMS

Title: Allusive. Change to descriptive title, e.g., 'US in Lebanon'? (If so, why?)
Syntax: Rather long sentences.
Possible grammatical shifts: 'to be seen to flinch' (l.1); 'has no such simplicity' (l.16); 'The bombings . . . killed' (l.8); 'four-country force' (l.16); 'In much more important Lebanon' (l.6).
Geographical terms: Falklands; Grenada (where?); American.
Metaphors:

(1) *Dead:* 'core' (l.17); 'moved in' (l.5); 'pulled back' (l.19); 'sailed away' (l.20).
(2) *Standard:* 'flinch' (l.1); 'knees knock' (l.2); 'get into bad trouble' (l.4); 'shambles' (l.18); 'shot their way into' (l.15); 'cordon' (l.18); lean back (l.37).
(3) *Original:* 'slide into politics' (l.24); 'protect with one arm while removing his trousers with the other' (ll.31–2).

(4) *Obscure:* 'between the rock and the hard place' (1.7); (American metaphor); 'tiny unit to hold a little finger' (ll.25–6).

Lexis: Assorted' (1.1); 'fine' (1.10); 'business' (1.13); 'straightforward' (1.14); 'marines' (1.17); 'inexorably' (1.24); 'militia' (1.27); 'bland' (1.35).

Colloquialisms: 'shambles' (1.18); 'mishmash' (1.21).

Re-creations: 'rejected the flinch' (1.5).

Repetition: 'clear plan of action' (ll.11–12).

CONCLUSION

How (1) accurate, (2) economical is the translation likely to be? How much meaning will be lost by translating the numerous metaphors, few colloquialisms and informal phrasal verbs? Should the translator supply any additional information for, e.g., Grenada? Falklands? anything else?

Note: The difficulties (meaning and translation) of all problems must be *discussed* – a list will not do; e.g., 'assorted' *implies* 'different'; 'various', 'of many odd kinds'. Will it be translated by one, two or three adjectives?

Papers and Originals

Upper gastrointestinal endoscopy: its effects on patient management

C. D. Holdsworth, K. D. Bardhan, G. V. Balmforth, R. A. Dixon, G. E. Sladen

SUMMARY AND CONCLUSIONS

Out of 95 patients referred for upper gastrointestinal endoscopy after a barium-meal examination, 44 underwent a change in management. Some changes were minor but in 12 patients a decision on surgery was required. Seven of these patients were among a group of 13 for whom the referring consultant would have recommended laparotomy had endoscopy not been available, while the other five were subjected to an unplanned laparotomy.

These findings support the practice of performing endoscopy on patients whose symptoms are not fully explained by barium-meal examination, especially patients aged over 45. In such cases the procedure also seems to be cost-effective.

INTRODUCTION

Fibreoptic endoscopy is now widely used to investigate suspected upper gastrointestinal tract disease. In our four districts some 2500 examinations are done yearly, which represents a considerable load; thus an examination of the usefulness or otherwise of the technique seemed long overdue. Its value in acute upper gastrointestinal haemorrhage has been assessed but it has not been evaluated objectively in other conditions. Thus to determine the real rather than imagined value of endoscopy we have studied prospectively a consecutive series of patients referred for the procedure after having undergone a barium-meal examination.

Source: *British Medical Journal*, 24 March 1983.

234

METHOD

20   Of the four clinicians participating in this study, two work in district general hospitals and two in nearby undergraduate teaching hospitals. All accept patients for outpatient assessment from general practitioners, and also direct referrals for endoscopy from consultant colleagues. The patients studied represent a population usually seen for outpatient endoscopy – that is,
25   patients presenting with upper gastrointestinal symptoms and referred for endoscopy within three months after a normal barium-meal examination or one showing abnormalities that need to be elucidated. The doctor referring the patient for endoscopy (in the case of some outpatients this was the endoscopist himself) was asked, 'What immediate action would you take if
30   fibre endoscopy was not available?' He was allowed only one option in a check list (see table, first column). Endoscopy was carried out, the result recorded, and, one to three months later, the case records examined to determine the immediate course of clinical management adopted by the referring clinician. The post-endoscopy plan was then compared with the pre-endoscopy plan to
35   determine any change.

NOTES

The aim of these notes is: (1) to demonstrate the referential level of the text; and (2) to give some hints for translating it in accordance with natural usage.

GENERAL

The purpose of the paper is to present the results of a clinical trial into the value of upper gastrointestinal endoscopy. This is a procedure in which the linings of the oesophagus (the gullet, the part of the alimentary canal or digestive tract between the pharynx and the stomach) and the stomach are examined under direct vision by passing a flexible fibreoptic instrument which enables the operator to see round all bends and corners. The study attempted to ascertain whether use of this new procedure could be justified in terms both of results and of costs. The question posed was whether endoscopy would produce information important enough to affect the choice of treatment in a group of patients where the traditional X-ray method of investigation (with a barium meal) had failed to discover the reason for their intestinal symptoms. As a result of the endoscopy, seven out of the 13 patients previously due to have an exploratory operation were instead given less invasive treatment. In the remaining six, the need for operation was confirmed, and five others who had previously been assigned to non-operative treatment were now found to require an operation. Since these operations cost about £450 each and endoscopy £15 per case (in 1979), endoscopy proved to be cost-effective in this study.

PARTICULAR PROBLEMS

PARTICULAR PROBLEMS

Papers and originals, etc: See Chapter 14, 'Technical translation'. The house-style of the TL setting has to be followed.

Title: This is a completely descriptive title with stress on endoscopy, and should normally be followed in the translation – despite its length. It may alternatively be recast as 'Endoscopy of the upper gastrointestinal tract and its effect on patient management'. 'Management': A technical term here for the whole system of care and treatment of a disease or a patient, therefore a more general term than 'treatment'; probably translate as 'treatment' (or 'general treatment').

l.1   'referred': Here a technical term for patients sent by general surgeons to a specialised endoscopy unit. 'Refer' normally indicates a doctor sending a patient to another, normally a specialist (*adresser qn. à qn.*; *jn. an jn. verweisen*).

l.2   'barium-meal examination': Before X-ray pictures are taken, the patient is required to swallow a quantity of barium a radio-opaque substance which produces an outline of the intestinal tract on the X-ray films. Can be translated as *bouillie barytée* or *transit baryté*.

l.2   'underwent a change in management': Clumsy writing. Translate perhaps as 'had their treatment changed'.

l.3   'a decision on surgery was required': 'endoscopy resulted in a decision to operate'.

ll.4–5 'referring consultant': 'the specialist referring them'.

l.6   'laparotomy': The surgical opening of the abdomen in order to discover what is wrong.

l.6   'unplanned': 'not previously intended'.

l.7   'support': 'are evidence in favour of'.

l.10   'cost-effective': A vogue-economic term associated with Mrs Thatcher's governments: defined as 'providing adequate financial return in relation to outlay', the sense here is presumably more humane (but there is a saving of two laparotomies!). Translate as *rentable* (F), *rentabel* (G).

l.11   'fibreoptic' (Am. 'fiberoptic'): A fibreoptic endoscope is a flexible bundle of synthetic fibres which transmit an image around any number of corners or contortions. The term is likely to become a (naturalised) internationalism (*fibreoptique*, *fibroptisch*) but I have not found it. Therefore, if I cannot find an informant, I 'coin' the term, putting it in inverted commas and adding a brief explanatory note. At present the German equivalent is *flexible Fiberglasendoskopie*.

l.12   'districts': The reference is to the districts covered by the four hospitals employing the authors.

l.13   'done': Usually 'performed'.

l.13   'load': Combines 'tasks' with 'large number'.

l.14   'usefulness or otherwise': 'degree of usefulness'.

l.14   'value in': Translate 'value in cases of'.

1.17   'prospectively': Methodological term referring to the prospect of new cases to be found and followed up after the trial has been designed.

1.20   'clinicians': Doctors specialising in treatment of patients directly rather than in laboratory or research work.

1.21   'undergraduate': Translate 'students taking first degrees', 'students', or perhaps omit as redundant in this context.

1.21   'accept': A descriptive term. Note the technical terms 'admit' (*admettre, aufnehmen*), 'discharge' (*renvoyer*), 'in-patient' (*malade hospitalisé*), 'out-patient' (*malade en consultation externe*); 'hospitalise' = 'admit as in-patient' – all of which should have standard translations.

1.25   'present with': Technical term: *présenter avec.*

ll.29–30 A direct question is rare in academic papers but justified here and should be reproduced in the translation.

11.30–1 'check list': *liste de contrôle, Prüfliste.*

1.32   'case records': *dossiers médicaux* (note that *observations* (F) if often used for 'case records'.

Brideshead Revisited

Evelyn Waugh

Julia left Sebastian and me at Brideshead and went to stay with an aunt, Lady
Rosscommon, in her villa at Cap Ferrat. All the way she pondered her
problem. She had given a name to her widower-diplomat; she called him
'Eustace', and from that moment he became a figure of fun to her, a little
5 interior, incommunicable joke, so that when at last such a man did cross her
path – though he was not a diplomat but a wistful major in the Life Guards –
and fall in love with her and offer her just those gifts she had chosen, she sent
him away moodier and more wistful than ever; for by that time she had met
Rex Mottram.

10 Rex's age was greatly in his favour, for among Julia's friends there was a
kind of gerontophilic snobbery; young men were held to be gauche and
pimply; it was thought very much more chic to be seen lunching at the Ritz –
a thing, in any case, allowed to few girls of that day, to the tiny circle of Julia's
intimates; a thing looked at askance by the elders who kept the score, chatting
15 pleasantly against the walls of the ballrooms – at the table on the left as you
came in, with a starched and wrinkled old roué whom your mother had been
warned of as a girl, than in the centre of the room with a party of exuberant
young bloods. Rex, indeed, was neither starched nor wrinkled; his seniors
thought him a pushful young cad, but Julia recognized the unmistakable chic
20 – the flavour of 'Max' and 'F.E.' and the Prince of Wales, of the big table in
the Sporting Club, the second magnum and the fourth cigar, of the chauffeur
kept waiting hour after hour without compunction – which her friends would
envy. His social position was unique; it had an air of mystery, even of crime,
about it; people said Rex went about armed. Julia and her friends had a
25 fascinated abhorrence of what they called 'Pont Street'; they collected
phrases that damned their user, and among themselves – and often, discon-
certingly, in public – talked a language made up of them. It was 'Pont Street'
to wear a signet ring and to give chocolates at the theatre; it was 'Pont Street'
at a dance to say, 'Can I forage for you?' Whatever Rex might be, he was
30 definitely not 'Pont Street'. He had stepped straight from the underworld
into the world of Brenda Champion who was herself the innermost of a

Source: *A. D. Peters & Co. Ltd.*

number of concentric ivory spheres. Perhaps Julia recognized in Brenda
Champion an intimation of what she and her friends might be in twelve years'
time; there was an antagonism between the girl and the woman that was hard
35   to explain otherwise. Certainly the fact of his being Brenda Champion's
property sharpened Julia's appetite for Rex.

Rex and Brenda Champion were staying at the next villa on Cap Ferrat,
taken that year by a newspaper magnate and frequented by politicians. They
would not normally have come within Lady Rosscommon's ambit, but,
40   living so close, the parties mingled and at once Rex began warily to pay his
court.

NOTES FOR THE TRANSLATION OF AN EXPRESSIVE TEXT

General

The text is a description of some typical features of upper- and upper-middle-class
life in England and London in the inter-war years. The writer's attitude is sympa-
thetic to this society – the only approach to social criticism is in ll.21–2, but it is
observant and detailed; the triviality of the characters is self-evident.

The novel was written in 1950, and this passage contains some upper-class 1920s
'slang' (vogue-words). The writing is individual, careful, beautifully composed –
some long sentences (notably ll.12–23), with parentheses, perceptibly influenced
by Proust.

Particular problems

l.1   'Lady': Aristocratic title, specifically English (opaque), therefore usually
        transferred. Other titles that are transparent ('earl', 'duke', 'count'
        'marquess', 'marchioness') may have recognised equivalents and be trans-
        lated in some European languages.
l.2   'villa': Here probably large detached mansion, close to the sea. In
        European languages, the word is often transferred, but not when it means a
        'semi-detached suburban house'.
ll.2–3 Alliteration deliberate, but not all that important in translation.
l.3   'widower-diplomat': A coinage but, if unnatural, translate as 'widowed
        diplomat'.
l.4   'Eustace': Slightly comic upper-class first name, rare now. Transfer as it
        stands.
l.4   'figure of fun': Recognised phrase (dead metaphor); translates as 'comic
        figure'.
l.5   'interior joke': Unusual collocation. Translate literally.
ll.5–6 'cross her path': Standard metaphor. 'Path' becomes 'way' in most
        standard equivalent translations, e.g. *se trouva sur son chemin*.

l.6   'wistful': 'No-equivalent' word. By CA (in order of importance): 'sad', 'thoughtful', 'vague', 'yearning', 'disappointed'. Translate perhaps by coupled adjectives ('sad and thoughtful', 'thoughtful and yearning') or adverb plus adjective ('sadly thoughtful').

l.6   'Life Guards': Translates into European languages as *garde du corps*, *Leibwache*, etc. However, as it is not an important cultural reference, it could be translated by a functional/descriptive equivalent: 'a (royal) cavalry regiment'. I see no point here in transferring the term.

l.8   'moody': Translates 'straight' into German (*launisch*) but not French (*d'humeur changeante*). Not important enough for a CA.

l.11   'gerontophilic': Internationalism.

l.12   'Ritz': Transfer. Add 'Hotel' for a culture where it is not known.

ll.10–18 The structures of this long sentence should be preserved after the standard shifts have been made; the extraordinary gap between 'more' (l.12) and 'than' (l.17) should be kept.

l.14   'a thing': Replace by *ce que*, (F) *was* (G) or 'a practice'.

l.14   'kept the score': Standard metaphor, probably from cricket: 'kept the account'.

l.16   'roué': No longer roué in French! *Débauché*.

l.18   'bloods': 'Dashing young men'. No longer used in this sense, except ironically.

l.18   'starched': 'starchy', *guindé*. Connotation of 'starched shirt'.

l.18   'seniors': (obsolescent): 'elders'.

l.19   'pushful' (rare): 'pushing', 'self-assertive', 'pushy'.

l.19   'cad': Colloquial, upper-middle-class for 'nasty, ungentlemanly person'. Now mainly ironical.

l.19   'chic': Transfers in French and German (*Schick*).

l.20   'flavour': Here 'atmosphere'.

l.20   '"Max"': Refers to Max Beerbohm (1872–1956), English wit and caricaturist. I suggest you give full name, and provide biographical information in a glossary.

l.20   '"F.E."': Refers to F.E. Smith (1870–1930), lawyer and orator. As for '"Max"'.

l.20   'Prince of Wales': Later Edward VIII. Use recognised translation, also through-translation.

l.21   'Sporting Club': Transfer or translate as 'gambling club' (*not* 'sports club').

l.21   'magnum': Perhaps add 'of champagne'.

l.25   '"Pont Street"': in Knightsbridge, a fashionable London shopping area. Transfer and gloss.

l.29   'forage': 'look for food'.

l.30   'underworld': Criminal underworld.

ll.31–2 'innermost of a number of concentric ivory circles': Not clear, unless 'ivory' (cf. 'ivory tower') means 'remote' and 'spheres' are 'social circles'. In theory, you could translate literally and leave the problem to your readers but I'd follow my interpretation, as I do not think it is important.

l.38   'Taken': 'rented'.
ll.40–1   'pay his court': Variant of 'pay court', *faire sa cour*.
l.40   'warily': 'cautiously, diffidently', possibly 'suspiciously'. If one synonym
          is used, under-translation is inevitable.

Inevitably there will be semantic loss in the translation, since the passage contains a large number of cultural and 'non-equivalent' words; if the full meaning of these were rendered, the version would be cumbersome. It is also difficult to retain the binary balanced style.

Une certaine idée de la France
Charles De Gaulle

Toute ma vie, je me suis fait une certaine idée de la France. Le sentiment me l'inspire aussi bien que la raison. Ce qu'il y a, en moi, d'affectif imagine naturellement la France, telle la princesse des contes ou la madone aux fresques des murs, comme vouée à une destinée éminente et exceptionnelle. J'ai, d'instinct, l'impression que la Providence l'a créée pour des succès achevés ou des malheurs exemplaires. S'il advient que la médiocrité marque, pourtant, ses faits et gestes, j'en éprouve la sensation d'une absurde anomalie, imputable aux fautes des Français, non au génie de la patrie. Mais aussi, le côté positif de mon esprit me convainc que la France n'est réellement
10 elle-même qu'au premier rang; que, seules, de vastes entreprises sont susceptibles de compenser les ferments de dispersion que son peuple porte en lui-même; que notre pays, tel qu'il est, parmi les autres, tels qu'ils sont, doit, sous peine de danger mortel, viser haut et se tenir droit. Bref, à mon sens, la France ne peut être la France sans la grandeur.

COMMUNICATIVE TRANSLATION

All my life I have created a certain idea of France for myself. My feeling, as well as my reason, inspires me with this idea. In my mind I imagine France as a fairy-tale princess or a madonna painted on frescoes, as though destined for a distinguished and exceptional future. Instinctively I feel that Providence has created France to have consummate successes or exemplary failures. If, however, it sinks to mediocrity in its actions, I feel this is an absurd anomaly which is due to the faults of the French and not to the genius of the country. Moreover, I am convinced that France only really reaches its full stature when it stands in the first rank; that only vast undertakings can make up for the seeds of dispersal that its people carry in themselves; that our country must have high aims and have a name for honesty and act according to its lights; otherwise it will be in mortal danger. In short, as I see it,

---

Source: *Mémoires de Guerre. L'Appel*. Librairie Plon.

France cannot be France unless it is great.

Commentary

This translation 'normalises' the original, and I cannot set it in a real context, since the original presents few linguistic or cultural difficulties. A few conventional idioms ('sinks to mediocrity', 'reaches its full stature', 'act according to its lights') replace De Gaulle's individual expressions.

Note that this text is both 'authoritative' and 'expressive' in that it has authority and expresses a personality. Many other authoritative statements, poorly written, clichéd, commonplace, unimaginative, are 'expressive' only in the sense that they demonstrate atrophied personalities, but they still have to be translated 'semantically'.

SEMANTIC TRANSLATION

All my life, I have devised for myself a certain idea of France. Feeling inspires me with it as well as reason. What is emotional in me naturally imagines France, like the princess in the fairy-tales or the madonna on the frescoes of the walls, as dedicated to an eminent and exceptional destiny. I have, instinctively, the feeling that Providence has created France for complete successes or exemplary misfortunes. If it happens, however, that mediocrity marks her deeds and her actions, I experience the feeling of an absurd anomaly, attributable to the faults of the French, not to the genius of the motherland. But further, the positive side of my thought persuades me that France is really only herself when in the first rank; that vast enterprises alone are capable of compensating for the leaven of dispersal which her people carries in itself; that our country, as it is, among the others, as they are, must on pain of mortal danger, aim high and stand upright. In short, in my opinion, France cannot be France without greatness.

Commentary

This translation assumes that the original is authoritative. The translation is at the author's level, but since, unlike many expressive texts, it is implicitly addressed to a large readership, viz. the entire French nation, this readership cannot be ignored: in particular, the phonaesthetic side of the original has to be kept. However, for some common idioms, I have brought out their 'full' rather than their standard sense. The style is personal, lofty, formal, old-fashioned, superb.

PARTICULAR PROBLEMS

1.1   *je me suis fait* (*se faire une idée*): Translates as 'get some idea'. In this more formal text, the sense of *faire* is strengthened.

1.2   *affectif*: Has a wider semantic range than the technical 'affective' (from 'affect', a psychological term). Hence 'emotional'.

1.4   *des murs*: Virtually redundant, but is reproduced to obtain equivalent effect.

1.5   *l'a créée*: 'France' is recovered from the previous sentence for clarity and impressiveness.

1.7   *faits et gestes*: An established tautologous nominal, meaning 'conduct'.

1.8   *patrie*: Has the natural sense of 'motherland' or 'homeland'. If 'motherland' sound unnatural, try 'homeland'.

1.11 *les ferments*: Used materially and figuratively, in a restless sense. De Gaulle's plural is idiosyncratic, and could perhaps be modified.

1.12 *tel que, tels que*: 'just as' could replace 'such', which is too negative.

1.13 *à mon sens:* The normal 'in my opinion' is strengthened to 'to my mind'.

A 'faithful' translation would retain the plural 'ferments'; it might replace 'emotional' with 'affective' and even transfer *la patrie*.

Le Parti Socialiste

Le PS revient à la thèse qu'il y a une classe dominante, et même une 'minorité' dominante contre une majorité d''exploités'. Cette résurgence du manichéisme, ce 'retour du sacré' sont-ils destinés à compenser la frustration de certains éléments qui avaient été invités par le premier secrétaire à se tenir
5   tranquilles pendant l'élection présidentielle? Toujours est-il que le 'front de classe' redevient le mot de passe.

SEMANTIC TRANSLATION

The French Socialist Party is returning to the thesis that there is one dominant class, and even one dominant 'minority' against a majority of 'the exploited'. This resurgence of Manichaeism, this 'return of the sacred' – is this intended to compensate for the frustration of some individuals who had been invited by the first secretary to keep quiet during the Presidential election? Be that as it may, the 'class front' is again becoming the password.

Commentary

This translation would only be appropriate if the original were an extract from an authoritative statement (it is not), say a party chairman's speech or an attempt to show the rhetoric of French political writings. The SL syntactic structures have been retained, but this text is distinguished from literal translation in rendering *certains éléments* as 'some individuals' rather than 'certain elements', which is not the meaning in this context. The only concession made to the readership is the translation of *PS* as 'French Socialist Party', thus distinguishing it from 'faithful translation' where no concessions are permitted. Note that the translation is at the author's level; no attempt is made to transfer the SL culture or to neutralise it, and it is written as though to express an individual personality, even if it does not in fact do so.

COMMUNICATIVE TRANSLATION

The French Socialist Party is again taking up the argument that there is one dominant class, and even one dominant minority opposed to an exploited majority. It may be that this revival of a simple black and white concept, and the return to classical Marxism, are intended to make up for the frustration of some members whom the party leader had invited to keep quiet during the Presidential election. The fact remains that 'class solidarity' has again become the Party slogan.

Commentary

The method of translation is appropriate, as the original is an extract from a French political magazine, and I am assuming that the 'setting' of the translation is an English weekly review, or a client who wants a readily comprehensible translation: therefore an educated but not a specialised readership.

Deviations from literal translation are made (a) to convert to natural usage or (b) to clarify the text on the referential level.

PARTICULAR PROBLEMS

l.1   *le PS*: As in the semantic translation, this acronym has to be explained.
l.1   *revient*: The phrasal verb 'take up' is preferred, to achieve a slightly more familiar register.
l.1   *la thèse*: 'Thesis' is coming into general educated vocabulary but still not as common as *thèse* or 'argument'.
l.2   Inverted commas: Used perhaps to indicate established Marxist key-terms, possibly quotations from Marx. The TL readership, being less familiar with Marxism, the inverted commas are omitted here. Additional ironical connotation possible but unlikely.
l.2   *contre* and *exploités*: Modified to achieve natural usage, which is usually more neatly done grammatically (through shifts) than lexically. Lexical modification often makes too great a change in meaning, but may be justified by the collocation.
ll.2–5 The sentence has been recast, because (a) rhetorical sentences are more common in Romance languages than in English and (b) the French word-order is effective but oratorical and would reproduce strangely in the English setting. The question form is partly compensated by 'it may be that' but the English is not as emphatic as the French.
l.3   *manichéisme*: First I make the assumption that the English readership will not be as familiar with the word as the French 'Catholic' readership. Secondly, the relevant meaning here is functional, not descriptive: Mani's third-century Persian heresy is irrelevant. The functional meaning is the existence and opposition of the principles of good and evil: 'the concept of

the opposition between good and evil' is a possible translation, but appears too heavy. 'The idea of good and evil', 'the conflict between good and evil' are among a number of other possible options.

1.3   *retour du sacré*: Strictly 'return of the sacred' but in the context 'return to the sacred' is more natural and overlaps in meaning. I assume the inverted commas are used half-apologetically to show that the author is making up his own collocation, but it may be an obscure quotation. *Le sacré* may have an ironical connotation; the reference is to the sacred texts of Marxism. Alternative: 'pure Marixism'.

1.3   *compenser*: 'make up for'; cf. 'take up'.

1.4   *certains éléments*: In my opinion, *certains* translates as 'some' six times out of ten! *Eléments* is negative only in a negative context. 'Party members' makes the reference clearer.

1.4   *invités*: Used ironically.

1.4   *le premier secrétaire*: Chief post in some Communist and Socialist parties abroad. The term is easily deculturalised, though it is transparent, either as 'party leader' or 'party secretary'.

1.5   *toujours est-il que*: 'the fact remains that' is not so 'refined' (used in the sense of 'slightly precious', 'faded', 'literary') as 'be that as it may'.

1.5   *'front de classe'*: No longer as current as 20 years ago, but 'class solidarity' may be too remote.

1.6   *mot de passe*: Means only 'pass-word', but the wider 'slogan' may be intended.

Note that if *contre* had translated as 'at odds with', *se tenir tranquille* as 'keep their mouths shut', etc., the translation would be 'idiomatic' rather than 'communicative'. Usually I oppose both 'faithful' and 'idiomatic' translation methods.

A la Recherche du Temps Perdu
Marcel Proust

J'étais dans une de ces périodes de la jeunesse, dépourvues d'un amour particulier, vacantes, où partout – comme un amoureux, la femme dont il est épris – on désire, on cherche, on voit la Beauté. Qu'un seul trait réel – le peu qu'on distingue d'une femme vue de loin, ou de dos – nous permette de
5   projeter la Beauté devant nous, nous nous figurons l'avoir reconnue, notre cœur bat, nous pressons le pas, et nous resterons toujours à demi persuadés que c'était elle, pourvu que la femme ait disparu: ce n'est que si nous pouvons la rattraper que nous comprenons notre erreur.

SEMANTIC TRANSLATION

I was in one of those periods of youth, that are lacking in a particular love, that are vacant, where everywhere – as a lover the woman he is in love with – one desires, one seeks, one sees Beauty. Let just one real feature – the little that one can distinguish of a woman seen from afar, or from behind – allow us to project Beauty before us, and we imagine that we have recognised her, our heart beats, we hurry on, and we shall remain always half-convinced that she was the one, provided the woman has disappeared; only if we can overtake her do we understand our mistake.

Commentary

This translation is appropriate if the original is a serious literary text, therefore an expressive text and *ipso facto* authoritative. The translation attempts to preserve the original's degree of deviation from natural language: long sentences, compressed parenthesis, two sets of three simple main clauses, romantic words, strong rhythmic emphases. Where the original follows the SL norm, the translation follows the TL norm: thus 'that are' is put in twice between nouns and adjective/ present participle; the French perfect infinitive (1.6) shifts to object noun clause; 'can' (1.3) precedes 'distinguish'; *persuadé* perhaps has the same currency as 'convinced'. In a 'faithful' translation, these modifications would probably have been avoided, and *c'était elle* 'preserved' as 'it was she' (last-ditch aristocratic stand) rather than 'it was her'.

COMMUNICATIVE TRANSLATION

For me it was one of those times in youth when we are without a special love, and which are empty. Here we desire, look for and see beauty everywhere, just like lovers in search of the women they are in love with. We have only to let a single real feature, say the little we can make out of a woman seen from a distance or from behind, show us a picture of beauty for us to think we have recognised her. With hearts beating, we hurry on. We shall always remain half-convinced we've seen Beauty herself, as long as she has disappeared; we can only understand our mistake when we catch up with her.

Commentary

This communicative translation is mainly 'academic'; it might help someone who is trying to read the French original and cannot understand it. It converts to natural usage, under-translates, and concentrates on the 'message'.

l.1   *dépourvu de*: This often translates as 'without', but the semantic translation (q.v.) brings out more of its meaning.

ll.2–8 Here, as throughout, there is gross oversimplification. This translation overlooks the three parallel successive acts or movements, desiring, searching, seeing; beauty is personalised rather than personified; the register becomes informal; the second sequence of four verbs is also fudged. Various little words have been put in to make the translation more commonplace. In an 'idiomatic' translation, *vacantes* might translate as 'empty as a drum'; *pressons le pas* as 'run quick as lightning'; *disparu* as 'melted into thin air'. Such changes caricature the position of translators and linguists who believe idioms to be the essence of a language.

Présentation d'un cas de toxoplasmose associée à une maladie de Hodgkin

par MM. J. Chauvergne, C. Meuge, Ch. de Joigny et B. Hœrni

La toxoplasmose et la maladie de Hodgkin peuvent réaliser des tableaux cliniques très voisins, caractérisés essentiellement par une altération de l'état général, un syndrome fébrile, une polyadénopathie.

L'examen histologique d'un prélèvement biopsique permet en général de porter le diagnostic exact, mais certains aspects ganglionnaires réalisés parfois par la toxoplasmose sont très proches de ceux de la 10 lymphogranulomatose. C'est dire que la détection sérologique de la toxoplasmose constitue un appoint appréciable pour ce diagnostic et il faut souligner l'intérêt de sa réalisation systématique, au même titre que 15 d'autres explorations sérologiques, chez tout malade porteur d'une maladie de Hodgkin.

Ces problèmes diagnostiques déjà assez complexes peuvent être rendus plus 20 difficiles encore quand les deux affections sont associées, comme dans l'observation que nous présentons:

OBSERVATION

Mme D . . . Lucette, vingt-six ans. D.M. Fondation Bergonié, 66.599.

C'est en novembre 1965 que cette jeune

A case of toxoplasmosis associated with Hodgkin's disease*

J. Chauvergne, C. Meuge, Ch. de Joigny, B. Hœrni

Toxoplasmosis and Hodgkin's disease may present a very similar clinical picture, which is characterised primarily by a deterioration in general health, fever and generalised lymphadenopathy.

An accurate diagnosis can generally be 5 made on the basis of a histological examination of a biopsy specimen. However, the appearance of the lymph nodes which are sometimes found in toxoplasmosis closely resembles that of those in Hodgkin's disease. Serological tests for toxoplasmosis are therefore of considerable assistance in diagnosis, and should be carried out as a matter of routine, like other serological investigations, in all patients with Hodgkin's disease.

These diagnostic problems are rather complex in themselves, and may become even more difficult when both disorders occur in association, as in the following case report.

CASE REPORT

Mme D . . . Lucette, 26 years. Medical file number: Fondation Bergonié, 66,599.

In November 1965 this young woman's health began to deteriorate, with slight 25 fever. Her condition worsened, particularly after a spontaneous abortion that

---

Source: *Bordeaux Médical*, No.10 (October 1968).

*Translation by Sheila Silcock (adapted).

femme commence à présenter une altération de l'état général, avec fébricule, qui
s'accentue surtout après un avortement
survenu le 17 mars 1966. En avril 1966, 30
l'apparition d'un prurit et d'une adéno-
pathie sus-claviculaire gauche conduit à la
biopsie d'un ganglion dont l'examen histologique permet de porter le diagnostic de
maladie de Hodgkin, devant des aspects 35
tout à fait typiques et indiscutables.

occurred on March 17, 1966. In April 1966,
she developed pruritus and left supra-
clavicular adenopathy. Hodgkin's disease
was diagnosed after a lymph node biopsy, as
the appearance of the tissue was entirely
characteristic of the disease.

NOTES

This text illustrates some of the main features of French to English medical
translation: *faux amis*, jargon, tense changes, shifts, referential synonyms and
typical terminology (listed p. 288).

Toxoplasmosis is an infection with the parasitic micro-organism *toxoplasma
gondi*. It is fairly common (a worldwide disease) and usually harmless, but
congenital infection is fatal. Hodgkin's disease is an uncommon disorder of the
lymph nodes, and occasionally of other organs. No microbe has as yet been
incriminated. It is an unusual form of cancer. If it is diagnosed in the early stages, it
can be effectively treated.

Association between toxoplasmosis and Hodgin's disease is rare, but patients
suffering from the latter are particularly prone to infections. The article discusses
the factors underlying the association of the two diseases.

PARTICULAR PROBLEMS

Title: A descriptive title; English titles are often shorter than others: *associée*:
'associated', i.e. 'accompanying', not 'linked' (*liée*), which implies a causal
connection.

Authors: English deletes *par*, *MM.*, etc. and *et*.

1.2   *réaliser*: Blanket term for 'show', 'produce', 'accomplish', 'make'. Note
        1.0, *réaliser un aspect*, which is odd and has to be normalised; also 1.00,
        réalisation.

1.4   *altération*: Other meanings: 'degeneration', 'damage', 'falsification',
        'change for the worse'. A common *faux ami*. The meaning 'alteration' is
        rare and not possible in a medical context (cf. *alterazione*, *Veränderung*, and
        the sinister 'modification', which translates 'alteration').

1.4   *état*: A clear example of a case-gap. State of what?

ll.4–5 *syndrome fébrile*: *Syndrome*, 'syndrome' are both overused jargon words. In
        fact fever is a symptom, usually a feature of a syndrome, which is a
        collection of symptoms and signs.

1.5   *polyadénopathie*: Disease ('-pathy') affecting several ('poly-') glands
        ('-aden(o)-') at once. 'Polyadenopathy' existed, but the 'lymph' com-

ponent has to be shown, as lymphatic tissue is not glandular. 'Poly-' is covered by 'generalised'.

l.6   *histo-*: 'of the tissue'.

ll.6–7 *prélèvement biopsique*: As usual, the French adjective of substance (*biopsique*) becomes an English pre-modifying noun ('biopsy'). *Prélèvement* (literally 'pre-removal') can mean 'specimen', 'sample', 'swab', and, outside medicine, 'levy', 'imposition', 'deduction', 'removal', e.g., *prélèvement bancaire*, 'standing order'.

l.7   *permet*: When *permettre* and verbs such as *consentir, inciter, faciliter, empêcher, défendre, pousser, laisser* are used with a non-human subject (Halliday's 'metaphorical grammar'), the syntax is frequently remodelled in the translation, with the following illustrative variations: *L'examen permet de porter un diagnostic* – 'On the basis of the examination, a diagnosis can be made'; 'We can make a diagnosis after examining the patient.' Therefore the SL infinitive becomes the TL main verb, either as a passive or as an active verb, and *permettre* becomes a modal verb. But you do not have to make the shift, if you do not want to. You can translate: 'The examination allows/permits us to make a diagnosis.'

l.8   *certains aspects*: *certains* usually translates as 'some', and *aspect* is often 'appearance'. 'Some signs' is too pernickety.

l.9   *ganglion/naire*: Another adjective of substance. This is one of the main *faux amis* in medical language. *Ganglion* (a round swelling) is translated as 'ganglion' when it is a collection of cells in a nerve; also when it is a cyst in a tendon, as in the wrist; but here, as commonly, it is 'lymph node' or 'lymph gland' or simply 'gland' ('enlarged glands are swollen lymph glands'). Lymph glands are small bean-like bodies along the course of the lymphatic vessels. Lymph, a transparent slightly yellow liquid, is collected from all parts of the body, and returned to the blood via the lymphatic system. The only way you can 'guess' this is by noting that Hodgkin's disease is concerned with lymph nodes and not with ganglia.

l.11   *lymphogranulomatose*: 'lymphogranulomatosis' ('granule', small particle; '-oma', '-osis', swelling, usually morbid process), a generic term which includes Hodgkin's disease; it is sometimes used by Continental European writers as a synonym for Hodgkin's disease.

l.11   *C'est dire que*: 'Therefore'. French medical texts are less formal than English, which are less formal than German medical texts.

l.12   *détection*: Variant: 'identification'.

l.13   *appoint*: 'additional help'.

l.14   *il faut souligner l'intérêt de sa réalisation systématique*: Overblown jargon. Note that here, as often, *intérêt* means 'value' or 'importance'.

l.15   *au même titre que*: Ponderous.

l.16   *exploration*: 'investigation'. More generic than *examen, détection*, etc.

l.17   *porteur*: Not 'carrier', since Hodgkin's disease is not infectious. In other contexts, *porteur* may be a 'carrier' or, for animals, 'bearing', e.g. *rats porteurs de tumeurs.* Note that Romance adjectives, present and past participles and relative clauses are often used, as here, where English has a preposition (between two nouns), provided an 'empty' verb is used (this is the 'house-on-the-hill' construction).

l.19   *déjà*: Rather over-translated here as 'in themselves' – it could be omitted.

l.20   *peuvent être rendus*: Alternative: 'may be made'.

The sentence is co-ordinated by 'and' in English to reinforce in *déjà complexes*, which could be alternately rendered by a relative clause: 'These problems, which are . . .'

l.21   *affections*: 'disorders' is the best non-committal general word: 'disease' often suggests infection or stress; 'illness' is rather informal, and not often used in the plural; 'affection' in this sense is not so common, but can be used to avoid repetition.

l.24   *observation*: 'observation' as well as 'case report', 'case history'. Note that these are usually written in the present in French, in the past in English. English case-histories do not mention the patient's name or number.

l.25   *D.M.*: May or may not stand for *dossier médical*.

l.27   *présenter une altération*: The sentence is recast, the French empty verb plus verb-noun being as usual turned to a verb.

l.28   'Pruritus' includes irritation as well as itching. Note the spelling!

l.28   *fébricule*: *-icule* is a diminutive ('slight'). 'Febricula' is obsolete in British English, and the term would be affected for such a slight and common symptom.

l.29   *s'accentue*: Refers to *altération*!

l.29   *avortement*: The distinction between 'abortion' (up to 16 weeks) and 'miscarriage' (16-28 weeks) is obsolete in medical language. An abortion is either 'spontaneous' (*spontané*), accidental (indicated by *survenu* here) or 'induced' (*provoqué*), deliberate. For *survenu* see also l.17, *porteur* ('house-on-the-hill' construction).

l.32   *sus-claviculaire*: 'above the collar-bone'. *Sus-* is 'supra-'; *sous-* is 'sub-'.

ll.31–6 The sentence has been recast. For *permettre* and *aspects* see ll.6 and 7.

l.36   *tout à fait typiques et indiscutables* ('unmistakable') has been collapsed into 'entirely characteristic'.

(Notes by Sheila Silcock and the author.)

Dialysebehandlung bei akutem Nierenversagen im Kindesalter*

H. G. Sieberth, M. Bulla, W. Hübner, M. Mennicken und G. Siemon

Medizinische Universitätsklinik (Direktor: Prof. Dr. R. Gross) und Universitäts-Kinderklinik (Direktor: Prof. Dr. C. Bennholdt-Thomsen †), Köln

Von 1966 bis 1969 wurden 14 Kinder im Alter von 7 Wochen bis 14 Jahren mit der extrakorporalen Hämodialyse oder Peritonealdialyse behandelt. Indikationen waren akutes Nierenversagen (n=7), Coma hepaticum (n=2), Arzneimittelvergiftungen (n=2), hämolytisch-urämisches Syndrom (n=1), hyptertone Enzephalopathie bei pyelonephritischen Schrumpfnieren (n=1) und hyperpyretische Grippe (n=1). In acht Fällen führte die Behandlung zur Rückbildung der Krankheitssymptome. Bei dem Kind mit hyperpyretischer Grippe konnte die Entwicklung einer schweren Zerebralschädigung nicht verhindert werden. Fünf Kinder starben. Die Indikation zur Dialyse ist immer dann gegeben, wenn sich erste Zeichen einer Urämie einstellen oder einer Überwässerung, die nicht auf Saluretika ansprechen. Das Verfahren ist stets nur Teil einer Gesamtbehandlung.

Das akute Nierenversagen, besonders im engeren Sinne (6), wird im Kindesalter viel seltener beobachtet als bei Erwachsenen. Das ist deshalb bemerkenswert, weil

Treatment of acute renal failure in children by dialysis*

H. G. Sieberth, M. Bulla, W. Hübner, M. Mennicken, G. Siemon

Medizinische Universitätsklinik (Director: Prof. Dr R. Gross) and Universitäts-Kinderklinik (previous Director: the late Prof. Dr C. Bennholdt-Thomsen), Cologne

Between 1966 and 1969 haemodialysis or peritoneal dialysis was performed on 14 children aged from 7 weeks to 14 years. The indications were: acute renal failure (7 children), hepatic coma (2), drug poisoning (2), haemolytic–uraemic syndrome (1), hypertensive encephalopathy in chronic pyelonephritis (1) and hyperpyretic influenza (1). In eight cases, treatment produced regression of the symptoms. In the child with hyperpyretic influenza, severe cerebral damage could not be prevented. Five children died. Dialysis is indicated whenever there are the first signs of uraemia or of fluid retention not responding to diuretics. Dialysis is only part of a programme of treatment.

Acute renal failure is much less commonly seen in children than in adults. This is all the more remarkable, because disturbances in fluid balance, shock and poisoning are certainly not less common in children than among adults. The reason for this disparity is assumed to be the greater resistance of children to the kind of insult which in an adult would lead to renal insufficiency. Schubert and Köberle explained

*Professor Dr. H. Sarre zum 65, Geburtstag.

*Dedicated to Professor H. Sarre for his 65th birthday.

Störungen im Wasser- und Elektrolyt-haushalt, Schockzustände und Intoxi-kationen bei Kindern sicher nicht seltener als bei Erwachsenen auftreten. Als Ursache wird eine erhöhte Resistenz des kindlichen Organismus gegenüber Noxen angenom-men, die beim Erwachsenen bereits zu einer akuten Niereninsuffizienz führen können (24, 25). Schubert und Köberle (51) erklärten die geringe Fallzahl damit, daß das akute Nierenversagen im Kindesalter häufiger nicht diagnostiziert wird.

Da nur wenig Berichte über die Dialyse-behandlungen beim Kind vorliegen, soll im folgenden über 14 behandelte Fälle mit akuter Niereninsuffizienz berichtet werden.

KASUISTIK

Fall 1: *Arantil®-Vergiftung.* Der 1⁴/₁₂ Jahre alte, bewußtseinsklare Junge hatte etwa zehn Tabletten Arantil (0,075g Amino-phenazon, 0,125g Aminophenazon-Abkömmling pro Tablette) eingenommen. Trotz Magenspülung und Infusionstherapie wurde das Kind zunehmend somnolent. Zwölf Stunden nach der Aufnahme traten generalisierte Krämpfe auf. Gleichzeitig entwickelte sich eine Oligurie mit kompensierter Acidose. Da bei Pyrazolon-Intoxikation fast regelmäßig mit einem tödlichen Ausgang zu rechnen ist, sobald Krampfanfälle auftreten (4, 27), erfolgte nach Anlage eines arteriovenösen Shunts über die Femoralgefäße sofort eine sechsstündige Hämodialysebehandlung. Während der Dialyse hörten die Krampf-anfälle auf, und das Bewußtsein wurde wieder klar. Zwei Tage nach der Behand-lung ließen sich am Augenhintergrund fleckförmige Blutungen nachweisen, die sich nach einer Woche vollkommen zurückgebildet hatten. Im EEG fanden sich vier Tage nach dem ersten Krampfanfall noch erhebliche δ-Dysrhythmien, die im weiteren Verlauf eine gute Rückbildungs-tendenz zeigten. Das Kind konnte zwölf Tage nach der akuten Intoxikation in gutem Allgemeinzustand nach Hause entlassen werden.

the lower incidence on the ground that acute renal failure is less frequently diag-nosed in children.

As there are few reports on dialysis in children, fourteen cases of acute renal insufficiency will be discussed.

CASE REPORTS

Case 1: *'Arantil' intoxication*

A sixteen-month-old boy, who was fully conscious, had taken about ten tablets of Arantil (0.075g aminophenazone, 0.125g aminophenazone derivatives per tablet). In spite of gastric wash-out and infusion treat-ment, the child became increasingly drowsy. Generalised convulsions appeared twelve hours after admission. Oliguria with a compensated acidosis developed at the same time. As pyrazolone poisoning is almost always fatal, once convulsions occur, the insertion of an arteriovenous shunt over the femoral vessels was immediately followed by six hours' dialysis. In the course of the dialysis, the attacks stopped and the child's conscious level returned to normal. Two days after the treatment, retinal dot-haemorrhages were observed, but these completely receded in a week. Four days after the onset of convulsions there were still considerable delta-wave abnormalities in the EEG, which tended to disappear with time. Twelve days after ingestion, the child was discharged in good health.

Source: *Deutsche Medizinische Wochenschrift*, No. 24 (11 June 1971).

NOTES

The paper describes the use of dialysis in fourteen children over a period of three years, reporting the indications for and effectiveness of the treatment in each case. Dialysis took the form of either haemodialysis or peritoneal dialysis. The former involves purifying the blood by filtering out waste products across a membrane in a kidney machine. The latter implies instilling and removing litres of fluid from the peritoneal cavity through a plastic tube in the abdominal wall, the peritoneum itself acting as a dialysing membrane. Half the children involved died.

PARTICULAR PROBLEMS

Name of periodical: Transfer. Put literal translation in brackets only if readership is unlikely to understand it: 'German Medical Weekly Review'.

Title: English title conveniently stresses last word ('dialysis'). 'Renal' slightly preferable to 'kidney failure' in professional register. 'Dialysis': Filtering of circulating blood through a semi-permeable membrane in an artificial kidney, in order to eliminate waste products.

Authors: Transfer locations as parts of addresses. The † has to be explained.

l.3   *extrakorporalen*, i.e. with artificial kidney. More commonly called 'haemodialysis'. Change of word-order puts more stress on the subject – dialysis.

ll.4–11 Repunctuation clarifies stress.

l.6   *Coma hepaticum*: Conveniently anglicised to be consistent with the other indications.

l.8   *hypertone*: Can mean 'hypertonic' or 'hypertensive'. Collocated with 'encephalopathy' it is 'hypertensive'.

l.10   *Schrumpfnieren*: Atrophic kidneys, resulting from pyelonephritis (inflammation of kidneys); the tautology is avoided in the translation.

l.13   *Symptome*: 'symptoms' is used generically to include 'signs' found by examining the patient, and 'symptoms' reported by the patient.

l.14   *konnte*: Translated with 'full' meaning. More frequently (e.g. l.00) *konnte* is not translated; it is often used to avoid a past tense.

ll.18–9 *sich einstellen*: 'appear'. (*Einstellen* has many meanings, including 'start', 'stop' and 'adjust'.)

l.19   *Urämie*: Accumulation in the blood of waste products normally excreted in the urine.

l.20   *Uberwässerung*: Apparently a coinage, literally 'excessive watering'; translate as 'fluid retention' or (technical) 'oedema'.

l.20   *Saluretika*: Saluretics promote excretion of sodium in urine. They act as a diuretic, which increases flow of urine.

l.22   *Gesamt-*: Superfluous.

ll.23–4 *im engeren Sinne* (6): The (6) refers to a reference book in the bibliography, where I assume that acute renal failure is defined in the broad and also in the narrow sense of the term. If this reference work (H. Schweigk's *Handbuch der innerin Medizin*, Vol. 7, Nos. 1–2) is available, you should reproduce its definition in the narrow sense, deleting the words 'in the narrow sense', since this distinction is metalingual and does not appear to be generally used in English medicine. If the book is not available, you delete the parenthesis altogether, as here.

l.25   The modulation ('less commonly') is more natural.

ll.27–8 'fluid balance': The standard term, also referred to as 'water' or 'fluid and electrolytic balance'. French *équilibre liquide*. *Haushalt* is also 'budget', 'household', 'housekeeping', 'economy'.

l.28   *Schockzustände*: *-zustände* ('conditions') is superfluous.

ll.28–9 The general distinction between 'intoxication' and 'poisoning', which largely overlap, is that 'intoxication' tends to be systemic (affecting the whole system) and professional (referring also to drunkenness), and 'poisoning' local and more familiar.

ll.28–9 The variant, 'shock, poisoning and disturbances in . . .' is better balanced.

l.30   *Ursache*, being isolated from its anaphoric reference by a longish sentence, perhaps needs a case partner, which I have supplied.

ll.31–2 *des kindlichen Organismus*: A piece of typical, formal scientific German.

l.32   *Noxe*: 'noxa' appears to be rare in German and English; 'noxious agents' would imply particular entities; 'insult' is a technical term for attack.

l.33   *bereits*: Modal connective. Either delete (under-translation), as here, or translate as 'themselves' (over-translation); cf. *déjà*.

l.36   'the lower incidence' emphasises that this is in relation to adults.

ll.29,   I have used three modulations for *nicht seltener, häufiger nicht, nur wenig*, as
39,40   they appear more natural in English.

l.41   *-behandlungen*: As dialysis is a treatment, *-behandlungen* is superfluous.
        Kasuistik: Standard term for 'case reports'; cf. *anamnesie* and English 'anamnesis', which is more comprehensive.

l.45   'Arantil': Not found, but as its composition is stated, there are no problems for the reader. The quotation marks imply that it is not an English drug.

l.46   *bewußtseinsklar*: Standard term for 'conscious'.

l.46   *Junge*: 'infant' or 'boy' will do here. The term 'infant' is paradoxical in British English, referring at school to children aged 5 to 7, but generally to children under 3.

l.50   *Magenspülung*: Stomach irrigation (stomach pump).

l.50   'infusion': Of a liquid, glucose or a saline solution, into a vein.

l.51   *somnolent*: Variant, 'sleepy'.

l.52   *Aufnahme* (admission) contrasts with *Entlassung* (discharge). Standard terms.

l.53   *Krämpfe*: Can mean 'cramps' (involuntary muscle contractions) or 'spasms', 'convulsions', 'paroxysms'.

l.65   *Augenhintergrund*: Standard term. Variant, 'fundus of the eye', 'eyeground', *fundus oculi* for the back of the eye. The retina is its inner lining.

1.66   *fleckförmige*: 'dot' is a more common medical term than 'speck' or 'spot'.

1.68   'level' is put in to show that consciousness does not switch on and off but is a gradient.

1.70   '-disrhythmias' refers to irregular rhythms of the delta waves with a frequency below 3½ per second in the electroencephalogram (EEG), a graph of the electrical activity of the brain. In English, one refers to 'disrhythmias'   in the electrocardiograms, and 'wave abnormalities' in electroencephalograms.

1.73   Variant 'after the episode of poisoning'. 'Acute' is superfluous.

Alexander von Humboldt: Leben und Werk

W.-H. Hein

Alexander von Humboldt: His Life and Work*

W.-H. Hein

EXTRACT 1 (p. 36)

Der Sankt Gotthard mit Hospiz und Kapuzinerkapelle

Kolorierte Aquatinta von Charles Melchior Descourtis um 1780. 22cm × 32,5 cm, HSH.

Zweimal überquerte Humboldt 1795 auf seiner Reise durch die Schweiz den Sankt Gotthard-Paß. Auf der Route Genua – St. Gotthard untersuchte er das Streichen und Fallen der geologischen Schichten und entwarf später ein Profil, in dem er erstmals die oberen Erdschichten in Form eines Querschnittes darstellte. »Ich begriff die Idee, ganze Länder darzustellen wie ein Bergwerk« schrieb er dazu. Mit dieser Arbeit waren die Voraussetzungen für seine späteren großen Profile Spaniens und Mexikos geschaffen.

EXTRACT 2 (pp. 38–9)

Man hätte annehmen müssen, daß diese tiefgründige Betrachtung über Leben und Sterben Schiller ansprach. Doch seltsamerweise äußerte er sich abfällig über sie, und der erst von Alexander so eingenommene Dichter rückt nun deutlich von ihm ab. Zwei Jahre später, im August 1797, urteilt er dann in einem Brief an Christian Gottfried Körner vernichtend über ihn: »Ich

EXTRACT 1 (p. 36)

The St Gotthard Pass with the hospice and the Capuchin chapel

Coloured aquatint by Charles Melchoir Descourtis, *c.* 1780, 22 cm × 32.5 cm, HCH.

During his tour of Switzerland Humboldt twice crossed the St Gotthard Pass. On the way from Genoa to St Gotthard he investigated the strikes and dips of the geological strata, and later designed a topographical profile, in which he showed the upper layers of the earth for the first time as a cross-section. 'I conceived the idea of representing whole countries like a mine', he wrote. This work anticipated his later major profiles of Spain and Mexico.

EXTRACT 2 (pp. 38–9)

One might have assumed that this profound study of life and death would have appealed to Schiller. Oddly enough, he judged it unfavourably, and the writer who had at first been so taken by Alexander now clearly dissociated himself from him. Two years later, in August 1797, he made a devastating appraisal of him in a letter to

*Translated by John Cumming; edited by Pauline Newmark and the author.

kann ihm keinen Funken eines reinen, objektiven Interesses abmerken, – und wie sonderbar es auch klingen mag, so finde ich in ihm, bei allem ungeheuren Reichtum des Stoffes, eine Dürftigkeit des Sinnes, die bei dem Gegenstande, den er behandelt, das schlimmste Übel ist. Es ist der nackte, schneidende Verstand, der die Natur, die immer unfaßlich und in allen ihren Punkten ehrwürdig und unergründlich ist, schamlos ausgemessen haben will und mit einer Frechheit, die ich nicht begreife, seine Formeln, die oft nur leere Worte und immer nur enge Begriffe sind, zu ihrem Maßstabe macht. Kurz, mir scheint er für seinen Gegenstand ein viel zu grobes Organ und dabei ein viel zu beschränkter Verstandesmensch zu sein. Er hat keine Einbildungskraft, und so fehlt ihm nach meinem Urteil das notwendigste Vermögen zu seiner Wissenschaft, denn die Natur muß angeschaut und empfunden werden, in ihren einzelnsten Erscheinungen wie in ihren höchsten Gesetzen.«

25 Christian Gottfried Körner: 'I cannot observe any spark of pure, objective interest in him – and, however strange it may sound, I find in him, in spite of all the immense abundance of matter, a meagre 30 quantity of sense, which is a disaster, given the subject he is concerned with. It is naked, cutting reason, which shamelessly claims to have taken the measure of nature, which is always incomprehensible and in all 35 its aspects worthy of respect and unfathomable. Yet here reason, with an impudence which I do not understand, turns its own formulas, which are often only empty phrases and always only narrow concepts, 40 into the yardstick of nature. In short, it seems to me far too coarse an instrument for his subject-matter and at the same time, as a man of reason, he is far too limited. He has no imagination, and therefore in my judge- 45 ment he is without the most necessary capacity for his science, for nature has to be observed and felt, both in its most isolated phenomena and in its highest laws.'

NOTES

These two extracts, written by the editor, are from *Alexander von Humboldt: Leben und Werk*, an illustrated collection of essays edited by Wolfgang-Hagen Hein.

Extract 1

The first extract is a factual caption for an illustration.

Particular problems

Title: *Kapuziner*: 'Capuchin', *not* 'capucin' (*Collins German Dictionary!*). cm: The metric dimension is appropriately retained in this non-cultural context. (l.5) *HSH*, 'HCH': The acronym refers to the editor's Humboldt Collection (*Humboldt Sammlung, Hein*), and is rather covertly explained on the page after the frontispiece, which the reader would not usually notice. The translator can lose a lot of time by pursuing (in the various SL or TL dictionaries of abbreviations) acronyms coined by the author and/or specific to the SL text.

l.6   'Twice' is displaced to a more natural but still emphatic position.

l.6   *überquerte*: 'Cross a pass' seems to me more natural than 'go through' or 'pass through', which jars with the 'pass'.

l.8   *Route*: 'way' or 'route' ('route' suggests a map).

ll.9–10 *Streichen und Fallen*: No problem for a geologist and not much for other non-specialists if you have the *Wörterbuch der Geowissenschaften* (GDR). Otherwise, you first have to consider whether these are technical or descriptive terms. I found *Streichen* in its 26th (geological) sense in the *Langenscheidt*. I suspected that *Fallen* must be in opposition to *Streichen*, but it was not in the *Langenscheidt* or *Collins*. (Opposition or antithesis or contrast are essential and neglected aspects of discourse analysis, particularly (not here) when they go from negative to positive.) Finally I found 'horizontal direction of a stratum – perpendicular to the direction of the dip' which confirmed the opposition and produced the correct technical term. The opposition was also nicely shown in the *Penguin Geological Dictionary* but not in the *Encyclopaedia Britannica*. Therefore I abandoned previous ideas of 'range or stretch' contrasted with 'declivity or descent' as descriptive rather than technical terms.

l.10   *Schichten*: 'strata' rather than 'layers' in this technical collocation.

ll.12–13 *in Form*: 'as' is more natural than 'in the form of'.

l.14   *begriff*: 'conceived' appears to me to be the 'idiolectal' sense of the word here. 'Apprehended' is in 1987 a 'dictionary word' (word to be found only in dictionaries). But it is not easy to get the precise sense of a word written in 1795.

l.15   *dazu*: Superfluous in English; cf. *J'y pense, Ich danke Dir dafür*, etc.

ll.16–8 *die Voraussetzungen waren geschaffen*: 'anticipated' is an under-translation, but anything like 'the preconditions, prerequisites, bases, requirements (etc.) were created' is too heavy. Alternatively, 'with this work he anticipated', but the 'metaphorical grammar' (Halliday) exemplified in my version (i.e. the personification of 'this work') is a little extravagant.

Extract 2

The second extract quotes a letter of Schiller's about Humboldt. The translator has to follow the process of Schiller's thinking as intimately as he can. Any deviation from literal translation has to be justified, as I see it, reluctantly; at the same time, idiomatic language in the original has to be recognised. When Hein, a subtle writer, says of Humboldt's many honours: *Im Alter von 24 Jahren als botanischer Autodidakt so herausgestellt zu werden, wer erlebt das schon?* any word-for-word translation would be a disaster, and 'Who has had the experience of such a public dedication, while only a self-taught botanist of 24 years of age' is ponderous, mis-stressed and distorted. You have to plunge and hold tight: 'What other young man could ever have received such honours as this 24-year-old self-taught scientist?' Alternatively, 'Could any young man ever have . . .' (Twelve skilled translators would always offer twelve different versions of such a sentence.)

Particular problems

This text is written in formal, educated, slightly old-fashioned German, by W.-H. Hein, an elderly (he says so) polymath academic who loves his topic and the German language. The translator has to follow every waywardness when possible.

l.20   *tiefgründig*: 'profound' is an (inevitable?) under-translation.

l.20   *Betrachtung*: 'reflection on . . .' is too refined.

l.21   *Doch* omitted: Connectives are commoner in German than in English, and *doch* is covered by 'enough'.

l.22   *äuerte er sich abfällig*: Reflexive verbs are less common in English. 'Unfavourably' slightly under-translates *abfällig*. Alternatively, 'adversely'.

l.23   *eingenommen* is stronger than 'taken by'.

l.24   *rückt*: The German present tense is mor vivid (as in French), but this is journalistic (commentator style) in English.

ll.25–7 *urteilt vernichtend*: 'Standard' shift from German 'verb plus adverb' to English 'empty verb plus adjective plus verb-noun', to give the verb-noun more force. (See many of Firbas's papers on functional sentence perspective.) 'Devastating' (alternatively 'crushing') is strong, but not stronger than *vernichtend*.

l.28   keinen: Negative is possibly more forceful when transferred to the verb.

l.28   *Funken*: Dead metaphor in both languages, equally frequent.

l.28   *rein*: 'pure' shows up a lexical gap in English.

l.29   *abmerken*: Neat German *ab-* shows up a lexical gap in English and all Romance languages.

l.30   *klingen*: 'seem' may sound more natural, but 'sound' is what Schiller wrote.

ll.31,32 *ungeheuren*, *Reichtum* and *Dürftigkeit* deserve literal lexical translation, but 'meagreness' for *Dürftigkeit* would be too odd, so, as often, the adjectival noun is split into adjective plus general word.

l.32   *Stoff* and *Sinn* are contrasted, best realised by 'matter' (alternatively 'material') and 'sense'.

l.34   *das schlimmste Übel*: This is now, and hopefully then, a colloquialism, and has to be boldly translated for sense ('a real disaster'?).

ll.34,35 *der nackte, schneidende*: My reasons for translating both words literally are: (a) words used outside their normal collocations return to their primary senses; (b) both words are negative in this context; (c) 'naked' is used in the sense of 'unmodified', 'unmitigated', 'undisguised' ('bare' is not forceful enough), 'cutting' as 'sharp', 'thin', 'like a blade'.

l.35   *Verstand* and *Vernunft* are one of the trickiest couplets in all German (and *Vernunft* as 'reason' in Kant doesn't help). Basically, in my opinion, *Verstand* ('understanding') relates to thinking, *Vernunft* ('common sense') to behaviour. There is no word for 'reason' except the rather technical *Ratio* (used by Brecht, who must have noticed the lexical gap). In this context, *Verstand* is used negatively, and rather than 'understanding'. I have translated it as 'reason', which is often used negatively by the Romantics.

1.36   *unfalich*: It is tempting to put 'immeasurable', since it is physical and transparent, like the German (typically), but the German word will not quite stretch as far, and it plays on 'measure', which is not in the Schiller.

ll.36–7   *in allen ihren Punkten*: Alternatively, 'in every respect'.

1.37   *ehrwürdig*: Not 'venerable' here. Alternatively, 'worthy of honour', which spells it out. The sentence is split into two, on the ground that German sentences are usually longer than English, and it has too many conjunctions (*und*).

1.38   *ausgemessen*: 'measure out'. Schiller's word is in fact more physical than mine, but I am making a concession here.

1.40   *Worte*: 'phrases' rather than 'words' (*Wörter*) or 'phraseology'.

1.42   *ihrem Mastab*: *ihrem* has to be replaced by the appropriate noun (as often) as 'its' would be misleading. The single gender of English objects follows common sense but can be grammatically confusing. *Mastab*: Alternatively, 'criterion'.

1.43   *Organ*: 'Organ' in the sense of 'instrument' is old-fashioned and heavy in English also, but less so in modern German. Such general words often modulate in translation (cf. *qualité*, 'property', etc.).

1.44   *und dabei*, etc.: Schiller's German is strange! Up to now, the anaphoric subject has been *Verstand*. From now on, it becomes Humboldt! The translation is accordingly corrected. Further, the emphasis in the translation is transferred from *Verstandesmensch* (a collocation with a recognised translation 'man of reason', which supports the previous interpretation of *Verstand*, to *beschränkt* (alternatively 'narrow-minded', 'dull').

1.48   *die Natur*: Could be personified ('her most isolated, . . . her highest') to show the late-eighteenth-century concept-world.

1.50   *einzelnsten*: Alternatively 'most individual', 'most particular'.

L'Adoration
Jacques Borel

Cette rue, cette place ressemblent à la rue, à
la place d'alors: elles ne sont pas les mêmes,
et, les autres, je puis avoir l'impression
qu'elles existent encore, mais dans une
autre ville que j'aurais quittée il y a
longtemps et où je ne serais pas revenu
depuis. Même, les souvenirs postérieurs à
cette époque de l'Occupation, ceux, si
proches encore, de certaines promenades,
de certaines minutes, semblent se trans-
poser d'eux-mêmes, et comme naturellement, à la fois dans le temps et dans ce
même espace reconnaissable et pourtant
autre.

Peut-être parce que, depuis, il m'a
semblé vivre avec moins d'acuité que je
vivais alors? Qu'il me semble, aussi, y avoir
eu dans ma vie moins d'événements, et que,
du coup, ce temps, dont le mouvement s'est
sensiblement accéléré, qui s'est écoulé
depuis le temps nourri et privilégié où j'étais
un jeune homme, me paraît n'avoir été
qu'un même courant uniforme, inconsis-
tant et mou où rien n'a marqué? Peut-être
enfin parce que, ma première passion, c'est
dans le Paris de l'Occupation que je l'ai
connue, et que le climat, l'intense isolement
de la passion restent liés pour moi à ces
images qui se gravaient alors en moi et dans
lesquelles je m'apparais à moi-même,
penché vers un visage radieux ou, seul,
longeant à pas pressés les boîtes fermées des
bouquinistes, et en même temps immobile
et comme entré, avec ces images mêmes
dont je fais partie, dans une espèce
d'éternité.

TEXT **10**

The Bond*
Jacques Borel

Those places look as they did then, but they
are not the same; and as for the others, I
have the feeling that they still exist but in
some other town that I left long ago and
have never been back to. Even the memory
of things that happened after the Occupation, some still recent, walks for instance,
and certain moments spent, seem to transpose themselves into that other time and
place, recognisable yet different.

Is it because I have since lived less
intensely than I did then? Or because I feel
that there has been less incident in my life,
and this latter time, its pace so palpably
accelerated, following the sheltered and
favoured days when I was young, has
seemed to me one of monotony without
substance, unmarked by any notable event?
But finally, perhaps, it is because I underwent my first passionate experiences in
Occupied Paris, and the climate, the
extreme isolation of passion, remains linked
for me with the images that were then
imprinted on my mind, in which I see myself bent over a glowing face or hurrying
alone past the closed stalls of the book-
sellers, myself unchanging and fixed in a
sort of eternity with those pictures of which
I am part.

---

*Translation by Norman Denny, Editions
Gallimard.

TRANSLATION CRITICISM

SL text analysis

This is a lyrical elegiac expression of a regret for vanished past: the place is the same but the time, youth, the charged and intense atmosphere of passion and excitement have gone. It is an interior monologue, written in simple language. The passage includes four long sentences, each marked by strongly balanced noun groups and clauses, all with the implications of spoken rather than any standard written discourse. The stresses are important.

The passage is not strongly 'marked' culturally, and should be translated 'semantically'.

Notes on the translation

The translator has done his best to normalise the text. He asks himself not 'What did Borel say?', but 'how would one say this in English, how would this usually be expressed?' The result is that passages of normal usage are correspondingly translated, but oddities are prosaically ironed out, and an emotional dramatic challenging utterance becomes a calm normal factual statement.

Close comparison of TL with SL text

Title: Note the complete change in the translation of the 'allusive' title.

Opening (grammar): The translator has rejected the challenging repetitions and the punctuation of the original: 'This street (and?) this square resemble the street (and?) the square of that time: they are not the same and, as for others, perhaps I have the feeling . . .' It is difficult to justify a prosy change which both cuts down and deflates the tone of voice of the original.

The rest of the paragraph is more closely translated, although *comme naturellement* (l.11), a common adverbial if ever there was one, is ignored, and *autre* (l.14), a vogue word, can only 'other'.

The second paragraph keeps the grammar but makes unnecessary changes in the lexis.

l.12   'less intensely': Why not 'less acutely'?

l.13   'less incident': Why not 'fewer events'?

l.14   'so palpably': 'perceptibly'?

l.15   *du coup* ('suddenly') is inexplicably omitted.

      'sheltered and favoured': 'Sheltered' is linguistically and referentially misleading, since it is inappropriate during the Occupation and it is outside the semantic range of *nourri*. The sentence components are: packed, dense, sustained and, I suggest, eventful here.

ll.16–8 This is a paraphrase. Admittedly the French (*courant . . . mou*) is weak, but even the grammatical feature *ne . . . que* is ignored. I would see no need to withdraw from: 'appears to me to have merely been one uniform, inconsistent and slack trend, marked by nothing of consequence'.

The last long sentence reverses the emphasis of the original.

1.20   'my first passionate affair, I experienced that in occupied Paris . . .'

1.22   'and at the same time motionless, as though I had now entered with these same images of which I am a part, a kind of eternity'. It seems to me that the translator's last sentence is a peculiar mixture of good and bad. 'Bent over a glowing face' is warmer than 'leaning toward a radiant face'; the 'book-sellers' clause is excellent, but why is the repeated *images* not respected? The translator, by normalising the clause-order, has lost the suspense and tension of the original. The rendering of *immobile* as 'myself unchanging and fixed' is peculiarly arbitrary.

Conclusion

The translator has lowered the tone of the text and given it the flavour of natural usage. In fact the more normal passages in the original and the lexical words are sometimes sensitively translated.

The translation is uneven, and the translator has skirted at least two of the more vivid and challenging passages in the original.

The text is memorably written, and deserved a closer translation.

Die Blasse Anna
Heinrich Böll

Erst im Frühjahr 1950 kehrte ich aus dem Krieg heim, und ich fand niemanden mehr in der Stadt, den ich kannte. Zum Glück hatten meine Eltern mir Geld hinterlassen. Ich mietete ein Zimmer in der Stadt, dort lag ich auf dem Bett, rauchte und wartete und wußte nicht, worauf ich wartete. Arbeiten zu gehen, hatte ich keine Lust. Ich gab meiner Wirtin Geld, und sie kaufte alles für mich und bereitete mir das Essen. Jedesmal, wenn sie mir den Kaffee oder das Essen ins Zimmer brachte, blieb sie länger, als mir lieb war. Ihr Sohn war in einem Ort gefallen, der Kalinowka hieß, und wenn sie eingetreten war, setzte sie das Tablett auf den Tisch und kam in die dämmrige Ecke, wo mein Bett stand. Dort döste ich vor mich hin, drückte die Zigaretten an der Wand aus, und so war die Wand hinter meinem Bett voller schwarzer Flecken. Meine Wirtin war blaß und mager, und wenn im Dämmer ihr Gesicht über meinem Bett stehen blieb, hatte ich Angst vor ihr. Zuerst dachte ich, sie sei verrückt, denn ihre Augen waren sehr hell und groß, und immer wieder fragte sie mich nach ihrem Sohn. «Sind Sie sicher, daß Sie ihn nicht gekannt haben? Der Ort hieß Kalinowka – sind Sie dort nicht gewesen?»

Aber ich hatte nie von einem Ort gehört, der Kalinowka hieß, und jedesmal drehte ich mich zur Wand und sagte: «Nein, wirklich nicht, ich kann mich nicht entsinnen.»

Meine Wirtin war nicht verrückt, sie war eine sehr ordentliche Frau, und es tat mir weh, wenn sie mich fragte. Sie fragte mich sehr oft, jeden Tag ein paarmal, und wenn ich zu ihr in die Küche ging, mußte ich das Bild ihres Sohnes betrachten, ein Buntphoto, das über dem Sofa hing. Er war ein

Pale Anna*
Heinrich Böll

It wasn't until spring 1950 that I came back from the war, and I found there was nobody I knew left in the town. Luckily my parents had left me some money. I rented a room in the town, lay there on the bed, smoked and waited, and didn't know what I was waiting for. I didn't want to work. I gave my landlady money and she bought me everything and cooked my food. Every time she brought coffee or a meal to my room, she stayed there longer than I liked. Her son had been killed at a place called Kalinovka, and when she had come in she would put the tray on the table and come over to the dim corner where my bed stood. There I dozed and vegetated, stubbed the cigarettes out against the wall, and so all over the wall by my bed there were black marks. My landlady was pale and thin, and when her face paused over my bed in the half-light, I was afraid of her. At first I thought she was mad, for her eyes were very bright and large, and again and again she asked me about her son. 'Are you certain you didn't know him? The place was called Kalinovka – didn't you ever go there?'

But I'd never heard of the place called Kalinovka, and each time I turned to the wall and said: 'No, really I didn't, I can't remember.'

My landlady wasn't mad, she was a very decent woman, and it hurt me when she asked me. She asked me very often, several times a day, and if I went to her in the kitchen I had to look at her son's picture, a coloured photograph which hung over the sofa. He'd been a laughing, fair-haired boy, and in the coloured photograph he wore an infantryman's walking-out uniform.

---

*Translation by Christopher Middleton.

lachender blonder Junge gewesen, und auf dem Buntphoto trug er eine Infanterie-Ausgehuniform.

«Es ist in der Garnison gemacht worden,» 45 sagte meine Wirtin, «bevor sie ausrückten.»

Es war ein Brustbild: er trug den Stahlhelm, und hinter ihm war deutlich die Attrappe einer Schloßruine zu sehen, die von künstlichen Reben umrankt war. 50

«Er war Schaffner,» sagte meine Wirtin, «bei der Straßenbahn. Eine fleißiger Junge.» Und dann nahm sie jedesmal den Karton voll Photographien, der auf ihrem Nähtisch zwischen Flicklappen und 55 Garnknäueln stand. Und ich mußte sehr viele Bilder ihres Sohnes in die Hand nehmen: Gruppenaufnahmen aus der Schule, wo jedesmal vorne einer mit einer Schiefertafel zwischen den Knien in der 60 Mitte saß, und auf der Schiefertafel stand eine VI, eine VII, zuletzt eine VIII. Gesondert, von einem roten Gummiband zusammengehalten, lagen die Kommunionbilder: ein lächelndes Kind in 65 einem frackartigen schwarzen Anzug, mit einer Riesenkerze in der Hand, so stand er vor einem Transparent, das mit einem goldenen Kelch bemalt war. Dann kamen Bilder, die ihn als Schlosserlehrling vor 70 einer Drehbank zeigten, das Gesicht rußig, die Hände um eine Feile geklammert.

«Das war nichts für ihn,» sagte meine Wirtin, «es war zu schwer.» Und sie zeigte mir das letzte Bild von ihm, bevor er Soldat 75 wurde: er stand in der Uniform eines Straßenbahnschaffners neben einem Wagen der Linie 9 an der Endstation, wo die Bahn ums Rondell kurvt, und ich erkannte die Limonadenbude, an der ich so 80 oft Zigaretten gekauft hatte, als noch kein Krieg war; ich erkannte die Pappeln, die heute noch dort stehen, sah die Villa mit den goldenen Löwen vorm Portal, die heute nicht mehr dort stehen, und mir fiel das 85 Mädchen ein, an das ich während des Krieges oft gedacht hatte: sie war hübsch gewesen, blaß, mit schmalen Augen, und an der Endstation der Linie 9 war sie immer in die Bahn gestiegen. 90

Jedesmal blickte ich sehr lange auf das Photo, das den Sohn meiner Wirtin an der

'It was taken at the barracks,' my landlady said, 'before they went to the front.'

It was a half-length portrait: he wore a steel helmet, and behind him you could see quite distinctly a dummy ruined castle, with artificial creepers all over it.

'He was a conductor,' my landlady said, 'in a tram. A hard-working boy.' And then she took, each time, the box of photographs which stood on her sewing-table between patches and tangles of thread. And always she pressed lots of pictures of her son into my hands: school groups, on each of which one boy sat in the middle of the front row with a slate between his knees, and on the slate there was a 6, a 7, finally an 8. In a separate bundle, held together by a red rubber band, were the Communion pictures: a smiling child in a black suit like a dress suit, with a giant candle in his hand, that was how he stood, in front of a diaphane on which a gold chalice was painted. Then came pictures which showed him as a locksmith's apprentice at a lathe, with smudges on his face and his hands gripping a file.

'That wasn't the job for him,' my landlady said, 'the work was too heavy.' And she showed me the last picture of him, before he became a soldier: there he stood, in a tramconductor's uniform, beside a number 9 tram at the terminus, where the tracks curve round the circle, and I recognized the refreshment stand at which I'd so often bought cigarettes, when there had still been no war; I recognized the poplars, which are still there today, saw the villa with the golden lions at the gate, which aren't there any more, and I remembered the girl whom I'd often thought of during the war: she'd been pretty, pale, with slit eyes, and she'd always boarded the tram at the number 9 terminus.

Each time I would have a long look at the photo which showed my landlady's son at the number 9 terminus, and I thought of a lot of things: of the girl and of the soap factory where I used to work in those days; I heard the tram's screeching, saw the red lemonade which I drank at the stand in the summer, green cigarette advertisements,

Endstation der 9 zeigte, und ich dachte an vieles: an das Mädchen und an die Seifenfabrik, in der ich damals gearbeitet hatte, ich hörte das Kreischen der Bahn, sah die rote Limonade, die ich im Sommer an der Bude getrunken hatte, grüne Zigarettenplakate und wieder das Mädchen.

«Vielleicht», sagte meine Wirtin, «haben Sie ihn doch gekannt.»

Ich schüttelte den Kopf und legte das Photo in den Karton zurück: es war ein Glanzphoto und sah noch neu aus, obwohl es schon acht Jahre alt war.

«Nein, nein,» sagte ich, «auch Kalinowka – wirklich nicht.»

Ich mußte oft zu ihr in die Küche, und sie kam oft in mein Zimmer, und den ganzen Tag dachte ich an das, was ich vergessen wollte: an den Krieg, und ich warf die Asche meiner Zigarette hinters Bett, drückte die Glut an der Wand aus.

Manchmal, wenn ich abends dort lag, hörte ich im Zimmer nebenan die Schritte eines Mädchens, oder ich hörte den Jugoslawen, der im Zimmer neben der Küche wohnte, hörte ihn fluchend den Lichtschalter suchen, bevor er in sein Zimmer ging.

Erst als ich drei Wochen dort wohnte, als ich das Bild von Karl wohl zum fünfzigsten Mal in die Hand genommen, sah ich, daß der Straßenbahnwagen, vor dem er lachend mit seiner Geldtasche stand, nicht leer war. Zum ersten Mal blickte ich aufmerksam auf das Photo und sah, daß ein lächelndes Mädchen im Inneren des Wagens mitgeknipst worden war. Es war die Hübsche, an die ich während des Krieges so oft gedacht hatte. Die Wirtin kam auf mich zu, blickte mir aufmerksam ins Gesicht und sagte: «Nun erkennen Sie ihn, wie?» Dann trat sie hinter mich, blickte über meine Schulter auf das Bild, und aus ihrer zusammengerafften Schürze stieg der Geruch frischer Erbsen an meinem Rücken herauf.

«Nein,» sagte ich leise, «aber das Mädchen.»

and again the girl.

'Perhaps', my landlady said, 'you knew him after all.'

I shook my head and put the photo back into the box: it was a glossy photo and still looked new, though it was eight years old.

'No, no,' I said, 'Kalinovka too, really I didn't.'

I had to go to her in the kitchen often, and she often came to my room, and all day I was thinking of what I wanted to forget: the war – and I flicked my cigarette ash off behind the bed, stubbed out the butt against the wall.

Sometimes as I lay there in the evening I heard a girl's footsteps in the next room, or I heard the Jugoslav who lived in the room beside the kitchen, heard him cursing as he hunted for the light switch before going into his room.

It wasn't until I'd been there three weeks and had taken Karl's picture into my hands for about the fiftieth time, that I saw that the tram-car, in front of which he was standing with his satchel, smiling, wasn't empty. For the first time I looked attentively at the photo, and saw that a smiling girl inside the car had got into the picture. It was the pretty girl whom I'd often thought of during the war. The landlady came over, looked attentively into my face and said: 'Now do you know him, do you?' Then she went behind me and from her tucked-in apron the smell of fresh green peas came up over my back.

'No,' I said quietly, 'but I do know the girl.'

German Short Stories I, 1964, Richard Newnham (ed.).

TRANSLATION CRITICISM

SL text analysis

The author's intention is to describe, typically, the life of a returned soldier in a rented room in a provincial town.

The language is simple and natural, informal. There are many co-ordinate sentences with stress on verbs. It is at the material rather than the mental pole of language, therefore easier to translate; further, it contains few culturally-specific words, and no sound-effects; no metaphors, few idioms. The author expresses himself through emphasis and one or two 'wayward' words, but uses mainly a simple factual style.

Translation method: semantic in principle, but here almost indistinguishable from communicative.

Translator's intention and method

The translator's intention was to reproduce the precise contextual meaning of the translation. In such a plain text, the unit of translation is often the word. Informality was easy to achieve in English with its phrasal verbs (e.g. 1.0, *wußte nicht, worauf ich wartete* – 'I didn't know what I was waiting for'). Most shifts from SL to TL are in conformity with the norms of the target language and do not require innovative expression.

Comparison of TL with SL text

Possible mistranslations

1.45   *Garnison*: 'garrison' ('barracks' = *Kaserne*).
1.52   *bei der Straßenbahn*: Strictly 'with the trams' (i.e. the company).
1.68   *Transparent*, 'diaphane' – both obsolete. 'Banner'.
1.79   *Rondell*: round flower-bed.
1.80   *rote Limonade*: red soft drink.

Under-translation

1.2   Omission of *heim* (emphasised at end of clause) is regrettable.
1.84   *das Portal*: 'large gate'.
1.113   *die Glut ausdrücken*: 'extinguish the glow'.

Over-translation

1.88   *schmal*: 'narrow'.
1.90   *gestiegen*: 'got on'.

Change of emphasis

ll.5–6   *dort lag ich auf dem Bett*: 'there I lay on the bed' ('lay there on the bed').

l.8   *Arbeiten zu gehen, hatte ich keine Lust*: 'As for going out to work, I didn't feel like it' or 'I wasn't in the mood' ('I didn't want to work').

l.22   *im Dämmer*: Emphasis changed.

l.108   *Ich mußte oft zu ihr in die Küche*: 'I often had to go to her in the kitchen' ('I had to go to her in the kitchen often').

l.121   *Erst als ich drei Wochen dort wohnte*: 'Only when I'd' or 'I'd only lived there three weeks' ('It wasn't until I'd been there three weeks').

Expressive renderings

ll.17–8 *ich döste vor mich hin*: 'I dozed and vegetated' (i.e. 'lying stretched out there').

l.20   *voller schwarzer Flecken*: *voller* transferred to 'all over the wall'.

l.36   *sehr ordentlich*: 'very decent' (connotation also of 'orderly' and 'ordinary').

l.73   *Das war nichts für ihn*: 'That wasn't the job for him'; alternatively, 'That wasn't right for him'. Note the German is an idiom, therefore a deviation from literal translation is virtually essential.

l.76   *er stand*: 'There he stood' (but the new emphasis is the translator's).

ll.138–9 *aber das Mädchen*: 'but I do know the girl' (brilliant use of emphatic present, often neglected by translators).

Quality of translation

A close accurate translation, always on the level of language as well as reference, free from synonyms and added idioms. A few changes of emphasis seem unnecessary, and point to the usefulness of functional sentence perspective to a translator. But there is little 'ideology' in the translation; it is, paradoxiclly, 'scientific' and can be contrasted with Text 10.

The future of the translation in the TL culture

A good story, well observed *Zeitgeschichte* (contemporary history), but slight, without a strong impact. It gives an insight on post-war life in Germany; it is unlikely to influence anglophone writing.

La Société Française
G. Dupeux

Un historien contemporain écrivait, il y a quelques années, que l'histoire sociale de la France au XIXe siècle était encore 'terra incognita'. Un jugement aussi sévère ne pourrait plus être porté aujourd'hui. La publication récente de thèses de doctorat tout orientées vers l'histoire sociale et d'excellents ouvrages de synthèse ont grandement amélioré nos connaissances, au moins pour certaines régions françaises et pour une partie du XIXe siècle. Il n'est pas moins vrai que des lacunes considérables subsistent, et qu'il reste beaucoup à faire.

Les raisons de ce retard sont diverses. Il se pourrait que l'une des plus importantes tienne à la difficulté de définir avec précision le domaine de l'histoire sociale. Le désir, fort louable, de décrire dans tous ses détails la vie quotidienne des Français à diverses époques, aboutit trop souvent à une accumulation de détails pittoresques, mais dont on n'est nullement assuré qu'ils expriment une réalité vécue par tel ou tel groupe. A l'opposé, la description de modèles sociologiques, systématiques et abstraits, inspirés de conceptions a priori, aboutit à dresser l'écran d'une construction artificielle devant les événements et les individus.

Nous avons conçu cette histoire de la société française à l'époque contemporaine comme une histoire des groupes sociaux, définis par la place occupée dans le processus de production et la division sociale du travail, comme une histoire aussi de leurs rapports, et de l'évolution, dans le temps, de ces rapports. Nous avons cherché à montrer comment, dans cette évolution, certains groupes sociaux défavorisés et mécontents ont réussi à améliorer leur position et assuré, pour quelque temps au

French Society*
G. Dupeux

Some years ago it was remarked by a contemporary historian that the social history of France in the nineteenth century was still uncharted territory. Nobody could make 5 such a drastic statement today. In recent years the publication of doctoral theses devoted to social history and some excellent works of synthesis have enormously increased our knowledge of several regions 10 of France, and of much of the nineteenth century. But there are still big gaps and plenty of scope for further research.

There are various reasons for this. One of the principal ones may be the very difficulty 15 of defining the scope of social history. A praiseworthy ambition to describe in detail the daily life of Frenchmen can simply end up with an accumulation of picturesque details without any certainty that they 20 reflect the realities of life for any particular social group. On the other hand, simply to describe a series of systematized sociological models, constructed on an *a priori* basis, is to interpose a dark screen between 25 the reader and the events and the people he is reading about.

The conceptual aim of the present work is to provide a history of the various groups that constitute French society, classified 30 according to the position they occupy in the production process and in the social division of labour, of their relationship with each other, and with the way these relationships have changed in the course of time. 35 We have tried to show how certain underprivileged and malcontent social groups have managed to better their social position and even for a time achieve a sort of

40 *Translation by Peter Wait.

moins, leur domination, parcourant ainsi toute la courbe qui les a menés de la revendication au conservatisme, puis à la réaction et à la peur sociale; comment 45 d'autres groupes, autrefois prépondérants, ont été rejetés définitivement dans l'ombre tandis que d'autres encore se constituaient et exigeaient leur part de bien-être, sinon de pouvoir. 50

domination, running the whole course from radical challenge to conservative acceptance, ending with reactionary fears for the future of society; how other groups that once dominated the scene have been totally eclipsed, while others again are emerging from the shadows and demanding their share of the good things of life and even power.

TRANSLATION CRITICISM

SL text analysis

The SL text attempts to demonstrate the alternating periods of success and failure of three large social groups in contemporary French social history; it uses a Marxist but apparently non-partisan approach.

The language is formal, educated, cool and non-technical; the text is well-written; it shows cultural overlap and always follows a natural sophisticated usage. One would expect semantic and communicative translation methods to largely coincide here, but since this is a rather general non-literary text, the communicative translation method should predominate. The text is authoritative in being written by an acknowledged authority, but it is not sacrosanct, its 'expressive' aspect being unimportant.

Translator's intention and general method

The translator has attempted an accurate, smooth and natural version of the original, strengthening certain emphases and boldly over-translating many lexical details which, as he saw it, appeared to be too abstract, weak and vague in the original French. He uses phrasal verbs and present participles to achieve a rather more informal style than the original.

Comparison of TL with SL text

Grammar

The sentence punctuation is preserved, thereby keeping sentences as units of translation. The larger clauses are mainly preserved, but passives and actives interchange in the main clauses of the first and second sentences (*écrivait* – 'it was remarked'; *ne pourrait plus être porté* – '(Nobody) could make'): the first sentence of the translation stresses 'social history'; the second is strengthened by the active voice. At the group rank, there are various verb shifts:

1.22   *on n'est nullement assuré*: 'without any certainty'.

1.23 *réalité vécue*: 'the realities of life'.
1.24 *la description*: 'simply to describe'.
1.30 *Nous avons conçu*: 'the conceptual aim'.
1.33 *la place occupée*: 'the position they occupy'.
1.36 *l'évolution . . . de ces rapports*: 'the way these relationships have changed'.
Note several cases where French verbs (*restent, subsistent, tiennent à, aboutit à*) are rendered by 'is' or 'are'. 'To be' and 'to have' are English all-purpose verbs!

Lexis

The sense is sharpened in:
1.4   *sévère*: 'drastic'.
1.7   *orientées*: 'devoted'.
1.8   *grandement*: 'enormously'.
1.10   *certaines*: 'several'.
1.11   *une partie*: 'much of'.
1.13   *beaucoup à faire*: 'plenty of scope for further research'.
1.15   *importantes*: 'principal'.
1.17   *le domaine*: 'scope'.
1.18   *désir*: 'ambition'.
1.20   *trop souvent*: 'simply'.
1.23   *expriment*: 'reflect'.
1.29   *les individus*: 'the people he is reading about'.
1.33   *définis*: 'classified'.
1.40   *position*: 'social position'.
1.42   *leur domination*: 'a sort of domination'.
1.46   *autrefois prépondérants*: 'that once dominated the scene'.
1.49   *bien-être*: 'the good things of life'.
1.49   *sinon*: 'even'.

Some of this strengthens the original, filling it out without changing the sense and giving it greater vigour. 'Scope' and the 'good things of life' demonstrate French lexical gaps. Only in the case of *une partie* ('much of'), *domination* ('a sort of domination') and *trop souvent* ('simply') does the change seem unnecessary.

De la revendication au conservatisme, puis à la réaction et à la peur sociale demands bold recasting, and the translator's is consistent with his general method. A closer less particular treatment would go to 'the whole course from protest to conservative attitudes, and later to reactionary positions and fear for their social position'.

Metaphors

ll.27–8 *dresser l'écran d'une construction artificielle*: 'interpose a dark screen' seems awkward. Possibly 'erect an artificial screen'.

ll.42–3   *parcourant toute la courbe*: 'running the whole course'. A brilliant example
           of modified metaphor. The dead metaphor 'course' is revived by
           'running'.
l.47   *rejetés dans l'ombre*: 'totally eclipsed'. A standard metaphor rendered
           more powerfully by another.
l.48   *se constituaient*: 'are emerging from the shadows'. The metaphor is
           brilliantly restored.

Cultural metaphor

ll.3–4   *terra incognita*: 'uncharted territory'. The Latin tag would seem contrived
           in the English text. The rendering is excellent.

Omissions and additions

ll.11–12   *Il n'est pas moins vrai*: 'but'. 'Nevertheless' or 'The fact remains that'?
l.14   *ce retard*: 'this'. Difficult! Possibly 'these omissions'.
ll.19–20   *à diverses époques*: Omitted as unnecessary.
l.26   *abstraits*: Since *systématiques* has been changed to 'systematized', there is
           no place for 'abstract', which is perhaps a pity.
l.31   *à l'epoque contemporaine*: Barely covered by 'that constitute'. 'Now' or
           'today' could be put after 'society' (l.29).
l.36   *leurs rapports*: 'their relationships with each other' (case-grammar
           applied).

Change of tenses

ll.48–9   *se constituaient . . . exigeaient*: On balance, the change from imperfect to
           continuous present is justified.

Quality of translation

The translator has succeeded brilliantly and with verve in what he set out to do. All
the propositions of the original are reproduced, often with stronger contrasts and a
greater impact. In some instances he has gone, I think, excessively beyond the
original. Possibly Dupeux, reading the translation, might react by saying it
exaggerates and commits itself too much; it is not as cautiously worded as he
intended it to be. Possibly he would envy the translator the greater resources of
English.

The translator would not accept my principle that fundamentally translation is
an enforced deviation from literal translation. (Why should he?) He appears to give
a marked preference to the referential level in his bold sweeping outline, so that the

textual level is regarded and incorporated at a remove. He makes me nervous – there is 'ideology' that goes beyond the universals of accuracy and economy in this translation. I applaud his audacity and admire his skill in writing.

The translation's place in the TL culture

Dupeux's book appears to be interesting and important, and may also afford an insight into British nineteenth-century social history. The translation is serious and was worth doing.

TEXT **13**

Zum Wohle aller

Sind die Deutschen fleißiger als andere, wenn es um die Arbeit geht – und fauler, wenn nach Streik gerufen wird? Wer vor dreißig Jahren, kaum daß die Bundesrepublik Deutschland gegründet war und Elend und Schuttberge noch das Bild prägten, dem Land, seinen Menschen eine Generation später Wohlstand vorausgesagt hätte, wäre ungläubigem Staunen und verständnislosem Kopfschütteln begegnet. Doch von Angang an waren die politischen Entscheidungen in der jungen Bundesrepublik Deutschland darauf ausgerichtet, das Land zu einem sozialen Rechtsstaat auszubauen. Bestimmt hat es den Deutschen dabei nicht an Fleiß gemangelt – doch auch das Glück stand ihnen zur Seite: die großzügige Marshallplan-Hilfe der Vereinigten Staaten, die lange Periode des Friedens in Europa, der Aufbau der Europäischen Gemeinschaft und der Abbau der Zölle und anderer Handelsschranken.

Heute, im Rückblick, zeigt sich, daß der vor dreißig Jahren eingeschlagene Weg kein Irrweg war. Die Verfassung gewährleistet das Eigentum, fordert aber auch zugleich, daß sein Gebrauch dem Wohle der Allgemeinheit zu dienen habe. Obwohl es in der Bundesrepublik Deutschland eine Reihe von staatlichen und halbstaatlichen Unternehmen gibt, herrschen grundsätzlich Privateigentum an Produktionsmitteln und unternehmerische Entscheidungsfreiheit. Und dennoch sind Arbeitskämpfe in der Bundesrepublik Deutschland selten – weil die sozialen Gegensätze sich in Grenzen halten. Daß alle radikalen Parteien in der Bundesrepublik Deutschland ohne jede Chance sind, steht dazu in einem engen Zusammenhang.

TEXT **13**

To the benefit of all

Are the Germans more industrious than others in respect of their work – and slower to answer the call to strike? Thirty years ago, shortly after the birth of the Federal Republic of Germany, when poverty and mountains of rubble were normal, anyone who prophesied that this country and its people would reach prosperity only a generation later would have been looked upon with astonishment, disbelief, a sad shaking of heads. Political decisions in the young Federal Republic of Germany however had the objective of making the country a social, constitutional state from the very outset. Certainly the Germans worked hard, but they also had luck: the generous Marshall Plan aid granted by the United States, the long period of peace in Europe, the development of the European Communities and the gradual elimination of duty and other restrictions to trade.

Looking back, we can now say that the approach taken thirty years ago was not a mistake. The Constitution guarantees property rights, but also demands that property should be used to benefit all. Although the Federal Republic of Germany has a number of companies that are completely or partly owned by the state, the general principle is that the means of production should remain private property and that entrepreneurial powers of decision should not be limited. Nevertheless, strikes are rare in the Federal Republic of Germany – because the social differences are not all too great. This is one of the main reasons why radical parties have no hope of building up a large following in the Federal Republic of Germany.

Source: *SCALA*, Deutsche Ausgabe, Nr. 2 (1980
SCALA, English Edition, No. 2 (1980).

TRANSLATION CRITICISM

SL text analysis

The text's intention is to state that since the War the Federal Republic's political direction has been sound and that the country has become a prosperous, hard-working, orderly and moderate nation.

SCALA represents a West German establishment view and is published by a Frankfurt publisher (subsidised?) for an educated non-specialist readership. It is translated into five languages. The text is written in cultivated 'quality press' language, relying on a few emotive words and restrained standard metaphors to attain its persuasive, indeed propaganda effect. Culturally there are one or two problems. This is an 'anonymous' text, following normal and natural usage, and it is fairly well written. The translation method should be 'communicative' throughout. This is a journalistic text, where finely accurate translation is not as important as in many other text-types. A clean impact is essential – the translation must not be cluttered with detail.

Translator's intention and method

The translator's intention, as in all 'vocative' texts, is to produce the same effect on his readership as was produced on the readership of the original. As there is much cultural overlap, this is theoretically possible.

An English readership would however be unlikely to react like a German readership to this text and one assumes that the translator should attempt to make his readership envious.

The translator showed himself aware of the importance of achieving a strong emotive effect and of using idiomatic language.

Comparison of TL with SL text

Title

The 'allusive' title is translated by its standard equivalent; alternatively, 'For the benefit of all'. A descriptive equivalent could be 'West German prosperity'.

Grammar

ll. 1–3   The rhetorical question, whose function here is to introduce the topic, is retained in the English, although this device is not so common in English as in other European languages.

1.2   *wenn es um die Arbeit geht*: The shift from clause to adverbial group unnecessarily increases the formality and decreases the emphasis of this item. Alternative: 'when they have to work'.

l.3   *wenn nach Streik gerufen wird*: More typically, the shift from the passive to a standard metaphor makes for a less formal tone.

l.5   *gegründet*: 'birth'. It is natural in English to prefer verb-nouns to verbs for concision and emphasis.

l.8   *Wohlstand vorausgesagt*: Expanded to 'prophesied that (they) would reach prosperity'. The collocation 'reach prosperity' is awkward; 'achieve prosperity' is preferable.

l.9   *ungläubigem Staunen*: 'astonishment, disbelief'. The shift strengthens the translation.

l.13 *ausgerichtet*: Converted to verbal-noun: 'objective'.

l.24 *im Rückblick*: 'looking back' is less formal than 'in retrospect'.

l.33 *grundsätzlich*: 'the general principle is that'.

ll.35–6 *es in der Bundesrepublik gibt*: 'the FRG has' is less formal.

Modulations

ll.15–6 *hat es nicht an Fleiß gemangelt*: 'they worked hard'. The modulation is justified since the German is a considerable understatement.

l.35 *Freiheit*: 'not be limited'. The modulation is influenced by the linguistic context; it dangerously overstresses the point. It would have been wiser to keep to 'freedom of . . . powers'

l.38 *sich in Grenzen halten*: 'are not all too great'. A less formal but inadequate rendering of the German dead metaphor, 'are kept in bounds', gets the sense.

ll.40–1 *steht dazu in einem engen Zusammenhang*: 'This is one of the main reasons': a bold, rather free but successful modulation, since it is less muted and formal than the original.

Metaphors

l.6   *Schuttberge*: Standard literal translation of standard metaphor.

l.6   *das Bild prägten*: 'were normal'. Rather unusual metaphor ('characterised the general picture') is normalised to sense. Here the original's powerful effect is lost.

l.10 *Kopfschütteln*: Concrete and figurative literally translated, with 'sad' replacing *verständnislos*.

l.17 *das Glück stand ihnen zur Seite*: 'they were lucky'. Adequate reduction to sense of standard metaphor.

ll.25–6 *eingeschlagene Weg . . . Irrweg*: Standard translations as 'approach' and 'mistake' respectively. 'Take an approach' is acceptable – 'path' would be too refined.

Lexis

l.2   *fauler*: 'slower'. The clever ironical contrast with 'industrious' is lost, which seems a pity, but the version is normalised.

1.4   *kaum*: 'shortly'. Under-translation required by linguistic context.
1.5   *gegründet*: The change from 'foundation' to 'birth' is in the taste area.
1.6   *Elend*: 'poverty' is an under-translation for 'distress'.
1.15   *ausbauen*: 'make' is an under-translation for 'strengthen', 'consolidate'.
1.20   *Aufbau*: 'development'. Under-translation for 'building up'.
1.22   *Abbau*: 'gradual elimination'. A perceptive componential analysis of *Abbau*.
1.27   *Eigentum*: 'property rights'. Strengthens the sense.
ll.28–9 *Gebrauch . . . dienen*: The two words are successfully conflated as 'used'.
1.36   *Arbeitskämpfe*: Familiar alternative ('industrial action') for 'strikes'.
1.38   *Gegensätze*: Usually a stronger word than 'differences' ('contrasts', 'antitheses', 'oppositions', 'antagonisms'). Suggests that the translator is trying to tone down the original.
1.40   *ohne jede Chance*: Could have been translated as 'no prospects' or 'no future'. The translator appears to be spelling out the sense for propaganda reasons.

Misprint?

1.22   *Zölle*: Should read 'duties'(?) unless 'duty' is seen as a collective noun.

Institutional terms

` 1.14   *einem sozialen Rechtsstaat* is a quotation from the Federal Republic's Basic Law or Constitution. A 'social, constitutional state' is the official translation and has to be retained. *Rechtsstaat*, defined as a state where the authority of the government is limited by a system of law (Wahrig), is a recognised technical term. 'Constitutional state' is merely a descriptive equivalent or a label. Note that *Collins' German Dictionary* deals inadequately with this term. *Sozialen*, 'a social . . . state', is an ambiguous unusual descriptive term but it is comprehensible in the context of *Sozialstaat*, 'welfare state'.
1.34   *unternehmerisch*: 'entrepreneurial' is the closest technical equivalent.

Sound-effect

ll.20,22 *Aufbau* and *Abbau* as sound-effect is lost.

Word-order

1.11   *Doch von Angang an*: This phrase has been shifted to the end of the sentence in the translation. The English phrase 'from the very outset' is a dead metaphor, is more idiomatic and therefore stronger than the German. Whether it is put at the end or the beginning of the sentence is a matter of taste.

Addition

ll.37–8 'of building up a large following' strengthens *Chance* but 'have no future' would be decisive and concise.

Quality of the translation

The translator has successfully realised his intention. Referentially, the main ideas of the SL text are reproduced. The language is rather more informal than it is in the original, which is in line with the difference between educated English and German. There are several instances of under-translation, sometimes inevitable in the context of different collocations and normal and natural usage. In fact the use of more general words helps to strengthen the pragmatic effect, since, being common and frequently used, they have more connotations and are more emotive than specific, let alone technical, words which are purely referential. Only in one or two instances is the translator's response inadequate.

A 'vocative' text such as this one which uses much emotional language offers a wider range of translation solutions than many other text-types, particularly on the grammatical level and, provided it appears to fulfil its aims, its choice of language need not be strictly assessed.

The propaganda and publicity areas of vocative (or social) texts normally require more creative or inventive translation than, say, informative texts.

The translation's future in the TL culture

Since this is an ephemeral but official text, the question of its 'enduring' merit does not arise. The translation has two interesting traces of the 'group loyalty factor' (Ivars Alksnis, 1983) which suggest that the translation (unconsciously?) puts the Federal Republic in a better light than does the original ('slower' for *fauler*; 'the Germans worked hard').

Glossary

In some cases, I give terms a special sense which is I think appropriate, transparent and operational for translation. These terms are indicated with an asterisk.

*ACRONYM: A word formed from the first letters or first syllables of its component words (e.g. UNO, BTT (q.v.), Komsomol).

ACTUAL: The sense used in the particular context, as opposed to 'potential'.

ADJECTIVAL CLAUSE (or RELATIVE CLAUSE):   Subordinate clause qualifying or describing a noun or pronoun (e.g. 'the man who came in'; 'the house (that) I saw'; 'the man (who/whom) I saw').

*ADJECTIVAL NOUN: Noun formed from an adjective, (e.g. 'kindness', 'redness').

*'ANONYMOUS' TEXT: (Delisle's (1981) term). A text where the name and status of the author is not important. Usually a run-of-the-mill 'informative' text.

*AUTHORITATIVE TEXT (or STATEMENT);   An official text, or a text where the status of the author carries authority.

BACK-TRANSLATION TEST (BTT):   Translating a stretch or lexical unit of TL text back into the SL, for purposes of comparison and correction. A useful test for assessing the semantic range of the SL passage. If the retranslation doesn't correspond with the SL text, a translator can justify his version: (a) if it shows up a SL lexical gap; (b) the wider context supports a non-corresponding version. However, if the SL lexical unit has a clear one-to-one TL equivalent, a different version is usually hard to justify.

BLEND (or 'PORTMANTEAU' WORD):   The fusion of two words into one (e.g. 'motel', 'brunch' and common technical language).

CASE-GAP: Where a 'CASE-PARTNER' (q.v.) is missing.

CASE-PARTNER: A noun GROUP (q.v.) or pronoun dependent on a verb, adjective or noun; it may be the subject, object, indirect object, etc., of a verb; in the possessive or genitive case (e.g. 'a row of books', 'a student group') or dependent on a VERB ADJECTIVE (q.v.) (e.g. 'responsible to me'). In translation, case-partners are sometimes added to fill SL 'case-gaps'.

CLASSIFIER: A generic or general or superordinate term sometimes supplied by the translator to qualify a specific term (e.g. 'the city of Brno').

CLAUSE: A complete stretch of words including a subject and a verb. A main clause can be used on its own in a sentence; a subordinate clause can only be used with a main clause and is often introduced by a subordinating conjunction or relative pronoun.

COLLOCATION: Two or more words ('collocates') that go 'happily' or naturally with each other (see pp. 212–3).

COMMUNICATIVE TRANSLATION: Translation at the readership's level.

COMPENSATION: Compensating for any semantic loss (e.g. undertranslation, metaphor, pun, sound effect) in one place at another place in the text.

*CONFLATE or *COLLAPSE: To bring two or more SL words together and translate by one TL word.

CONNECTIVES: Words used to connect two sentences to secure **cohesion**: conjunctions, pronouns, adverbs, such as 'further, 'yet', etc. Also called 'link(ing) words' or 'connectors'.

CORRESPONDENT: Corresponding stretch of text in SL and TL text.

CULTURAL EQUIVALENT: A cultural word translated by a cultural word, e.g. *bac* by '"A" level'. Always approximate.

CULTURE: Objects, processes, institutions, customs, ideas peculiar to one group of people.

*CURRENCY: The status of a word, idiom or syntactic structure at the period of writing (SL or TL), either within or outside the context, as exemplified first in its frequency of use, and also in its degree of novelty, validity and obsolescence. (A more comprehensive account is offered by STATUS (q.v.).)

DEICTIC WORD: A word indicating time or space like a pronoun: e.g. 'the', 'this', 'my', 'your', 'here', 'there'.

*DELETE, *DELETION: Means 'omit, don't translate'.

*DICTIONARY WORD: A word only found in (usually bilingual) dictionaries and therefore to be avoided by translators.

*EMPTY VERB: (a) A verb such as 'do', 'give' (an order), 'deliver' (a speech), 'take' (action), collocated with a verb-noun, to which it gives greater force; (b) any verb that can be deleted in translation (see 'HOUSE-ON-HILL' CONSTRUCTION).

*EPONYM: Any word derived from a proper name.

EQUAL FREQUENCY RULE: Any corresponding features of the SL and TL text should be approximately equally frequent in the appropriate language register. Features include words, metaphors, collocations, grammatical structure, word order, proverbs, institutional terms.

EQUATIVE or EQUATIONAL VERB or COPULA: A verb that expresses equivalence or change, such as 'be', 'seem', 'become', 'grow', 'turn', 'get', which has adjective or noun complements.

FALSE FRIEND or *FAUX AMI*: An SL word that has the same or similar form but another meaning in the TL; therefore a deceptive cognate.

FREAK EXAMPLE: An exceptional example, often inadequately offered as evidence.

*FUNCTIONAL TRANSLATION: A simple natural translation that clarifies the purpose and meaning of the SL passage (in the best sense, a 'paraphrase').

GENERAL WORD: A noun, verb, or adjective with a wide referential range, e.g., 'thing', 'do', 'good', 'development', 'affair', 'business', *phénomène, élement*. Also called 'hold-all words'.

GRAECO-LATINISM: A modern word derived from a combination of Latin and/or ancient Greek words.

GRAMMATICAL (or FUNCTIONAL) WORD: A word indicating relations, e.g. a preposition, pronoun, connective, a PRE-NOUN (q.v.), a DEICTIC WORD (q.v.). A component of a limited or 'closed' language system, that includes or excludes 'grey area' words such as 'in respect of', *dans le cadre de*, 'to the point that', etc.

GROUP, also called PHRASE: A constituent part of a clause or a sentence; there are noun groups ('a (nice) lad'), verb groups ('went to see', 'would have done'), adverbial groups ('extremely well', 'in the morning'). Groups initiated with a preposition, like the last example, are often called 'prepositional groups'.

*'HOUSE-ON-HILL' CONSTRUCTION: An SL structure that uses an EMPTY VERB (q.v.), usually a participle or an adjectival clause, or a preposition to qualify a noun, usually translated into English by 'noun plus preposition plus noun' (examples on p. 87).

*HOUSE-STYLE or FORMAT: The conventions of format peculiar to a publication or a publisher, including titling or sub-titling, punctuation, capitalisation, spelling, footnotes, length of paragraphs, dates, illustrations, arrangement.

*'ICEBERG': All the work involved in translating, of which only the 'tip' shows.

*INTENSIFIERS: Adverbs or adjectives used, usually in clichéd collocations, to intensify or stress meaning: e.g. 'totally', 'highly', 'incredible', 'deeply', 'immensely', 'profoundly'. Often deleted in natural usage.

INTERFERENCE: Literal translation from SL or a third language that does not give the right or required sense (see TRANSLATIONESE).

INTERNATIONALISM: Strictly a word that keeps the same meaning and the same form in many languages, therefore normally a technical term. (Concept-words such as 'liberalism' could be described as 'pseudo-internationalisms'.)

JARGON: Here used in the sense of overblown and pretentious groups and words, e.g. Graeco-latinisms with double or triple suffixes or multi-noun compounds used unnecessarily to replace simple words – not in its other sense of 'technical Language'.

LEXICAL WORD: A descriptive word referring to objects, events or qualities, usually a noun, verb, adjective or adverb. Unlimited (an 'open' set) in number in any language.

LEXIS: The sum of 'lexical words' in a language.

LINGUISTIC SYNONYMS: Two or more words that resemble each other in meaning, e.g. unlawful, illicit, illegal.

METALANGUAGE: Language used to describe language about language, or to exemplify one of its features (cf. metalingual)

METAPHOR: A word or phrase applied to an object, action or quality which it does not literally denote, in order to describe it more accurately or vividly – a degree of resemblance is therefore implied.

*MODULATION: A translation procedure converting SL double negative to TL positive or vice versa, qualifying a verb, adjective or adverb (e.g. 'not unmindful' → 'mindful'). The procedure is available as an option for any clause, though 'in principle' (i.e. out of context) it produces either a stronger or a weaker TL equivalent.

MONOSEMOUS: Having only one sense. Also called 'univocal' or 'monosemantic'.

MORPHEME: A minimal unit of language that has meaning. Includes roots, prefixes, suffixes and inflections ('endings').

NATURALIZE: Means *either* 'convert to natural usage' *or* 'convert to normal TL spelling or pronunciation.'

NEGATIVE: Lexically, a word used in an unfavourable or pejorative or disparaging sense; a 'snarl' word.

NEOLOGISM: A newly formed word or an old word in a new sense.

NO-EQUIVALENT WORD: An SL word for which there is no clear one- (word) to one- (word) equivalent in the TL, that shows up a lexical gap in the TL. Often has no cognate in the TL. Often translated, after componential analysis, into two or more TL words.

NOUN COMPOUND: The combination of two or more nouns, usually unhyphenated, referring to one concept.

NOUN GROUP: See GROUP.

ONE-TO-ONE: One word translated by one word.

OPAQUE: SL form whose TL meaning is not apparent from its morphology, etymology etc.

OVER-TRANSLATION: A translation that gives more detail than its correspondng SL unit. Often a more specific word.

PHATIC LANGUAGE: Used to establish social contact and to express sociability with interlocutors or readers rather than referential meaning. All communication has a phatic element.

*PHATICISM: (neolog): A standard phatic phrase.

POSITIVE: Used in a favourable, approving 'ameliorative' sense (opposed to 'negative'). A 'purr' word.

POTENTIAL: Possible or latent, of meaning, only out of context, as opposed to 'actual' in context.

PRAGMATIC: Affecting the readership; the communicative, emotive element in language, as opposed to the referential, informative element (cf. the contrast between 'mind' and 'reality'). The two elements are always present in language, but in varying degree. (Note that 'pragmatic' has other senses.)

*PRE-NOUN: All the functional or grammatical words that are used to qualify a noun, e.g. articles, deictic and possessive adjectives, 'other', 'some', etc.

REFERENT: The object, event or quality that a word denotes in the context of an utterance.

REFERENTIAL SYNONYMS: Two or more words that refer to the same thing or person, e.g. Disraeli, the 19th Century Tory Prime Minister, the first Earl of Beaconsfield, he etc.

REGISTER: A variety of 'social' language at one period, characterised by a particular degree of formality, emotional tone, difficulty, dialect and social class; occasionally by other factors such as age and sex.

ROMANCE LANGUAGES: Portuguese, Spanish (Catalan, Castilian), French, Italian, Romansh, Romanian.

*'SACRED' TEXT: (contrast with 'anonymous' text): An authoritative or expressive text where the manner is as important as the matter.

SCRAP EXAMPLE: A small example, illustrative rather than demonstrative.

SEMANTIC TRANSLATION: Translation at the author's level.

*SETTING: The place where the SL text appears and the TL text is likely to appear: i.e. name of periodical, publisher, type of client, etc. The setting dictates the HOUSE-STYLE (q.v.).

SL (SOURCE LANGUAGE): The language of the text that is to be or has been translated.

*STATUS (of a construction, idiom or word): A more comprehensive term than CURRENCY (q.v.); a complete statement for the translator, including frequency, acceptance, milieu, degree of formality, technicality, emotional tone, favourableness (positive/ negative), likely future – in and outside the context!

SUB-TEXT: The thought under the text, sometimes in contradiction to what is stated ('sub-text' appears to be an actor's term popularised by the translator and biographer of Ibsen and Chekhov, Michael Meyer). A dangerous concept. Every translator likes to think he has just occasionally translated what the author meant rather than what he wrote.

TL (TARGET LANGUAGE): The language of the translated text.

TOPIC: Always used in the sense of the subject-matter or area of knowledge of a text.

TRANSFERENCE (called 'TRANSCRIPTION' in Newmark, 1981): The transfer of an SL word or lexical unit into the TL text, as a translation procedure.

TRANSLATIONESE (sometimes called 'TRANSLATORESE'): A literal translation that does not produce the appropriate sense. Usually due to INTERFERENCE (q.v.) if the TL is not the translator's language of habitual use, or to automatic acceptance of dictionary meanings.

*TRANSPARENT: An SL word whose meaning 'shines through' in the TL, owing to its form, etymology, etc. Therefore usually a non-*faux ami*, a faithful friend. Used also of SL compounds whose components translate literally into the TL, sometimes referred to as semantically motivated words.

TRANSPOSITION (or SHIFT): A change of grammar in the translation from SL to TL.

*UNDERLIFE: The personal qualities and private life of a writer that can be deduced from a close reading of the SL text.

UNDER-TRANSLATION: Where the translation gives less detail and is more general than the original. Most translations are under-translations, but their degree of under-translation is too high.

'UNFINDABLE' WORD: A word that cannot be found in a reference book or be identified by an informant.

UNIT OF TRANSLATION (UT): The smallest segment of an SL text which can be translated, as a whole, in isolation from other segments. It normally ranges from the word through the collocation to the clause. It could be described as 'as small as is possible and as large as is necessary' (this is my view), though some translators would say that it is a misleading concept, since the only UT is the whole text.

VERBAL ADJECTIVE: An adjective derived from a verb, with the force of a verb: e.g. 'responsible', 'dependent', 'helping'.

VERB-NOUN: ('VERBAL NOUN', 'DEVERBAL'): A noun formed from a verb, e.g. 'establishment', 'promotion', 'progress', 'cry', 'laugh'. Often collocated with an EMPTY VERB (q.v.). One verb-noun sometimes indicates state or process, active or passive, or a concrete object: thus five possible meanings. Animate verb-nouns (e.g. 'eater') may have no one-to-one equivalents in other languages.

Abbreviations

ALPAC	Automatic Language Processing Advisory Committee
Am.	American
AT	automatic translation
BBC	British Broadcasting Corporation
BSI	British Standards Institution
BTT	back-translation test (or of text)
CA	componential analysis
CAT	computer-aided translation
CD	communicative dynamism
CMEA	Council for Mutual Economic Assistance
COD	*Concise Oxford Dictionary*
COI	Central Office of Information
Cz.	Czech
E	English
EB	*Encyclopaedia Britannica*
EEC	European Economic Community
ESIT	Ecole Supérieure d'Interprétation et de Traduction (Paris)
F	French
FL	foreign language
FRG	Federal Republic of Germany
FSP	functional sentence perspective
G	German
GDR	German Democratic Republic
ISO	International Standards Organisation
It.	Italian
IT	information technology
LSP	language for special (or specific) purposes
MAT	machine-aided translation
MT	machine translation
O	original
OECD	Organisation for Economic Co-operation and Development
OED	*Oxford English Dictionary*
R	Russian
SI	Système International (d'Unités)
SL	source language
Sp.	Spanish
SVO	subject–verb–object
T	translation
TL	target language
TME	temporal and modal exponent
UK	United Kingdom
UN	United Nations
UT	unit of translation
WP	word-processor

Author's Published Papers

1971 'Teaching Italian translation', *Incorporated Linguist*, April 1971.

1975 'European languages: some perspectives' Curriculum Development (10) 8–33, University of Sussex, Winter 1975.

1976 'A Layman's approach to medical translation, part 1', *Incorporated Linguist* 15(2) 41–43.

1976 'A Layman's approach to medical translation, part 11', *Incorporated Linguist* 15(3) 63–68.

1976 'A tentative preface to translation' *AVLA Journal* 14(3), Winter 1976.

1978 'Some problems of translation theory and methodology', *Fremdsprachen* (Leipzig) 1978.

1978 'Componential analysis and translation theory', *Papers in Traductology*, University of Ottawa.

1979 'A layman's view of medical translation' (1405–8) *British Medical Journal* No. 6202. 1st Dec.

1982 'The Translation of authoritative statements' pp. 283–303 in J-C. Gémar. *The Language of the Law and Translation*, Linguatech, Quebec. (*Meta* Vol. 27/4).

'Translation and the Vocative function of Language' pp. 29–37 *Incorporated Linguist*, Vol. 21/1 London.

'A further Note on Communicative and Semantic translation' 18–21 *Babel* Vol. XXVIII.

1983 'Introductory Survey' (1–21) in ed. C. Picken, *The Translator's Handbook*. (Aslib).

'Criteria for evaluating the translation of informative texts' *Fremdsprachen* Leipzig.

1984 'General Aspects of Italian – English Translation pp. 381–404 in *La Traduzione nell' insegnamento delle lingue straniere* La Scuola. Brescia.

1985 'The translation of Metaphor' (295–327) in *The Ubiquity of Metaphor* ed. R. Dirven and W. Paprotte. John Benjamin, Amsterdam.

1986 'Criteria for evaluating the translation of informative texts' *Fremdsprachen*.

1986 'Translation studies: eight tentative directions for research, and some dead ducks'. (37–50) in ed. L. Wollen and H. Lindquist *Translation Studies in Scandinavia*. Lund.

'Translation in language teaching and for professional purposes' in *German in the United Kingdom* (129–131) (UK Conference on German) CILT.

'The Translation of political language' (43–65) in *Dimensioni linguistiche e distanze culturali*. Trieste.

1987 'How you Translate' in *Translation in the modern language degree* ed. H. Keith and J. Mason Heriot Watt, CILT.

1988 'Translation today' in *Translation Studies: State of the Art* Vol. 1 ed. Anderman and Rogers. University of Surrey Press.

1988 'Systemic Grammar and Translation' (M.A.K. Halliday. Festschrift) *Language Topics*. ed. Steele and Threadgold. Benjamins. Amsterdam.

'Translation and Mistranslation' (forthcoming) AILA. Hildesheim.

'Teaching Translation' Stockholm University in *Teaching Translation* ed. Magnusson and Wahlen.

'Modern Translation Theory' (forthcoming) *Lebende Sprachen*.

'The use and abuse of a text-bound approach to translation' FIT transactions (forthcoming).

'Translation and interpretation: retrospect and prospect' in *Applied Linguistics in Society* ed. P. Grunwell for BAAL. CILT. London.

'Pragmatic Translation and Literalism'. Canadian Association for Translation Studies. Windsor, Ontario.

'The Word and its degree of context in translation'. (forthcoming) University of Surrey Press.

'Word and Text: narrowing the gap between the two approaches to Translation'. BAAL Conference, Exeter.

'Translation as literary and linguistic criticism'. Belgian Association of Anglicists in Higher Education. Namur, Belgium.

'Teaching Translation Theory'. *International Journal of Translation*. University of Delhi. (forthcoming).

'The Virtues and Vices of Translationese' Festschrift for Albrecht Neubert, Leipzig. (forthcoming).

Medical terminology

aden(o)-	gland
cephalo-	brain
dia-	apart, across, through, thorough
drom-	running
dys-	abnormal, faulty, bad
femur-	thigh
fus-	pouring
gnost-	know, perceive
-gram	graph
haemo-	blood
hepatic	liver
histo-	tissue
hyper-	excessive
hypo-	insufficient
-lysis	loosening
nox-/noc-	harmful
olig-	little
-oma	swelling
-osis	formation or increase of
-pathy	disease
peri-	around
poly-	several
pyr-	fire, fever
renal	kidney
sal-	salt, sodium
syn-	together
therap-	treatment
ton-/ten-	stretch
toxic	poisonous
ur(o)-	urine

Bibliography

(See also Chapter 16 – Reference books and their uses)

Alksnis, I. (1980) 'The Hazards of Translation'. *Parallèles*. No. 3. Geneva.
Bettelheim, B. (1983) *Freud and Man's Soul*. London: Chatto & Windus.
Brinkmann, H. (1971) *Die deutsche Sprache*, Düsseldorf.
Buhler, K. (1965) *Die Sprachtheorie*. Jena.
Burling, Robbins (1970) *Man's Many Voices*. NY: Holt, Rinehart & Winston.
Cairncross, J. (1968) *Three Racine Plays*. Harmondsworth: Penguin.
Catford, J.C. (1915) *A Linguistic Theory of Translation*. Oxford: OUP.
Chukovsky, K. (1984) *A High Art: the art of translation*, tr. L.G. Leighton. Knoxville: Univ. of Tennessee.
Crystal, D. (1981) 'How dare you talk like that?' *The Listener* **106** (27/9).
Delisle, J. (1981) *L'Analyse du discours comme méthode de traduction*. Ottawa: Ottawa University Press.
Dressler, W. (1973) *Einführung in die Textlinguistik*. Tübingen: Niemeyer.
Dressler, W. (1981) *Current Trends in Text Linguistics*. Berlin: De Gruyter.
Duff, A. (1981) *The Third Language*. Oxford: Pergamon.
Ferguson, C.A. (1975) 'Diglossia', in *Language and Social Context*, ed. P. Giglioli. Harmondsworth: Penguin.
Fillmore, C. (1968) 'The case for case', in *Universals in Linguistic Theory*, eds E. Bach and R. Harms. NY: Holt, Rinehart & Winston.
Fillmore, C. (1977) 'The case for case reopened', in *Syntax and Semantics*, eds P. Cole and J.M. Sadock. NY: Academic Press.
Firbas, J. (1972) 'Interplay in functional sentence perspective', in *The Prague School of Linguistics and Language Teaching*, ed. V. Fried, London: OUP.
Firth, J.R. (1957) *Papers in Linguistics 1934–51*. London: OUP.
Folkart, B. (1984) 'A thing-bound approach to the practice and teaching of technical translation', *Meta* **XXIX** No. 3. Montreal.
Gadamer, H.G. (1976) *Philosophical Hermeneutics*. Los Angeles: University of California Press.
Gowers, E. and Fraser, R. (1977) *Fowler's Modern Usage*. Oxford: Clarendon Press.
Graham, A.C. (1965) *Poems of the Late Tang*. Harmondsworth: Penguin.
Graham, J. (1985) (ed.) *Difference in Translation*. Cornell University Press, Ithaca.
Grévisse, M. (1986) *Bon Usage: Grammaire Française*. London: Collins.
Grice, H.P. 'Logic and conversation', in *Syntax and Semantics 3: Speech acts*, eds P. Cole and J.L. Morgan. NY: Academic Press.
Guillemin-Flescher, S. (1981) *Syntaxe comparée du français et de l'anglais*. Ophrys: Paris.
Haas, W. (1968) 'The theory of translation', in G.R.H. Parkinson. *The Theory of Meaning*. London: OUP.
Halliday, M.A.K. (1973) *Explorations in the Functions of Language*. London: Arnold.

Helbig, G. (1969) *Wörterbuch zur Valenz und Distribution deutscher Verben*. Leipzig: VEB Enzyklopädie.

Holman, M. (1985) 'Translation or transliteration?' *Supostavitelno Ezikoznanie* 5/10. Sofia.

Hönig, H.G. and Kussmaul, P. (1982) *Strategie der Übersetzung*. Tübingen: Narr.

House, J. (1977) *A model for Translation Quality Assessment*. Tübingen: Narr.

Jakobson, R. (1967) 'On linguistic aspects of translation', in *On Translation*, ed. R.A. Brower. Cambridge, Mass.: Harvard University Press.

Joos, M. (1962) *The Seven Clocks*. Indiana University; and the Hague: Mouton.

Ladmiral, J.-R. (1979) *Traduire: théorèmes pour la traduction*. Paris: Payot.

Lakoff, G. and Johnson, M. (1980) *Metaphors We Live By*. Chicago: Univ. of Chicago Press.

Lecuyer, M.F. (1978) *Practice in Advanced French Précis*. London: Harrap:

Levy, J. (1969) *Die literarische Übersetzung*. Frankfurt.

Loffler-Lorian, A.M. (1985) 'Traduction automatique et style'. *Babel* **XXI**(2).

Maillot, J. (1981) *La Traduction scientifique et technique*. Paris: Eyrolles.

Malblanc, A. (1980) *Stylistique comparée du français et de l'allemand*. Paris: Didier.

Masterman, M. (1982) 'Limits of innovation' in MT', in *Practical Experience of MI*, ed. V. Lawson. Amsterdam: North Holland.

Mathiot, M. (1979) *Ethnolinguistics: Boas, Sapir and Whorf revisited*. The Hague: Mouton.

Meyer, M. (1974) 'On translating plays', *Twentieth Century Studies*.

Mounin, G. (1963) *Les Problèmes théoriques de la traduction*. Paris: Gallimard.

Neubert, A. (1984) 'Text-bound translation teaching', in *Translation Theory and its Implementation*, ed. W. Wilss. Tübingen: Narr.

Nida, E.A. (1975) *The Componential Analysis of Meaning*. The Hague: Mouton.

Nida, E.A. (1975) *Exploring Semantic Structures*. Munich: Fink.

Osgood, C.E., Suci, G. and Tannenbaum, P.H. (1967) *The Measurement of Meaning*. Univ. of Illinois.

Paepcke, F. (1975) 'Gemeinsprache, Fachsprachen und Übersetzung', in *Im Übersetzen, Leben*, eds K. Berger and H.-M. Speier. Tübingen: Narr.

Palkova, Z. and Palek, B. (1981) 'Functional sentence perspective and text linguistics', in *Current Trends in Text Linguistics*, ed. W. Dressler. Berlin: De Gruyter.

Pottier, B. (1964) 'Vers une sémantique moderne', *Travaux de linguistique et de litterature 2*. Strasbourg.

Quine, W.V.O. (1959) 'Meaning and translation', in *On Translation*, ed. R.A. Brower. Cambridge, Mass.: Harvard.

Quirk, R. (1984) *The Use of English*. London: Longman.

Ritchie, R.L.G., Simons, C.I. (1952) *Essays in Translations from French*. Cambridge: CUP.

Rose, M.G. (1982) 'Walter Benjamin as translation theorist: a reconsideration'. *Dispositio* **8** (19–21). Univ. of Michigan.

Seleskovitch, D. (1985) *Interpréter pour traduire*. Paris: Didier.

Sinclair, J. McH. and Coulthard, R.M. (1975) *Towards an Analysis of Discourse*.

Tesniere, L. (1965) *Elements de syntaxe structurale*. Paris: Klincksieck.

Thiel, G. (1980) Übersetzungsbezogene Textanalyse', in *Übersetzungswissenschaft*, eds W. Wilss and S.A. Poulsen.

Toury, G. (1980) *In Search of a Theory of Translation*. Tel Aviv: Porter Institute.

Tytler, A.F. (1962) *Essay on the Principles of Translation*. London: Dent.

Vinay, J. P. and Darbelnet, J. (1965) *Stylistique comparée du français et de l'anglais*. Paris: Didier.

Voegelin, C. (1960) 'Casual language', in *Style in Language*, ed. T. Sebeok. Cambridge, Mass.: MIT Press.

Waldron, R.A. (1979) *Sense and Sense Development*. London: Deutsch.

Weinrich, H. (1970) *Linguistik der Lüge*. Heidelberg.

Wilss, W. (1982) *The Science of Translation*. Tübingen: Narr.

Name Index

Alksnis, 185

Benjamin, 45
Bettelheim, 132
Buhler, 39, 55
Burling, 121

Cairncross, 166–70
Catford, 65, 85, 86
Chukovsky, 194, 225
Crystal, 204, 212

Delisle, 47, 55, 63, 76, 153–4, 190
Dillon, 167–9
Dressler, 60, 81
Duff, 208

Ferguson, 203
Fillmore, 131–2, 135
Firbas, 60–2, 127, 137
Firth, 38, 108
Folkart, 155–6, 160
Frost, 194

Gadamer, 79
Gowers and Fraser, 205
Graham, 167
Grévisse, 65
Grice, 55
Guillemin-Flescher, 62, 65

Haas, 54
Halliday, 125, 131–2
Hamburger, 71
Helbig, 129, 131, 139
Holman, 183
Hönig and Kussmaul, 78, 198
Hudson, 62

Jakobson, 38, 42
Joos, 14

Ladmiral, 8
Leyris, 71

Lakoff and Johnson, 207
Lecuyer, 178
Levy, 42
Longacre, 63
Lorian, 196

Maillot, 152
Malblanc, 138
Masterman, 24
Mathiot, 203
Meyer, 77–8, 172–3
Mounin, 101

Nabokov, 45, 185
Neubert, 68, 164, 192
Nida, 125, 134, 139, 188, 195

Osgood, 21

Paepcke, 152
Palkova and Palek, 63
Pottier, 117

Quine, 66
Quirk, 14

Ritchie, 52–3
Rose, 70

Sager, Dungworth and McDonald, 151
Segal, 167
Seleskovitch, 47, 72, 219
Sinclair, 58

Tesniere, 131, 133, 138
Thiel, 133
Tytler, 95, 188

Vinay and Darbelnet, 54, 55, 67, 85–91, 138
Voegelin, 27

Waldron, 179
Wandruzska, 39
Weightman, 168
Weinrich, 78
Wilss, 82, 85

Subject Index

acronyms, 148, 198
additions to text, 91–3
ambiguity, 206, 218

case grammar, 125–38
clichés, 107–8, 208, 214
cohesion, 23, 59
collocations, 145, 212
communicative dynamism, 61, 137–8
communicative translation, 47–9, 242, 246, 249
componential analysis, 90, 96, 114–23

eponyms, 110–11, 198
equivalent effect, 83

familiar alternatives, 89, 99, 180, 201
formality, scale of, 14

idiolect, 206

jargon, 209–11

menus, 97
metaphor, 104–13, 167–8, 207–8, 232, 274–5, 279
misprints, 209
modulation, 88–9, 279

neologisms, 122, 140–50
non-equivalent words, 11, 117

phrasal words, 147
poetry, 70, 163–9
proper names, 35, 214
puns, 217

readership, 13, 15, 41–2, 55
redundancy, 208
revision, 36, 221–4
rhetorical questions, 64

scholarship, 37–8
semantic translation, 46–9, 243, 245, 248
service translation, 52

technical translation 151–61
tensions of translations, 4–5
titles, 56–7, 156, 232
transference, 81, 96, 147
translation, 6–7
    levels of theory, 8–10
translationese, 3, 50

unit of translation, 54, 66

writing quality, 3–4, 16